## Troubleshooting Photoshop

Sometimes Photoshop doesn't do what you want it to do. Sometimes Photoshop won't do *anything*. Here's how to handle the problem:

### Tools don't work

1. **Deselect.** Unless you're trying to work within an active selection, press ⌘+D (on a Mac) or Ctrl+D (on a PC) to deselect. (An active selection elsewhere may be restricting your work.)
2. **Reset the tool.** Control/Ctrl-click the tool icon at the left end of the Options bar and select Reset Tool.
3. **Check the Layers and Channels palette.** Make sure you have the correct layer active and that the layer (not a layer mask) is active. Check the Channels palette to make sure you have the color channels active.

### Commands aren't available

You move the cursor to the menu and click, only to discover that the command you want is grayed out! Your next stop should be the Image➪Mode menu. Check to make sure that the image's color mode and color depth are appropriate for the command you want to use. (Many of Photoshop's filters, for example, can be used only with 8-bit/RGB images.)

### Filter Gallery acts funny

If a filter produces unusual or unexpected colors in your image, check your foreground and background colors. Many of the filters use the foreground color, the background color, or both. Here's the list of filters for which you should set your colors before entering the Filter Gallery:

| *Filter* | *Color(s)* |
|---|---|
| Artistic➪Colored Pencil | Background |
| Artistic➪Neon Glow | Foreground + background |
| Brush Strokes➪Accented Edges | Foreground + background |
| Distort➪Diffuse Glow | Background |
| Sketch➪Bas Relief | Foreground + background |
| Sketch➪Chalk & Charcoal | Foreground + background |
| Sketch➪Conte Crayon | Foreground + background |
| Sketch➪Graphic Pen | Foreground + background |
| Sketch➪Halftone Pattern | Foreground + background |
| Sketch➪Note Paper | Foreground + background |
| Sketch➪Photocopy | Foreground + background |
| Sketch➪Plaster | Foreground + background |
| Sketch➪Reticulation | Foreground + background |
| Sketch➪Stamp | Foreground + background |
| Sketch➪Torn Edges | Foreground + background |
| Texture➪Stained Glass | Foreground |

# Photoshop® CS2 For Dummies®

## Photoshop is broken

When Photoshop just won't work properly, try replacing Photoshop's Preferences file using this procedure:

1. **Open Photoshop and save your custom goodies.** Use Edit⇨Preset Manager to save sets of styles, brushes, and other such bits and pieces you created. Use the Save Actions command in the Actions palette menu to save any sets of custom Actions.
2. **Review your Preferences.** Open Photoshop's Preferences and go through each pane, noting your preferred settings so that you can restore your work environment later.
3. **Quit Photoshop.**
4. ***On a Mac***
   - **Hold down ⌘+Shift+Option and restart Photoshop.** When prompted, release the modifier keys and confirm that yes, you do want to replace Photoshop's settings.

   ***On a PC***
   - **Restart Photoshop; then immediately press and hold down Ctrl+Shift+Alt.** When prompted, release the modifier keys and confirm that yes, you do want to replace Photoshop's settings.

## Selection tricks

Photoshop provides you with an army of selection tools and commands — and here are some auxiliary troops to join the fray!

| *To:* | *Do:* |
|---|---|
| Make a selection of all pixels on a layer | ⌘-click/Ctrl-click the layer thumbnail. |
| Load a layer mask as a selection | ⌘-click/Ctrl-click the mask thumbnail. |
| Load an alpha channel as a selection | ⌘-click/Ctrl-click the channel thumbnail. |
| Load all pixels according to luminosity | ⌘-click/Ctrl-click the RGB channel thumbnail. |

## Layer-merging tricks

Sometimes the Layers palette gets too crowded. Sometimes you need to apply the same filter to multiple layers. Merge layers to streamline your Layers palette or to work with multiple layers as a single entity.

| *To:* | *Do:* |
|---|---|
| Merge the active layer into the layer below | ⌘+E/Ctrl+E |
| Merge all visible layers into the active layer | ⌘+Shift+E/Ctrl+Shift+E |
| Merge a copy of all visible layers into the active layer | ⌘+Shift+Option+E/Ctrl+Shift+Alt+E |



Item 9571-7.

For more information about Wiley Publishing, call 1-800-762-2974.

# Photoshop® CS2 FOR DUMMIES®

**by Peter Bauer**

Wiley Publishing, Inc.

**Photoshop® CS2 For Dummies®**

Published by
**Wiley Publishing, Inc.**
111 River Street
Hoboken, NJ 07030-5774
www.wiley.com



Published by Wiley Publishing, Inc., Indianapolis, Indiana

Published simultaneously in Canada



For general information on our other products and services, please contact our Customer Care Department within the U.S. at 800-762-2974, outside the U.S. at 317-572-3993, or fax 317-572-4002.

For technical support, please visit www.wiley.com/techsupport.

Wiley also publishes its books in a variety of electronic formats. Some content that appears in print may not be available in electronic books.

Library of Congress Control Number: 2005923073

ISBN-13: 978-0-7645-9571-4

ISBN-10: 0-7645-9571-7

Manufactured in the United States of America

10 9 8 7 6 5 4 3 2 1

1K/SW/QV/QV/IN

# About the Author

**Peter Bauer:** Best known as the Help Desk Director for the National Association of Photoshop Professionals (NAPP), Pete is also the author of a half-dozen books on Adobe Photoshop and Illustrator, a contributing writer for *Photoshop User* and *Mac Design* magazines, featured columnist for PlanetPhotoshop.com, and software documentation writer for a variety of Photoshop- and Illustrator-related products. An Adobe Certified Expert, he also appears regularly as a member of the Photoshop World Instructor Dream Team. As NAPP Help Desk Director, Pete personally answers tens of thousands of e-mail questions annually about Photoshop and computer graphics. He has contributed to and assisted on such projects as feature film special effects, major book and magazine publications, award-winning Web sites, and fine art exhibitions. He has taught computer graphics at the university level and serves as a computer graphics efficiency consultant for a select corporate clientele. Pete and his wife, Professor Mary Ellen O'Connell, of the University of Notre Dame Law School, live in South Bend, Indiana. Despite being considered a world-class techno-geek, Pete still plays organized ice hockey.

# Dedication

For my wife — I am continually in awe of all you have accomplished, and all you continue to accomplish! Your dedication to the law governing armed conflict makes the world a safer and more civilized place.


# Author's Acknowledgments

First and foremost, I thank Photoshop Hall of Fame member Deke McClelland for suggesting me for this project. I also thank Matt Wagner (formerly of Waterside Productions, and now an independent literary agent) and Bob Woerner of Wiley (the guys who put the deal together) as well as the superb crew at Wiley that put the book itself together. I would certainly be remiss if I didn't give a public thank-you to Stephanie Elder Robey at PhotoSpin.com, who keeps me so well supplied with high quality images. (You'll see a number of PhotoSpin images on these pages.) And I have certainly benefited during the production of this book from the insights and experiences of those colleagues (who must remain nameless) who participated in the development of this excellent new version of Photoshop. The whole team at Adobe and the volunteers who risk crashes and lost projects in order to stomp out pre-release bugs: I salute you!

On a more personal note, there are quite a few folks not directly associated with the production of this book whose contributions I'd like to acknowledge. Scott and Kalebra Kelby, Jim Workman and Jean Kendra, Jeff Kelby, and Dave Moser of the National Association of Photoshop Professionals (NAPP) make my professional life what it is today. Without them, I'd be just another techno-geek who knows far too much about a couple of computer programs. With their support, I'm the Help Desk Director for NAPP — and get to share all that geek-knowledge with tens of thousands of NAPP members and with you. I also thank my colleagues, the instructors of the Photoshop World Dream Team, for always sharing their techniques and experience. I've learned much from each and every one of you. (Okay, well, Julieanne Kost of Adobe has to move to the top of that list!)

Needless to say, I thank my wife, the incredible Professor Mary Ellen O'Connell, for her unceasing support through yet another book project.

## Publisher's Acknowledgments

We're proud of this book; please send us your comments through our online registration form located at www.dummies.com/register/.

Some of the people who helped bring this book to market include the following:

*Acquisitions, Editorial, and Media Development*

**Senior Project Editor:** Paul Levesque

**Senior Acquisitions Editor:** Bob Woerner

**Senior Copy Editor:** Teresa Artman

**Technical Editor:** Dennis R. Cohen

**Editorial Manager:** Leah Cameron

**Media Development Manager:** Laura VanWinkle

**Media Development Supervisor:** Richard Graves

**Editorial Assistant:** Amanda Foxworth

**Cartoons:** Rich Tennant (www.the5thwave.com)

*Composition Services*

**Project Coordinator:** Maridee Ennis

**Layout and Graphics:** Ron Terry, Lauren Goddard, Lynsey Osborn, Kathie Rickard, Heather Ryan

**Proofreaders:** Betty Kish, Jessica Kramer, Judith McMullen, Joe Niesen

**Indexer:** Joan Griffitts

***Special Help***

Andy Hollandbeck, Rebecca Senninger

---

*Publishing and Editorial for Technology Dummies*

**Richard Swadley,** Vice President and Executive Group Publisher

**Andy Cummings,** Vice President and Publisher

**Mary Bednarek,** Executive Acquisitions Director

**Mary C. Corder,** Editorial Director

*Publishing for Consumer Dummies*

**Diane Graves Steele,** Vice President and Publisher

**Joyce Pepple,** Acquisitions Director

*Composition Services*

**Gerry Fahey,** Vice President of Production Services

**Debbie Stailey,** Director of Composition Services

# Contents at a Glance

# Table of Contents

# Introduction

Adobe Photoshop is one of the most important computer programs of our age. It's made photo editing a commonplace thing, something for the everyperson. Still, Photoshop can be a scary thing (especially that first purchase price!), comprising a jungle of menus and palettes and tools and options and shortcuts as well as a bewildering array of add-ons and plug-ins. And that's why you're holding this book in your hands. And why I wrote it. And why Wiley published it.

You want to make sense of Photoshop — or, at the very least, be able to work competently and efficiently in the program, accomplishing those tasks that need to get done. You want a reference that discusses how things work and what things do, not in a techno-geek or encyclopedic manner, but rather as an experienced friend might explain something to you. Although step-by-step explanations are okay if they show how something works, you don't need rote recipes that don't apply to the work you do. You don't mind discovering tricks, as long as they can be applied to your images and artwork in a productive, meaningful manner. You're in the right place!

## About This Book

If you're familiar with the *For Dummies* series, you surely have noticed already that there's something, well, different about this book. It looks like a *For Dummies* book, but it doesn't. The cover's color scheme and the cartoons are there, but there's a lot more color. And the layout is, well, not as boxy as the *For Dummies* books you've seen in the past. Welcome to the new age of *For Dummies!*

It's been quite a collaborative effort over these weeks and months, brainstorming, discussing, negotiating, finding middle ground — all to present you with the best possible format for *Photoshop CS2 For Dummies.* This is a completely new book, from the ground up. New author, new text, new images, new layout, new format. New Photoshop, too.

One thing hasn't changed, though: This book was produced with an eye toward you and your needs. From Day One, the goal has been to put into your hands the book that makes Photoshop understandable and useable. You won't find a technical explanation of every option for every tool in every situation, but rather a concise explanation of those parts of Photoshop you're most likely to need. If you happen to be an astrophysicist studying the origins of the universe, your Photoshop requirements might be substantially more specific than you'll find here. (Yes, I do know at least two of those folks — and I'm sure they bought this book, too.) But for the overwhelming majority of the people who have access to Adobe Photoshop CS2, this book provides the background you need to work efficiently and competently with Photoshop.

As I wrote this book, I intentionally tried to strike a balance between the types of images with which you are most likely to work and those visually stimulating (yet far less common) images of unusual subjects from far away places. At no point in this book does flavor override foundation. When you need to see a practical example, that's what I show you. I included a number of images from PhotoSpin.com, my favorite subscription stock art source. But, again, I worked to ensure that each piece of artwork illustrates a technique and does so in a meaningful, nondistracting way for you, the reader.

You'll see that I used mostly my Apple computers in producing this book. That's simply a matter of choice and convenience. Other than the buttons in the corners of the windows, the modifier keys, and a few choices in terminology (such as *pop-up menu* versus *drop-down menu*), Photoshop works pretty much the same on a Mac as it does in Windows. (Okay, well, one other difference: I find color management on Apple computers to be *much* simpler and more reliable.) You'll also see (if you look closely) that I shoot mostly with Canon cameras and use Epson printers. That doesn't mean that you shouldn't shoot with Nikon, Sony, or Fuji, or that you shouldn't print with HP or Canon. If that's what you have, if it's the equipment with which you're comfortable, if it fulfills your needs, stick with it!

One additional note: If you're brand new to digital imaging and computers, this probably isn't the best place to start. I do indeed make certain assumptions about your level of computer knowledge (and, to a lesser degree, your knowledge of digital imaging). But if you know your File➪Open from your File➪Close and can find your lens cap with both hands, read Chapter 1, and you'll have no problem with *Photoshop CS2 For Dummies*.

## How This Book Is Organized

*Photoshop CS2 For Dummies* is primarily a reference book. As such, you can check the table of contents or the index for a specific subject, flip to those pages, and get the information you need. You can also start at the beginning and read cover to cover (just to make sure you don't miss a single tip, technique, or joke). To give you an indication of the type of information in each chapter, I organized the book into parts. Here's a quick look at what sort of content you'll find in each part.

## Part I: Breezing through Basic Training

The first set of chapters presents the basic operation of Photoshop, what you need to know to get around in the program, and the core process of getting images into Photoshop and back out again. If you're new to digital imaging, and particularly unfamiliar with Photoshop, make sure to read Chapter 1 through Chapter 3. If you've worked with Photoshop or another image editing program and aren't quite sure about the concept of resolution or which file formats are best for which purposes, don't overlook Chapter 2. Chapter 4 is the meat and potatoes of Photoshop: scanning and downloading images from cameras, cropping to fit specific print and frame sizes, and printing or posting your images on the Web. All in one nice, tidy package.

## Part II: Easy Enhancements for Digital Images

In Chapters 5 through 9, you discover ideas and techniques for improving the appearance of your images. You read about *tonality* (the lightness and darkness of the image), *color correction* (making the image's color look natural), and making selections to isolate individual parts of your image for correction. Part II also includes a full chapter on the Raw file format for digital cameras — what it is, why it's important, and how to determine whether it's right for you. At the end of this part, I include a chapter on the most common problems in digital photos (red-eye, wrinkles, and unwanted objects and people). And, yes, that chapter includes what to do about those problems, too!

## Part III: Creating "Art" in Photoshop

The chapters in Part III take a walk on the creative side. Although not everyone wants to use Photoshop as a digital painting program, everyone should understand how to get around in the complex and daunting Brushes palette. *Compositing* images (making one picture from two or more), adding text (whether a simple copyright notice or an entire page), using paths, and adding layer styles are all valuable skills for just about all folks who work with Photoshop (even if they don't consider their work to be art).

## Part IV: Power Photoshop

The two chapters in Part IV are more specialized than the rest of the book. If you don't work in a production environment (even cropping to the same dimensions regularly can count as production), you might not need to use Actions in Photoshop. But there's far more to Chapter 16 than just Actions and scripting! It also shows you how you can create an onscreen presentation that anyone can view, automatically generate a single page with small thumbnail images of all your photos, and save paper by printing multiple images on a single sheet. Chapter 17 is a Web-only chapter. If you don't create graphics for the Web, you probably don't need to read it. However, if you skip it, you might never see how to create cool little animated movies.

### Part V: The Part of Tens

The final part of this book, The Part of Tens, was both the easiest and most difficult section to prepare. It was easy because, well, the chapters are short. It was incredibly tough because it's so hard to narrow any Photoshop-related list to just ten items. Photoshop is such a beautifully complex and deep program that I had a very hard time (as you'll read) restricting myself to just ten favorite tips and tricks, just ten bits of hardware and software to make your work in Photoshop easier, and just ten reasons to own a digital camera. But I did it (more or less — beware of hidden tips and tricks)!

## Conventions Used in This Book

In order to save some space and maintain clarity, I use an arrow symbol as shorthand for Photoshop menu commands. I could write this:

> Move the cursor onto the word Image at the top of your screen and press the mouse button. Continuing to press the mouse button, move the cursor downward to the word Adjustments. Still pressing the mouse button, move the cursor to the right and downward onto the words Shadow/Highlight. Release the mouse button.

But it makes more sense to write this:

> Choose Shadow/Highlight from the Image➪Adjustments menu.

Or even to use this:

> Choose the Image➪Adjustments➪Shadow/Highlight command.

You'll also note that I include keyboard shortcuts (when applicable) for both Mac and Windows. Generally the shortcuts are together, with Mac always first, and look like this:

> Move the selection to a separate layer with the shortcut ⌘+Shift+J/Ctrl+Shift+J.

The Mac shortcut comes first, with the Windows version following. And, in a just barely revolutionary step, I assume that some Mac users have discovered the joys of a multibutton mouse. So instead of writing

> Control-click (Mac) or right-click (Windows).

I write this

> Right-click (multibutton mouse) or Control-click (single-button mouse).

If you use an Apple computer and haven't yet tried a multibutton mouse, put that right on the top of your wish list — it's a great timesaver.

## Icons Used in This Book

You'll see icons in the margins as you read this book, icons that indicate something special. Here, without further ado, is the gallery:

This icon tells you I'm introducing a new feature, something just added to the program with Photoshop CS2. If you're brand new to Photoshop yourself, you can ignore this icon — it's *all* new to you. If you're an experienced Photoshop user, take note.

When I have a little secret or shortcut to share with you — something that can make your life easier, smoother, more convenient — you see the Tip icon.

This icon doesn't appear very often, but when it does, read carefully! I reserve the Warning icon for those things that can really mess up your day — things that can cause you to lose work by ruining your file or messing up Photoshop. If there were to be a quiz afterward, every Warning would be in the essay section!

The Remember icon shows you good-to-know stuff, things that are applicable in a number of different places in Photoshop, or things that can make your Photoshop life easier.

You might notice this icon in a place or two in the book. It's not common because I exclude most of the highly technical background info: you know, the boring techno-geek concepts behind Photoshop. When I do use it, you know that the material is included to help clarify a complex or important concept.

## How to Use This Book

This is a reference book, not a lesson-based workbook or a tips and tricks cookbook. When you have a question about how something in Photoshop works, flip to the table of contents or the index to find your spot. You certainly can read the chapters in order, cover to cover, to make sure that you get the most out of it. Nonetheless, keep this book handy while you work in Photoshop. (Reading cover to cover not only ensures that you find out the most about Photoshop, but it guarantees that you don't miss a single cartoon or joke.)

Unless you're borrowing a friend's copy or you checked this book out of the library, I suggest you get comfortable with the thought of sticky notes and bent page corners. Photoshop is a very complex program — no one knows everything about Photoshop. And many concepts and techniques in Photoshop are hard to remember, especially if you don't use them often. Bookmark those pages so they're easy to find next time because you're sure to be coming back time and again to *Photoshop CS2 For Dummies*.

# Part I

# Breezing through Basic Training

"Well, well! Guess who just lost 9 pixels?"

## In this part . . .

A solid understanding of certain basic concepts and techniques makes learning Photoshop much easier. Heck, it's difficult to understand a discussion of feathered selections when you don't know your pixels from a hole in the ground, right?

In Chapter 1, I introduce you to Adobe Photoshop. Chapter 2 focuses on the basic concepts of digital imaging and offers a look at the primary file formats in which you save Photoshop images. If you're upgrading to CS2, just skim Chapter 3, which presents the Photoshop interface. If you're new to Photoshop or are upgrading from Photoshop Elements/an earlier version of Photoshop, though, make sure to read Chapter 3. Finally, Chapter 4 covers bringing images into Photoshop from digital cameras or scanners, organizing those files, and basic output through printing or a Web site.

# Chapter 1

# Welcome to Photoshop!

### In This Chapter

- What Photoshop does very well, kind of well, and just sort of, well . . .
- Taking a look at what you need to know to work with Photoshop

Adobe Photoshop is, without question, the leading image editing program in the world. Photoshop has even become somewhat of a cultural icon. It's not uncommon to hear Photoshop used as a verb ("That picture is obviously Photoshopped!"), and you'll even see references to Photoshop in the daily comics and cartoon strips. And now you're part of this whole gigantic phenomenon called Photoshop.

You might have purchased Photoshop as a new full version, as an upgrade, or as part of the Adobe Creative Suite. The Creative Suite (that's where the CS comes from) comes in two versions. The Standard Edition includes Photoshop, Adobe Illustrator (for creating vector-based artwork), and Adobe InDesign (for page layout work). The Premium Edition also includes Adobe GoLive (for Web design) and Adobe Acrobat (to create PDF documents).

Whether you're new to Photoshop, upgrading from Photoshop CS or earlier, or transitioning from Elements to the full version of Photoshop, you're in for some treats. Photoshop CS2 has some intriguing new capabilities that enable you to do more, and more easily, than ever. Before I take you on this journey through the intricacies of Photoshop, I want to introduce you to Photoshop in a more general way. In this chapter, I tell you what Photoshop is designed to do, what it can do (although not as capably as job-specific software), and what you can get it to do if you try really, really hard. I also review some basic computer operation concepts, and point out a couple of places where Photoshop is a little different than most other programs. At the end of the chapter, I have a few tips for you on installing Photoshop to ensure it runs properly.

# Exploring Adobe Photoshop

Photoshop is used for an incredible range of projects, ranging from editing and correcting digital photos to preparing images for magazines and newspapers to creating graphics for the Web. You'll also find Photoshop in the forensics departments of law enforcement agencies, scientific labs and research facilities, and dental and medical offices, as well as in classrooms, offices, studios, and homes around the world. As the Help Desk Director for the National Association of Photoshop Professionals (NAPP), I solve problems and provide solutions for Photoshop users from every corner of the computer graphics field and from every corner of the world. People are doing some pretty amazing things with Photoshop, many of which are so far from the program's original roots that it boggles the mind!

## What Photoshop is designed to do

Adobe Photoshop is an image editing program. It is designed to help you edit images, digital or digitized images, photographs, and otherwise. This is the core purpose of Photoshop. Over the years, Photoshop has grown and developed, adding features that supplement its basic operations. But at its heart, Photoshop is an image editor. At its most basic, Photoshop's workflow goes something like this: You take a picture, you edit the picture, and you print the picture (as illustrated in Figure 1-1).

**Figure 1-1:** Basic Photoshop: take photo, edit photo, print photo. Drink coffee (optional).

Whether captured with a digital camera, scanned into the computer, or created from scratch in Photoshop, your artwork consists of tiny squares of color, which are picture elements called *pixels.* (Pixels and the nature of digital imaging are explored in depth in Chapter 2.) Photoshop is all about changing and adjusting the colors of those pixels — collectively, in groups, or one at a time — in order to make your artwork look precisely how you want it to look. (Photoshop, by the way, has no *Good Taste* or *Quality Art* filter. It's up to you to decide what suits your artistic or personal vision and what meets your professional requirements.) Some very common Photoshop image editing tasks are shown in Figure 1-2: namely, correcting red-eye and minimizing wrinkles (both discussed in Chapter 9); and compositing images (see Chapter 10).

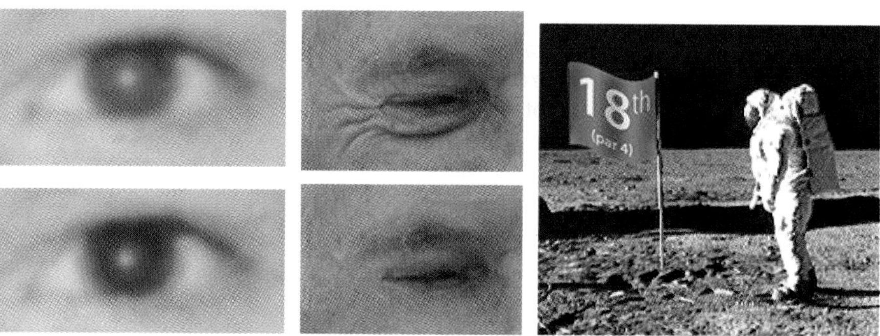


*Astronaut image courtesy of NASA*

**Figure 1-2:** Some common Photoshop tasks.

Over the past few updates, Photoshop has developed some rather powerful illustration capabilities to go with its digital imaging power. Although Photoshop is still no substitute for Adobe Illustrator, Photoshop certainly can serve you well for smaller illustration projects. (Keep in mind that Photoshop is a *raster art program* — it works with pixels — and vector artwork is only simulated in Photoshop.) Photoshop also has a very capable brush engine, which makes it feasible to paint efficiently on your digital canvas. Figure 1-3 shows a comparison of raster artwork (the digital photo, left), vector artwork (the illustration, center), and digital painting (right). The three types of artwork can appear in a single image, too. (Simulating vector artwork with Photoshop's shape layers is presented in Chapter 11, and you can read about painting with Photoshop in Chapter 14.)

**Figure 1-3:** You can use Photoshop with raster images, vector artwork, and even to paint..

By using *ImageReady,* the partner program to Photoshop (installed with Photoshop into the same Photoshop folder), you can create advanced Web graphics, such as rollover buttons and animations (see Chapter 17). Photoshop even includes special features to help you create an entire Web site to display your artwork (Web Photo Gallery), and a feature to prepare onscreen presentations, complete with transition effects between slides (PDF Presentation). (Read about Web Photo Gallery in Chapter 4 and PDF Presentation in Chapter 16.)

## Other things you can do with Photoshop

Although Photoshop is not a page layout or illustration program, you certainly can produce simple brochures, posters, greeting cards, and the like using only Photoshop. (See Figure 1-4.) One of the features that sets Photoshop apart from basic image editors is its powerful type engine, which can add, edit, format, and stylize text as capably as many word processing programs. Photoshop even has a spell check feature — not bad for a program that's designed to work with photos, eh?

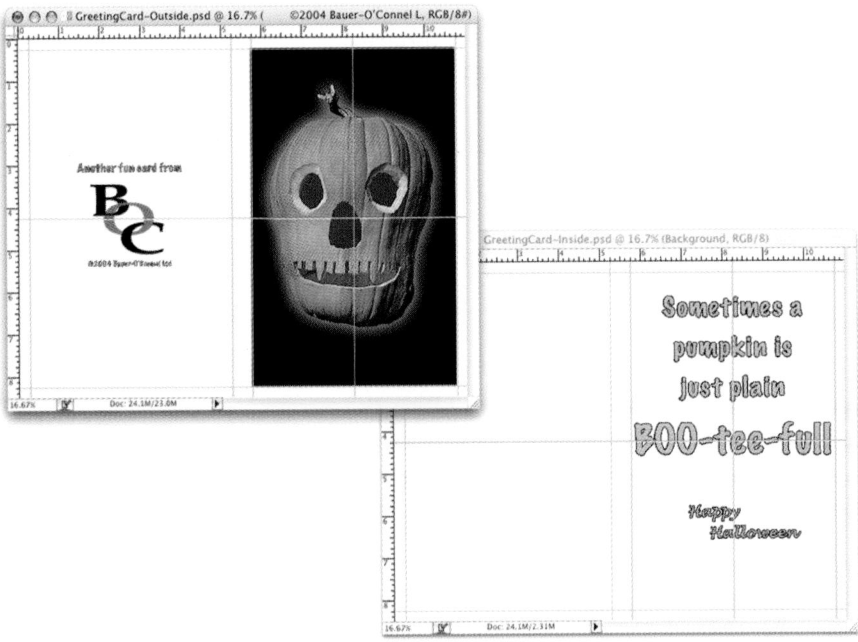


Figure 1-4: You can use Photoshop to create cards, posters, and brochures.

Photoshop CS2 takes yet another giant step toward filling in for InDesign or Illustrator with the introduction of Smart Objects. Smart Objects can be created in Photoshop through the Layers palette or pasted into your artwork from Illustrator. A Smart Object is a designer's dream. You add the Smart Object to your project; then, you can edit the original file and have the Smart Object updated to match. For example, suppose you add a sponsor logo to a poster as a Smart Object, and then use that same Smart Object in a direct-mail piece, a flyer, a magazine ad, and a couple of other related projects. Just before the approval date for the project, however, the sponsor drops out and is replaced by a new sponsor. You simply change the original file from which you created the Smart Object and then update the various instances of the Smart Object in your various projects. Done! Not only is this approach faster than manually changing each instance of the logo, but it ensures accuracy. Each Smart Object retains any effects you've applied, but those effects are applied to the updated artwork.

On the subject of special effects, Photoshop CS2 also introduces *object warping,* which you use to bend and twist elements in your artwork. As Photoshop moves more toward an object-based interface, it provides you with more ways to work with the content of a layer as a single unit rather than as independent pixels. Sure, you can still work with pixels, but treating a layer as an object certainly can be convenient. Take a look at Figure 1-5. Using a warp mesh to manipulate the artwork makes short work of what would otherwise have been a difficult edit. Click and drag an intersection within the mesh to reform the shape.

**Figure 1-5:** Warping the content of a layer is faster than selecting and moving pixels.

You can certainly supplement your video editing program with Photoshop (even if Photoshop can't open and play movies you capture with your video camera). From Adobe Premiere (or other professional video programs), you can export a series of frames in the FilmStrip format, which you can open and edit in Photoshop. Photoshop even provides support for nonsquare pixels, just in case you find yourself developing a project for television. You can create new documents that use nonsquare pixels and, through Photoshop's View menu, work on them as if they were regular old square-pixel digital images. No more "guesstimating" distortion factors or trying to calculate what is round or square in the artwork.

When you install Photoshop CS2, you also install a separate program named Adobe Bridge. (Unlike ImageReady, Bridge isn't inside the Photoshop folder.) Bridge is a standalone version of the File Browser from the previous version of Photoshop. As an asset management tool, it's even more capable. And because it's a separate program, it can be used throughout the Adobe Creative Suite or even independently to organize your images and artwork. (Figure 1-6 shows Adobe Bridge.) See Chapter 4 for more on Adobe Bridge.

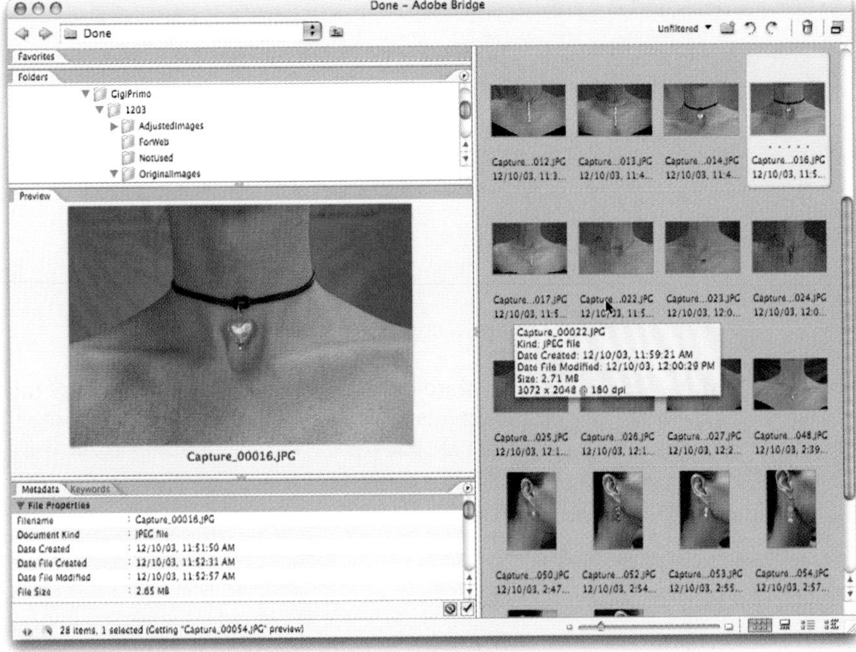


Figure 1-6: Use Adobe Bridge to manage your collection of images and artwork.

## If you don't have specialized software

Admittedly, Photoshop CS2 just plain can't do some things. It won't make you a good cup of coffee. It can't press your trousers. It doesn't vacuum under the couch. It isn't even a substitute for iTunes, Microsoft Excel, or Netscape Navigator — it just doesn't do those things.

However, there are a number of things for which Photoshop isn't designed that you *can* do in a pinch. If you don't have InDesign, you can still lay out the pages of a newsletter, magazine, or even a book, one page at a time. (With PDF Presentation, you can even generate a multipage PDF document from your individual pages.) If you don't have GoLive, you can use Photoshop to create a Web site, again one page at a time, complete with rollover buttons, image maps for links, and animations. You also have tools that simulate 3-D in Photoshop.

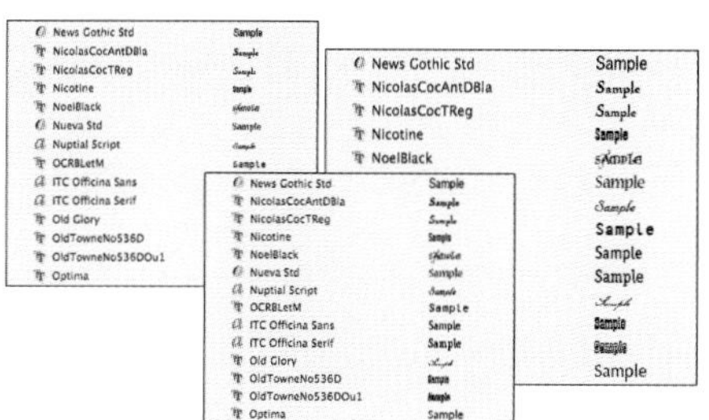
Figure 1-7: Being able to finally see typeface samples is definitely a plus.

Page layout in Photoshop isn't particularly difficult for a one-page piece or even a trifold brochure. Photoshop has a quite-capable type engine, considering the program is designed to push pixels rather than play with paragraphs. And, for the first time, Photoshop shows you a sample of each typeface in the Font menu — no more trying to remember which fonts are which! Choose from three sizes of preview in Photoshop's Preferences (as shown in Figure 1-7). However, you can't link Photoshop's type containers, so a substantial addition or subtraction at the top of the first column requires manually recomposing all following columns. After all, the biggest advantages of a dedicated page layout program are the continuity (using a master page or layout) and flow from page to page. If you work with layout regularly, use InDesign CS2.

Adobe GoLive CS2 is a state-of-the-art Web design tool, whose interoperability with Photoshop is exquisite. It's a piece of cake to use Photoshop and ImageReady to create complex Web graphics, including rollover buttons (buttons that change appearance when clicked) and animations, and then drop those PSD files right into a GoLive Web page. (Read about creating complex Web graphics in Chapter 17.) However, if you don't have GoLive and you desperately need to create a Web page, Photoshop comes to your rescue. After laying out your page and creating your slices, links, and rollovers in ImageReady, use the Save Optimized As command to generate an HTML document (your Web page) and a folder filled with the images that form the page (see Figure 1-8). One of the advantages to creating a Web page in GoLive rather than Photoshop is HTML text. (Using Photoshop and ImageReady, all the text on your Web pages is saved as graphic files. HTML text not only produces smaller Web pages for faster download, but it's resizable in the Web browser.)

Although Photoshop doesn't actually work in three dimensions (digital images have width and height, but not depth), you can use it in conjunction with your 3-D software. In addition to creating textures, Photoshop now includes the very powerful Vanishing Point feature, which lets you map artwork onto simulated 3-D surfaces. (Read about Vanishing Point in Chapter 10.)

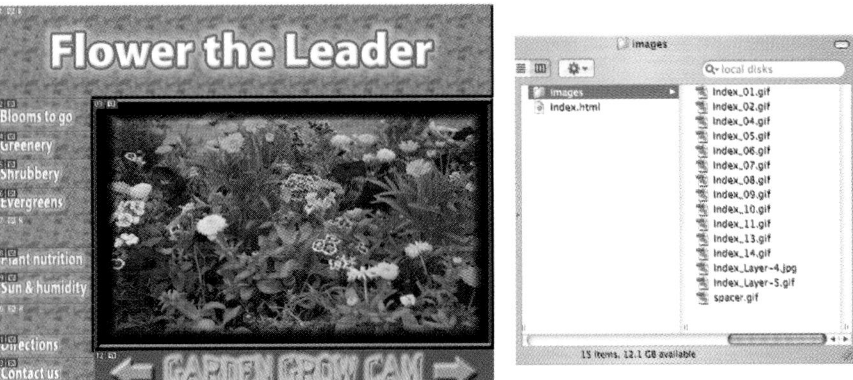


Figure 1-8: You can create an entire Web page in Photoshop/ImageReady.

# Viewing Photoshop's Parts and Processes

In many respects, Photoshop CS2 is just another computer program — you launch the program, open files, save files, and quit the program quite normally. Many common functions have common keyboard shortcuts. You enlarge, shrink, minimize, and close windows as you do in other programs.

## Reviewing basic computer operations

Chapter 3 looks at Photoshop-specific aspects of working with floating palettes, menus and submenus, and tools from the Options bar, but I want to take just a little time to review some fundamental computer concepts.

### Launching Photoshop

You can launch Photoshop (start the program) by double-clicking an image file or through the Applications folder (Mac) or the Start menu (Windows) — and Mac users can drag the Photoshop program icon (the actual program itself) to the Dock to make it available for one-click startup. Figure 1-9 shows both the Dock and the Start menu. You'll find the file named Adobe Photoshop CS2 inside the Adobe Photoshop CS2 folder, inside the main Applications folder. You can open a file in ImageReady either by launching the program directly or by

Figure 1-9: Start Photoshop through the Start menu (Windows) or the Dock (Mac).

clicking the button at the bottom of the Toolbox in Photoshop. (Chapter 3 shows you the Photoshop interface and how to get around in the program.)

Never open an image into Photoshop from removable media (CD, DVD, your digital camera or its Flash card, Zip disks, jump drives, and the like) or from a network drive. Always copy the file to a local hard drive, open from that drive, save back to the drive, and then copy the file to its next destination. You can open from internal hard drives or external hard drives, but to avoid losing your work (or the entire image file) because of a problem reading from or writing to removable media, always copy to a local hard drive.

### Working with images

Within Photoshop, you work with individual image files. Each image is recorded on the hard drive in a specific file format. Photoshop opens just about any image consisting of pixels as well as some file formats that do not. (File formats are discussed in Chapter 2.) Remember that to change a file's format, you open the file in Photoshop and use the Save As command to create a new file. And, although theoretically not always necessary on the Mac, I suggest that you *always* include the file extension at the end of the filename. If Photoshop won't open an image, it might be in a file format that Photoshop can't read. It cannot, for example, open an Excel spreadsheet or a Microsoft Word DOC file because those are not image formats — and Photoshop is, as you know, an image editing program. If you have a brand new digital camera and Photoshop won't open its Raw images, check for an update to the Adobe Camera Raw plug-in at

```
www.adobe.com/products/photoshop/cameraraw.html
```

You will also find installation instructions for the update there.

### Saving your files

You must use the Save or Save As command to preserve changes to your images. And after you save and close an image, those changes are irreversible. When working with an important image, consider these two tips:

- **Work on a copy of the image file.** Unless you're working with a digital photo in the Raw format (discussed in Chapter 7), make a copy of your image file as a backup before changing it in Photoshop. That ensures that should something go horribly wrong, you can start over. (You never actually change a Raw photo — Photoshop can't rewrite the original file — so you are always, in effect, working on a copy.)
- **Save your work as PSD, too.** Especially if your image has layers, save it in Photoshop's PSD file format (complete with all the layers) before using Save As to create a final copy in another format. If you don't save a copy with layers, going back to make one little change can cost hours of work.

If you attempt to close an image or quit Photoshop without saving your work first, you will get a gentle reminder asking whether you want to save, close without saving, or cancel the close/quit (as shown in Figure 1-10).

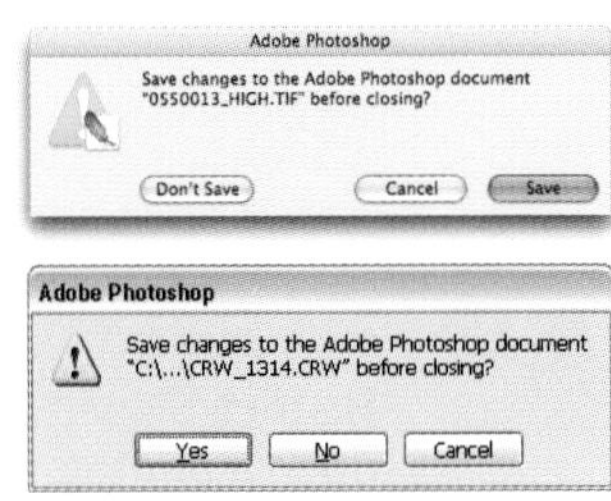


**Figure 1-10:** Photoshop reminds you if you haven't saved changes to an image.

### Keyboard shortcuts

Keyboard shortcuts are customizable in Photoshop (check out Chapter 3), but some of the basic shortcuts are the same as those you use in other programs. You open, copy, paste, save, close, and quit just as you do in Microsoft Word, your e-mail program, and just about any other software. I suggest that you keep these shortcuts unchanged, even if you do some other shortcut customization.

## Photoshop's incredible selective Undo

Here is one major difference between Photoshop and other programs you use. Almost all programs have some form of Undo, enabling you to reverse the most recent command or action (or mistake). Like many programs, Photoshop uses the ⌘+Z/Ctrl+Z shortcut for Undo/Redo (but remember that you can change the shortcut, as described in Chapter 3). Photoshop also has, however, a couple of great features that let you *partially* undo.

### Painting to undo with the History Brush

You can use the Photoshop History Brush to partially undo just about any filter, adjustment, or tool by painting. You select the History Brush, choose a history state (a stage in the image development) to which you want to revert, and then paint over areas of the image that you want to change back to the earlier state.

You can undo as far back in the editing process as you want, with a couple of limitations: The History palette (where you select the state to which you want to revert) holds only a limited number of history states. In the Photoshop Preferences➪General pane, you specify how many states you want Photoshop to remember (to a maximum of 1,000). Keep in mind that storing lots of history states takes up computer memory that you might need for processing filters and adjustments. That can slow things down. The default of 20 history states is good for most projects, but when using painting tools or other procedures that involve lots of repetitive steps, a larger number (perhaps as many as 60) is generally a better idea.

The second limitation is pixel dimensions. If you make changes to the image's actual size (in pixels) with the Crop tool or the Image Size or Canvas Size commands, you cannot revert to prior steps with the History Brush. You can choose as a source any history state that comes *after* the image's pixel dimensions changed but none that come before.

©2002 PhotoSpin, PhotoSpin image #0770118

**Figure 1-11:** Painting to undo with the History Brush.

Here's one example of using the History Brush as a creative tool. You open a photograph in Photoshop. You desaturate the image to make it appear to be grayscale, which gives it the appearance of a black-and-white photo. In the History palette, you click in the left column next to the Open step to designate that as the *source state,* the appearance of the image to which you want to revert. You select the History Brush and paint over your eyes, lips, and hair, restoring them to the original (color) appearance (see Figure 1-11). There you have it — a grayscale image with a couple of areas of color, compliments of the History Brush!

### Reducing to undo with the Fade command

Immediately after applying a filter or adjustment or using most of Photoshop's tools, you can choose the Edit➪Fade command and change the opacity or blending mode with which the previous step was performed. You might, for example, apply a sharpening filter and then use the Edit➪Fade Unsharp Mask command to change the blending mode from Normal to Luminosity. (Sharpening only the luminosity of your image, whether with this technique or in the L*a*b color mode, prevents unwanted color shifts along edges in your images. Color modes are discussed in Chapter 6.) Or you might apply the Motion Blur filter and then use Edit➪Fade Motion Blur (yes, the name of the command

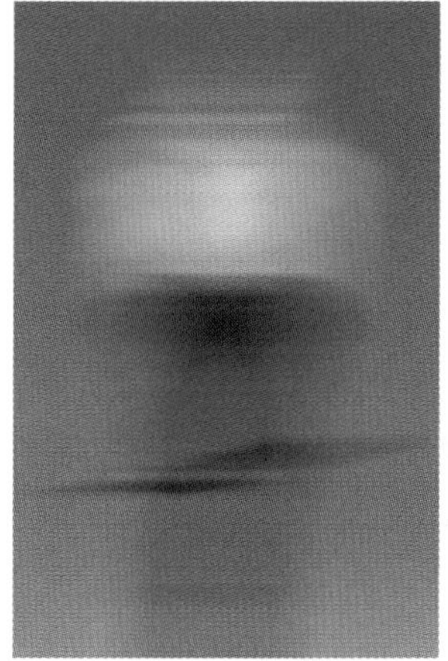

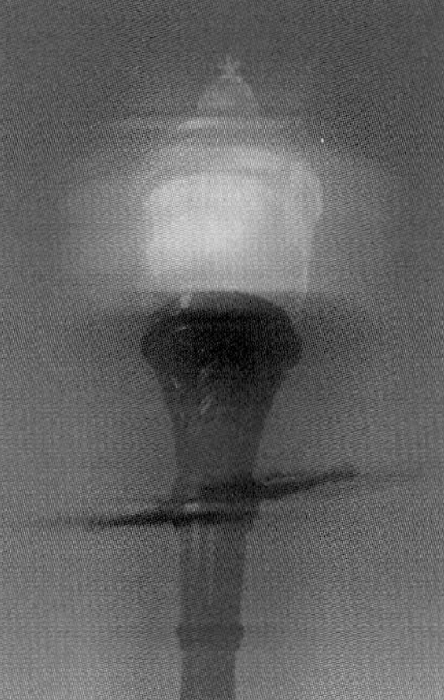

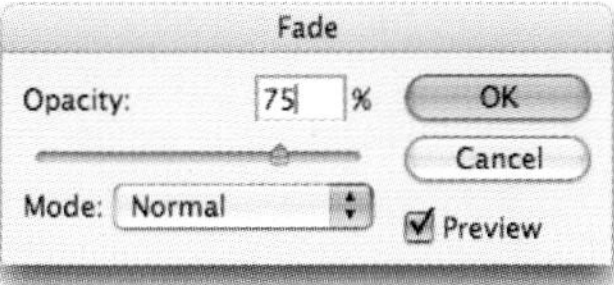


**Figure 1-12:** Compare the original blur with a reduction using the Fade command.

actually changes for you) to reduce the opacity of the blur to 75%. That gives you the appearance of a back-and-forth motion while leaving the subject recognizable (see Figure 1-12).

## Installing Photoshop: Need to know

If you haven't yet installed Photoshop CS2 (or the Adobe Creative Suite), here are a few points to keep in mind:

- **Install only into the default location.** Photoshop is a resource-intensive program. Installing it into the default location (Applications on a Mac/Program Files for Windows, as shown in Figure 1-13) ensures that it has access to the operating system and hardware as necessary. Installing into any other location or attempting to run Photoshop across a network can lead to frustrating problems and loss of work in progress.

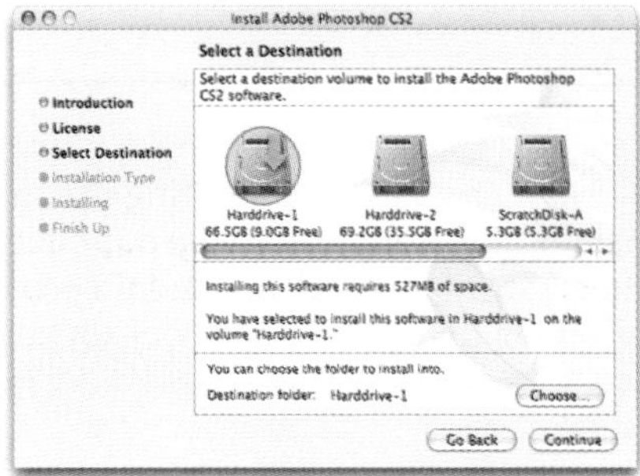


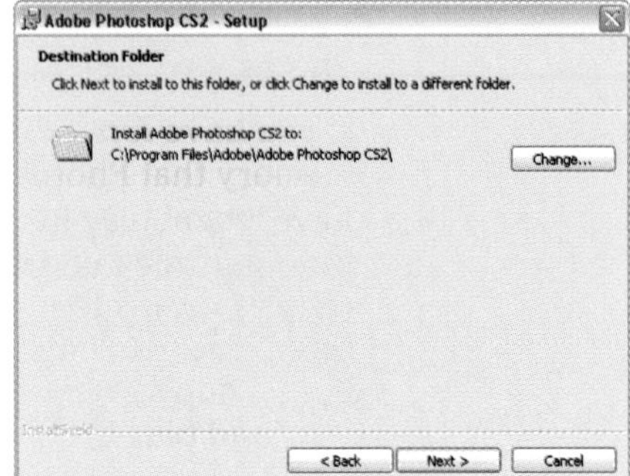


Figure 1-13: Install into the default location to avoid future problems.

- **Disable all antivirus software before installing.** Antivirus software can intercept certain installation procedures, deeming them to be hazardous to your computer's health. That can lead to malfunctions, crashes, lost work, frustration, and what I like to call Computer Flying across the Room Syndrome. If you use antivirus software (and if you're on Windows, you'd better!), turn it off before installing any program, especially one as complex as Photoshop. You might find the antivirus program's icon in the Windows taskbar; or you might need to go to the Start menu, use All Programs to locate the antivirus software, and disable it. On Mac, check the Dock. And don't forget to restart your antivirus software afterward! If you already installed Photoshop and antivirus software was running at the time, I urge you to uninstall and reinstall. (On Mac, drag the Adobe Photoshop CS2 folder from the Applications folder to the Trash and empty the Trash. On Windows, choose Start⇨Control Panel⇨Add/Remove Programs.)

- **If you use auto-backup software, shut it down, too.** Never run auto-backup software when installing software. Like antivirus software, it can also lead to problems by interfering with the installer.
- **Connect to the Internet and activate right away.** It's best to run the Photoshop installer while your computer is connected to the Internet. That enables Photoshop's activation process to happen right away, making sure you can get started as soon as the installer finishes.
- **If you have third-party plug-ins, install them elsewhere.** Third-party *plug-ins* — those filters and other Photoshop add-ons that you buy from companies other than Adobe — can be installed into a folder outside the Photoshop folder. You can then make an alias (Mac) or shortcut (Windows) to that folder and drag the alias/shortcut to Photoshop's Plug-Ins folder. (If you have a multibutton mouse, right-click the folder to create an alias/shortcut; Control-click if you're still using a one-button mouse.) Why install outside the Photoshop folder? Should you ever need to (gasp!) reinstall Photoshop, you won't need to reinstall all your third-party plug-ins. Just create a new alias/shortcut and move it into Photoshop's new Plug-Ins folder.
- **If you have *lots* of plug-ins, create sets.** Plug-ins require *RAM* (computer memory that Photoshop uses to process your editing commands). If you have lots of plug-ins, consider dividing them into groups according to how and when you use them. Sort (or install) them into separate folders. (***Hint:*** Plug-ins that you use in many situations can be installed into multiple folders.) When you need to load a specific set, do so through Photoshop's Preferences⇨Plug-Ins & Scratch Disks pane by designating a second plug-ins folder and relaunching Photoshop.
- **If you love fonts, use a font management utility.** If you have hundreds of fonts (over the years, I've somehow managed to collect upward of 3,000 fonts), use a font management utility to create sets of fonts according to style and only activate those sets that you need at any given time. The Mac OS has Font Book built right in, and Windows users might want to take a look at Suitcase (`www.extensis.com`). Too many active fonts can choke Photoshop's type engine, slowing performance.

# Chapter 2

# Knowing Just Enough about Digital Images

### In This Chapter

- Understanding digital images
- Discovering resolution
- The many file formats of Photoshop

In the early days of photography, some less-advanced cultures viewed a photo with great suspicion, and even fear. Was that an actual person, trapped in the paper? Did taking a photo steal a person's soul? We know that a camera doesn't trap anyone inside the paper — and we're pretty sure about the stolen soul issue — but how much does the average shooter know about digital images? And how much do *you* need to know about digital images to work effectively in Photoshop?

The answers to those two questions are "Not as much as he/she should" and "Not as much as you might fear." In this chapter, I give you some basic information about how digital images exist in Photoshop, a real understanding of that critical term *resolution,* and an overview of the different ways that you can save your images. But most importantly, I help you understand the very nature of digital images by explaining the world of pixels.

Welcome to the Philosophy Chapter!

## What Exactly Is a Digital Image?

Whether you take a picture with a digital camera or use a scanner to bring a photo (or other artwork) into Photoshop, you are *digitizing* the image. That is, *digit* not as in a finger or toe but as in a number. Computers do everything — absolutely *everything* — by processing numbers, and the basic language of computers is *binary code.* Whether it's a photo of a Tahitian sunset, a client's name in a database, or the latest box score on the Internet, your computer works on it in binary code. In a nutshell, binary code uses a series of zeros and ones (that's where the numbers part comes into play) to record information. (In Photoshop, this is a critical concept for color, as you can see in Chapter 6.) Binary code might look like this:

```
00100101 01010011 00011011 11010100 11101000 11000110
10101001 10010011 11010101 01011010 00101100 11101110
```

This example, of course, would be complete gibberish to a computer — if those two lines turn out to be the launch code for some missile, it's just a coincidence.

So what does binary code have to do with the wedding photos that you took this weekend or the masterpiece you must print for your thesis project? An image in Photoshop consists of tiny squares of color called *pixels* (short for *picture element*), as you can see in the close-up to the right in Figure 2-1. Each pixel is recorded and processed by the computer in binary code. These pixels replicate a photo the same way that tiles in a mosaic reproduce a painting.

Figure 2-1: That's not really an ugly old dog; it's a bunch of tiny colored squares.

A tile in a mosaic isn't *face* or *sky* or *grass;* rather, it's beige or blue or green. The tiles individually have no relationship to the image as a whole; rather, they require an association with the surrounding tiles to give them purpose, to make them part of the picture. Without the rest of the tiles, a single tile has no meaning.

Likewise, a single pixel in a digital image is simply a square of color. It doesn't become a meaningful part of your digital image until it's surrounded by other pixels of the same or different color, creating a unified whole — a comprehensible picture. How you manipulate those pixels, from the time you capture the image digitally until you output the image to paper or the Web, determines how successfully your pixels will represent your image, your artwork, your dream.

## The True Nature of Pixels

Here are some basic truths about pixels that you really need to know. Although reading this next section probably won't improve your love life, let you speak to the dead, or give you the winning lottery number, it will help you understand what's happening to your image as you work with it in Photoshop.

- **Each pixel can be exactly one color.** That color can change as you edit or alter the image, but each pixel consists entirely of a single color — there's no such thing as a two-tone pixel. Figure 2-2, at 1600% zoom, shows each pixel distinctly.

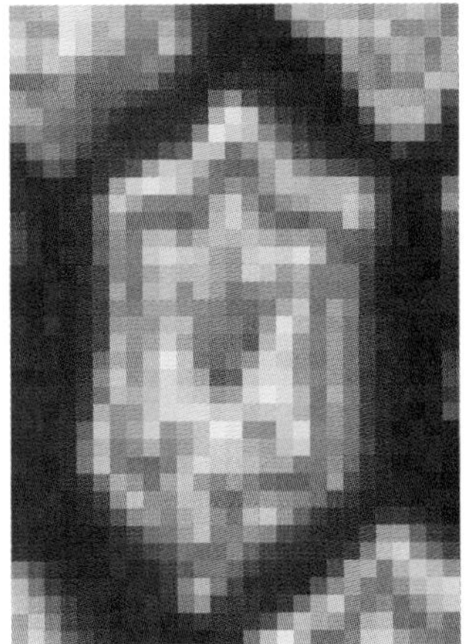

Figure 2-2: Each pixel is monotone, containing a single color throughout the pixel.

- **Each pixel is independent.** You might think that you see a car or a circle or a tree or Uncle Bob in an image, but the image is actually only a bunch of little colored squares. Although you can read about various ways to work with groups of pixels throughout this book, each pixel exists unto itself.
- **Each pixel is square (except on TV).** Really! Each pixel in a digital image is square except when creating images for television, which uses nonsquare pixels. (That's a rather specialized field, which I very briefly address in Chapter 3.) It's important that you understand the squareness (totally, like L7, Daddy-O) of pixels because you sometimes have to deal with those pointy little corners.
- **Smaller is better (generally speaking).** The smaller each pixel, the better the detail in an image. (However, when preparing images for the Web, you need smaller images that invariably have less detail.) If you capture an image of a dog in a park with two million pixels and capture the same shot with only 30,000 pixels, it's pretty obvious which image will better show the individual blades of grass and the fur. Take a look at Figure 2-3 for an example of this critical concept.

  Smaller pixels also help hide those nasty corners of pixels that are sometimes visible along curves and diagonal lines. When the corners of pixels are noticeable and degrade the image, you call it a bad case of the *jaggies*.

Figure 2-3: More pixels (top) means better detail.

- **Pixels are aligned in a *raster*.** The term *raster* appears regularly when you discuss images created from pixels. Raster, in this case, refers to the nice orderly rows and columns in which pixels appear. Each image has a certain number of rows of pixels, and each row is a certain number of pixels wide — the columns. Within the raster, the pixels perfectly align side-to-side and top-to-bottom.
- **Every picture created with pixels is rectangular.** Some images might appear to be round, or star-shaped, or have a hole cut from the middle, but they don't unless you print them out and grab your scissors. The image file itself is rectangular, even if it appears round. There are actually pixels in those seemingly empty areas; the pixels are, however, transparent.

# How Many Pixels Can Dance on the Head of a Pin?

You hear the term *resolution* a lot when working with digital images. (And you see it, too, like the examples in Figure 2-4). Digital cameras have so-many megapixels of *resolution;* inkjet printers have so-much by so-much *resolution;* to work in Photoshop CS2, your monitor must have a *resolution* of at least 1024 x 768 pixels; you must scan your line art at a very high *resolution;* when printing your images, you must use 300 pixels per inch (ppi) as your *resolution* (wrong!), but your Web images must have a *resolution* of 72 ppi (again wrong!); and don't forget your New Year's *resolution!*

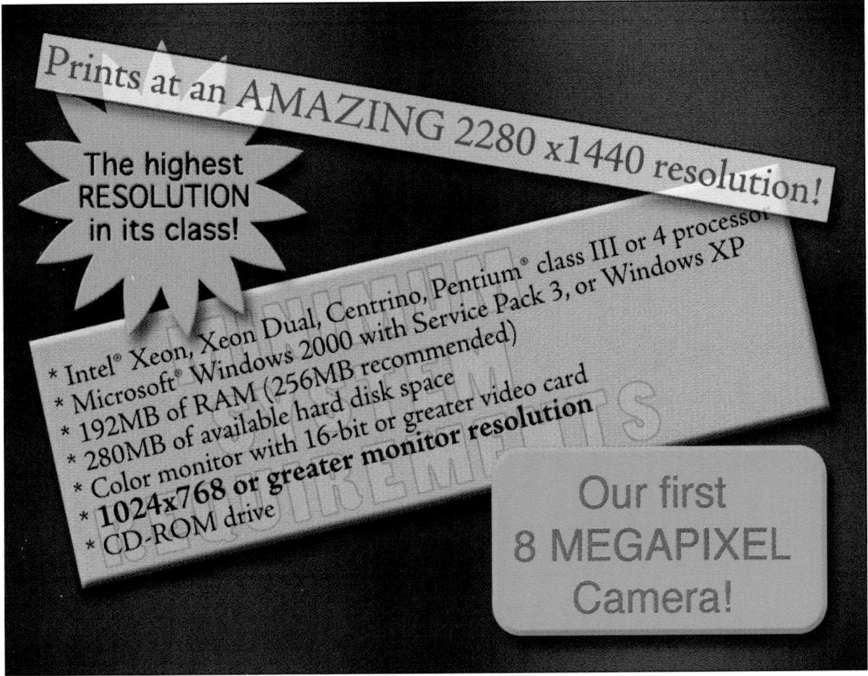


Figure 2-4: Resolution to the left of me, resolution to the right of me. . . .

What are all these *resolutions,* and what do they have to do with you?

## Resolution revelations

In this wonderful world of digital imaging, you see *resolution* used in four basic ways:

- **Image resolution:** *Image resolution* is the size of your image's individual pixels when you print. I go into greater detail about this concept later in the upcoming section, "Picking an image resolution."
- **Camera resolution:** Digital cameras capture each image in a specific number of pixels. Check your camera's user guide or open one of the images in Photoshop and go to Image➪Image Size. Take a look at the number of pixels that your camera records for the width and for the height. Multiply the numbers together, divide by one million, and round off the result. (If you're in the camera maker's marketing department, make sure that you round up.) That's the megapixel (MP) rating for the camera. Use it as a general guideline when shopping. If you create Web graphics or snapshot-size prints, 3 or 4 megapixels is fine. For large prints, you need at least 6 megapixels.
- **Monitor resolution:** *Monitor resolution* determines how many pixels are visible onscreen. Whether you use a Mac or a PC, you set the monitor resolution at the system level, as shown in Figure 2-5.

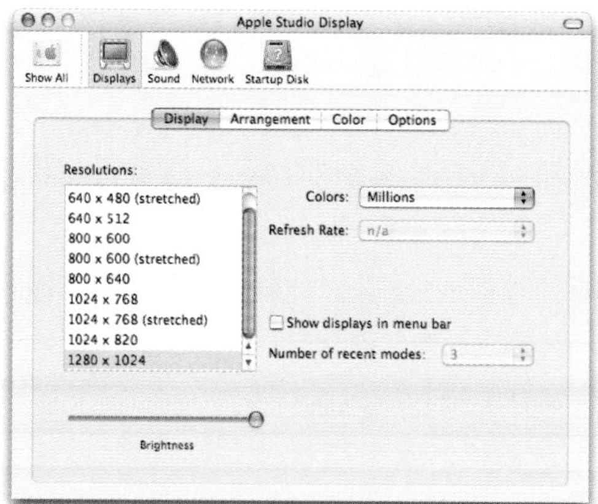

Figure 2-5: Set a Mac's resolution through the System Preferences (left), a PC's resolution through the Control Panel (right).

  - **Mac:** On a Mac, click the blue Apple menu in the upper-left corner of the screen and choose System Preferences. Then click Displays. (Some Apple monitors have a button on the bezel that automatically opens the window for you.) When you use a higher monitor resolution, you get a larger workspace, but each pixel is smaller, which might make some jobs tougher. Experiment to find a monitor resolution that works just right for you.

   - **Windows:** Go to Start➪Control Panel and then double-click Display. Click the Settings tab to see what monitor resolutions are available.

- **Printer resolution:** Unlike the three preceding terms, printer resolution doesn't involve pixels. Rather, a *printer's resolution* tells you how many tiny droplets of ink are sprayed on the paper. Remember that it takes several droplets to reproduce a single image pixel — you certainly don't need an image resolution anywhere close to the printer's resolution! (See the following section for more on this.)

## Resolving image resolution

*Image resolution* is nothing more than an instruction to a printing device about how large to reproduce each pixel. Onscreen, when working in Photoshop, your image has no resolution at all. An image that's 3000 pixels wide and 2000 pixels tall looks and acts exactly the same in Photoshop whether you've got the image resolution at 300 ppi or 72 ppi. Same number of pixels, right?

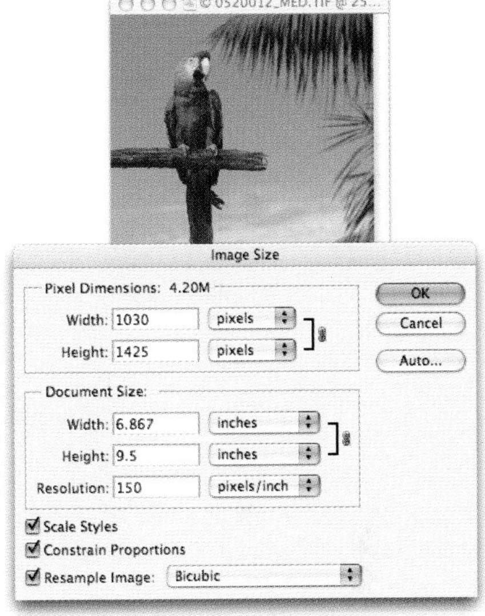


©2001 PhotoSpin, PhotoSpin image #0520012

**Figure 2-6:** At the top, real information about your image. Below, simply printing instructions.

You can always check — or change — a picture's resolution by using the Photoshop Image➪Image Size command. The Image Size dialog box (which you can see in Figure 2-6) has two separate but related sets of information about your image. At the top, you see information about the actual image itself, in the Pixel Dimensions area. Below, in the Document Size area, you see instructions for a printing device — that "size" pertains only to printing and has no impact on what you do in Photoshop.

You'll find it very handy to change the pixel dimensions *and* the print size at the same time in the Image Size dialog box. And, much to the delight of the math-challenged among us, Image Size does most of the calculations for you.

### *Changing the size of your artwork with Image Size*

You have a number of ways to change the size of your photos and other art. In Chapter 4, I introduce you to *cropping* (chopping off part of the artwork to make it fit a certain size or to improve its overall appearance and impact). You can use Photoshop's Image Size command to change the image dimensions (or printing instructions) without altering the *composition* (the visual arrangement of the image or artwork). All the content of the original image is there, just at a different size. Of course, as you can see in Figure 2-7, if you reduce the size of an image *too* much, some of that original content can become virtually unrecognizable.

Figure 2-7: As the smaller image shows, reducing an image *too* much isn't good.

If you know the specific pixel dimensions that you need for the final image — say for a Web page — you can simply type a new number in one of the upper fields in the Image Size dialog box and click OK. In most cases, you select all three check boxes at the bottom of the dialog box, enter your desired print width or height (letting Photoshop calculate the other dimension), enter your desired print resolution, and click OK. Of course, you probably want a little more control over the process, don't you? Figure 2-8 gives you a closer look at the Image Size dialog box.

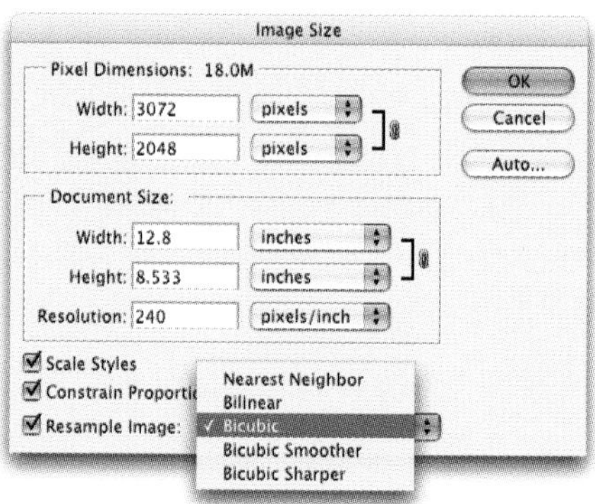

Figure 2-8: Your choices can have a substantial impact on the appearance of your final image.

In the lower part of the Image Size dialog box, you have three decisions to make. The first is rather easy: If you're resizing an image that uses layer styles (see Chapter 12), you want to mark the Scale Styles check box to preserve the image's appearance as it shrinks or grows. In a nutshell, layer styles (such as shadows, glows, and bevels) are applied to a layer at a specific size. You can scale the image without changing those sizes or you can scale the image and change the style sizes proportionally. Not scaling layer styles can dramatically alter the appearance of a resized image, as you can see in Figure 2-9. A slight bevel combined with a small drop shadow produces a subtle 3-D effect in the original (upper). Below, when the image is scaled down to one-fourth the original size without scaling the effects, your chips change to chumps, and the artwork is ruined.

Figure 2-9: Scaling an image without scaling its layer styles can ruin your image.

The middle check box, Constrain Proportions, should almost always remain checked. There might be some exceptions, but you normally want to preserve an image's *aspect ratio* (the relationship between height and width) when resizing to prevent distorting the image. Figure 2-10 shows you what can happen when you scale one dimension without constraining the image's proportions.

Figure 2-10: Resizing an image without constraining proportions. Interesting, yes, but useful?

The third check box, Resample Image, is the one that most often requires the attention of that gray matter within your skull. Not only do you need to decide whether you want to *resample* the image (change its pixel dimensions), but you also need to decide *how* you want to resample. Refer to Figure 2-8 to see that you have five different ways to calculate the change (called *resampling algorithms*).

Before I talk about those choices, let me explain what happens when the Resample Image box is left unchecked. The top portion of the Image Size dialog box becomes unavailable — you can no longer make changes in the Pixel Dimension fields (as you see in Figure 2-11). The information is there, but it won't change. When you clear the Resample Image check box, you protect the original pixels, preventing any change to the image itself.

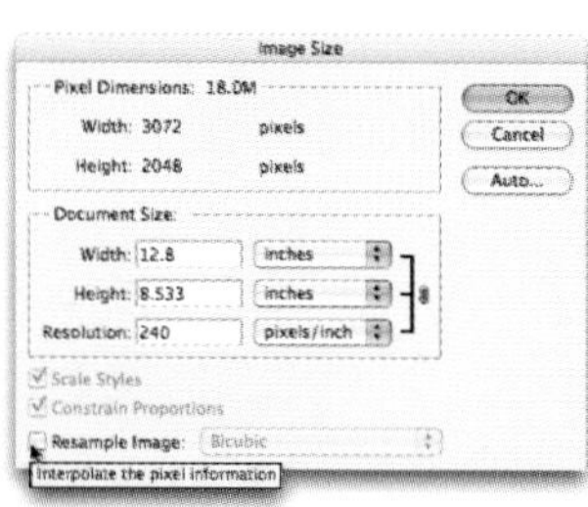

Figure 2-11: Clear the Resample Image check box to change print size, not pixel dimensions.

So what's left? When using Image Size without resampling, you're simply changing the instructions recorded in the image for your printing device. When you enter one dimension, either width or height, Photoshop does the math and fills in both the other dimension and the new resolution. Or, if you'd like, you could change the Resolution field and have Photoshop recalculate the print dimensions although it generally makes more sense to specify a desired print size.

Take a look at Figure 2-12. I cleared the Resample Image check box and entered **10** and **inches** for my new print width in order to print this image to a letter-size (8.5" x 11") sheet of paper. Photoshop fills in the new height (6.667 inches) and a new resolution (307.2 ppi). But what if I want an 8 x 10 print? If I enter **8** and **inches** for the height, Photoshop recalculates the width to 12 inches (and enters a resolution of 256 ppi). If I want a true 8 x 10, I have to crop some of the image because a digital photo and an 8 x 10 have different aspect ratios. (You can read more about that in Chapter 4.)

Okay, then, back to the subject of resampling! When you resample an image (change the pixel dimensions), Photoshop takes the image and maps it to the new size, attempting to preserve the image's appearances as much as possible at the new size, using the new number of pixels. Of course, if you take an image that's more than 3000 pixels wide and resample it to 300 pixels wide, you're going to lose some of the detail. (Remember what happened to Hugo the Bulldog earlier in this chapter in Figure 2-3!)

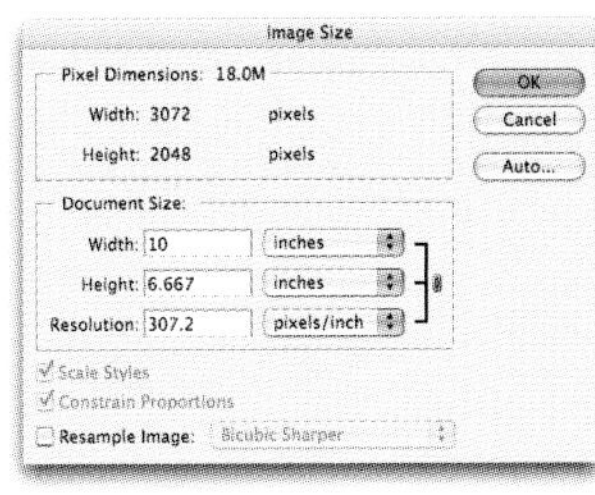


Figure 2-12: Enter a value, and Photoshop recalculates the fields automatically.

## To resample or to crop: That is the question

In order to better understand the difference between resampling an image and cropping an image, consider this situation:

1. **A painter paints a picture.** He or she paints it at whatever size he or she thinks is appropriate. (Or, perhaps, on the only piece of canvas he or she can afford on that particular day.)
2. **A patron likes the artwork, but the painting is too large for the frame that works best with the dining room table.** Yeah, patrons can be like that, can't they?
3. **The patron asks the artist to make the painting fit the frame.**
4. **The artist decides between cropping and resampling.** He or she can grab a pair of scissors and cut off some of the painting (cropping) or the artist can re-create the painting from scratch at a smaller size, repainting the scene. Thankfully, Photoshop does the "repainting" for us, using Image Size with its resampling algorithms.

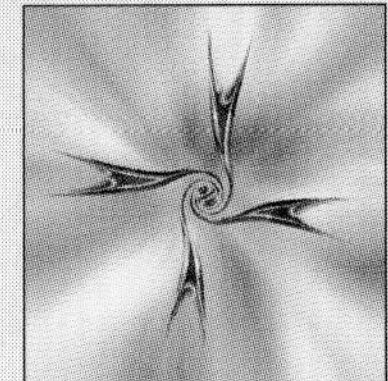

5. **The artist charges the patron for the extra work.** (Let's not forget this final, crucial step!)

Cropping cuts away part of the image to meet a target size. Resampling retains all the image but shrinks or enlarges it to meet the target size.

### Choosing a resampling method

After you decide to change the pixel dimensions of your image via the Image Size command, you need to select one of the five resampling algorithms (take another peek at Figure 2-8). Table 2-1 sums up my advice on choosing the right one.

If you'll be resizing a number of images in the same way, either upsampling or downsampling, open Photoshop's Preferences➪General and select the optimal resampling method in the Image Interpolation menu. That algorithm then becomes the default in Image Size, saving you the trouble of changing the algorithm each time.

Keep in mind that the resampling method that you select in the Preferences is also used for the Edit➪Transform commands, which you use to scale, rotate, and otherwise alter individual elements within your artwork. (You can read about the Transform commands in Chapter 10.)

**Table 2-1 Selecting a Resampling Algorithm**

| *Algorithm Name* | *Use It For* | *Results* |
|---|---|---|
| Nearest Neighbor | Artwork containing large areas of solid color like a pie chart or a simple logo; avoid using with photos | Maintains pixel color |
| Bilinear | Artwork having horizontal and vertical lines and blocks of color, such as Web page buttons; avoid using with photos | Maintains the sharpness of your edges |
| Bicubic | General-purpose resampling for minor changes in image size | Calculates the average of surrounding pixels when generating a new pixel |
| Bicubic Smoother | Increasing the size of photographic images or artwork with gradients and gradual shifts in color | Gives the most pleasing result when increasing the number of pixels (upsampling) |
| Bicubic Sharper | For reducing the number of pixels in a photo (down sampling) | Maintains the crispness of your image |

### *Picking an image resolution*

After you have resampling under your belt, how do you know what size you should be resampling *to?* How many pixels do you need? Here are your general guidelines:

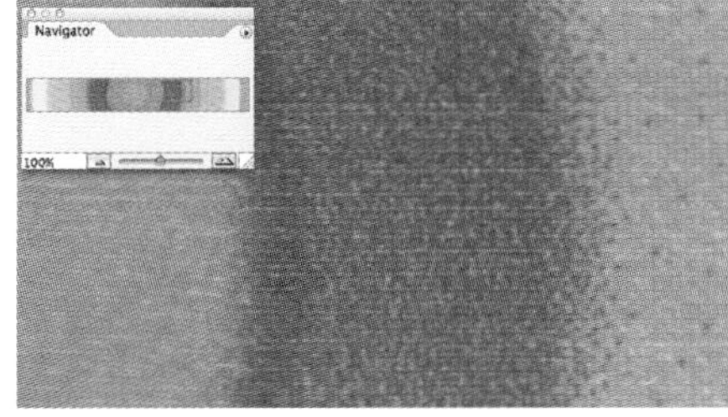

Figure 2-13: The close-up shows inkjet printer droplets.

- **Photos for your inkjet printer:** Inkjet printers are *stochastic* printing devices: That is, they use a series of droplets to replicate each pixel in your image, as shown in Figure 2-13. In theory, the optimal image resolution is one-third of the printer's rated resolution. For example, a printer rated at 720 ppi works best with images at 240 ppi. For a 1440 ppi printer, the formula calls for an image resolution of 480 ppi (and that goes for the 2880 x 1440 printers, too). However, most folks find that regardless of the printer's rating, they never need an image resolution higher than 300 ppi.
- **Web images:** Ignore resolution. Ignore the entire Document Size area of the Image Size dialog box. Consider only the image's pixel dimensions. Determine what area of the Web page the image will occupy and then resize to exactly those pixel dimensions.
- **Page layout programs and commercial printing:** If your image is to be placed into a page layout program's document and sent to a commercial printing facility, you need to know the *line screen frequency* (the resolution, so to speak) of the printing press on which the job will be run. Ask the print shop or the person handling the page layout. Your image resolution should be either exactly 1.5 times or exactly twice the line screen frequency, either one. (You shouldn't notice any difference in the final printed product with either resolution.)
- **PowerPoint presentations and word processing documents:** Generally speaking, 72 ppi is appropriate for images that you place into a presentation or Word document. You should resize to the exact dimensions of the area on the page or slide that the image fills.

Sometimes resampling an image to 300 ppi does more harm than good. You might get a better print at the image's original resolution than you will at the higher resolution after resampling. If your image's original resolution is 240 ppi or more, consider printing at that resolution rather than upsampling to 300 ppi. When in doubt, work on a copy of your image so that you can return to the original if necessary.

# File Formats: Which Do You Need?

After working with your image in Photoshop, you need to save the changes. Using the File⇨Save command updates the current file on your hard drive, maintaining the current file format when possible. If you added some feature to the file that is not supported by the original file format, Photoshop automatically opens the Save As dialog box and shows you which features are not supported by the selected file format. In Figure 2-14, the lower part of the Save As dialog box shows you the yellow warning triangles that identify options being used in the image that are not available when saving as a JPEG.

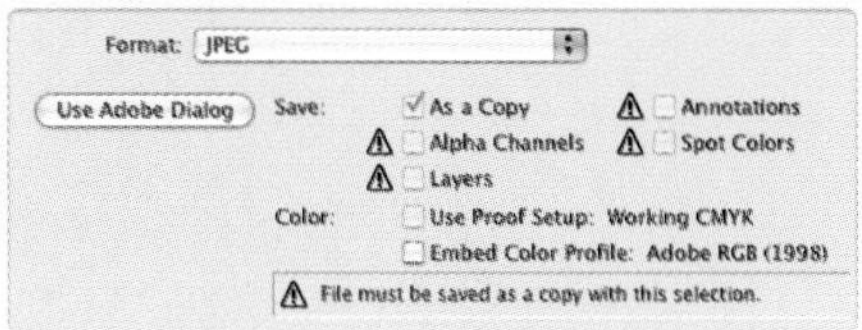


Figure 2-14: Photoshop shows you which image features are not available in your selected file format.

You can go ahead and save the image in that format, but your file will no longer contain those unsupported features. In the example shown in Figure 2-14, I can click the Save button and create a JPEG file, but that JPEG won't have the alpha channel (a saved selection), the spot channel (a custom printing color), or the annotations (sort of electronic sticky notes you add to images with the Notes and Audio Annotation tools); and it will be flattened to a single layer. If I want to retain those features in the file, I need to choose a different file format, such as Photoshop's own PSD format. (Read more about alpha channels in Chapter 8 and about spot channels in Chapter 6.)

No matter which of the file formats you choose, if you add layers, type, adjustment layers, channels, or paths to your image, keep the original as an unflattened/unmerged (all the layers are preserved) Photoshop (PSD) or layered TIFF file. In the future, should you ever need to make changes to the image — or duplicate an effect in the image — you won't need to start from scratch.

## Formats for digital photos

If you print your images yourself at home or office, you can stick with the original format or use the PSD Photoshop format. If you send the photos to the local camera shop (or discount store) for printing, stick with JPEG — or, if they accept it, TIFF. Here are the pros and cons of the major formats that you should consider for photos:

- **PSD:** Photoshop's native file format is great for saving your images with the most flexibility. Because the PSD format supports all of Photoshop's features, you don't need to flatten your images — and keeping your layers lets you make changes later. If your file size is very large (4MB or larger), make a TIFF or JPEG copy before printing, flattening all the layers. Do not send PSD files to the local shop for prints.

- **TIFF:** Although the TIFF file format (as you use it in Photoshop) can save your layers and most other Photoshop features, make sure to use the Layers➪Flatten Image command before sending files out for printing. Layered TIFF files are compatible only with Photoshop. If you don't flatten the image prior to saving as TIFF, or if you elect to include layers when saving as TIFF, Photoshop presents you with a gentle reminder, as show in Figure 2-15.
- **JPG:** JPEG, as it's called, is actually a file compression scheme rather than a file format, but that's not important. What *is* important is that JPEG throws away some of your image data when it saves the file. Save important images in PSD or TIFF and use JPEG only for copies. When should you use JPEG? When sending images to a photo lab that doesn't accept TIFF files and when sending images (perhaps by e-mail or on CD) to people who don't have Photoshop. Unlike PSD and TIFF, you can open JPEG images in a Web browser and print from there — and so can Granny, and Cousin Jim, and that overseas soldier you adopted. When saving JPEGs, the lower the Quality setting you choose in the JPEG Options dialog box, the smaller the file but also the more damage to the image. I discuss saving as JPEG in more detail in the sidebar, "Resaving images in the JPEG format."
- **PDF:** It's easy to overlook Adobe's PDF format when talking about photos, but you should consider using this format. Although the local photo lab probably won't accept it, it's a great format for sharing your pictures with folks who don't have Photoshop. Unlike JPEG, your images won't be degraded when saving as PDF; and like JPEG, just about anyone with a computer can view the files. (Adobe Reader, which you can use with PDFs, is found on just about every computer now, just like Web browsers for JPEG.) Keep in mind, however, that PDF files are larger than JPEGs.

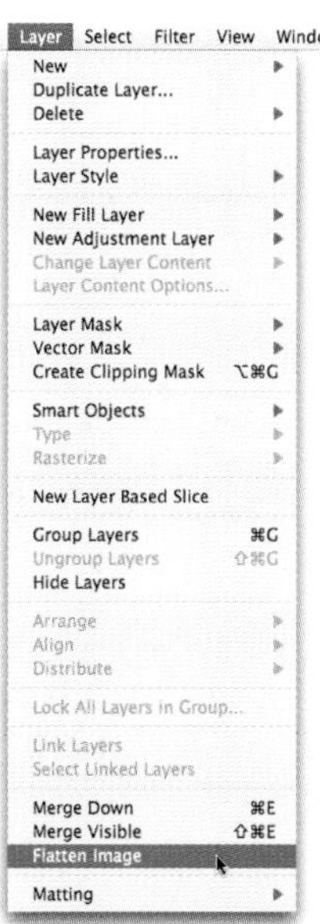


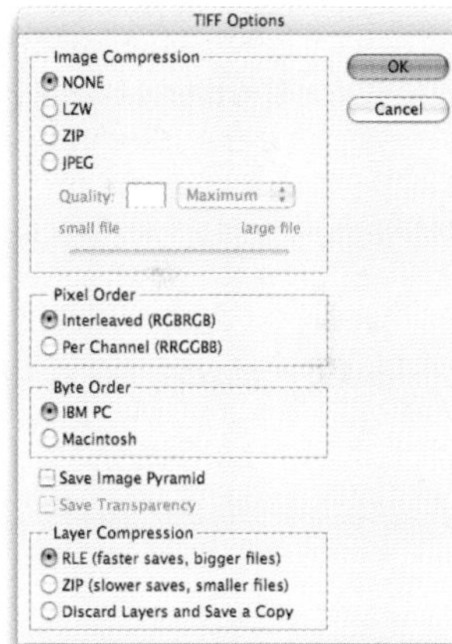


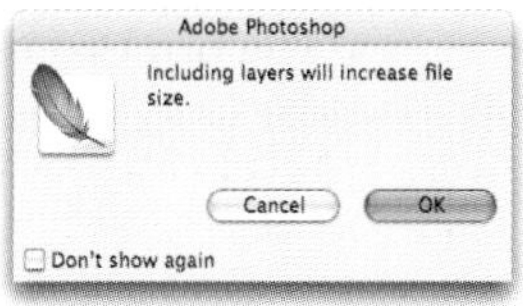


**Figure 2-15:** Flatten layers before saving a TIFF for use in other programs.

- **Large Document Format (PSB):** Really, really, *really* big pictures — over 30,000 pixels wide or long or both — need to be saved in the PSB file format. Before you can do that, however, you need to activate the format in Photoshop's Preferences➪File Handling, as shown in Figure 2-16. Will you ever need this format? Consider that 30,000 pixels at a photo-quality resolution of 300 ppi is 100 inches long. At a resolution of 85 ppi, more appropriate for a long banner to hang in a hallway, you're talking about artwork that stretches almost 30 feet! Can your printer do that? If not, you probably don't need the PSB file format.

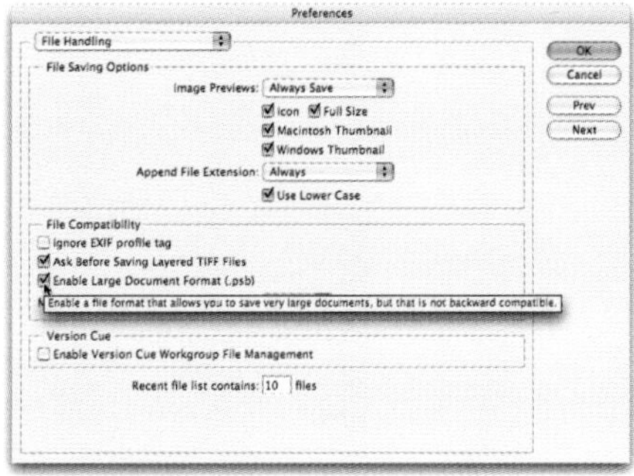


**Figure 2-16:** Activate the Large Document Format (PSB) for huge projects.

You could theoretically use a number of other available formats, such as DCS, PNG, and Photoshop Raw, but there's no real need with the more common and more versatile formats about which you just read.

If you're working with photos from your digital camera and you want to save them as JPEG but that format isn't available in the Save As dialog box, convert the image to 8-bit color with Image➪Mode➪8-Bits/Channel. You shot the image in Raw (or TIFF) and need to convert to 8-bit color if you want to save as JPEG, because JPEG doesn't support 16-bit color.

## Formats for Web graphics

Generally speaking, you use Photoshop's Save for Web command (or ImageReady's Save Optimize As command) rather than Save As to generate copies of your images for use on a Web site. Chapter 17 explores Web graphics in detail, but here are the three file formats that you need for the Web:

- **JPG:** Use JPEG for photos. Remember to resize the photo so that it fits on a Web page. When selecting a Quality setting, you need to balance image appearance with file size. A smaller file downloads (and displays in a Web browser) faster, but a larger file generally looks better. Reduce the Quality setting until just before the image doesn't look great and you've hit the *sweet spot* — the compromise between file size and image quality.

- **GIF:** GIF is more appropriate for items like Web buttons and banners (such as those shown in Figure 2-17) than it is for photos. If you save a photo that's more than perhaps 100 pixels x 100 pixels in size, you might see some degradation of the image quality as similar colors become one color. When you save an image as GIF, it can contain no more than 256 distinct colors. JPEG and the other common file formats can have thousands of different colors.
- **PNG:** PNG comes in two types: PNG-8 (which is a substitute for GIF) and PNG-24 (which is a substitute for JPEG). PNG has a couple of advantages for Web designers, such as support for transparency, but not all Web browsers can display PNG graphics. Generally speaking, it's safer to use JPEG and GIF.

**Figure 2-17:** Use GIF for Web interface items.

## Formats for commercial printing

You're the Photoshop master of your office. Everyone knows that you understand everything about digital images. So you're the right person to create the company's new brochure. Except you're a photographer. Or you're a Web designer. Or you're actually pretty new to Photoshop. And you don't have a clue about preparing images for a commercial printing press.

Here's what you need to know about file formats for those CMYK (cyan, magenta, yellow, black) color images that you're sending to the print shop:

- **TIFF:** TIFF is generally a solid choice. Use TIFF for photographic images that don't contain any type layers.
- **EPS:** Choose EPS if your image has type. Don't flatten or merge the type layers before using Save As to create the EPS. In the EPS options, make sure to select the Include Vector Data check box to ensure that your type prints perfectly.

## Resaving images in the JPEG format

JPEG uses a *lossy* compression scheme: That is, as part of the compression process, it actually permanently throws away some data when you save your image. The lower the Quality setting, the more image degradation. Take a look at the figure here. The original image is on the left. In the middle is the same image saved in JPEG format with high quality and then on the right with low quality. See what I mean by *degradation?*

If you save by using JPEG a second time, even more data is thrown away. Every time this happens, your image quality suffers. Yes, indeed, there are times when you need to open a JPEG image, make some changes, and save as JPEG again (perhaps for the Web, perhaps to share with non-Photoshop friends and family). To minimize damage to the image, either use the highest setting (12) for the Quality setting or (if you know it) the exact same setting used last in Photoshop.

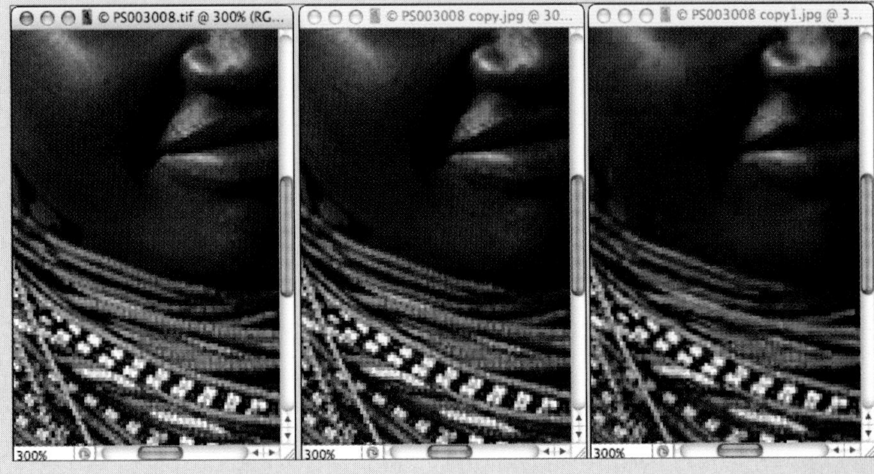


©1997 PhotoSpin, PhotoSpin image #PS003008

If you reopen an EPS file in Photoshop, your type layers get merged. Don't! Instead, make sure to save your original file as PSD and, should you need to make changes, open the PSD and create a new EPS file when done editing.

- **PDF:** PDF offers the same disadvantage (don't reopen in Photoshop) as the EPS file format. But it also offers support for spot color channels, alpha channels, and paths — options not supported by EPS. (*Spot channels* are used with custom colors, and *alpha channels* store information about transparency in the image.) If your file uses any of these features, choose PDF over EPS (if your print shop accepts PDFs).

When saving as PDF, the PDF Options dialog box offers you Preserve Photoshop Editing Capabilities. If you select the option, the PDF file will reopen in Photoshop CS2 with layers and editable type. However, this option is not compatible with earlier versions of Photoshop and can cause problems in a page layout program other than InDesign CS2.

- **PSD:** Use PSD only if you are adding the image file to a project in Adobe InDesign. Do not send PSD files to a print shop.
- **DCS:** DCS 2.0 is a variation of the EPS file format that supports spot color channels and alpha channels. Use it primarily with QuarkXPress.

## Formats for PowerPoint and Word

If the final destination of your image is PowerPoint or Microsoft Word, use the PNG file format. If your image has areas of transparency in it, PNG is *definitely* the way to go. (Read about the two types of PNG files in "Formats for Web graphics," earlier in this chapter.)

And what about all that neat clip art that you've got on your hard drive? How do you use those images when Photoshop won't open the vector-based WMF and EMF clip art files? Here's how you get clip art into Photoshop, quick and easy:

1. **Open a new document in Microsoft Word (or a comparable word processing program).**
2. **Add the clip art.**

   In Word, use the command Insert➪Picture➪Clip Art (or your word processor's comparable command). Click directly on the artwork and drag the lower-right corner to resize it to the dimensions that you need in Photoshop. (The artwork comes into Photoshop at 300 ppi.)
3. **Choose Edit➪Copy.**

   This copies the image to the Clipboard (the computer's memory) in Word.
4. **Switch to your Photoshop document.**
5. **Paste.**

   You've got your clip art, ready to use in Photoshop! Use the Edit➪Transform commands to scale, rotate, and otherwise fit the clip art into your design. (See Figure 2-18.)

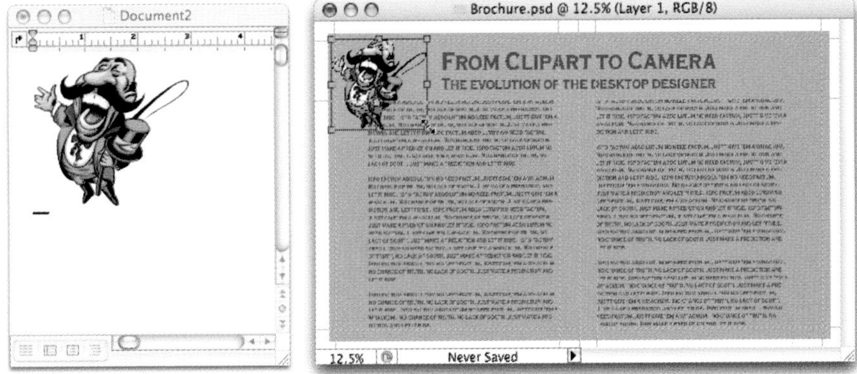


Figure 2-18: Copy vector artwork from Word and paste into Photoshop.

# Chapter 3

# Taking the Chef's Tour of Your Photoshop Kitchen

### *In This Chapter*

- Understanding the general guidelines for working in Photoshop
- Working more efficiently with customization
- Determining your preferences and color settings

I know you're hungry to dive right in and start mixing up some masterpieces, but before you fire up the stove, look around the kitchen. Get to know your spoons from your ladles, your pots from your pans, figure out how to turn on the blender . . . that sort of thing.

In this chapter, rather than going through all the Photoshop CS2 menus, palettes, and tools (which would take several hundred very boring pages), I show you some basic operational concepts. (But don't worry — you can read about how to use specific commands and tools throughout the book, in the chapters most appropriate for them.) Here you discover such things as how to spot which menu commands have dialog boxes, what the little triangle in the corner of a palette does, and which tools don't use the Options bar. You also read about customizing your Photoshop environment for faster and more efficient work. Next I show you how to set up Photoshop's Preferences and Color Settings. And to wrap up the chapter — perhaps the most important section in this entire book — I explain what to do when Photoshop doesn't seem to be working properly.

# Food for Thought: How Things Work

A good understanding of certain fundamental operations and features in Photoshop provides you with the background that you need to follow the recipes or get creative and whip up some delicious artwork.

And don't forget about Photoshop's Tool Tips. If you don't know what something or some option does, park your cursor over it for a couple of seconds, and Photoshop provides its information in a little box.

## Ordering from the menus

When you're working in Photoshop, you see a horizontal list of menus spread across the very top (Mac) or near the top (Windows) of the screen: File, Edit, Image, Layer, Select, Filter, View, Window, and Help. (On the Mac, the program also has a menu named Photoshop, just to the left of the File menu.) As with most programs you use, you click the name of a menu to reveal its commands. For both Mac and Windows, you can click and hold the mouse button down until you're over the command you want; or, you can click and release, move the cursor, and then click again. Some commands, such as Crop and Reveal All, are executed immediately after you choose them. When a command name in the menu is followed by an ellipsis (...) — the Apply Image command shown in Figure 3-1, for example — you know that a dialog box will open in which you input variables and make decisions. A triangle to the right of a command name, such as what you see next to Rotate Canvas, indicates a *submenu.* Click the command name, and another menu appears to the right. The cryptic set of symbols to the right of the Image Size command is the keyboard shortcut for opening the command's dialog box. (I show you how to assign keyboard shortcuts later in the section, "Sugar and spice, shortcuts are nice.")

As you read in the upcoming section, "Clearing the table: Custom workspaces," Photoshop CS2 menus are customizable — you don't have to see commands that you never use. You can also color-code your menu commands, making it easier to spot those that you need regularly.

When a specific command appears *grayed out* in the menu (in gray type rather than black), that command isn't available. Some commands (such as Reveal All in Figure 3-1) are available only under specific circumstances (like part of the image being hidden with the Crop tool). When working with Photoshop's creative filters, you'll find that many aren't available unless you're working with an 8-bit RGB (red/green/blue) image. (Color modes and bit depth are discussed in Chapter 6.)

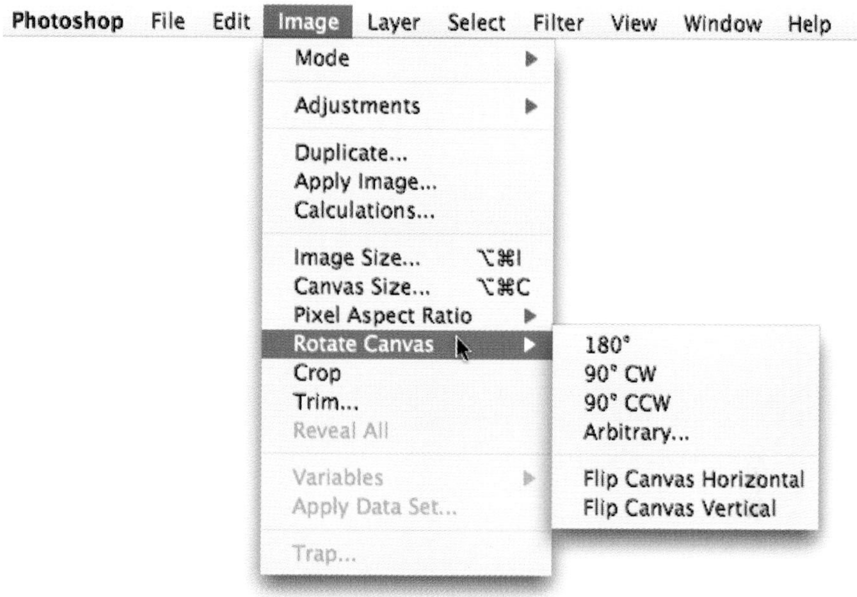


Figure 3-1: Some commands have submenus, and some have dialog boxes.

## Your platter full of palettes

Photoshop (and the other programs of the Adobe Creative Suite) uses *floating palettes.* The palettes, many of which you see along the right edge of your screen, always appear on top of (float over) your image window. The image window will never hide your palettes. (Palettes, however, can hide other palettes.) The Options bar (across the top of the work area) and the Toolbox (or toolbar) along the left edge of the screen are also palettes.

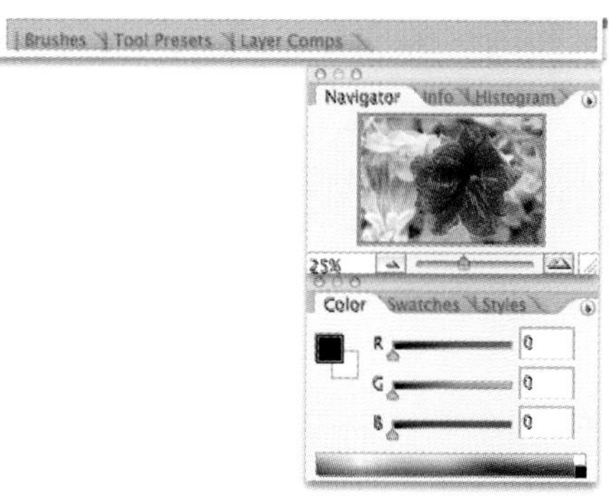


Figure 3-2: Nesting palettes and using the Palette Well prevents crowding the work area.

Palettes contain Photoshop features that you might need to access regularly enough to make it inconvenient to use a menu command. (I can't imagine having to mouse to a menu command every time I wanted to change tools or select a specific layer!) You don't always need to have your palettes visible. In Photoshop, press the Tab key to hide all the palettes or press

Shift+Tab to hide all but the Toolbox and the Options bar. With fewer palettes visible, you provide more room for your image. You can selectively hide and show palettes via the Window menu.

As you see in Figure 3-2, several palettes can be *nested* (grouped together). To bring a palette to the front, click its tab. You can also drag a palette's tab to move it out of a group to any location onscreen or into another group. Also, at the right end of the Options bar is the Palette Well, which contains (by default) the Brushes, Tool Presets, and Layer Comp palettes. Drag a palette's tab into the Palette Well to get it out of your way yet leave it easily accessible.

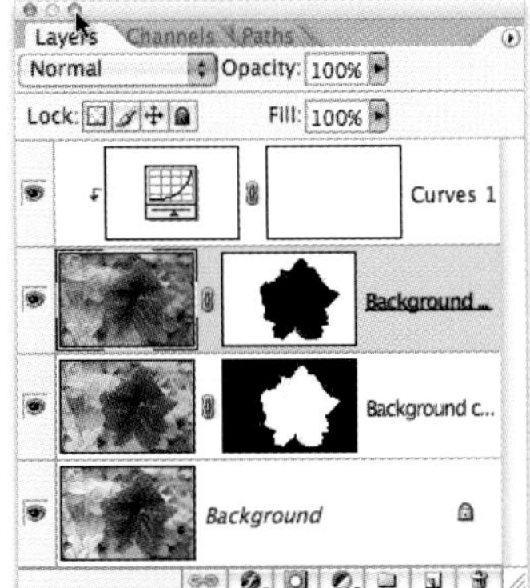


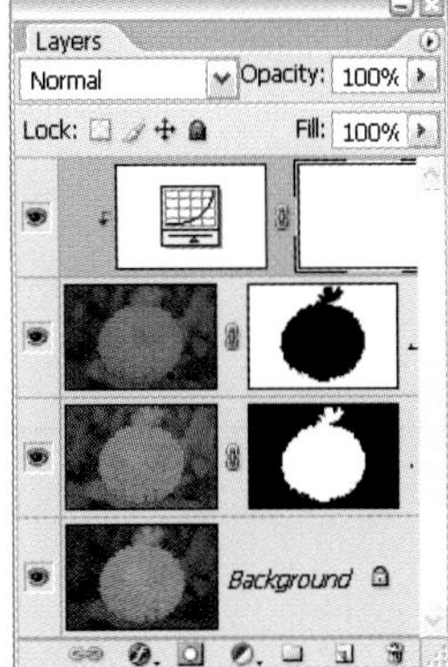


Figure 3-3: Mac and Windows have the same functional buttons, just on opposite sides.

Many of Photoshop's palettes are resizable. Like an image window, you drag the lower-right corner of the palette to expand or contract it. You also have a couple of buttons to control the visibility and size of the palette or palette group. Take a look at Figure 3-3. Macintosh users have three buttons in the upper-left corner of the palette, and Windows users have a pair of buttons to the upper right.

- **Mac**
  - Click the red button on the right to *optimize* the palette size, shrinking or expanding to show only the palette content.
  - Click the green button on the left to hide the palette (or palette group).
  - Click the red button a second time to minimize the palette.

    Don't bother clicking the middle button — it's just for show, making the palettes match image windows.
- **Windows**
  - Click the right button to hide the palette (or palette group).
  - Click the left button to optimize.

Isn't the coincidence eerie?

Almost all the Photoshop palettes have a palette menu, in which you select various options. (The Toolbox and Options bar do not have menus.) You open the palette menu by clicking the small triangle in the upper-right corner of the palette. The palette menu contains such options as thumbnail size (for example, the Layers, Channels, and Paths palettes), how to display items in the palette (Swatches, Styles, and Brushes among others), or even the size and content of the palette (Info and Histogram). When the palette is docked in the Palette Well, the triangle that opens the menu appears in the palette's tab.

The content of some palettes changes automatically as you work with your image. Add a layer, and the Layers palette shows a new layer. Save a selection, and the Channels palette shows a new alpha channel. Drag a shape tool, and the Layers palette gets a new layer and the Paths palette shows the layer's vector mask. You control some other palettes by loading (and deleting) content through the palette menus or with the Edit➪Preset Manager command. Use the Preset Manager (as shown in Figure 3-4) to save sets of your custom bits and pieces as well as to load and delete items from the palettes.

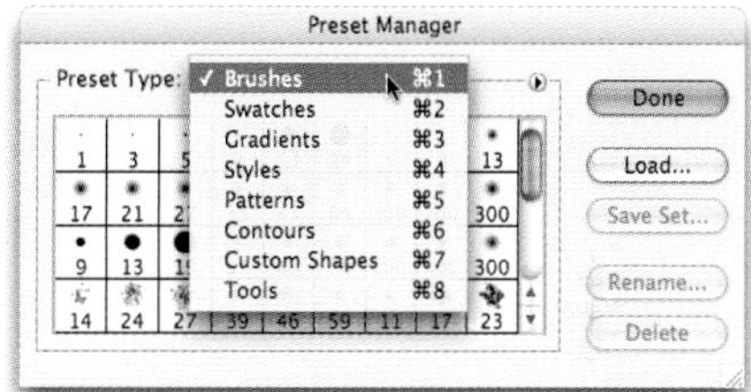


Figure 3-4: Use the Preset Manager to control the content of a number of palettes.

In addition to the content of the Brushes, Swatches, Styles, and Tool Presets palettes, you use the Preset Manager with a number of pickers. *Pickers* are sort of mini-palettes, available only with certain tools or features. The Gradient and Custom Shape pickers are accessed through the Options bar when those tools are in use. The Pattern picker is found in the Fill dialog box, the Layer Style dialog box, and (with some tools) in the Options bar. The Contour picker is used with a half-dozen of the effects in the Layer Style dialog box.

When you create custom layer styles, brushes, gradients, and the like, use the Preset Manager to protect your work. Create sets of the items and save those sets with the Preset Manager. Then remember to save copies of the sets someplace on your hard drive *outside* the Photoshop folder so that you don't accidentally delete them if you ever *(oh, no!)* have to reinstall Photoshop. Remember that new content of your palettes is stored only in Photoshop's Preferences file (introduced later in this chapter) until you create and save sets.

Photoshop CS2 introduces some important changes to the Layers palette, as shown in Figure 3-5. Layer sets are no more. The Link column is gone, too. Instead, Photoshop CS2 gives you the power to select multiple layers by Shift-clicking and ⌘-clicking/Ctrl-clicking. You can transform multiple layers, but you can't add content to multiple layers at the same time — say, filling a selection on two or three layers — nor can you apply a layer style to multiple layers all at once. You can link and create layer groups (the functional equivalent of layer sets) from selected layers through the Layers menu.

Figure 3-5: There is no longer a link column in the Layers palette.

## The tools of your trade

You control the behavior of Photoshop's tools through the Options bar. With the exception of a few path-related tools (Direct Selection, Add Anchor Point, Delete Anchor Point, and Convert Point), every tool in Photoshop has options. The Options bar changes as you switch tools. And in some cases, the Options bar changes while you work with the tool. In the case of the Crop tool, as shown in Figure 3-6, you have one set of options before you drag the tool and another set after establishing the bounding box.

*©1998 PhotoSpin, PhotoSpin image #0080045*

Figure 3-6: The Options bar changes when you have any active crop marquee.

The behavior of some tools changes when you add one or more modifier keys (⌘, Shift, and Option for the Mac; Ctrl, Shift, and Alt for Windows). As an example of how modifier keys can affect tool behavior, consider the Rectangular Marquee and Elliptical Marquee tools:

- **Hold down the Shift key while dragging.** Normally the marquee selection tools are *freeform* — you drag however you like. When you hold down the Shift key while dragging, on the other hand, you constrain the proportions of the selection to a square or circle (rather than a rectangle or ellipse).
- **Hold down the Option/Alt key while dragging.** When you hold down the Option/Alt key while dragging a marquee selection tool, the selection is centered on the point at which you first clicked. Rather than being a corner of a selection, that starting point is the center of the selection.
- **Hold down the Shift and Option/Alt keys while dragging.** You can select from the center while constraining proportions by using the Shift and Option/Alt keys together.
- **Use the Shift key to add to an existing selection.** If you already have an active selection in your image, Shift-dragging a selection tool adds to that selection. (Press Shift before you click and drag.)
- **Use the Option/Alt key to subtract from an existing selection.** When you have an existing selection and you hold down the Option/Alt key, you can drag to subtract from the selection. Note in Figure 3-7 that the selection tool's cursor shows a small minus sign when subtracting from a selection.

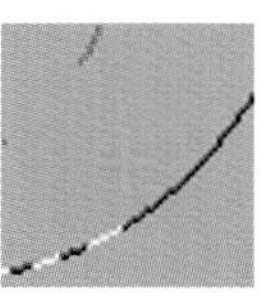

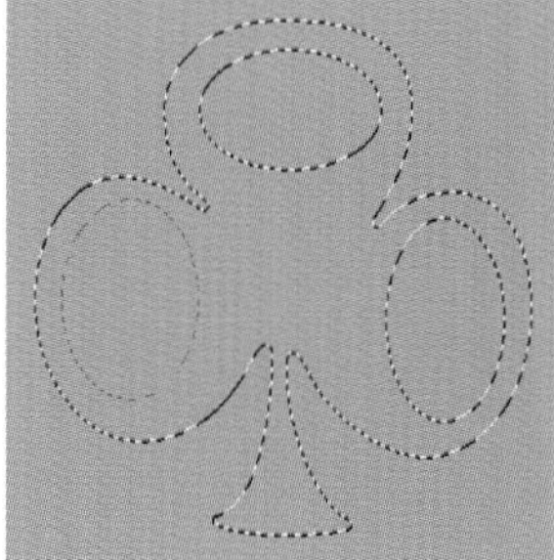

Figure 3-7: Use the Option/Alt key with a selection tool to subtract from a selection.

- **"Double-clutch" with the Shift or Option/Alt key.** You can even constrain proportions or select from the center *and* add to or subtract from a selection. Press the Shift key (to add to the existing selection) or the Option/Alt key (to subtract from the existing selection). Click and start dragging the marquee selection tool. While continuing to hold down the mouse button, release the modifier key and press and hold Shift (to constrain proportions) or Option/Alt (to center the selection) or both; then continue to drag your selection tool. You might want to use this technique, for example, when creating a donut-shaped selection. Drag the initial circular selection, and then subtract a smaller circular selection from the center of the initial circle.

Don't be afraid to experiment with modifier keys while working with tools. After all, you always have the Undo command (⌘+Z/Ctrl+Z) at hand!

# Get Cookin' with Customization

Customizing Photoshop not only helps you work faster and more efficiently, but it can also help you work more precisely and prevent tragic errors. Consider using a Crop tool preset to create a 5 x 7 print at 300 pixels per inch (ppi). Such a preset will *always* produce exactly those dimensions, every single time. Setting up the Crop tool each time you need a 5 x 7 at 300 ppi doesn't only waste time, but it also opens the door for time-consuming or project-wrecking typos. ("Oops! I guess I made a mistake — this image is 5 x 7 at only *30* pixels per inch!")

## Clearing the table: Custom workspaces

One of the easiest ways to work more efficiently is to see your image better. Generally speaking, bigger is better, so the more room you have on the monitor to display your artwork, the better you can zoom in and do precise work. The easiest way to gain workspace? Press the Tab key to hide Photoshop's palettes. Pressing Shift+Tab hides all the palettes except the Options bar and the Toolbox.

Keep in mind that you should always use 100% zoom when evaluating your image for banding or moiré and when applying filters. Any other zoom factor is a simulation of the image's appearance.

You can also drag the palettes that you need regularly to the Palette Well and hide the others. And don't forget that the major palettes have keyboard shortcuts assigned to show and hide. Although keyboard shortcuts are customizable (as you can read later in this chapter), here are the primary palettes' assigned F keys (the *function keys* that appear at the top of your keyboard):

- **Actions:** Option/Alt+F9
- **Brushes:** F5
- **Color:** F6
- **Info:** F8
- **Layers:** F7

Any palettes nested with the palette that you show/hide are also shown and hidden. And don't forget that you can always restore all palettes to their default locations with Photoshop's Window➪Workspace➪Reset Palette Locations command.

The most efficient way to customize your work area is to create and save specialized workspaces. Arrange the palettes exactly as you need them for a particular job you do regularly, choose Window⇨Workspace⇨Save Workspace, and name the workspace for that type of job. Then you can make a specialized workspace for each type of work you do. For example, perhaps when you do color correction, you need to see the Histogram palette (in the expanded view), the Info palette, and the Channels palette. Arrange those palettes how you need them and then hide the rest, saving the workspace named as *Color Correction.* Or, perhaps when you create illustrations in Photoshop, you need to see the Layers and Paths palettes at the same time. Drag one out of the group to separate it, position them both where convenient, and save the workspace as *Illustration.*

To access a saved workspace, go to the Window⇨Workspace menu and select it from the list at the bottom of the menu, as shown in Figure 3-8. You'll see some preset custom workspaces in the menu as well.

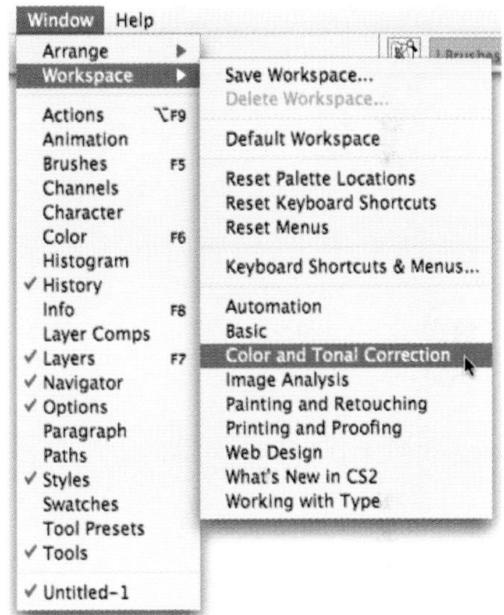

**Figure 3-8:** Select a workspace from the menu to instantly rearrange your palettes.

You can also save the current state of the customizable keyboard shortcuts and menus in your workspace. Although streamlining the menus for the specific work you're doing is a great idea, it's probably not such a great idea to have more than one set of custom keyboard shortcuts. The time it takes to remember which shortcuts go with the current workspace (or to undo a mistake caused by the wrong shortcut) is time wasted.

To customize Photoshop's menus, choose the Edit⇨Menus command. (Alternatively, open Edit⇨Keyboard Shortcuts and click the Menus tab.) You'll find every menu command listed. You also have the option here of hiding a command or assigning a custom color to make it easier to identify in the menu. You might, for example, hide the artistic filters that you never use, and color-code the others according to how you like or use them (see Figure 3-9).

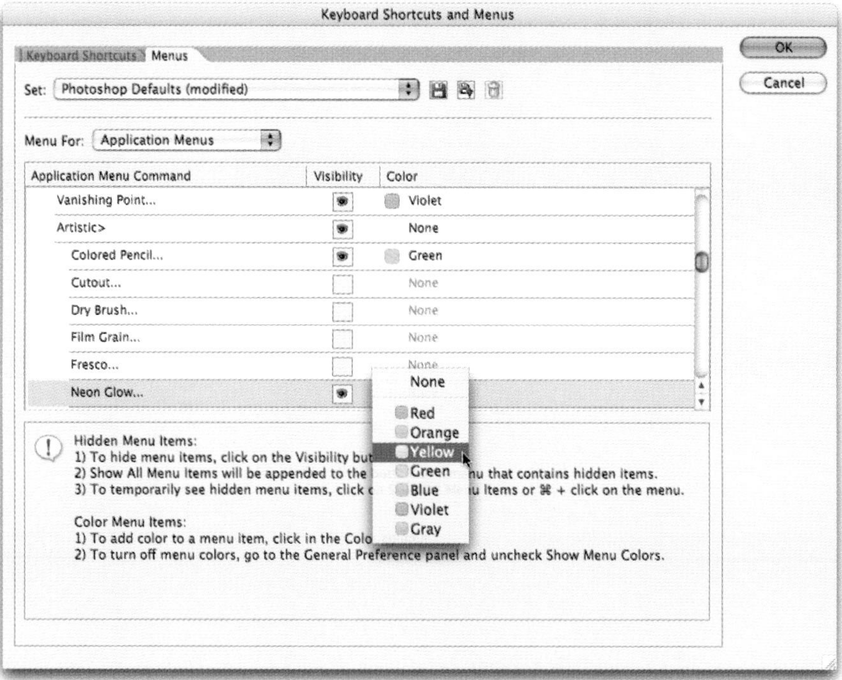


**Figure 3-9:** You can hide menu commands and color-code the visible commands.

In addition to the application menu commands (from the menus at the top of the screen), you can switch the Menus For pop-up to Palette menus and customize those menus, too. Don't forget to save your customized menu arrangements with the button directly to the right of the Settings pop-up. Your saved menu set will appear in that Settings pop-up for easy access.

## Sugar and spice, shortcuts are nice

Photoshop's keyboard shortcuts can save a bunch of time. Rather than mousing to the Toolbox to select the Brush tool, just press B on the keyboard. To open the Levels dialog box, press ⌘+L/Ctrl+L instead of mousing to the Image menu, down to the Adjustments submenu, and then over and down to Levels.

Photoshop CS2 has customizable keyboard shortcuts. Because the default set of shortcuts is pretty standard — not only throughout the Adobe Creative Suite but also with other major programs — you're probably best served by making only a couple of changes. Use the Edit⇨Keyboard Shortcuts command, as shown in Figure 3-10, to make these shortcut assignments:

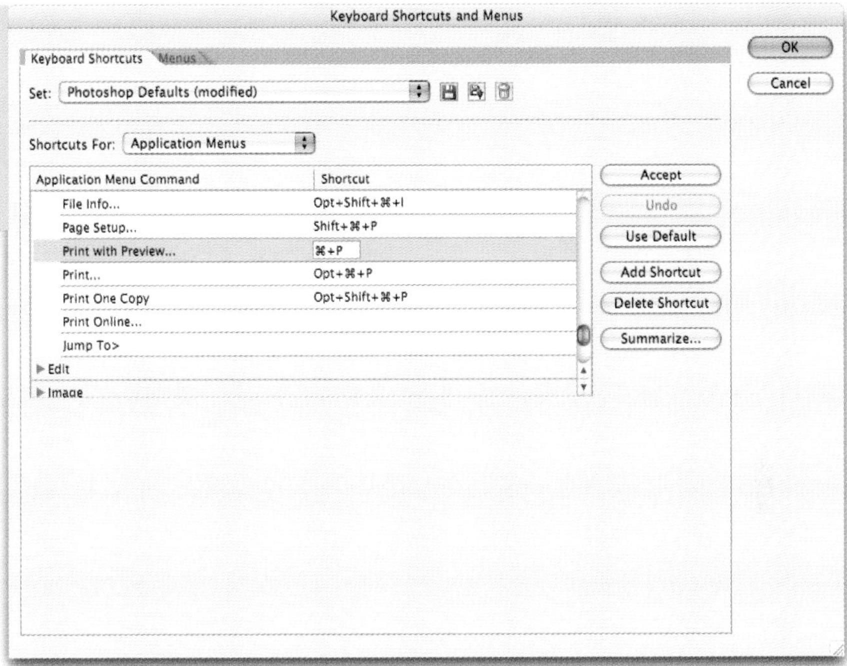


**Figure 3-10:** Assign custom keyboard shortcuts to speed your work.

- **Use ⌘+P/Ctrl+P to access Print with Preview.** As you read in Chapter 4, you have more control using Print with Preview than you do with the simple Print command. Therefore it makes more sense to use the simpler and more common shortcut for that command. Locate the Print with Preview command in the dialog box (under the File menu) and click the current shortcut. Type the new shortcut. Note that Photoshop warns you that the shortcut is already in use. Simply change the Print command to ⌘+Option+P/Ctrl+Alt+P to resolve the conflict.
- **Change ⌘+Z/Ctrl+Z to use Step Backward.** In most programs, pressing ⌘+Z/Ctrl+Z keeps *undoing* — reverting through a series of previous actions in the program. In Photoshop, however, that shortcut toggles an Undo/Redo function; that is, press once to undo, and press a second time to reverse the undo. Bah! Make Photoshop conform to the undo, undo, undo behavior common to other programs. In Keyboard Shortcuts, under Edit, change ⌘+Z/Ctrl+Z to Step Backward and then use ⌘+Option+Z/Ctrl+Alt+Z to toggle between Undo and Redo.

- **Assign shortcuts to often-used commands.** Smart Blur (or Gaussian Blur) can be assigned ⌘+Shift+Option+G/Ctrl+Shift+Alt+G. Smart Sharpen (or Unsharp Mask) can be assigned Shift+Option+U/Ctrl+Shift+Alt+U. Perhaps use ⌘+Shift+R/Ctrl+Shift+R for the Image Size command. As you work with Photoshop, pay attention to other menu commands that you access regularly and memorize their keyboard shortcuts or assign custom shortcuts.

## Spoons can't chop: Creating tool presets

One of the keys to efficient, accurate work in Photoshop is using the right tool for the job. The Patch tool, for example, copies texture only. If you need to cover a spot on a client's face, you need the Clone Stamp tool rather than the Patch tool. (You can read about how the tools work throughout this book.)

You can ensure that you're using not only the correct tool but also the correct settings for that tool by creating *tool presets,* which store your settings from the Options bar. You select the preset tool (and, of course, that's where the catchy name comes from) from the Tool Presets palette or from the left end of the Options bar, as shown in Figure 3-11.

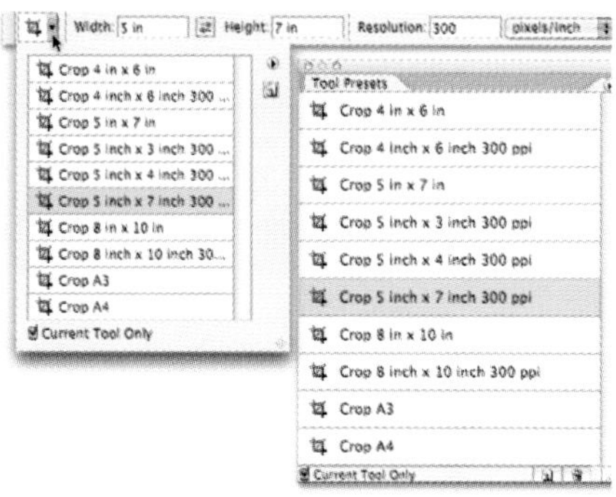


**Figure 3-11:** Tool presets help you work faster and more accurately.

Although just about any tool is a good candidate for tool presets, some are just plain naturals. Consider, if you will, the Type tool. When you consider all the options for the Type tool in not only the Options bar but also in the Character and Paragraph palettes, there's quite a bit to select and track. To ensure consistent text from project to project, consider creating tool presets for each project, including (as appropriate) headline and body text, special effects and accent type, and even your copyright information.

Another logical candidate for tool presets is the Crop tool. As I explain in Chapter 4, a photo from a high-end digital camera has an *aspect ratio* (relationship between width and height of the image) of 2:3, and common print and frame aspect ratios include 4:5 (for 8 x 10 prints), 5:7, and 13:19 (for large prints). (Some lower-cost cameras shoot in different aspect ratios.) You'll often find a need to crop an image to a specific size to meet your printing requirements. And, don't forget resolution — printing in the correct size at the wrong resolution is simply a waste of paper and ink! Set up a number of Crop tool presets for your typical print sizes and relax, knowing that you'll always be cropping correctly.

# Season to Taste: Photoshop's Settings

The program-level Preferences and the Color Settings flavor all your work in Photoshop. The options that you choose in Photoshop's Preferences (or simply the *Prefs*) control many facets of the program's basic behavior. Choices made in the Color Settings dialog box determine how your work looks, both onscreen and in print. And when you get down to brass tacks, that's what it's all about — the appearance of your artwork.

## Standing orders: Setting the Preferences

Photoshop's Preferences file stores a whole lot of information about how you use the program. Whether you prefer to measure in inches or pixels, how you like the grid and guides displayed, what size thumbnails you prefer in your palettes, which font you used last — all sorts of data is maintained in the Prefs. Much of the info in the Preferences is picked up automatically as you work (such as the size and color mode of the last new document you created, whether the Character palette was visible when you last shut down the program, and which tool options were selected in the Options bar), but you actively select a number of options in Photoshop's Preferences dialog box, as shown in Figure 3-12.

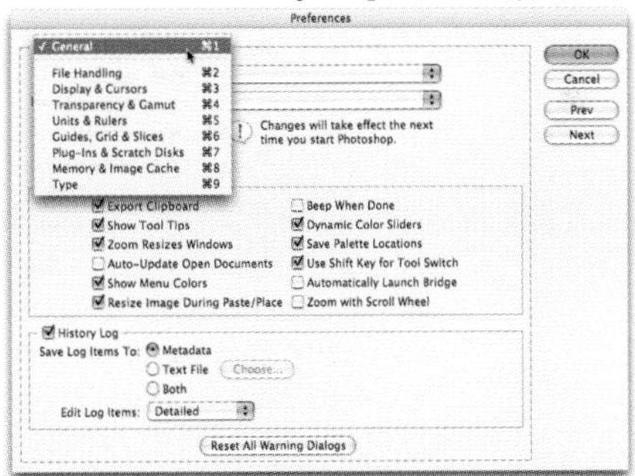


**Figure 3-12:** Use Photoshop's Preferences to establish many program behaviors.

Your custom styles, brushes, Actions, and the like are recorded only in Photoshop's Preferences until you actually save them to your hard drive. That makes them vulnerable to accidental loss. Use the Actions palette menu command Save Action to save sets of Actions (not individual Actions) and use the Preset Manager (under the Edit menu) to save sets of your other bits and pieces.

Open the Prefs on a Mac with the keyboard shortcut ⌘+K or use the Photoshop➪Preferences menu to select one of the nine specific subsets of Preferences to change. The shortcut for Windows users is Ctrl+K, and the Preferences submenu is under the Edit menu. The default settings are perfectly acceptable (after all, they are the defaults for a reason), but here are some changes to the Prefs to consider, listed by the section of the Preferences dialog box in which you find them.

### Preferences➪General

If you'll be doing a lot of resizing and scaling in Photoshop, consider changing the Image Interpolation method. Use Bicubic Smoother if you'll be increasing pixel dimensions regularly; select Bicubic Sharper when downsizing. If you work on a monitor set to a resolution of 1024 x 768 pixels, consider changing the UI (user interface) Font Size to Small. That shrinks palettes and gives you a little more room to work.

If you use Adobe Bridge regularly, mark the check box to launch the program automatically. (I explain how to use Bridge in Chapter 4.) And consider whether you want to automatically save the history log with each file, in a text file, or not at all. (The *history log* tracks all the changes you make to a file; however, as metadata, it does increase the file size. Read a metadata history log using the File➪File Info command.)

### Preferences➪File Handling

Image previews add a little to the file size, but in most cases, you want to include the preview. On Macs, you have the option of including a file extension or not (or having Photoshop ask you each and every time). Even if you don't plan on sharing files with a Windows machine, I strongly recommend that you always include the file extension in the filename by selecting the Always option. Likewise, I suggest that you always maximize PSD and PSB file compatibility. This ensures that your Photoshop CS2 files can be opened (with as many features intact as possible) in earlier versions of the program and that they'll function properly with other programs in the Creative Suite. If you're in a work group situation (with two or more people working on a single project), I urge you to use Version Cue (part of the Creative Suite) to manage work files. It's a truly great way to avoid singing the *Which Version Is Current Blues*.

### Preferences➪Display & Cursors

New in Photoshop CS2 are a couple of ways to display cursors for painting tools. In prior versions, you could show the tool icon (Standard), a small crosshair (Precise), or a representation of the tool's brush tip, indicating the size and shape of the brush (Brush Size). With soft-edged brushes, the brush size cursor shows where the tool will be applied at 50% strength or higher. That option is currently called Normal Brush Tip, and you have an alternative (Full Size Brush Tip) that always shows the full extent of the brush tip, regardless of the Hardness setting.

Also new is the option of adding a crosshair in the middle of either brush-size cursor. The crosshair option is great for keeping a brush centered along an edge or path, and just about eliminates the need for the Precise cursor option. As you can see in Figure 3-13, when working with a soft brush, showing all the pixels that are changed even a little (to the right) might not give you an accurate view of your work. (The Normal Brush Tip cursor is shown to the left and with the Show Crosshair in Brush Tip option to the lower-left.)

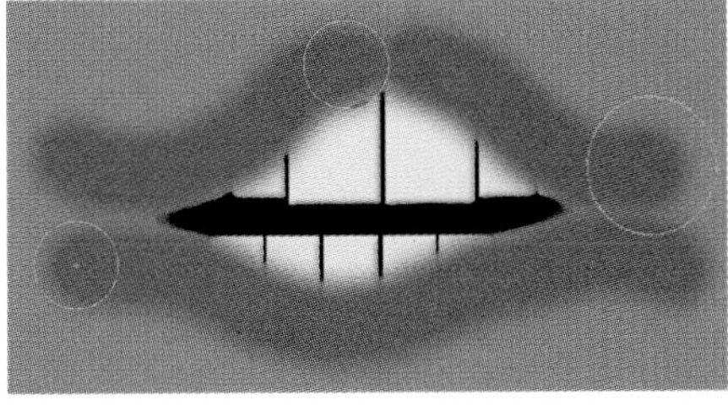

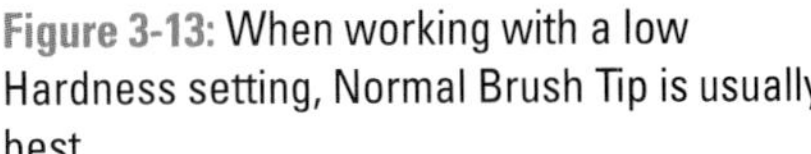

Figure 3-13: When working with a low Hardness setting, Normal Brush Tip is usually best.

When you're sure that you have a brush-size cursor selected in the Preferences but Photoshop shows you the precise cursor, check the CapsLock key on your keyboard. Pressing CapsLock toggles the painting cursors between precise and brush size.

### Preferences⇨Transparency & Gamut

If you find the gray-and-white checkerboard pattern distracting in images with transparency, you can set Grid Size to None, which gives you a plain white background in transparent areas of your artwork. If you work in grayscale regularly, you might want to change the color of the transparency grid to something that contrasts with your image, perhaps pale blue and pale yellow.

### Preferences⇨Units & Rulers

If you create Web graphics rather than print images, you probably want to change Photoshop's unit of measure from Inches to Pixels. Keep in mind that you can change the unit of measure on the fly by right-clicking (multibutton mouse) or Control-clicking (single-button mouse) the rulers in your image. If you regularly print at a resolution other than 300 ppi, you might also want to adjust the default resolution for print-size new documents.

### Preferences⇨Guides, Grid & Slices

Photoshop CS2 introduces *Smart Guides,* which appear and disappear automatically as you drag the content of one layer into and out of alignment with the content of other layers. Smart Guides (magenta in color by default), show when the content of the layer you're dragging aligns perfectly with the edges or center of other layers' content. See Figure 3-14.

Figure 3-14: The magenta guides show how the layer aligns with other layers.

The one thing you might want to change in this pane of the Preferences is the Show Slice Numbers option. The slice numbers appear in the upper-left corner of each slice when you're subdividing Web graphics (see Chapter 17). Unless you intend to edit the images individually later, you probably don't need to know which slice is which, so slice numbers are generally not necessary. Clear the check box to remove the distractions.

## Preferences⇨Plug-Ins & Scratch Disks

If you have third-party plug-ins, filters, and such that you purchased separately for use in Photoshop, consider using a second folder for the plug-ins, outside the Photoshop folder, and designate that folder as the Additional Plug-Ins Folder in the Preferences. Having your extra plug-ins outside the Photoshop folder means you won't have to reinstall them if you have to replace Photoshop. If any of those plug-ins date to Photoshop 5 — and still work — you might need to enter Photoshop 5's serial number as a *legacy* so that the plug-ins recognize the new version.

Photoshop's *scratch disks* are hard drive space used to support the memory. Use only internal hard drives as scratch disks — never an external drive, a network drive, or removable media! If you have multiple internal hard drives, consider a dedicated partition (perhaps 15GB) on the second drive — not the drive on which the operating system is installed. Name the partition Scratch, and use it exclusively as a scratch disk for Photoshop (and perhaps Adobe Illustrator). If you have a couple of extra internal drives, each can have a scratch partition, as shown in Figure 3-15. On a Windows computer, you might see a message warning you that the scratch disk and the Windows paging file (which serves the same basic purpose at the system level) are on the same drive. If you have only one internal hard drive, ignore the message.

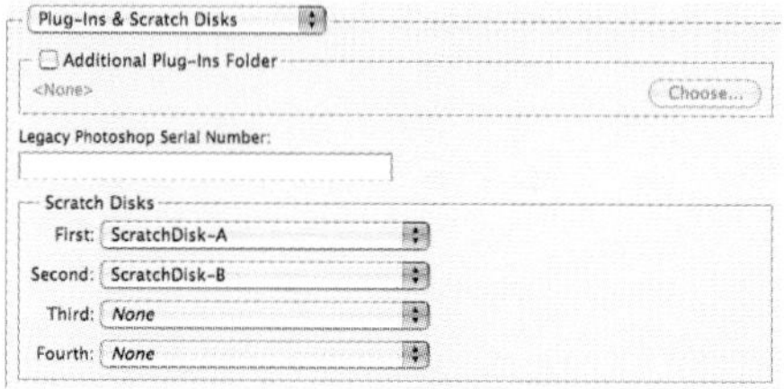


**Figure 3-15:** Use only internal hard drives for scratch disks.

## Preferences⇨Memory & Image Cache

The image cache stores low-resolution copies of your image to speed onscreen display at various zoom levels. Although this process speeds up screen redraw, the price is accuracy. Unless your video card has trouble driving your monitor at your selected resolution and color depth, you might be better served by Cache Levels: 1. That gives the most accurate picture of your work. (But remember to make critical decisions at 100% zoom, where one image pixel equals one screen pixel.)

Under most circumstances, Photoshop's memory allocation should remain set to 70%. If you have 4GB of RAM or more, you can likely increase Photoshop's memory usage to 80 or 85%. If you have a very small amount of installed RAM (say, 512MB) and the operating system is struggling to run, reduce Photoshop's maximum memory usage to 50%.

### Preferences⇨Type

Photoshop CS2 adds a new pane to the Preferences in which you select some type-related options. Photoshop (finally!) shows the font menu in each font's name in the actual typeface, and you can specify the size of that preview here.

## Ensuring consistency: Color Settings

If one term strikes fear deep in the heart of a typical Photoshop user, it's *color management.* Few aspects of the program are so misunderstood. Yet without wise color management decisions, your images won't print accurately. For most Photoshop users, color management can be implemented with a few key choices in the Edit⇨Color Settings dialog box (shown in Figure 3-16):

- **Select an RGB working space.** Open the Color Settings dialog box (under the Edit menu) and select your *RGB working space* — the color space in which you edit and create. If you primarily create Web graphics, send your images to a photo lab for printing, or print with an inkjet printer that uses only four ink colors (cyan, magenta, yellow, and black), choose sRGB as your color space. If you print to a mid-level or high-end inkjet printer or prepare artwork that will be converted to a CMYK color space, choose Adobe RGB. If you have hardware and software to create a custom profile for your computer's monitor, use that profile.

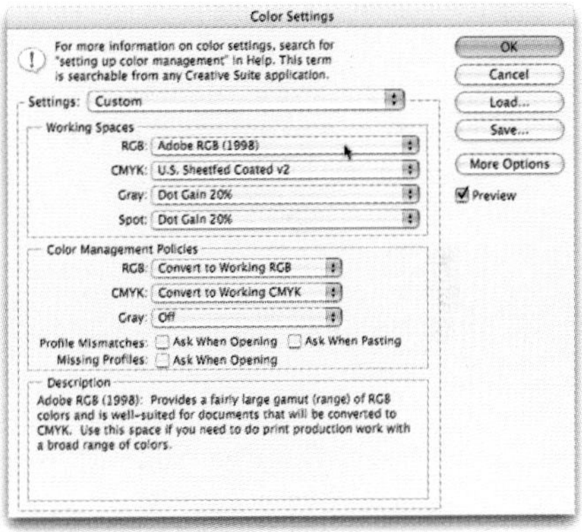


**Figure 3-16:** Choose wisely in the Color Settings dialog box for optimal printing.

- **Elect to convert images to your working space.** In the Color Management Policies area of the Color Settings dialog box, choose RGB: Convert to Working RGB. This ensures that the images you see onscreen actually use your working profile.

- **Turn off the mismatch warnings.** Clear the check boxes for those annoying and time-wasting warnings that pop up onscreen any time you open an image with a profile other than your working space. You are intentionally converting to your working space — you don't need to reaffirm the decision every time.
- **Output using Print with Preview.** When it's time to print, you'll get the most accurate and pleasing prints when you use File⇨Print with Preview. In the dialog box, click the More Options button. In the Color Management section's Print area, choose Document to keep the source space as your working space. In the Options area, choose Color Handling: Let Photoshop Determine Colors and select the printer's own profile for the paper on which you're printing as the Printer Profile. Use Relative Colorimetric as the rending intent and leave the Black Point Compensation check box marked.

The above guidelines are appropriate for most, but not all, Photoshop users. You might fall into a special category:

- **You *exclusively* create Web graphics.** In the Color Settings dialog box, choose Settings: Color Management Off. In the Save For Web dialog box, to the upper right of the preview area, choose Uncompensated Color. When saving images in the JPEG file format, do not embed ICC profiles. (*ICC profiles* make specific adjustments to the appearance of your images to compensate for vagaries of the hardware. I discuss color profiles in Chapter 4.) When you eliminate color profiles from the equation, you're creating Web graphics that any Web browser can show properly (or, more accurately, "as properly as the viewer's uncalibrated monitor can display").
- **You prepare images for offset or flexographic printing.** Your images end up in a CMYK color space. Communicate with the person preparing the page layout document in which your images will be placed or directly with the print shop. Find out what CMYK color profile you should be using (hopefully a custom profile designed for the specific press on which the job will be run). And, of course, there's the possibility that you will be expected to supply RGB images and let the conversion be handled by folks intimately familiar with the particular workflow through which your image will pass.
- **Your color management requirements are extreme.** If color in your images needs to be absolutely perfect — merely accurate won't do — you should consider purchasing hardware and software to calibrate and profile all the devices in your workflow. GretagMacBeth (`www.gretagmacbeth.com`), ColorVision (`www.colorvision.com`), and Monaco (`www.xritephoto.com`) are three sources to explore.

In order to achieve more consistency between Macs and PCs and among the programs of the Adobe Creative Suite, the Color Settings command is moved to the Edit menu for Macs.

# When Good Programs Go Bad: Fixing Photoshop

Sometimes things happen. Bad things. Tools don't work right. Simple commands take ages to execute. Photoshop (gasp!) *crashes*! Don't give up, and please don't toss the machine through the window. (Hey, I might be walking past at the time.) Start with the easy fixes and work your way up as necessary.

- **Check the palettes and selection.** If a tool isn't working as expected or is not working at all, check whether you're inadvertently preventing it from doing its job. See whether you have an active selection elsewhere in the image or press ⌘+D/Ctrl+D to deselect. Look at the Layers palette: Are you on the correct layer? Is the layer itself active or a layer mask? Check the Channels palette: Are the color channels active? At the left end of the Options bar, right-click (multibutton mouse) or Control-click (single-button mouse) the tool icon and select Reset Tool. Open another image — a flattened 8-bit RGB image — and try the tool or technique in that image. (If it works there, the problem isn't Photoshop but rather the specific image. Check the Image➪Mode menu to ensure you've got an appropriate color mode and depth.)
- **Reset Photoshop's Preferences file to the defaults.** Before replacing the Prefs, open Photoshop's Preset Manager (through the Edit menu) and save any custom styles, gradients, brushes, and so forth. Save them in a safe place, outside the Photoshop folder. Open the Actions palette and save any sets of custom Actions with the palette menu Save Actions command. (Remember that you must click a set of Actions — not an individual Action — to use Save Actions.) Open the Preferences and Color Settings and make notes about any special settings you're using. Quit Photoshop and restart the program with the ⌘+Option+Shift keys pressed (Mac); or, immediately after launching the program in Windows, press and hold the Ctrl+Alt+Shift keys. When asked whether you want to delete the Settings folder, release the modifier keys and confirm the deletion; then allow Photoshop to finish starting. Reset your Preferences and Color Settings and reload your custom bits and pieces.
- **Reinstall Photoshop.** If replacing the Prefs doesn't solve the problem, try reinstalling Photoshop. Save all your custom items (as described earlier) and then delete Photoshop and the related files.
    - *Mac:* Drag the Adobe Photoshop folder from the Applications folder to the Trash. Go to [*hard drive*]➪Users➪[*username*]➪Library➪Preferences and delete the Adobe Photoshop Settings folder.
    - *Windows XP:* Choose Start➪Control Panel➪Add or Remove Programs to eliminate Photoshop and any third-party plug-ins. (Be careful about removing shared components if you have other programs of the Adobe Creative Suite installed — cautious is better.)

> After you remove the old copy, reinstall Photoshop from the original CD. Make sure to disable all antivirus software and any auto-backup software before installing, and install into the default location shown by the installer. Test Photoshop before installing any third-party plug-ins.

If reinstalling Photoshop won't solve the problem, the source might be at the operating system level or perhaps a hardware problem. Call in the big guns and contact Adobe tech support:

```
www.adobe.com/support/phonenumbers/main.html
```

# Chapter 4

# Getting Images into and out of Photoshop

### In This Chapter

- Mommy, where do pictures come from?
- Keeping track of your images
- Putting pictures on paper
- Using Web sites and e-mail to share your work

You could, theoretically, open a new empty Photoshop file, paint in it, save the file, and drive from house to house to show the artwork on your computer to friends and family. However, you have lots of ways to share your images that are *much* easier. You can print them, post them on your Web site, or even e-mail them. And e-mailing an image file across the country is much more convenient (and, of course, more eco-friendly) than driving hither and yon with your computer in the trunk.

In this chapter, I show you how to get images into Photoshop from your digital camera and your scanner, and then how to keep those images organized on your hard drive and CDs/DVDs. I discuss the basics of printing your images on inkjet printers (and alternatives) and tell you some things you need to know to make sure you get the prints you expect. I also explain how to use Photoshop's automation to create Web sites of your images as well as how to prepare images for sending by e-mail.

# Bringing Images into Photoshop

Artwork in Photoshop originates in one of three ways (as shown in Figure 4-1):

- You open an image.
- You import an image (typically through a scanning device).
- You create an image from scratch with the File➪New command.

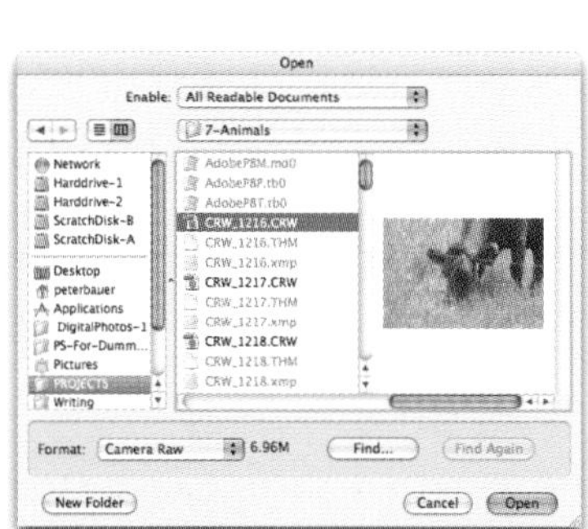

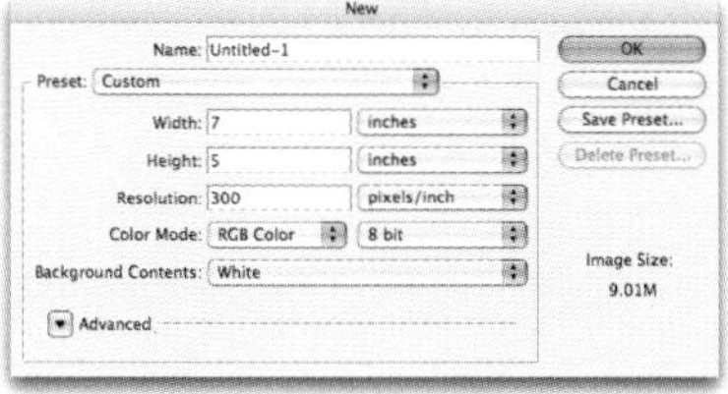


**Figure 4-1:** Open an image, scan an image, or create a new image to work in Photoshop.

You can open an image into Photoshop with the File➪Open command, through Adobe Bridge, or by double-clicking the image file. If you double-click a file and Photoshop doesn't launch or the wrong program launches, you need to associate the file format with Photoshop:

- **Mac file association**

    a. *In the Mac Finder, Control-click (one-button mouse) or right-click (multibutton mouse) a file of the type that you want to open in Photoshop.*

*b. From the contextual menu, choose Get Info.*

*c. In the Get Info dialog box, expand the Opens With area, choose Photoshop cs2 from the pop-up menu, and click Change All.*

*d. (Optional) Repeat for any additional file formats.*

If you double-click a file and Photoshop launches but the image doesn't open, you've likely made a change to the Mac OS and need to reinstall Photoshop.

- **Windows file association**

*a. In Windows Explorer/My Computer, right-click a file of the type that you want to change.*

*b. From the contextual menu, choose Properties.*

*c. To the right of Open With, click the Change button, choose Photoshop cs2, and click OK.*

*d. Click OK again to close the Properties dialog box.*

*e. (Optional) Repeat for any additional file formats.*

## Downloading from your digital camera

You can use the software that comes with your digital camera to transfer photographs from it to your computer's hard drive. Or, if you have the hardware, you can remove your camera's memory card, memory stick, or other media from the camera and use a *card reader,* which is a small device designed to read camera storage media. Transferring via the Mac Finder or Windows Explorer is generally much faster and usually just as reliable as transferring using the camera manufacturer's software.

*Never* open an image into Photoshop directly from a camera, Flash card, or CD/DVD. Doing so can slow down your work, and you also risk losing your work if Photoshop isn't able to immediately and efficiently read the original file while you work. And, of course, you can't save from Photoshop back to most removable media, so you need to create a new file (on a writable drive), anyway. Open images from a network drive only when working with Adobe's *Version Cue,* the Adobe Creative Suite's project management software.

After the images are safely stored on your local hard drive (or a high-speed external hard drive), you open them in Photoshop using one of the three methods that I describe earlier in the chapter. Depending on your color settings, you might see a warning that the image's color profile and the profile that you selected as your RGB working space don't match. Photoshop asks you what you want to do (see Figure 4-2). Generally speaking, you want to convert to your working space so that you see the most accurate color on your monitor. You might want to preserve the embedded profile if you'll be returning the image to the originating computer after looking at or working on it. The third option disregards all color profiles and works with uncorrected color. This is a good choice when working with images that you will later use with a noncolor-managed program, such as a Web browser or presentation program. (Without color management, you see the image as it will appear in the other program.) You can disable the color mismatch warnings in Photoshop's Color Settings dialog box.

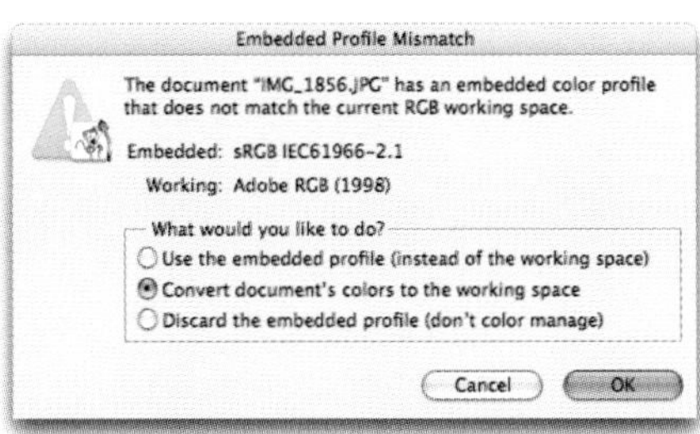


Figure 4-2: When color profiles don't match, you have to make a choice.

When opening an image that includes text, you might also get a message warning you that the type layers need to be updated. Generally speaking, you do want to update unless the image contains fonts not available on your computer.

## Purchasing commercial images

Some projects require images that you can't run out and shoot yourself. Say, for example, that you're preparing a poster or brochure about a ski trip to Japan. In your office or studio. In the United States. In July. Pretty tough to shoot what you need, eh? Turn to stock photography. You can purchase or license stock images (photos, illustrations, video, even audio) from a wide variety of sources, including Internet-based services and collections on CD/DVD. In fact, you'll see images from PhotoSpin.com in a variety of places in this book. Through Adobe Bridge (you can read about this elsewhere in this chapter), you can access over 300,000 stock images from a number of major suppliers.

When you consider using stock images, keep in mind the difference between royalty-free and rights-managed. *Royalty-free images* are yours to use as you see fit (within the terms of your agreement — no resale as stock photos, no defamatory or pornographic use, and so on). You can use the images when you need them, as often as you need them. *Rights-managed photos,* on the other hand, are licensed for a specific use, in specific media, for a specified time. Rights-managed artwork does have one advantage over royalty free. Because usage is controlled, you can license *exclusive* rights to the image for that period of time — the image you use won't appear in some competitor's advertising at the same time. Royalty-free photos, on the other hand, are available to anyone who pays for them, and usage is not controlled.

## Scanning prints

You place a photo (face down) on the glass of your scanner. You push a button. It automatically appears on your computer screen. That's scanning at its most basic. If your scanner's software installed a Photoshop-compatible plug-in into the Import/Export folder inside Photoshop's Plug-Ins folder, you can scan from within Photoshop. (The File⇨Import menu will show your scanner by name.)

### Determining scan resolution

Before scanning an image, you need to make some decisions:

- How you want to use the image
- What its final size will be
- What resolution you need

By determining how many pixels you need beforehand, you eliminate the need to resize the image in Photoshop (and the resulting image degradation). Many scanner interface windows let you input the final size and resolution you need right in the scan window. If you find the need to calculate scan resolution manually, here's how:

1. **Determine the required pixel dimensions.**
   - *For print:* If you'll be printing the image, determine the size at which you want to print (in inches) and the resolution at which you want to print (typically 300 ppi [pixels per inch] is a good choice). Multiply the print width and height by the resolution to determine pixel dimensions.
   - *For the Web:* If the image is destined for your Web site, determine how much of your page the image will occupy (in pixels).
2. **Measure the original.**

   Before placing it on the scanner's glass, measure the original image. If you're using only part of the image, measure that part. (Be careful not to scratch the original with your ruler!)
3. **Do the math.**

   Divide your required pixel dimensions (Step 1) by the physical dimensions of the original (Step 2). The result is your *scan resolution.* (If you get different numbers for the width and height, use the larger and expect to do some cropping in Photoshop.)

Many flatbed scanners (scanners designed for use with documents and photos) have *transparency adapters* that let you scan film and slides. However, if you have a lot of negatives or slides to scan or if the best possible quality is required, consider a dedicated film scanner from Nikon, Minolta, or Kodak.

### Preventing moiré patterns

Unless you spent thousands of dollars on your scanner, you probably want to forget about the scanner software's color and tonal correction capabilities — Photoshop gives you more control. However, here is one thing that scanner software does much better than Photoshop, and it's a capability that you should use when appropriate: moiré (pronounced, roughly, *mwah-RAY*) reduction. A *moiré pattern* is a visible rosette pattern created by the pattern of dots placed by the printing press to reproduce color.

When you need to scan a color image or artwork that comes from a book, magazine, or newspaper (or other material printed on an offset printing press, such as product packaging or signs), you want to use the scanner's software to reduce moiré. The scanner's software compensates for the pattern (when you let the scanner know the pattern is there) and smoothes the scanned image (as you can see in Figure 4-3).

Figure 4-3: Scanning without (left) and with the scanner's moiré reduction option.

The moiré reduction feature in your scanner's software might not be immediately recognizable. It might be labeled Descreening, or it could be a choice between Color (Photo) and Color (Document). As always, refer to your hardware's User Guide for specific guidance.

If rescanning is out of the question and you have a moiré pattern to reduce in Photoshop, blur the image enough to disguise the problem, and then paint with the History Brush to restore areas of critical detail in the image.

Here's an important announcement from *The Department of An Ounce of Prevention is Worth a Pound of Cure:* Before doing any scanning, make sure that the scanner's glass is clean and free of dust. Likewise, check the inside of the scanner's lid. (What good is it to clean the glass if dust from the lid is going to contaminate it again as soon as you close it?) Remember that a minute or two spent cleaning the scanner could save hours of touch-up in Photoshop. Use a can of compressed air to dust the surface. If necessary, eliminate fingerprints or smears with appropriate glass cleaner. (Check the scanner's User Guide for cleaning instructions — and be careful when using liquid glass cleaner with an electrical device! I like to use the same premoistened wipes I use for my eyeglasses.) And use a burst of compressed air on the original, too, before placing it on the glass. Just be careful — hold the can of air some distance away from the photo and spray at an angle so that you don't damage the original.

# Keeping Your Images Organized

Because digital photography doesn't have a per-shot cost (as does shooting film), there is certainly a tendency to shoot more. And more. And more. Experimental shots, this-might-be-interesting shots, special effects shots, and (at least in my case) the same shot over and over and over again. They build up on your hard drive. (Who would have thought, even a few years ago, that a hard drive with a capacity of over 100 gigabytes could *ever* be filled up? Now, I'm not the youngest bull in the herd, but I remember backing up my hard drive to 3.5-inch floppy disks — and not that many of them either!)

It's pretty easy to stay organized after you choose a system. The hard part is actually deleting those digital photos that you really don't need to keep — you know, out-of-focus, shot at a bad angle, Aunt Betsy's eyes were closed and mouth was open, the 400th shot of the dogs sleeping all curled up, the 401st shot of the dogs sleeping all curled up, and the like. It takes discipline! (Or an optical drive that can burn CDs and/or DVDs.)

## Creating a folder structure

I generally recommend using a subject-based organization scheme, such as that shown in Figure 4-4. For example, inside the main folder named DigitalPhotos, you might have subfolders named Vacations, Work-Related, Holidays_2004, and FamilyPortraits. (Notice that none of the folder names use empty spaces or characters other than letters, numbers, a dash, and an underscore — that minimizes the possibility that Photoshop or another program won't be able to find a file.) Within the Vacations subfolder, you might have more subfolders with names such as Tahiti_2004, Snowmass_2005, Paris-Spring_2005, and Paris-Autumn_2004. Or you might have subfolders with names like Mom-and-Dad_2004, Akron_2004, Toledo_2005, and Cleveland_2004. Or, if you've got a work schedule like mine, the Vacations folder might be completely empty.

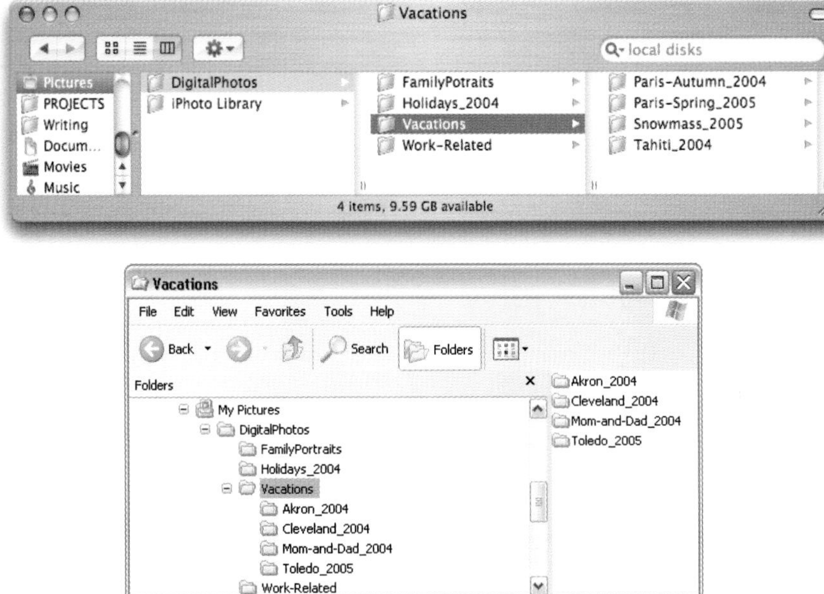


**Figure 4-4:** Organize with subfolders.

Don't overload your folders! If you find that your computer is slowing down when it tries to display the content of a folder, you've got too many files in the folder. Create a second folder of the same name and add -01 and -02 to the folder names. Generally speaking, 100MB is probably as large as you want in a single folder.

You can use your computer's CD/DVD drive (if it has the capability) to burn folders of images to disk. This not only provides you with a reliable backup (assuming you store the disks correctly and handle them carefully), but it can free up space on your hard drive. Your folder/subfolder structure can also be used when creating your disks.

## Using Adobe Bridge

New in Photoshop CS2 — oops, make that "new *out of* Photoshop CS2" — is *Adobe Bridge,* the standalone replacement for the File Browser to organize, preview, and open your images. The File Browser, introduced with Photoshop 7, was such a great hit that Adobe decided to expand the concept to the entire Adobe Creative Suite. Rather than adding a browser to each program in the Creative Suite, a single additional program was developed — one that would work with all the individual components. The result is Adobe Bridge.

Bridge is installed at the same time you install Photoshop CS2 or the Creative Suite. Unlike *ImageReady* (the standalone Web graphics program you

installed with Photoshop), Bridge has its own folder on your hard drive. (You'll find the Adobe Bridge folder inside the Applications folder on the Mac/in Program Files for Windows.) You can open Bridge independently, or you can use Photoshop's File➪Browse command to launch Bridge, which you see in Figure 4-5. You'll find one major change from the File Browser to Bridge: Bridge (because it's a separate program) has its menus across the top of your screen.

Figure 4-5: Adobe Bridge replaces the File Browser but serves the same function.

Here are a few tips for working with Adobe Bridge:

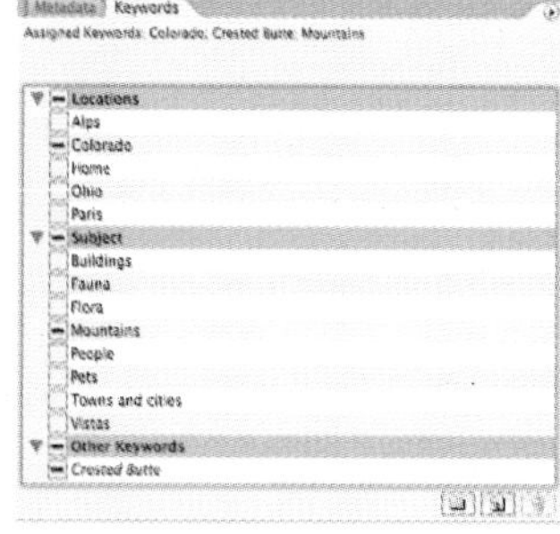


Figure 4-6: Assign keywords and categories to help organize (and locate) images.

- **Use keywords and categories.** Using the Keywords tab in the lower-left of the Bridge window (as shown in Figure 4-6), you can assign keywords and categories to images. *Keywords* and *categories* are descriptive terms that you assign to individual images. Down the road, you can use Bridge's Search feature to find all images with a specific assigned keyword.

You can select multiple images in Bridge by clicking and Shift-clicking (or ⌘-clicking/Ctrl-clicking) and then assign keywords to all the selected images at once.

- **Use labels and ratings.** Under the Label menu (which you see in Figure 4-7), you can assign a star rating to each image and assign colors to organize by subject or project. Use the View➪Sort menu to arrange images in the thumbnails area of Bridge according to either the label or the rating.

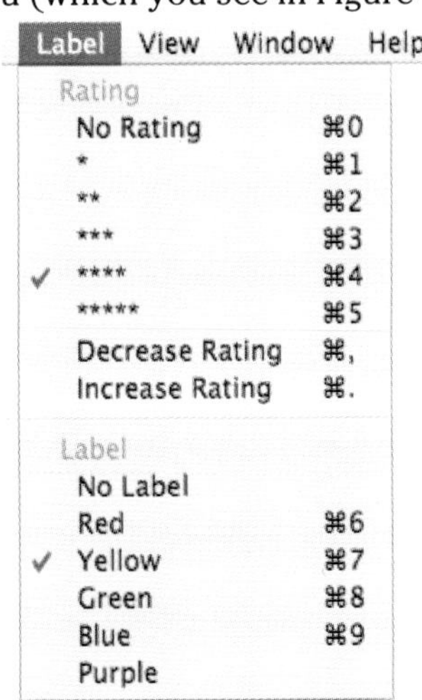


**Figure 4-7:** Use star ratings and labels as reminders and to sort your images.

- **Add folders to the Favorites.** You invariably will visit some folders on a regular basis. Use the File➪Add to Favorites command to get back to that folder faster and more easily. In the upper-left corner of the Bridge window, click the Favorites tab for one-click access. Keep in mind, too, that you can add a folder to the Favorites while working on a specific project, and then use the File➪Remove from Favorites command when the project is finished.
- **Change your view and workspace.** Use the View menu to customize what the Bridge window shows, and use the Window➪Workspace menu to determine how it is displayed. In Figure 4-8, you see the default workspace as well as the Lightbox workspace (which shows a number of fairly large images) and the Filmstrip Focus view (for seeing a number of thumbnails and a large preview).
- **Export the cache.** When the content of a folder is finalized — when the images in the folder won't change — use the Tools➪Cache➪Export Cache command. Exporting the cache drastically reduces the amount of time it takes to display thumbnails and metadata. If the content of the folder does change, purge the folder's cache and export again (both by using the Tools➪Cache menu). Remember to export the cache just before burning a folder of images to CD or DVD.

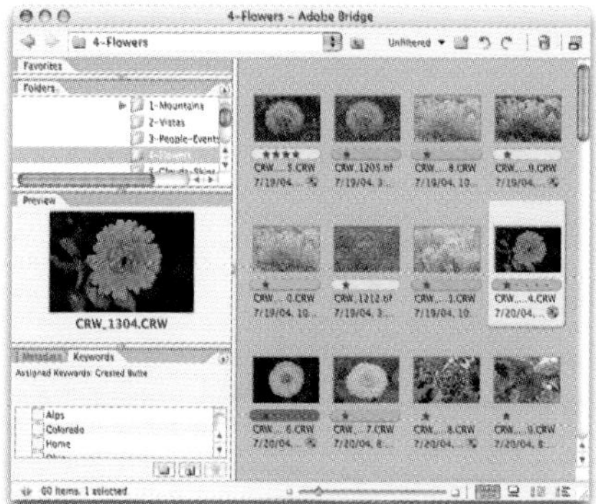

Figure 4-8: Use a workspace that fits your needs.

## Renaming image files easily

All right, then, you've arranged a hierarchy of folders and subfolders. You've sorted your images into those folders. You've assigned rank and label to the images. However, you still have no idea which is which in the File➪Open Recent menu. Filenames such as `CRW_1907.crw` and `PB270091.jpg` don't tell you much about the image content, do they? Use Bridge's Tools➪Batch Rename command (as shown in Figure 4-9) to assign more meaningful (and informative) names to your files. Select content from each field from the pop-up menu or type in a field.

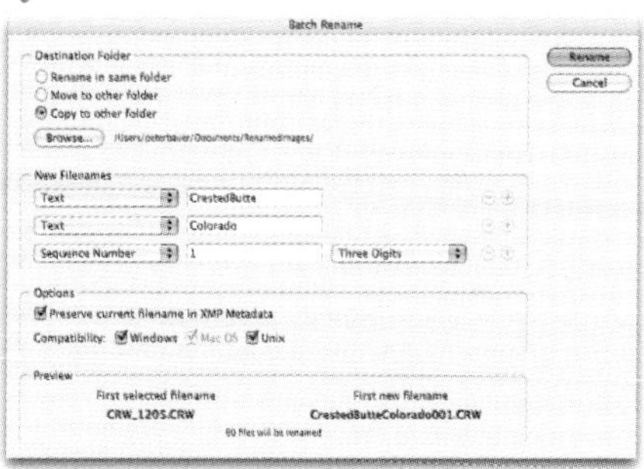


Figure 4-9: Use Batch Rename to assign informative names to files.

So that each of your original images gets a unique one-of-a-kind name, you *must* include a variable when using Batch Rename. (If you did try to rename all the images in a folder to say, `picture.jpg`, you would end up with only one image file in the destination folder — each would overwrite the previous.) Therefore, when using Batch Rename, you must choose one of the variables for one of the fields via the pop-up menu, be it the original document name or a sequence number/letter. Also keep in mind that you should not type a period (`.`) into any field. That character should be used only before the file extension. And, as a wonderful keep-us-from-creating-problems-for-ourselves improvement, Batch Rename now automatically adds the file extension for you.

# Printing Your Images

In the very recent past, the subject of printing images from Photoshop required a huge number of pages. Thankfully, improvements in hardware and software make printing much easier. Monitors are well calibrated out of the box, printers reproduce color more accurately, and inks and papers last for decades. Yes, things have come a long way in a short time. But before you click the Print button, you should make sure that your image is ready to print. Will it fit properly on the page and in the frame? Are the pixels small enough that they blend evenly into the overall picture? Will the colors you envision be the colors that appear on paper?

## Cropping to a specific aspect ratio

*Aspect ratio* is the relationship between the width and height of your image. An image in *landscape* aspect ratio is wider than it is tall, and an image in *portrait* aspect ratio is taller than wide. Although digital cameras capture in a variety of aspect ratios, including 3:4 and 4:5, SLR (single lens reflex) cameras typically use a 2:3 aspect ratio: One side is one-and-one-half times the size of the adjoining sides. Typical print (and picture frame) sizes are 8 x 10 inches (a 4:5 aspect ratio), 5 x 7 inches (5:7), 4 x 6 inches (2:3), and 3 x 5 inches (3:5). In Figure 4-10, the 2:3 aspect ratio is outlined in green, 5:7 is shown in yellow, and 4:5 is red.

Although an 8 x 10 print is physically larger than a 4 x 6 print, it actually prints less of your original image because it must be cropped. The 4 x 6 print, with a 2:3 aspect ratio, includes all the original image; the 8 x 10 print (with its 4:5 aspect ration) is missing two full inches of the image's longer dimension. To print 8 inches wide and retain the entire image, you'd be printing at 8 x 12.

Figure 4-10: Different print sizes encompass different amounts of your image.

In Photoshop, you can change the aspect ratio of your image with the Canvas Size command (if one dimension is already correctly sized), the Crop tool, or the Rectangular Marquee tool with the Image➪Crop command. The Crop tool can resample your image to the exact print dimensions and resolution in one step, but you generally need to use the Image Size command when changing aspect ratio with Canvas Size or the Rectangular Marquee.

With the Crop tool selected, you can enter specific dimensions and a target resolution on the Options bar. Drag the tool, position and adjust the bounding box, and then press Return/Enter on your keyboard to execute the crop. Whatever is within the bounding box is resampled to the exact size that you specify on the Options bar. (Remember to click the Clear button on the Options bar afterward to restore the Crop tool to its normal behavior.)

When cropping, Photoshop uses the resampling algorithm that you specify in Preferences➪General as the Image Interpolation method. For best results, choose Bicubic Smoother when increasing an image's size and Bicubic Sharper when decreasing the size.

When creating a cropping selection with the Rectangular Marquee tool, you can change the tool's Style pop-up menu (on the Options bar) from Normal to Fixed Aspect Ratio or Fixed Size. Generally speaking, use Fixed Aspect Ratio (as shown in Figure 4-11) and drag the marquee to encompass that part of the image you want to retain. After the selection marquee is how and where you want it, use the Image➪Crop command.

©2003 PhotoSpin, PhotoSpin image #0990134

**Figure 4-11:** Use the Fixed Aspect Ratio option for a specific width-height relationship.

Keep in mind that the Crop command doesn't resample the image — you've just changed the aspect ratio so far — so you need to also use the Image➪Image Size command (which is discussed in Chapter 2).

## Remembering resolution

Chapter 2 presents you with an in-depth look at resolution as it pertains to digital imaging. As a quick refresher, keep these points in mind when thinking about printing your images:

- **Images themselves have no resolution.** Whether in your camera, on your hard drive, or open in Photoshop, your images consist only of tiny colored squares called *pixels*. The image looks and acts the same within Photoshop, regardless of resolution. An image 3000 x 2000 pixels at 300 ppi is handled in Photoshop exactly as an image 3000 x 2000 pixels at 72 ppi.
- **Resolution is an instruction to a printing device.** The resolution value that you assign to an image in your digital camera or in Photoshop's Image Size dialog box is recorded with the image strictly as an instruction to the output device.
- **Resolution measures the size of individual pixels.** 300 ppi really means that each pixel will print at a size exactly 1⁄300 of an inch square. Likewise, 72 ppi equates to each pixel printing at 1⁄72 of an inch square. Some folks might find this reasoning uncomfortable (although they can deny neither the mathematics nor the logic). Should you run across such an individual, feel free to ask this question: "What if an image's resolution is 300 pixels per inch, but the image is only 299 pixels wide?" (Then smile and buy the next beverage.)
- **Web images use only pixel dimensions.** Web browsers aren't capable of reading the resolution information embedded in your simple graphics by Photoshop. Each image is displayed in the Web browser strictly according to the number of pixels in the image.

## Controlling color using Print with Preview

In the past few years, reproducing accurate color from monitor to printer has become much easier. Although the process of color management still strikes fear into the hearts of many, the actual need for complex hardware and software to control color is greatly reduced. Why? Simply because computer manufacturers recognized that we, the consumers, wanted better color. (Okay, maybe it was all the video gamers that got the attention.) Monitors ship from the factory calibrated and accurate. Printers use smaller droplets and better inks. Software does a better job of communicating color.

For most Photoshop users, accurate color is important. After spending hours tweaking an image's appearance onscreen, surely you want the print to look exactly like the monitor. Here's how to get that great color:

1. **When you're ready to output your image, use Photoshop's File➪Print with Preview command rather than the simple Print command.**

   Print with Preview gives you quite a few more options than you have in the regular Print dialog box, including the color management options used here. Compare the two dialog boxes in Figure 4-12.

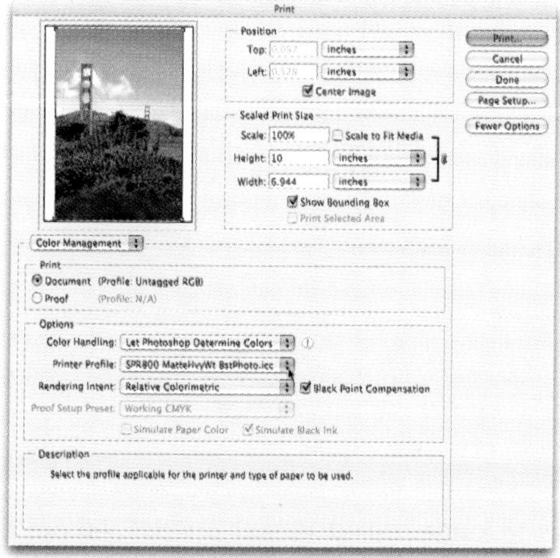


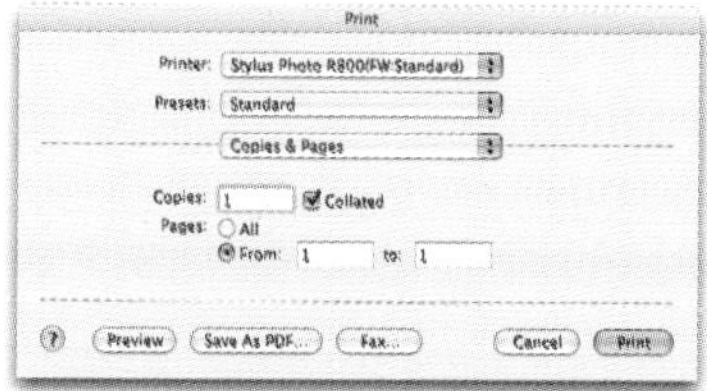


*©2004 PhotoSpin, PhotoSpin image #1440009*

**Figure 4-12:** Use the larger Print with Preview dialog box for more control over color.

2. **In the Print with Preview dialog box, click the More Options button to expand the dialog box.**

3. **Choose Print: Document.**

   In the Color Management section of the dialog box, make sure that the Print option is set to Document rather than Proof. The document's color profile should show in parentheses, and that profile should be your working RGB from Photoshop's Color Settings dialog box. Unless you have a custom monitor profile, use Adobe RGB (for mid- to high-end inkjet printers) or sRGB (for entry-level four-ink printers).

4. **Choose your options.**

   - *In the Options section* of the dialog box, select Color Handling: Let Photoshop Determine Colors.
   - *From the Printer Profile pop-up menu,* choose the printer's own profile for the paper on which you're printing.
   - *For Rendering Intent,* choose Relative Colorimetric and select the Black Point Compensation check box.

5. **When ready, click the Print button.**

   Clicking the Print with Preview Print button closes the dialog box and moves you to the printer's own Print dialog box.

6. **Disable the printer's color management.**

   Because you're doing all your color management in Photoshop, you want to disable all printer-level color management in the printer's own Print dialog box. (Check your printer's User Guide for specific instructions.)

7. **Print.**

   Clicking the Print button in the printer's dialog box sends the image to the printer and starts the actual process of putting ink on paper.

Don't forget that Photoshop CS2 offers you a couple of different ways to save paper (and time and money) by printing multiple images on a single sheet of paper. See Chapter 16 for information on Picture Package and Contact Sheet.

## Considering color management solutions

If your prints don't match your monitor, first evaluate your monitor's settings. Open an image with known color values (you know what the image should look like) in a noncolor-managed program. You might, for example, use Microsoft Word's Insert⇨Picture⇨From File command to add the image `Ducky.tif` from the Samples folder (inside the Photoshop folder) to a blank Word document. Use the monitor's own controls to make that image look the best possible, and then print. If the image prints accurately, great — you're all set.

If the monitor looks great but the print is strange, first try cleaning and calibrating the print head. And take another look at the Print dialog box to make sure that you're selecting the proper paper and color settings. (Again, refer to the User Guide for your printer for specific instructions.)

For those among us whose work (or play) requires extreme color fidelity, a number of companies offer hardware and software that regulate color. You can create custom profiles for monitors, printers, and even scanners and digital cameras. Although not inexpensive, skillful handling (in accordance with the User Guides!) not only results in better prints, but also reduces the amount of aw-shucks wasted paper and ink from bad output. If you fall into this category, explore the current offerings from GretagMacBeth (`www.gretagmacbeth.com`) and ColorVision (`www.colorvision.com`).

## Check your color (Mac only)

The Mac OS includes a great little program called DigitalColor Meter. You'll find it in the Applications➪Utilities folder. Open DigitalColor Meter and position the window in the lower center of your screen. Open Photoshop. Drag the Swatches palette to the center of the screen, above DigitalColor Meter. (If necessary, use the Swatches palette menu command Reset Swatches to make the default swatches visible in the palette.) Move the cursor onto the first swatch. If your selected monitor profile is accurate and your monitor is working properly, DigitalColor Meter will show RGB values of 255/0/0 (see the figure here). Try the next five swatches. You should see Yellow: 255/255/0; Green: 0/255/0; Cyan: 0/255/255; Blue: 0/0/255; and Magenta: 255/0/255.

If you have an Apple Cinema Display or an Apple Studio Display and DigitalColor Meter tells you something's not quite right, try the simple solution. Open Apple's System Preferences and click Displays. On the Color tab, select Adobe RGB as the system-level color profile and then close System Preferences. In Photoshop's Color Settings dialog box, select Adobe RGB as the RGB Working Space. Open DigitalColor Meter again and test that Swatches palette once more.

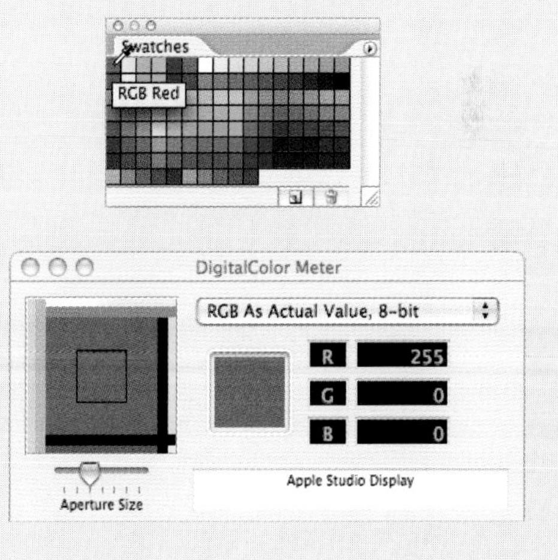

Keep in mind that all the color management hardware and software in the world doesn't do you a bit of good if you're not controlling your environment. If your work requires perfect color — not *good*, but *perfect* — you need to take some additional steps. In the office or studio, you need to regulate ambient light so that you have a consistent color-viewing situation, day in and day out, rain or shine, summer and winter. If you have windows, you need shades or drapes that you can close before doing color-critical work. The walls visible behind the monitor and the immediate work area should be neutral in color. (And that means no brightly colored sticky notes on the bezel of your monitor!) You probably need a hood for your monitor and perhaps a D50 (or D65) viewing station in which to evaluate your prints under optimal lighting conditions.

## Printing alternatives

Odds are that you use an inkjet printer to put your photos on paper. Although inkjet printers are the most popular and perhaps the most practical, you do have alternatives. If, for example, your work consists of brochures and flyers rather than photos, a color laser printer might better fit your needs. The initial cost is generally higher than all except wide-format inkjets, but the cost per page is much lower. Color laser printers generally don't print photographs as well as a mid- to high-end inkjet, and the prints are not archival (they won't last for a whole lot of years without fading), but such prints might be just fine for sharing snapshots among friends and family. The print options for a color laser printer (such as the Print dialog box you see in Figure 4-13) differ from an inkjet's options. Check the User Guide for the specific printer to set up your job correctly.

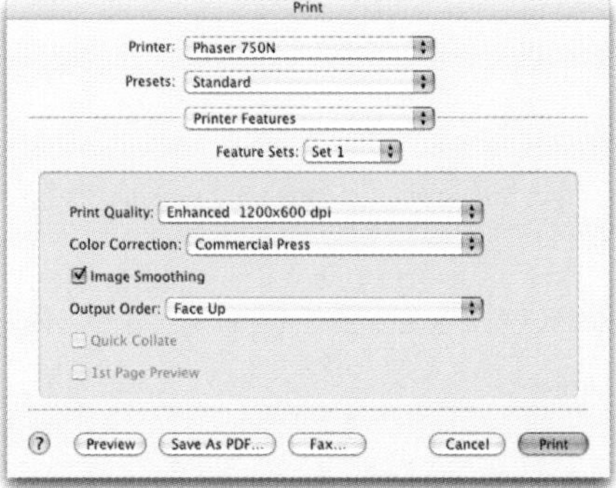


**Figure 4-13:** Color laser printer options differ from those for inkjet printers.

Dye sublimation printers use rolls of film impregnated with dyes to reproduce prints. Prices range from under $200 to several thousand dollars. The quality and longevity of the prints is generally tied to the price.

Here's another output alternative available to virtually all Photoshop users. Burn your images in JPEG format (highest quality, 300 ppi) onto a CD and take the CD to the local photo lab. Alternatively, use an online service with which you upload your JPEGs to the service's Web service to order prints. You'll get back glossy or matte prints at the size(s) requested. And the cost per print can be substantially less than using your inkjet printer. The local photo lab is often a great alternative for stacks of vacation photos and family reunion shots that need to be sent to a whole passel of kin.

Unless your inkjet printer is specifically designed to generate grayscale images, you might want to use the photo lab for such prints. Inkjet printers designed with grayscale in mind output using black ink plus a supplemental light-black or gray ink to increase the tonal range and ensure adequate detail in your shadows. Inkjets that aren't designed to print grayscale can either print using only black ink (which severely limits the detail and tonal range), or they use *rich black* (black ink supplemented with the additional color inks), which invariably leads to some color tint or color cast in the supposedly neutral grayscale images. It's the nature of the beast — ink droplets are placed near each other, not on top of each other, which leads to the visible tinting of a grayscale image when printed on an inkjet using colored inks. Check the User Guide for your printer: If it doesn't provide specific guidance for printing grayscale, send your black-and-white images to the local photo lab for output.

# Sharing Your Images on the Internet

To post your images on a Web site, you need a couple of things: a Web site and a Web server on which to post. Your Internet Service Provider (ISP) — the folks you pay to let you surf the Net and get e-mail — might have space reserved for you as part of your contract, or you might need to pay extra. Check your contract or call the ISP. (When it comes time to actually put your site on the Web, called *posting* the site, you need to check the ISP's Web site for specific instructions.)

## Using Web Photo Gallery

To get your site ready to post, you can use Photoshop's Web Photo Gallery feature. (If you have GoLive, you might want to use that program or perhaps generate a Web Photo Gallery and customize it in GoLive.) Web Photo Gallery creates the entire Web site from your folder of images and the guidance that you provide for customization of the site. You end up with a home page (named `index.htm` — the page you open in your Web browser) as well as folders named Pages, Thumbnails, and Images. Depending on the layout you select, you might also generate a few additional files. Remember that you must keep all these elements together for the Web site to function properly.

As you see in Figure 4-14, you have a rather long list of site layouts from which to choose. (Your list might vary.) Thankfully, the preview below the Cancel button gives you some idea of the layout, so you don't have to generate a full Web Photo Gallery only to change your mind.

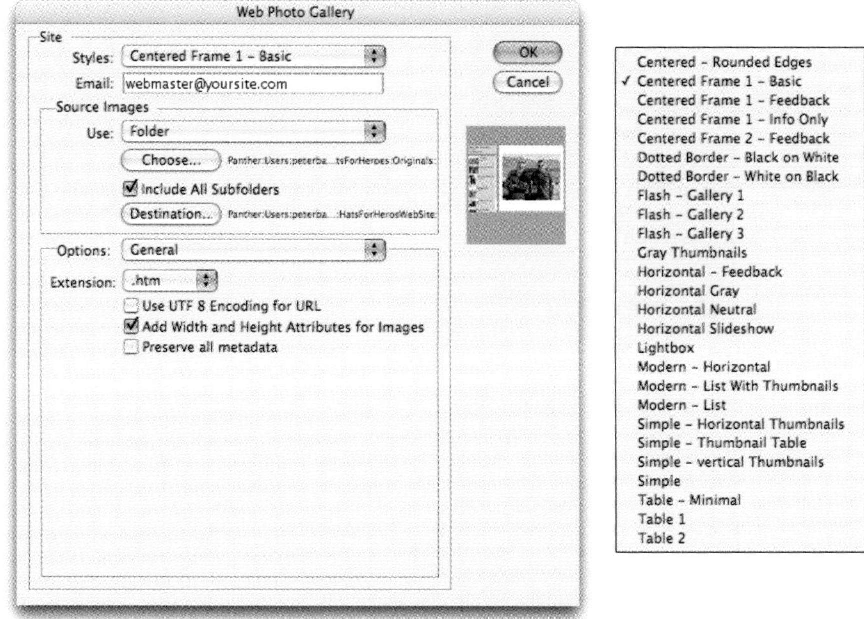


**Figure 4-14:** To the right, you see the substantial list of Web Photo Gallery templates.

In the top sections of the Web Photo Gallery dialog box, you choose the layout from the Style menu, enter your e-mail address so visitors to the site can tell you how wonderful it is, and select both a source folder (the images to post on the site) and the *destination* (a folder where the various parts of your new Web site can be saved — any place except the source folder).

In the Options area of the Web Photo Gallery dialog box, you make decisions about how you want to customize the template. In additional to the General options shown in Figure 4-14, you have five additional panels of options in which to work: Banner, Large Images, Thumbnails, Custom Color, and Security (shown in Figure 4-15). Note that not all options are available for all templates. If having the filename as a caption is critical to your concept, make sure you're using a template that includes that option.

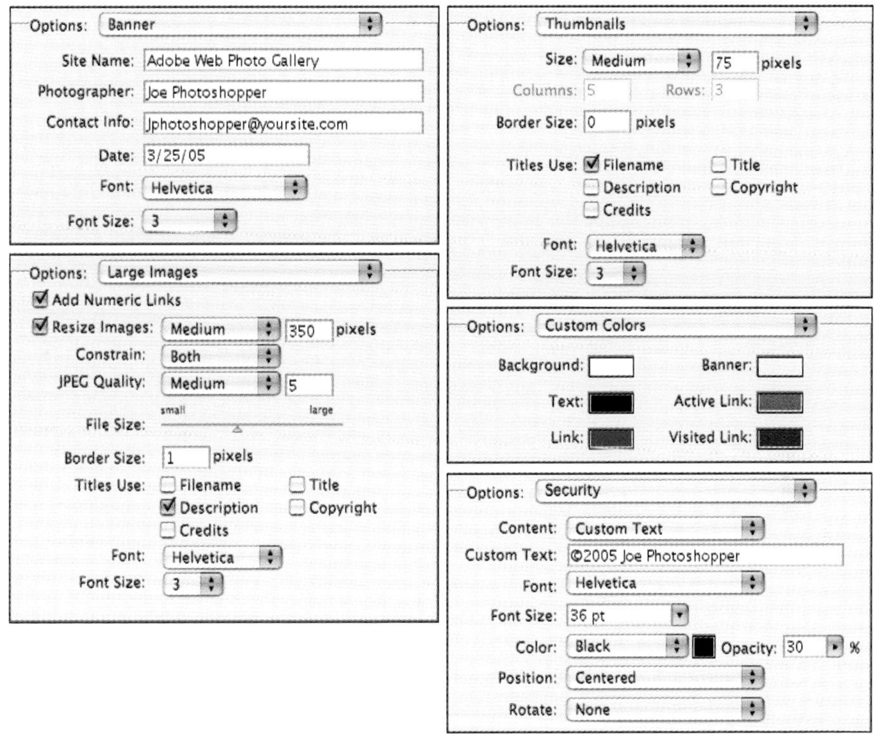


**Figure 4-15:** Not all options are available for every Web Photo Gallery template.

Prepare a folder of perhaps four or five images and create galleries from the layouts that look most interesting. By using only a few images, you save a bunch of time while experimenting. This also gives you a chance to preview the options you've selected, including the font size for Security. (It would be a shame to generate a gallery of hundreds of images only to find out that your copyright notice is wider than the images.) Remember, too, that you can manually create a replacement image (see Chapter 17) and substitute it in the Images folder (using exactly the same name). And as a great shortcut to generate small images for another program or a PDF Presentation, you can run Web Photo Gallery and then delete everything except the Images folder.

## E-mailing your images

In addition to posting your images on the Web as a Web Photo Gallery, you can use your e-mail program to share your images. However, if you like these folks enough to send them your images, you probably want to keep their friendship. And to that end, you want to be a responsible e-mailer — you don't want to send out an e-mail attachment so large that it disrupts service for the recipient. ("Hi Marge. You know those images from your vacation that you e-mailed me on Tuesday? They're still trying to download. Yeah, today is Saturday. Anyway, why don't I drive up to Maine and look at the snapshots — it's probably faster than waiting for the e-mail.")

As a general rule, your attached images should rarely (if ever) total more than 1MB in size (unless you verify through direct communication that everyone on your To: list can handle large attachments). Each individual image should be no more than 550 pixels tall (so that it can be viewed in a Web browser on any screen). You can certainly use your computer's compression utility — StuffIt (Mac) or WinZip (Windows) — to compress one or more images before sending. But if you do compress your attached images, make sure to include instructions to save the compressed file to the hard drive and double-click to expand.

# Part II

# Easy Enhancements for Digital Images

## In this part . . .

Some photos can be printed straight from the camera without ever seeing the light of Photoshop. However, most images need at least some adjustment, and many need a lot of adjustment. Here's where you discover how to work magic on your images.

The range of brightness from black to white is critical for most images. In Chapter 5, you read how to maximize and adjust that tonal range in your photos, and how to use the new Photoshop CS2 Histogram palette. And there's more to a great photo than shadows and highlights. Chapter 6 looks at adjusting the color in your images, making them look as natural as possible. More and more digital photographers are switching to the Raw file format because of the control it provides over the final image. Read Chapter 7 for the Raw lowdown.

Sometimes only part of an image needs to be adjusted. The key to making precise adjustments, as you can read in Chapter 8, is to tell Photoshop where to work with selections and masks. Chapter 9 examines many of the most common problems in Photoshop (and what to do about them). You can read about eliminating red-eye, reducing wrinkles, whitening teeth, and minimizing digital noise.

# Chapter 5

# Adding Dark Shadows and Sparkling Highlights

## *In This Chapter*

- Discovering tonality
- The easy Auto repairs
- Making adjustments with Levels and Curves
- Advanced tonality correction

It's the difference between an Ansel Adams print and the snapshot of your grandfather as a boy. It's the difference between high-definition TV and the local public access channel's broadcast. It's the difference between a Ferrari and a minivan. It's that *thing* — that special *something* — that tells you that you're seeing the real deal, the genuine article, all that it can be. And it's something that you can do for your images.

When an image really *pops* — when it jumps off the page at you — it's generally because the shadows are dark, the highlights are light, and the colors are rich. I'm sure it's no surprise to you that Photoshop can handle the job. (That's one of the reasons why you bought the program, right?)

In this chapter, I introduce you to the concept of *tonality,* which is the range of brightness in your image. I also introduce to you the various commands that Photoshop offers for you to adjust your image's tonality. There are even a couple of tools for pin-point control of shadows and highlights. And along the way, I offer you a look at the Histogram palette — what it tells you, what it *doesn't* tell you, and how to use it best.

## Adjusting Tonality to Make Your Images Pop

Most photos look better with a little tweaking. For pictures that look good to begin with, you might still want to perk them up a little with a tonal adjustment. Making the shadows a little darker and the highlights a bit lighter increases your image's perceived *tonal range,* which is sort of the distance between black and white. Take a look at Figure 5-1. It's a pleasant enough snapshot, with decent composition and an interesting subject (very interesting when you get to know her!). But it lacks pizzazz.

**Figure 5-1:** A nice snapshot, but not *art.*

With Photoshop, you can darken the shadows and lighten the rest of the image to make it more interesting. By intensifying the difference between what the eye sees as dark and what the eye sees as light in the image, you add some semblance of depth to this simple picture. Comparing Figure 5-1 with Figure 5-2, you can see that one basic tonal adjustment can also make the colors (such as the shirt) seem richer and even produce a perceived increase in detail or sharpness (the fur at the muzzle, ear, and top of her head).

**Figure 5-2:** One simple tonal adjustment darkens, lightens, enriches color, and brings out detail.

You might hear a number of words used for the same concept: the lightness and darkness of your image. Tonality, luminosity, and even brightness can be used virtually interchangeably when you're talking about the general subject. However, you generally use *brightness* when talking about specific pixels and *tonality* when referring to the image as a whole.

## Histograms Simplified

In most photographs of general subject matter, your eye sees the darkest neutral (gray) tone as black and the lightest neutral as white. (If the darkest color is obviously purple and the lightest a bright yellow, you probably wouldn't classify the photo's subject as "general.") In a given image, the shadow under the shoe might be just a dark gray, and the shirt looks like it might need some bleach, but your eye (in cooperation with your mind) compensates to some degree and lets you see black and white.

For a more accurate look at the tonal range of your image, Photoshop offers the Histogram palette (found nested with the Navigator and Info palettes in the upper-right corner of your screen), which displays the distribution of the pixels in your image at various luminosity values. The darker pixels *(shadows)* are stacked at the left end, the lighter pixels *(highlights)* are stacked at the right end, and the rest of the brightness values *(midtones)* are stacked between. The taller a column in the histogram, the more pixels at that luminosity value. Figure 5-3 shows an image with what some folks would call a near-perfect histogram distribution because of the beautiful bell curve centered in the graph.

Figure 5-3: This image has a very even distribution of pixels through the midtones.

But don't be seduced by a histogram distribution! Not every properly exposed image has such a bell curve. Many perfect images have wildly different histograms. The correct distribution in the histogram depends on two things: the image content and the artistic aims of the artist.

Consider, if you will, an image that consists primarily of white pixels, perhaps a beautiful Alpine snow scene or an ugly creepy-crawly thing on porcelain (as you can see in Figure 5-4). Either image has a histogram skewed dramatically to the right — what you call a *high-key* image. Nothing is wrong with the image (despite the histogram); it just happens to have a huge number of light-colored pixels.

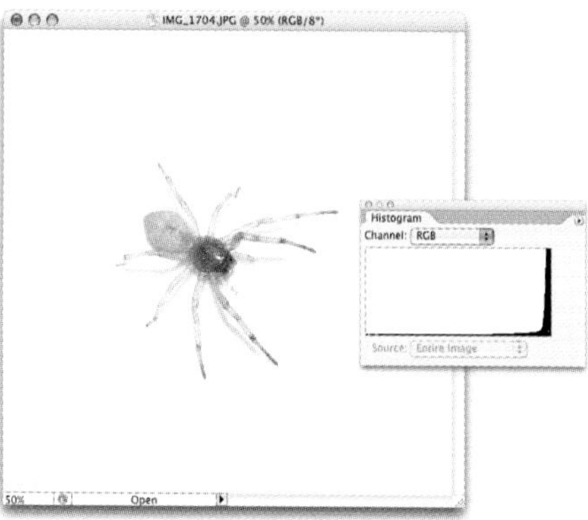


Figure 5-4: The histogram is skewed because of the many white pixels. Or maybe it's running away.

Likewise, a *low-key* image has a preponderance of dark pixels, which skews the histogram to the left. Just about any night scene has a very large number of very dark pixels, pulling the distribution to the left in the histogram. But many night scenes also include lights, which produce a spike at the far right end.

Keep in mind, too, that the heights of the individual columns in the histogram area are relative: The tallest goes all the way to the top of the box, and the others are scaled accordingly. For example, an image on a black background — say, a large black background — might have so many pixels in the left-most column that the other columns in the image appear tiny and almost unreadable, like the histogram shown in Figure 5-5.

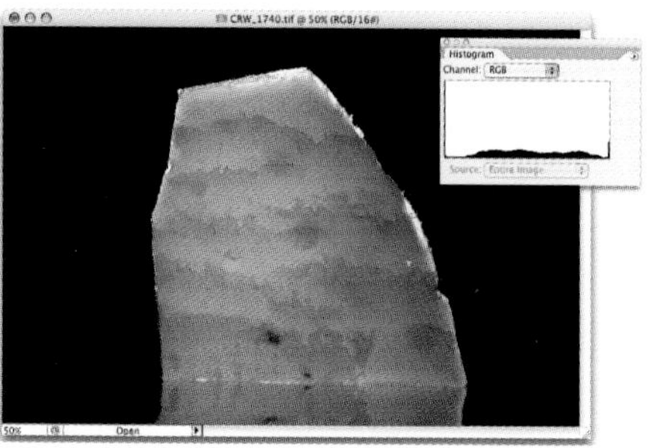

Figure 5-5: Too many pixels in the left-most column make the distribution for the midtones hard to see.

If the histogram is skewed to one end or the other, making it hard to read, you can make a selection within the image and the histogram updates to show information for only the selected area. (Read about making selections in Chapter 8.)

Sometimes a histogram seems to tell you absolutely nothing worthwhile. For example, take the histogram in Figure 5-6. The image doesn't have a bell curve distribution, with a gentle sloping to either side of the center peak. It's not a high-key image because the pixels aren't mashed together at the right. The image is somewhat low-key, but the histogram doesn't have a huge stack at the left end. It does tell you, however, that there are three distinct ranges of tonality in which you find most of the image's pixels.

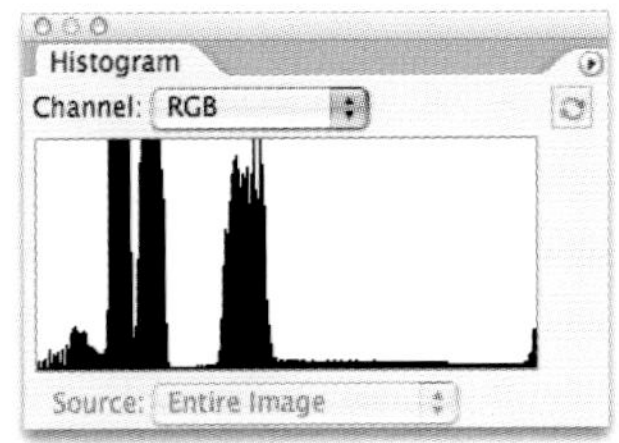


**Figure 5-6:** The histogram sometimes speaks to you in riddles.

When you click the triangle in the upper-right corner of the Histogram palette, you can change the palette's configuration. (So far in this chapter, I show the Expanded View, which offers a little better look at the graph than does the Compact View.) In this case, switching to the All Channels View, which shows you a histogram for each color channel, helps solve *The Mystery of the Wacky Histogram* (especially when seen with the image itself, as shown in Figure 5-7). The image contains a large number of pixels of a rather consistent color. If you mixed that color in the kitchen, the recipe would call for one part red, two parts green, and four parts blue.

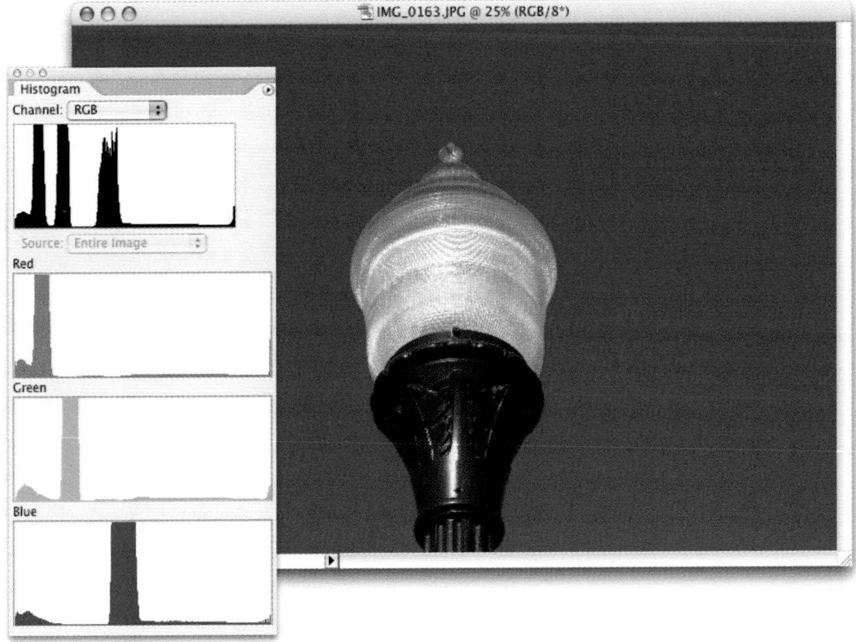


**Figure 5-7:** The All Channels View shows individual histograms for each color channel.

As you read later in this chapter in the section "Level-headed you!," you can use the histogram to help avoid degrading your image while making adjustments, and (as you read in Chapter 7) it's very important for working with the Camera Raw plug-in. But don't forget about your eyeballs — you don't need the Histogram palette to spot a low-key or high-key image.

# Using Photoshop's Auto Corrections

Adjusting the tonality of your image can be as simple as selecting one of the Auto commands from Photoshop's Image➪Adjustments menu. With many photos, the tonality (and even the color) jump to just the right look for your image. No muss, no fuss — just a great-looking picture with a single command.

If you need to do something special with the image (for example, create an unusual effect), or if the image is in bad shape to begin with, the Auto commands might not be your best bet. But remember this: It never hurts to try an Auto command first. At worst, you use the Undo command, and you've wasted only a couple of seconds and a pair of keystrokes.

Figure 5-8: The same photo, with and without an orange color cast.

From least sophisticated to most, here are your three Auto correction choices:

- **Auto Contrast:** Auto Contrast makes the dark pixels darker and the light pixels lighter, and tries to avoid introducing any *color shift* (an overall change in the color appearance). The same adjustment is applied to all three of your image's color channels. You can use Auto Contrast with an image in which the colors already look good and you perhaps just need a bit of a boost to the contrast.
- **Auto Levels:** Each of your image's color channels gets its own adjustment, maximizing the tonal range in the channel. If one of the color channels has very little to contribute to the original image, a *color cast* (an unwanted tint, as shown in Figure 5-8) might be introduced. Auto Levels is fine for most images that look good already and don't need to have exact colors.

- **Auto Color:** Rather than using a single brightest pixel and a single darkest pixel to determine what should be white and what should be black, Auto Color averages a few pixels at each end. That averaging prevents one single stray pixel from throwing off the calculation used to adjust your image. Auto Color is great for most typical images. You might need that Undo command, however, on some photos with very brightly colored objects or images that have extreme color casts.

# Levels and Curves and You

Sometimes you need (or simply want) more control than offered by the Auto commands. You might have a more demanding problem or a more expansive artistic vision. You might need to make major corrections or create stupendous effects. Photoshop, not surprisingly, offers that sort of control over your image. In fact (and also not surprisingly), you have several ways at your disposal to manipulate the tonality of your images. Two of the most commonly used are Levels and Curves, both found in your Image➪Adjustments menu.

Before I introduce you to those two commands, let me quickly explain and dismiss a couple of other available options. Since the early days of Photoshop, the Brightness/Contrast command has lurked among the Image➪Adjustments commands. In fact, it was *the* image adjustment command way back when. Now, however, the feature is somewhat lacking in control and sophistication and is perhaps of most use when fine-tuning an alpha channel or layer mask. (Alpha channels are discussed in Chapter 8, and layer masks appear in Chapter 10.) In both alpha channels and layer masks, you use a grayscale representation to identify specific areas of your image. Brightness/Contrast is perfectly adequate for many adjustments that you might make to those channels.

Also of limited use is the Equalize adjustment. It finds the lightest pixel in the image and calls that *white,* and also finds the darkest pixel and calls that *black.* The rest of the pixels in the image are distributed between those values, creating an extended tonal range. In practice, you'll find that the adjustment results in extreme highlights and extreme shadows, with a rather garish image overall as well as a lack of details in the midtones.

Always keep in mind that you don't have to make changes to the *entire* image. If only part of an image needs repair, make a selection of that area before opening the particular adjustment dialog box you want to use. (Read about making selections to isolate areas of your image in Chapter 8.) Say, for example, that you take a beautiful photo of a room in your house — "beautiful" except that the view out the window is far too bright. Isolate the window with a selection, and then use one of your image adjustment commands to tone it down.

You can apply Levels, Curves, and Brightness/Contrast as adjustment layers. *Adjustment layers* make the same changes to your images as the commands in the Image➪Adjustments menu but are far more flexible. By double-clicking the adjustment layer in the Layers palette, you can reopen the adjustment dialog box and make changes to your settings. When you use an adjustment layer, you can also restrict the effect of the adjustment to one or more layers through layer clipping and layer sets. (See Chapter 8 for more information on working with adjustment layers.) You can even delete an adjustment layer, thus eliminating its effect on your image, by dragging it to the Trash icon at the bottom of the Layers palette.

## Level-headed you!

The Image➪Adjustments➪Levels command (⌘+L/Ctrl+L) gives you control over shadows, highlights, and your image's overall tonality individually. Using a slider with three controls, you adjust the picture both to suit your eye, and with an eye on a histogram for reference. You even have numeric fields in which you can type exact values, should you find the need.

To perform the basic Levels correction, spreading the image's tonality over the full range of values available, you simply drag the slider controls under the histogram in the Levels dialog box inward until they're under the point where the histogram begins to rise in a mountain shape. Ignore those little flat tails that extend outward — they represent individual stray pixels — and drag the little pointers under columns that are at least a few pixels tall. The histogram in the Levels dialog box (as shown in Figure 5-9) is for reference as you make changes. Note, however, that while you work in Levels, the Histogram palette updates, showing you the "before" (in gray) and the "after" (in black).

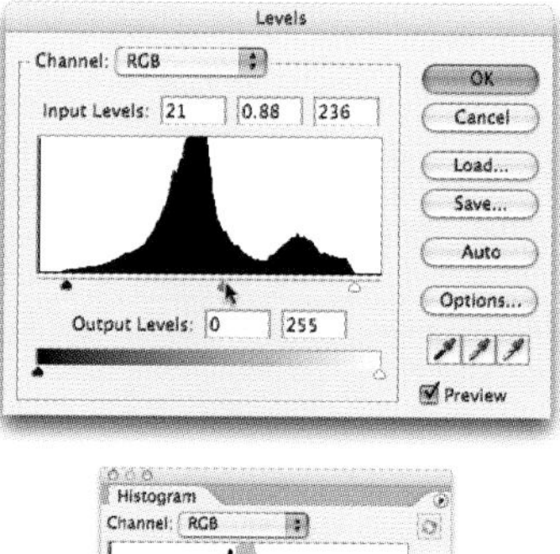


**Figure 5-9:** Compare the Levels histogram and the Histogram palette.

## Defining white and black

The Options button in the Levels (and Curves) dialog box opens a door through which you might never need to walk. However, should your path lead you to that door, I want you to know what lies behind. Neither pit nor tiger awaits you, only the possibility of controlling your highlights and shadows — or making a total mess of your image, of course. (Adobe does a good job of hiding those it-could-cost-me-a-fortune-if-I-screw-it-up features.) The Options button gives you control over the behavior of the Auto button (in both Levels and Curves), but I suggest that you leave the defaults alone. Even more importantly, the Options button lets you define what colors Photoshop should use for the lightest pixels and for the darkest pixels. That's right, white and black are not always the same.

If you print to an inkjet, you want the full tonal range of the printer, so you should leave white and black set to the extremes, as far apart as possible. However, if you prepare images for commercial offset presses, you might need to adjust the values used for highlights and shadows. If your white is too light, clouds and white blouses and snow have no detail — they are completely washed out. If your black is too dark, every shadow is impenetrable, and there's no texture to the surface on which the shadow falls.

If your print shop (or another person handling your images prior to press) asks you to redefine the highlights and shadows, open Levels (or Curves), click the Options button, click the highlight (white) color swatch to open the Color Picker, and then input the suggested values. Click OK and then repeat for the shadow swatch. Make sure to click the buttons that retain the values as your defaults as you OK your way back out of all those dialog boxes.

Dragging the middle slider to the right moves the bulk of the histogram toward the left, indicating that the overall appearance of the image is slightly darker.

Also note the lower Output Levels slider in Figure 5-9. You generally use that only when preparing an image for a commercial printing press that requires you to compress the image's tonal range. Otherwise, ignore that slider and its two fields except for special effects. And make a mental note of that pop-up menu at the top of the Levels dialog box — you can apply Levels to each color channel of your image individually, changing this tonal adjustment tool to a color correction feature. (Fixing the color in your image is covered in Chapter 6.)

When you're working in Levels (or just about any dialog box), remember that holding down the Option/Alt key changes the Cancel button to Reset. When you click Reset, all values in the dialog box are restored to the defaults, letting you start over without having to cancel and reselect the command.

Earlier in this chapter, I mention that you can use the Histogram palette to avoid introducing problems into the image. Note in Figure 5-9 that the Histogram palette shows slight gaps appearing among the darker columns in front. Technically called *posterization,* these gaps represent tonal values that are being squished together into a single value. The pixels at one brightness level are being shifted to the next higher or the next lower value, leaving that empty column in the Histogram. Is this a problem? No, as long as you don't see wide gaps, representing a number of consecutive tonal values not in use. (Extensive posterization ruins the subtle transitions between colors in your image.) And *that's* why you want to keep an eye on the Histogram palette — to make sure you're not creating wide gaps in the histogram and noticeable posterization in your image.

Here is an easy way to minimize that posterization, one that lets you make your Levels adjustment but keep a pretty histogram. Immediately after using Levels, use the Edit⇨Fade Levels command and change the blending mode from Normal to Luminosity. As you see in Figure 5-10, the posterization goes away with a minimal change in the effect of the Levels adjustment. Remember that the Fade command is available only *immediately* after applying an adjustment (or filter or tool) — you can't even use the Save command between. (Read more about the Fade command in Chapter 15.)

Figure 5-10: Change the Levels adjustment blending mode to Luminosity with Edit⇨Fade.

## Tonal corrections with the eyedroppers

The Levels dialog box (and the Curves dialog box, too) offers another way to make tonal corrections to your image — sort of a half-automated technique, using the three eyedroppers in the lower-right corner of the dialog box. Open your image, open the Levels dialog box, and correct both tonality and color in your image with three little clicks:

1. **Click the left eyedropper on something that should be black.**

   This might be a shadow, a piece of clothing, or the tire of a car. Generally, you click something in the image that's already quite dark.

2. **Click the right eyedropper on something that should be white.**

   A cloud, the bride's dress, perhaps an eye . . . all are likely targets for the highlight eyedropper. You usually click something that's already quite light.

3. **Click the middle eyedropper on something that should be gray.**

   Click something that should be neutral in color. It doesn't have to be mid-gray, just something that should be neutral. This reduces or eliminates any unwanted color cast in the image. If you don't like the result, click somewhere else in the image. Keep clicking until the colors in the image look right.

In Figure 5-11, the shadow under the bridge, the splash of water, and the weathered wood of the bridge itself provide excellent targets for the three eyedroppers.

Figure 5-11: Use the eyedroppers in Levels to set the black and white points; then neutralize your image's colors.

## Adjusting your curves without dieting

One step up from Levels in complexity, and about five steps ahead in terms of image control, is Image➪Adjustments➪Curves (⌘+M/Ctrl+M). Like Levels, you use Curves to adjust the tonality of your image. But rather than a slider with three adjustment controls, the Curves dialog box offers you the chance to control different parts of the tonal range independently. (Curves also offers eyedroppers for tonal and color correction. They're used the same way you use the eyedroppers in Levels.)

At the very beginning of this chapter, I show you how a simple tonal adjustment could add some drama, some interest to a rather bland image. Figure 5-12 shows you the simple Curves adjustment that I applied to that image. Dragging the curve downward in the shadows makes them darker, dragging upward for the highlights makes them brighter. The *midtones* (that section of the tonal range between shadows and highlights) also gets lightened a bit in this adjustment.

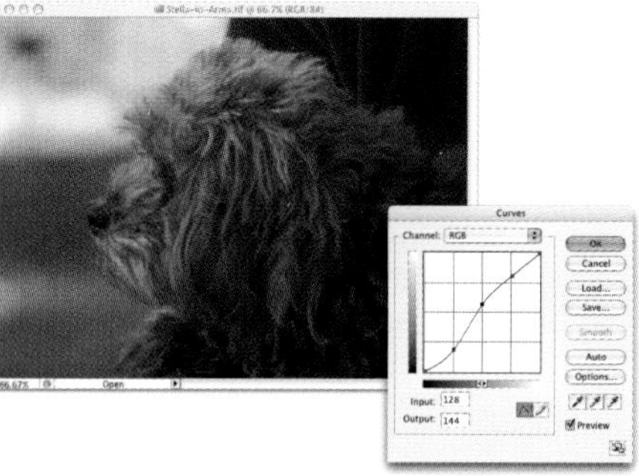

Figure 5-12: Remember little Stella from the beginning of the chapter?

When you first open the Curves dialog box, you see a graph with a diagonal line running from an anchor point in the lower left to another in the upper right. You click and drag that line up or down (not sideways) to add anchor points and make changes in the curve (and in your image). By default, the shadows are in the lower left, so dragging down darkens, and dragging up lightens. (See that two-headed arrow directly below the center of the graph? Click it to reverse the shadows and highlights in the Curves dialog box.) You can add more than a dozen anchor points to the curve — although you generally only need between one and three new points.

Most snapshots can benefit from a slight tweak in Curves. Click at the intersection of the first vertical and horizontal gridlines in the lower left (the *quarter tones*) and drag down slightly. The Input field should read 64, and the Output field should be somewhere between 55 and 60 for a shot that looks pretty good to start. Next, click at the intersection of the grid lines in the upper right (the *three-quarter tones*) and drag up slightly. The Input field should show 192, and the Output field can be anywhere from 195 to 205.

Both the Curves and Levels dialog boxes offer you the Load and Save buttons. If there's a correction that you'll use more than once, or a correction that needs to be precise time after time, use the Save button. Then, later, you can use the Load button to apply that adjustment to another image. If, for example, you used the wrong setting in your camera while taking a series of shots under the same lighting conditions, it's probable that they all need the same correction. Make the adjustment once, save it, and then apply it to the other images with the Load button.

If you want to correct a specific area in the image, hold down the mouse button and move the cursor into the image window (where it appears as the Eyedropper tool). You'll see a circle on the curve (like that near the middle of the curve in Figure 5-13), telling you where those pixels fall in the tonal range. To add an anchor point there, ⌘-click/Ctrl-click in the image window.

When your curve has multiple anchor points, the active anchor point shows as a filled-in square. Unselected anchor points are hollow squares. For precision, you can use the arrow keys on your keyboard to move the active anchor point, or you can type specific values in the Input field (starting position for the anchor point) and Output field (where you want the anchor point to go).

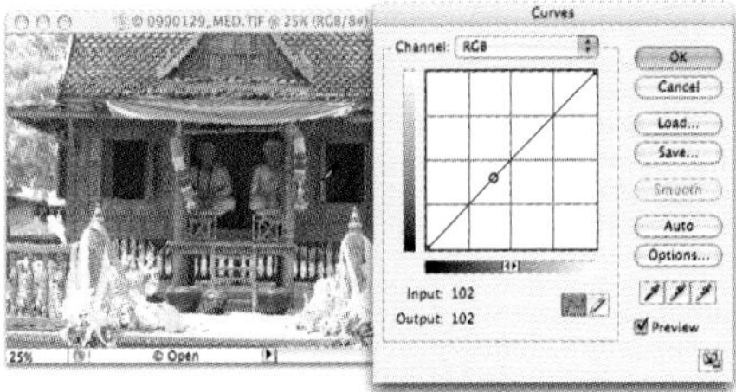

*©2003 PhotoSpin, PhotoSpin image #0990129*

**Figure 5-13:** Hold down the mouse button with the cursor over the image to see that point on the curve.

You have a couple of ways to customize the appearance of Curves, too. Click the button in the lower-right corner to toggle between the standard-size dialog box and a larger version. Option-click/Alt-click in the grid area to toggle between a 4 x 4 grid and a 10 x 10 grid. And, rather than clicking and dragging on the curve, you can activate the Pencil tool (shown in Figure 5-14) and draw your own curve by hand. When hand-drawing your curve, you've got the Smooth button available, too, to ensure that the transitions in your tonal adjustments are not too severe.

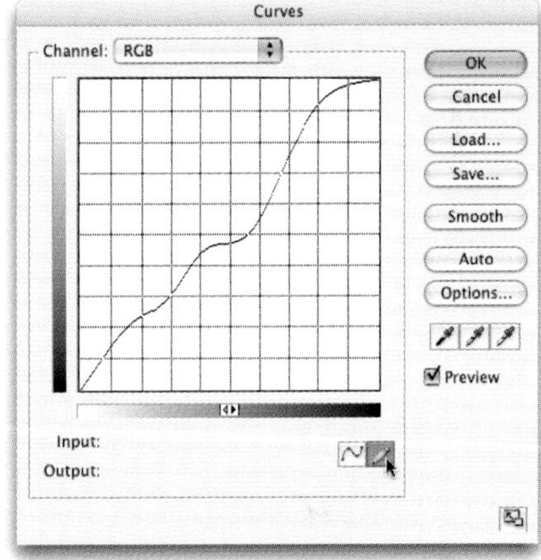


**Figure 5-14:** You can change the layout of Curves: handy when drawing a curve.

# Grabbing Even More Control

Photoshop CS2's Image➪Adjustments menu includes a couple more, extremely powerful, ways to work with tonality in your images. You can use the Shadow/Highlight adjustment to isolate and change whatever range of dark and light pixels you want. By specifying what range of tonal values that you want to be considered dark or light, you control how broadly or narrowly your change is applied. The Exposure feature lets you change the overall tonality of the image, as if you'd taken the photo with a different camera setting. And don't forget about making spot corrections with the Dodge and Burn tools!

The Shadow/Highlight and Exposure adjustments are *not* the same as working with Raw images in the Camera Raw plug-in (see Chapter 7). Camera Raw works with unprocessed image data, the so-called *digital negative.* Using Photoshop's Adjustment commands, you're working with image data that has already been manipulated in the camera, by Photoshop, or both. When working with unprocessed data in Camera Raw, you truly have control over the exposure, the shadows, the highlights, and much more.

The Shadow/Highlight and Exposure adjustments are not available as adjustment layers. Changes that you make with these features are a permanent part of your image.

## Using Shadow/Highlight

The Shadow/Highlight adjustment is designed to rescue two specific sorts of images — you've seen them (and maybe taken them): The background is perfectly exposed, and the person in the foreground is in horrible shadow. Or, equally bad, the background looks great, but the subject is washed out by a strong flash. (See both examples in Figure 5-15.) By controlling the shadows and highlights separately from the rest of the image, this feature helps you restore more balance to the image.

Figure 5-15: Shadow/Highlight does a rather good job with these all-too-common problems.

The default settings in Shadow/Highlight are intended to repair backlighting problems, as you see on the left in Figure 5-15. When the foreground lacks detail because of flash (as you can see on the right), minimize changes to the shadows and drag the Highlights slider to the right. (Pay more attention to the cheek than the neck — somebody needs a bath!) And, as you see in Figure 5-16, the two sliders in Shadow/Highlight can be used together.

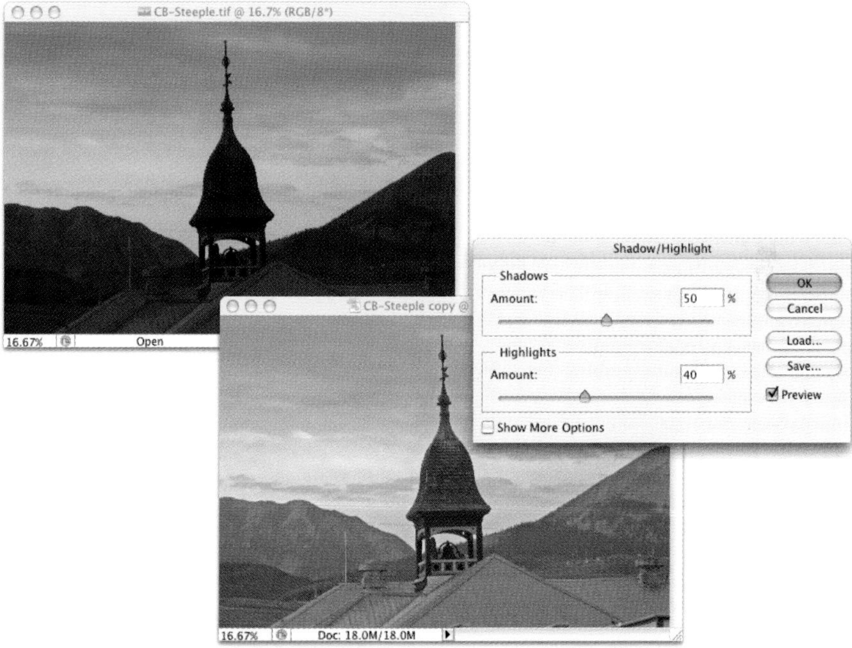


Figure 5-16: Some images need help for both shadows and highlights.

In the Shadows/Highlights dialog box, the Shadows slider lightens the darker areas of your image, and the Highlights slider darkens the lighter areas. Generally, you'll use one slider or the other to fix a specific problem in an image, but you can use both if you need to lighten shadows and tone down highlights in the same image.

You'll find that Shadow/Highlight is also a great tool for some other situations, especially when you select the Show More Options check box. Take a look, for example, at Figure 5-17. In the "before" picture on the left, the interesting subject matter is lost in the surrounding greenery. You don't pick out the sculpture immediately because both it and the leaves are rather dark. In the "after" shot, lightening with the Shadows slider, lowering the Midtone Contrast slider, and then boosting the saturation with the Color Correction slider works wonders. By lightening and increasing the saturation, the greens and browns separate themselves, helping you see the subject much better.

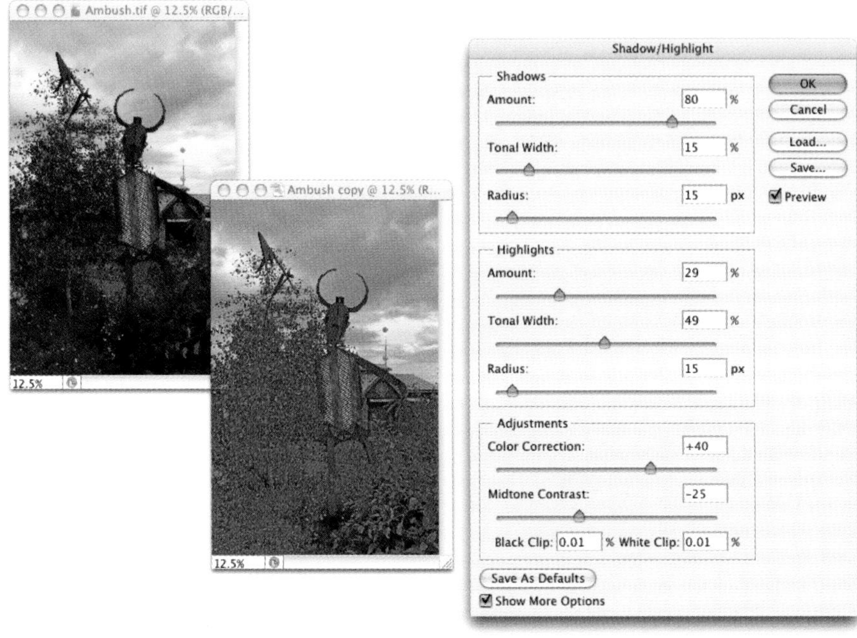


Figure 5-17: With lightening and saturation, Shadow/Highlight helps separate the subject and foliage.

When you enable the Show More Options check box, Shadow/Highlight has a rather intimidating set of controls. Not to worry! It's actually pretty simple:

- **Amount:** For both Shadows and Highlights, the Amount slider is how much of a correction you're making. This is the nuts and bolts of the Shadow/Highlight adjustment. For a backlit subject, you'll use the Shadows slider a lot and not the Highlights slider. When working with a washed-out subject, you'll probably move the Shadows slider to 0% and work with the Highlights slider.
- **Tonal Width:** Use the Tonal Width sliders to specify how much of the image's tonal range you want to include as shadows or highlights. If you drag either Tonal Width slider to 100%, you're working on the entire tonal range of the image — not a particularly appropriate job for Shadow/Highlight (use Curves instead). The default of 50% is rather too high most of the time. Instead, start your adjustment with a range of perhaps 20% and fine-tune from there.

- **Radius:** You adjust the Radius sliders to tell Shadow/Highlight which pixels should be identified as being in the shadow or highlight. With too low of a Radius setting, an individual black pixel stuck in the middle of a light area in your image might get classified as a shadow area. Too high of a setting has a tendency to apply the adjustment to the entire image. Generally speaking, start with a Radius of perhaps 10 pixels for very small images and 30 pixels for large digital photos. After adjusting your Amount and Tonal Width sliders, move the Radius slider back and forth while watching some of the smaller patches of shadow or highlight (whichever you're correcting) to make sure that those areas are being included in the adjustment.
- **Color Correction/Brightness:** This slider changes its name to match your image's color mode. When working with a color image, you see Color Correction. When you apply Shadow/Highlight to a grayscale image, the slider's name changes to Brightness. Don't bother with this slider until you make your Amount adjustment. In a color image, lightening the shadows or darkening the highlights shows the actual color of the pixels in those areas. Use this slider to increase (drag to the right) or decrease (drag to the left) the saturation of those pixels. Remember that Color Correction works only on the pixels that you identify with the Tonal Width and Radius sliders. (If you set both sets of Tonal Width and Radius sliders to 0%, Color Correction has no effect on the image at all.) When you correct a grayscale image, on the other hand, the Brightness slider affects all pixels except those that are already pure white or pure black.
- **Midtone Contrast:** You can increase or decrease the contrast throughout the image with the Midtone Contrast slider. Much like clicking in the middle of the curve in Curves and dragging up or down, you adjust the whole range of your image, including the shadows and highlights. When the overall appearance of your image needs improvement, start with Midtone Contrast and then work with your shadows and highlights individually.
- **Clip:** Most of the time, you don't want to change the clipping values. *Clipping* takes pixels that are *almost* black and forces them to pure black, or takes pixels that are *almost* white and forces them to pure white. Clipping your shadows or highlights reduces those subtle differences in color that provide the detail in the shadows and highlights. When would you want to clip shadows or highlights? When you don't care about detail in those areas of your image and need more contrast through the midtones.

## Changing exposure after the fact

Photoshop CS2 adds a new feature to the Image➪Adjustments menu called Exposure. It simulates how the image would have looked if you changed the exposure setting on your camera before clicking the shutter. Think of it as an across-the-board adjustment of tonality in the image. As you can see in Figure 5-18, even a minor adjustment can have a major impact on the image!

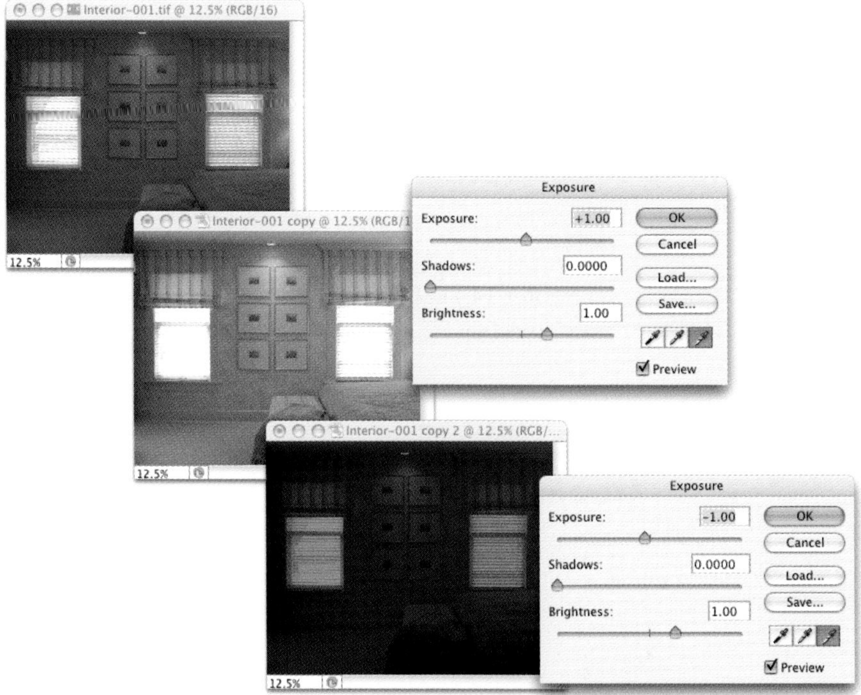


Figure 5-18: With the Exposure adjustment, a little change goes a long way!

Earlier in this chapter, I mention that sometimes you want to apply an adjustment to only part of an image. The windows in Figure 5-18 certainly qualify! To best repair this image, I would make a selection of the windows, improve their exposure, *invert* the selection (select the areas of the image other than the windows), and correct the room separately. (Chapter 8 has all the info on making selections.)

The Exposure dialog box offers a couple of additional controls, too. The Shadows and Brightness sliders are designed primarily to work with very high-bit images (the special 32-bit/channel high dynamic range images), and you likely will find them too sensitive to be of much use.

Exposure is a rather specialized tool, and you probably won't find it nearly as user-friendly or effective as Curves and Shadow/Highlight. If you do actually work with 32-bit/channel images, take it for a test drive; you might decide that it fills a need.

## Using Photoshop's toning tools

You have a couple more ways to work with tonality in Photoshop — the toning tools. These two brush-using tools let you paint corrections on your image, giving you incredible control over the appearance. Select the Burn tool to darken or the Dodge tool to lighten. Select a brush tip in the Options bar and drag the tool in your image to apply the correction. (Read about controlling the brush-using tools — and that incredibly-complex Brushes palette — in Chapter 14.) In Figure 5-19, you see the Burn tool darkening a specific area of the fence on the right.

**Figure 5-19:** "Painting" the fence with the Burn tool — where is Tom Sawyer when I need him?

The Dodge tool is great for minimizing (without removing) shadows in an image. You'll find it particularly useful for reducing wrinkles in faces and other such jobs that require lightening specific areas of an image. Figure 5-20 compares the original (left) with a working copy in which I'm using the Dodge tool to reduce the appearance of the wrinkles. By reducing rather than eliminating those wrinkles completely, I retain the character of the man's face as well as prevent that phony just-out-of-plastic-surgery look.

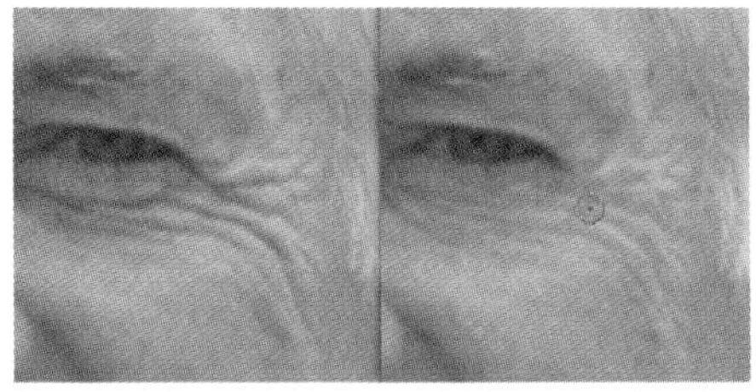



**Figure 5-20:** Use the Dodge tool to minimize wrinkles without removing them.

For most of the work that you do with the Dodge and Burn tools, the default Exposure setting of 50% is *way* too strong. In the Options bar, reduce the Exposure to about 12–15% for most work. And unless you're specifically working on lightening shadows or toning down highlights, set the tools' Range to Midtones in the Options bar.

# Chapter 6

# Making Color Look Natural

### In This Chapter

- Reds, greens, and in-betweens
- Photoshop's color correction armada
- Fixing flesh tones

In the end (and the middle and the beginning), your image in Photoshop is nothing but little squares of color. Each square — each pixel — can be exactly one color. Which color for which square is up to you. I'll say it again: There is no car or circle or tree or Uncle Bob in your Photoshop image — just a bunch of little squares of color.

In this chapter, I explain how those squares of color are formulated, how Photoshop works with those formulations, and — most importantly — how you can manipulate the colors of those squares. Toward the end of the chapter, you read about one of the biggest color-related challenges in Photoshop: achieving accurate skin color.

## What Is Color in Photoshop?

Photoshop works with digital images (including digital photos, images that have been digitized with a scanner, and artwork that you create from scratch in Photoshop). The *digits* are the computer code used to record the image's information. The number of pixels, the color of each pixel, and any associated information are all recorded in a series of zeros and ones on your hard drive. Color, therefore, is nothing more than numbers — at least as far as Photoshop is concerned. For you and me, however, color is far more than binary code on a hard drive. It's the image, the artwork, the message. The artwork is color, and color is the artwork, pixel by pixel.

## Color modes, models, and depths

Photoshop records the color of each pixel in your image in any of several different ways. Every pixel in any given image has all color recorded in a single *color mode,* which is the actual color format for the image file. While working with your image you might, however, define specific colors in any of a variety of *color models,* which are sort of the formula or recipes with which you mix color. And an image can have only one *color depth,* which is the limitation on the number of colors in an image.

Before I get into too many details, you need to understand one of the basic concepts of color: *gamut.* Consider gamut to be the range of colors that can be theoretically reproduced in a specific color mode or with a specific color profile. A wide gamut, therefore, has many more colors available than does a limited gamut. Those extra colors are generally the brighter, more vibrant colors . . . the ones that make an image come alive. The red/green/blue (RGB) color mode generally offers you a wider range of colors than does cyan/magenta/yellow/black (CMYK). (See, for example, the comparison in Figure 6-1.) And keep in mind that the specific *color profile* (the working space that you select — see Chapter 4), also has an impact on the colors in your image.

Figure 6-1: A wide-gamut image (on the left) and the same picture with a smaller gamut.

### *Which color mode should you choose?*

If you'll be printing to an inkjet printer or posting your image on the Web, you need RGB color mode. (Despite the CMYK inks that you load into your inkjet printer, the printer's software expects — and must receive — RGB color data.) If you're prepping an image for inclusion in a page layout document destined for a commercial offset press, you need CMYK. (You select the image's color mode from the Image➪Mode menu.) That's the simple summary. Here's a bit more detail, presented in the order in which you're likely to need the various color modes:

- **RGB:** RGB is the color mode for digital photos, computer monitors, the World Wide Web, and inkjet printers. All colors are recorded as proportions of the three component colors (red, green, and blue). RGB color is recorded in the three color channels (described a bit later in this chapter). RGB is an *additive* color mode — that is, the more of each component color you add, the closer you get to white.
- **CMYK:** CMYK is used primarily for printing on a commercial offset press, but you might need it for a color laser printer or a high-end inkjet printer with which you use a RIP (*raster image processor,* which is a specialized bit of hardware or software that lets your inkjet pretend it's a printing press). CMYK is the color mode of magazines, books, and other mass-produced printed material (such as the example in Figure 6-2). CMYK is a *subtractive* color mode — that is, the less of each component color you have, the closer you are to white.

Figure 6-2: You typically use CMYK images for bulk-print materials.

- **Grayscale:** When most people talk about a black-and-white photo, they really mean grayscale. The image does contain black and white but also a wide range of grays in between. You might use grayscale mode for Web-based images or for prints. Keep in mind that unless your inkjet printer is designed to reproduce grayscale images with black and gray inks (or black and light-black inks), you probably won't be happy with grayscale output. Using just one black ink doesn't reproduce the full range of grays in the image. Using the color inks adds a tint to the image. You do have an alternative for grayscale images: Send them to the local photo lab for printing.

- **Indexed Color:** Using a *color table,* or list of up to 256 specific colors, Indexed Color mode is for the Web. You save GIF and perhaps PNG-8 images in Indexed Color, but only those file formats require such a limited number of colors. Things like buttons on your Web page (which need only a couple of colors) should be created as GIFs using Indexed Color mode. That keeps the file size down, reducing the amount of space the image requires on your Web server and also speeding the *download time* (how long it takes for the image to appear on your site-visitor's monitor).
- **L*a*b:** Also known as *Lab* and *CIELAB* (and pronounced either *lab,* as the dog or a research facility, or verbally spelled out, as *el-ay-be*), this is a color mode that you might use when producing certain special effects or using certain techniques in Photoshop, but it's not one in which you'll save your final artwork. The three channels in an Lab image are
  - *Lightness*, which records the brightness of each pixel
  - *a*, which records the color of the pixel on a green-to-red axis
  - *b*, which records each pixel's color value on a blue-to-yellow axis

  You shouldn't print Lab images on an inkjet or post them on your Web site. You might see (elsewhere!) a tip that you should convert your RGB or CMYK images to Lab mode before using one of Photoshop's Sharpen filters. Bah! Apply the Unsharp Mask filter, use the Edit⇨Fade Unsharp Mask command, and change the blending mode from Normal to Luminosity. Same result, less work, and less potential for degradation of your image.
- **Duotone:** Duotone (including tritone and quadtone) is a very specialized color mode, exclusively for commercial printing, that uses only two (or three or four) inks spread throughout your image. Although that might sound good for an inkjet printer, in fact, Duotone is not an acceptable color mode for inkjets. Duotone images require that specific premixed inks are poured into the presses, which isn't something that you can do to your inkjet.
- **Multichannel:** Like Duotone, Multichannel is a color mode restricted to commercial printing because it depends on specific premixed colors of ink that are applied to the paper. Unlike Duotone, in which the inks are generally spread across the page, Multichannel images use certain inks in certain areas. You might need Multichannel mode when creating a logo for a client.
- **Bitmap:** Bitmap color mode is *true* black and white (as you see in Figure 6-3). Each pixel is either black or white. The placement of the black and white pixels produces shading, but the image doesn't really have any gray pixels. You might use Bitmap mode to create images for some wireless devices, use on the Web, or commercial print, but that's about it.

Converting between color modes or gamuts (done with the Image➪Mode menu) can reduce the quality of your image by compressing different colors into a single color value. You would not, for example, want to convert from RGB (which has a comparatively large number of colors available) to CMYK (with a more restricted color gamut) and then back to RGB. After colors are compressed by a conversion, you won't restore their original values by converting back to a wider gamut.

Figure 6-3: Bitmap images contain only black and white pixels: no grays, no colors.

### Does a color model make a difference?

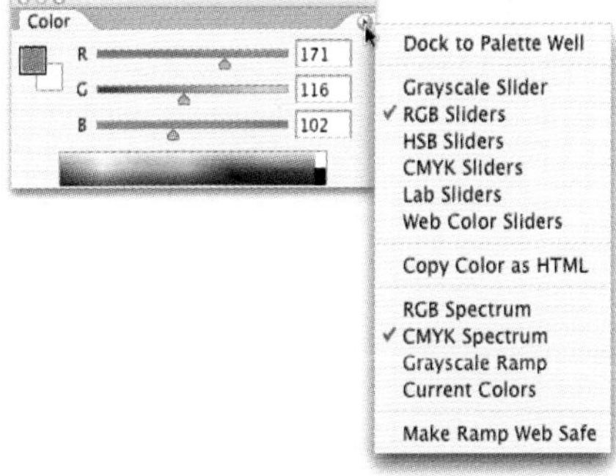


Figure 6-4: Choose your preferred color model from the Color palette menu.

Although the image itself has a single color mode, you can use any of the available color models when defining a color in Photoshop. Say, for example, that you're preparing to use the Brush tool to paint some artistic elements for your latest project. The project is in RGB mode because you'll be printing it with your inkjet printer. You can use the Color palette to define your foreground color any way you please — RGB, CMYK, Grayscale, Lab, or even HSB (hue/saturation/brightness, which is not available as a color mode, just a color model). It doesn't matter how you set up the Color palette, which you do through the palette's menu (as you see in Figure 6-4). When you add the color to your image, Photoshop uses the nearest RGB (or CMYK) equivalent. (Notice, too, that the Color palette menu in Figure 6-4 doesn't list Duotone or Multichannel. Those are color modes only, not color models.)

### Why should you worry about color depth?

*Color depth* is the actual number of different colors that you have available. (Remember that each pixel can be only one color at any one time.) When you work in *8-bit/channel* color (simply called *8-bit color*), each of the component colors is recorded with exactly 8 bits of information in the computer file. (At the beginning of this chapter, I mention digits. These are the actual numbers — the zeros and ones recorded on the hard drive to track each pixel's color.) In an 8-bit RGB image, each pixel's color is recorded with three strings of eight characters. When you work with *16-bit/channel* (or *16-bit color*), each of the component colors is recorded with 16 characters. The larger numbers mean more possible ways to record each color, which means more possible variations of color (as well as files that take up more space on your hard drive).

What that means to you, in practical terms, is possibly a better-looking image when working in 16-bit color. You'll have smoother transitions between colors throughout your image, no *banding* in gradients (those annoying areas in a gradient where you can actually see one color stop and the next color start), and no splotchy shadows. *Posterization,* which I explain in Chapter 5, is the degradation of your image's appearance when similar colors are forced to the same color, making transitions between colors more abrupt. Many tonal and color corrections that produce posterization in your 8-bit images won't harm a 16-bit image in the least. Take a look at Figure 6-5. A Levels adjustment is increasing the image's tonal range. When the same adjustment is applied to an 8-bit version of the image, some rather substantial posterization becomes visible in the Histogram palette (represented by the empty white gaps in the histogram).

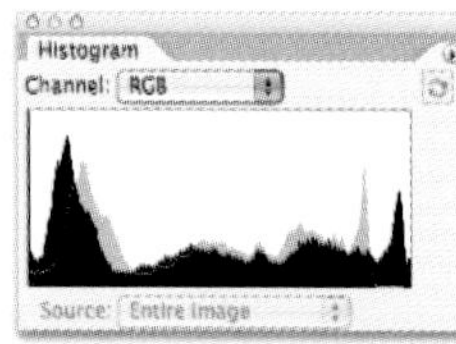

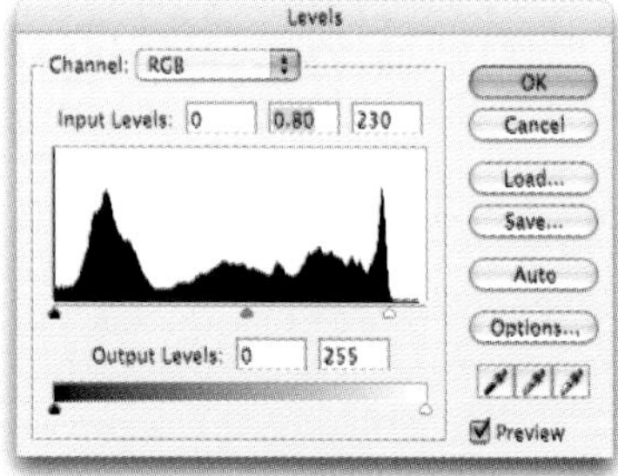


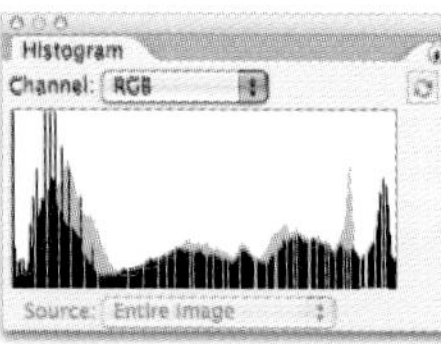


**Figure 6-5:** Compare the Histogram palettes to see posterization (right).

So, should you use 16-bit color all the time? No. You can't post a 16-bit image on the Web, and 16-bit color is rarely used for CMYK images. Digital photos taken in JPEG format are 8-bit (because that file format doesn't support 16-bit color). And with most inkjet printers, you won't see any improvement in the final print. (You might, however, see a dramatic increase in printing time because there's twice as much image data to process.)

If you shoot in 16-bit color, whether TIFF or Raw, it makes sense to process the image in 16-bit color. When the image is perfect, you might want to convert a copy of the file to 8-bit color for printing (Image➪Mode➪8-Bits/Channel). You might find some situations in which you'll convert an 8-bit image to 16-bit. Switching from 8-bit to 16-bit doesn't help you avoid posterization, but it might reduce banding if you add a sizable gradient.

One other note on color depth: Photoshop CS2 can work with 32-bit/channel images. These monstrous files are called *high dynamic range* (HDR) images and are typically constructed by combining different exposures of the same photo. In Photoshop CS2, you can work with a pair of exposures in the Merge to HDR feature (presented in Chapter 10). You probably will never be called upon to create an HDR image for any of the esoteric 3-D or video programs that use them, but you might find some benefit in combining multiple exposures of a difficult shot. Afterward, so that you have a file of reasonable size and access to more of Photoshop's features, use the Image➪Mode menu to convert to16-bit color or even 8-bit color.

### Recording color in your image

All your image's color data is saved in the Channels palette. When you're working with RGB or CMYK images, each color channel holds information for one of the component colors (red/green/blue or cyan/magenta/yellow/black). Each channel is a grayscale version of the image as a whole, using shades of gray, from white to black, to indicate where that channel's color appears (and how strongly) in the image. In RGB images, the lighter the pixel in a channel, the more of that color. When you work with a CMYK image, the light-dark in a channel is reversed, with darker areas showing where more of that color is applied.

## Color Adjustments in Photoshop

Sometimes you have an image that needs some help in the color department. It might have been shot with an incorrect camera setting, it might have a *color cast* (an unwanted tint of a specific color), or it might just be dull and dingy. Photoshop provides you with an incredible array of commands and tools to make the colors in your images look just right. You'll hear the term *color correction* being tossed about, but not all images have incorrect color. Some have very good color that can be *great* color. Instead of color *correction,* I like to think in terms of color *improvement.* And just about every image can use a little tweaking to improve its color.

## "Here, Spot!" What is a spot color?

Spot colors in your image are printed by using premixed inks of exactly that color. (We're talking commercial printing press here, not your run-of-the-mill inkjet printer.) To properly prepare a spot color for press, it needs to be in its own *spot channel,* which is a separate color channel in which you show where and how the ink will be applied. (Channels in your image are eventually used to create the actual printing plates that pick up ink and put it on paper.) Because spot channels are used with CMYK images, *dark* represents *more.* Where you need the spot color at 100% strength, paint directly in the spot channel with black. In areas where you want only a light tint of the spot color, use a light gray.

You create your spot channel by selecting the Spot Channel command from the Channels palette menu. Click the color swatch in the New Spot Channel dialog box to open the color libraries. (If you see the regular Color Picker, click the Color Libraries button.) Select the appropriate *book* (collection of colors; see the figure here) for your project; then select your color. Click OK in the New Spot Channel dialog box to accept the color, do *not* change the name of the spot channel, and then click OK. You can now paint or copy/paste into that new channel.

When saving images with spot channels, you can use the PSD file format (if the image will be placed into an InDesign document), PDF, TIFF, or DCS 2.0. Check with the person handling the layout or the print shop to see which is required.

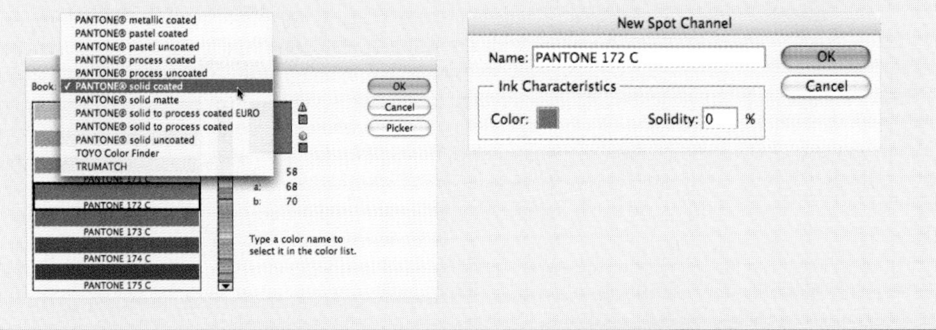


How do you know when the color is right? Your primary tool for the job is in your head. Literally. Make your decisions based primarily on what your eyes tell you. Sure, you can check the Info palette and the Histogram palette to make sure that your shadows are black and your highlights are white, but adjust your images until they look good to you — until you're satisfied with the color.

That little icon to the left is a little scary, but it does get your attention, doesn't it? This isn't a your-computer-will-blow-up sort of warning but more of a you-don't-want-to-waste-your-time-and-effort warning. Do your tonal adjustments before you start working with the image's colors. Go through the procedures in Chapter 5 first and then use the techniques here. Why? If you get perfect hue and saturation and then start making tonal adjustments, you're likely to knock your colors out of whack again. And, of course, there's also the possibility that adjusting your image's tonality will make the colors look perfect!

## Watching the Histogram and Info palettes

As you work with your various color adjustments in Photoshop, a couple of palettes can help you track the changes you're making. The Info and Histogram palettes are, by default, nested in the upper-right corner of your screen. (You can also show or hide them through Photoshop's Window menu.) You might want to drag one or the other out of the nested set so that both are visible at the same time. (Click the palette's tab and drag it away.) Keeping an eye on your Info and Histogram palettes while you're dragging sliders and entering numbers into various fields can help you spot potential problems before they develop.

The Histogram is useful for tracking changes in the distribution of pixels at various tonal ranges. You can read more about it in Chapter 5. The Info palette, while you've got an adjustment dialog box open, shows you "before" and "after" color values. Wherever you move the cursor in the image window (it will appear as the Eyedropper tool), the Info palette shows you the result of the adjustment — the consequences of your action, so to speak. You can also hold down the Shift key to change to the Color Sampler tool. Clicking in the image with the Color Sampler adds up to four markers in the image. The color values under those markers appear in the Info palette and, like the cursor location, show before/after values as you're making changes (see Figure 6-6).

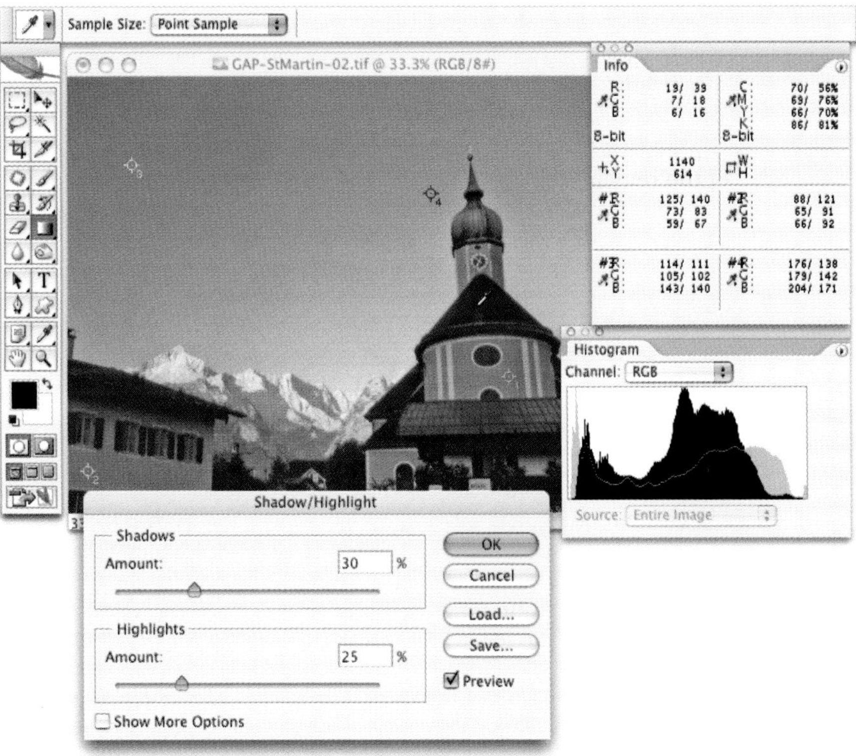


Figure 6-6: Each of the crosshairs in the image is tracked in the Info palette.

## Choosing color adjustment commands

Photoshop offers over a dozen different commands that you can use to improve the appearance of your images, all of which are easily accessed through the Image➪Adjustments menu (as you see in Figure 6-7). Some have specialized purposes, and some are extremely versatile, but all are worth understanding so that you choose the most appropriate feature for the problem staring at you from the screen. Most (but not all) of the commands that I discuss here can be added to your images as an *adjustment layer,* which gives you added flexibility. (Adjustment layers are discussed in detail in Chapter 8.)

Figure 6-7: Photoshop's flexibility is truly evident in the Image➪Adjustments menu.

### Auto Color

Auto Color is perhaps the simplest way to improve both color and *tonality* (the darkness of the shadows and the brightness of the highlights). Select the command, and Photoshop automatically finds the lightest and darkest pixels in the image. Then, on a channel-by-channel basis, it redistributes the values of the remaining pixels. For more information on Auto Color and the related Auto Contrast and Auto Levels commands, take a look at Chapter 5.

### Curves

The Curves command is also discussed at length in Chapter 5. However, for color correction (rather than tonal adjustment), you want to work on each channel individually, choosing each in turn from the pop-up menu at the top of the Curves dialog box (see Figure 6-8).

Although working on each channel with Curves can be very effective, it can also be rather time consuming, with lots of flipping back and forth among the channels as one adjustment makes another channel correction look like a bad decision. While it may be inconvenient, Curves is a very powerful color correction tool.

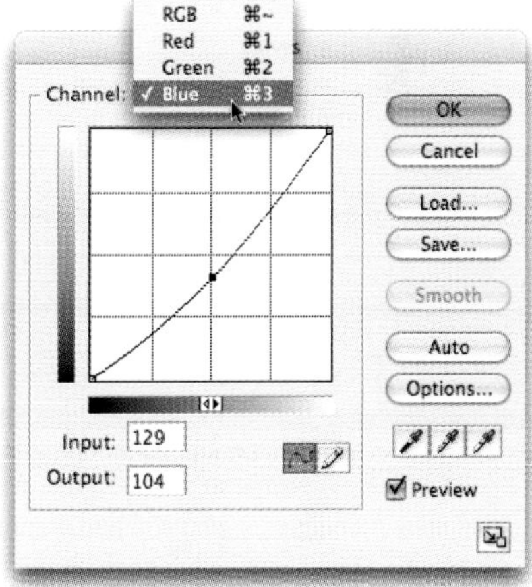


Figure 6-8: Correct each channel individually with Curves to adjust color in your image.

### Color Balance

The Color Balance command (as shown in Figure 6-9) presents you with three sliders that you use to make changes to the balance between your color opposites. If the image is too blue, you drag the third slider away from Blue and toward Yellow. (And this is a great way to remember which colors are opposite pairs!)

You can control the highlights, midtones, and shadows of your image individually by using radio buttons at the bottom of the Color Balance dialog box. And, in almost all cases, you'll want to leave the Preserve Luminosity check box marked so that the brightness of the individual pixels is retained.

You can also use Color Balance to throw an image out of whack for special effects or (getting back to the adjustment's roots) compensating for a color cast being introduced by the printing device.

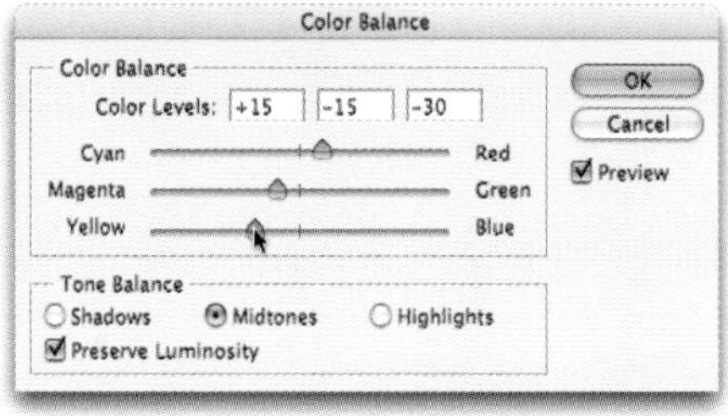


Figure 6-9: Color Balance gives you direct control over opposites.

## *Hue/Saturation*

Often overlooked and rarely exploited to the fullest, Hue/Saturation is a very powerful tool. Using the three sliders together, you can adjust the hue to eliminate a color cast, increase saturation so that your colors appear richer and more vibrant, and adjust lightness to improve your image's tonality. (See Figure 6-10.) Keep in mind that when you adjust something that's very dark, start with the Lightness slider so that you can evaluate the other changes (Hue and Saturation) properly. Remember, too, that you can apply Hue/Saturation (like a number of other adjustments) to a specific range of colors in the image, selected in the pop-up menu at the top of the dialog box.

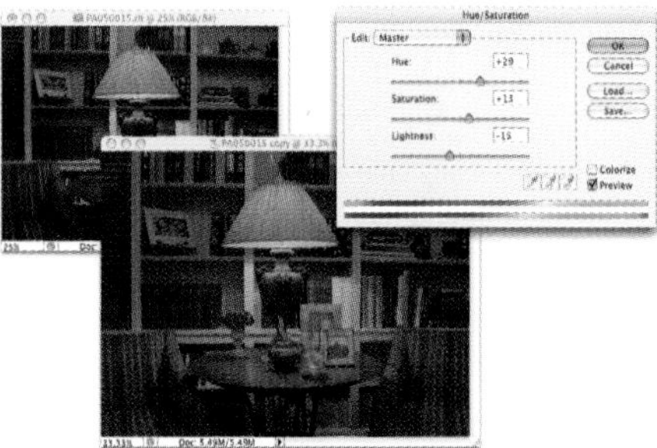

Figure 6-10: Hue/Saturation cures three problems at once.

If you need to simulate a *duotone image* (a picture created by using just two inks), apply a Hue/Saturation adjustment layer, mark the Colorize check box, adjust the sliders, save, and then print. If the inkjet printer introduces a color cast that changes the appearance of the image, reopen the adjustment layer and make the change necessary to compensate for the color cast.

### Desaturate

Photoshop's Desaturate command creates a grayscale representation of a color image without changing the color mode. This can be an extremely cool technique when you make a selection first, leaving some of the image in color and converting some to a simulated grayscale, as shown in Figure 6-11. However, there are better ways to go from color to grayscale, such as using the Channel Mixer (which I discuss later in this chapter).

©1998 PhotoSpin, PhotoSpin image #0150005

**Figure 6-11:** Create this effect by selecting most of an image prior to desaturating.

### Match Color

Now *this* is a feature to savor! There you are, adding Cousin Joe to the family photo (he wasn't bailed out in time), and you see that the lighting is all kinds of different and he sticks out like a sore thumb (or bum). Or you return from a major shoot, only to find that something wasn't set correctly in the camera, and *all* your images have a nasty color cast.

Match Color lets you adjust one image to another (and you can even use selections to identify areas to adjust or areas of the images to use as the basis for adjustment), but keep in mind that you get better results with images that are already rather similar. You can also fix one shot and use that shot as a standard by which others are corrected. (Like most image adjustments, you can record a change in an Action and use Photoshop's Batch command to apply that adjustment to a series of images. Read more about Actions in Chapter 16.) Take a look at Figure 6-12 to see the Match Color dialog box.

Because it's such a powerful tool, it's worth taking at look at what's going on in the Match Color dialog box:

- **Ignore Selection When Applying Adjustment:** If you have an active selection in the target layer or image (for calculating the adjustment, see the upcoming bullet on that) and you want the adjustment to be applied to the entire target, select this check box. If the box is left clear, the adjustment is applied only within the selection. Note that you can use selections to apply Match Color to only a portion of your image (such as flesh tones), or you can adjust sections of the image one at a time.

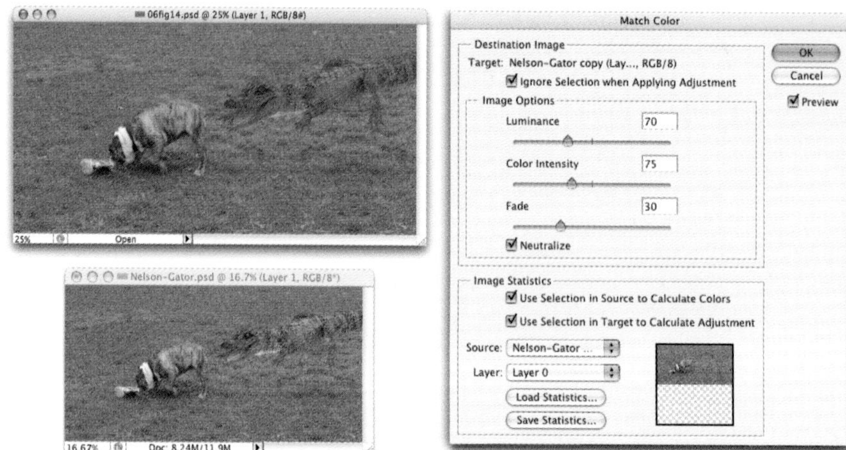


Figure 6-12: Matching the gator to the grass improves the lighting and his chances of lunch.

- **Luminance:** After the preview shows in your image window, you can tone down or brighten up the target area with the Luminance slider.
- **Color Intensity:** Think of this slider as a saturation adjustment.
- **Fade:** Using Fade lets you blend the adjustment, reducing its intensity.
- **Neutralize:** If a color cast is introduced by the adjustment, marking the Neutralize check box might eliminate it.
- **Use Selection in Source to Calculate Colors:** You can make a selection in the image to which you're trying to match (the *source*) and use the colors within that selection as the basis for the Match Color calculation. In Figure 6-12, an area of grass is selected on the lower layer so that the color of the dog and the bottle are not taken into account.
- **Use Selection in Target to Calculate Adjustment:** You can make another selection in the target layer or image that presents Match Color with a sample of those pixels to use for calculating the adjustment.
- **Source:** The Source pop-up menu lists all the open images that can be used as a basis for adjustment. Only images of the same color mode and color depth get listed. In the sample, the image itself is the source so that I can pick a specific layer to match. Think of *source* as the image whose colors you're matching. (The selected image or the active layer within an image is what you're adjusting.)
- **Layer:** When a multilayer image is selected in the Source pop-up menu, you can designate which layer (or a merged copy of the layers) is the actual source. In the example, the lower layer — the layer with the grass — is the source.

- **Load Statistics/Save Statistics:** If you're doing a series of images and you want to speed things up, click the Save Statistics button to record the adjustment you're making and then use the Load Statistics button with other images.

In Figure 6-12, an area of alligator scales is selected on the target layer and an area of grass is selected on the source layer. With the two selections, I tell Match Color to adjust the target layer based on the difference between the grass and the scales. But with the Ignore Selection When Applying Adjustment check box enabled as well, I make sure the entire target layer is adjusted. I could, however, make a selection of all the target layer except the tongue, clear the Ignore Selection When Applying Adjustment check box in Match Color, and have the adjustment applied only to the critter's hide.

### Replace Color

Sort of a cross between the Select➪Color Range command (see Chapter 8) and the Hue/Saturation adjustment, Replace Color is a great tool for swapping out one color for another. It's truly great in a production environment where, for example, a certain blouse is available in several colors. Shoot one color, and then use Replace Color to produce the additional product shots.

The Replace Color dialog box, as shown in Figure 6-13, has two separate parts: Selection and Replacement. Click with the left eyedropper, in either the preview area or in the image windows, and adjust the Fuzziness slider (how much variation counts as "selected") to make your initial selection. Use the middle eyedropper to add additional colors (or shades of your initial color), and use the right eyedropper to subtract from the selection. (Choose only variations of one color.) Then drag those Hue, Saturation, and Lightness sliders in the Replacement section of the dialog box to produce your new look.

Rather than switching eyedroppers back and forth, use the left eyedropper and the Shift key (to add) and the Option (Mac)/Alt (Windows) key (to subtract). You can also hold down the Shift key and drag through an area to select all the colors in the area. If you accidentally select some colors you don't want, release the Shift key and click once to start over.

### Selective Color

Although designed to help you compensate for the vagaries of printing presses, Selective Color can do other great things for you! The command's dialog box, which you can see in Figure 6-14, has a pop-up menu that offers the six basic colors of Photoshop, as well as Whites, Neutrals, and Blacks. You select which range of colors to adjust and then drag the sliders. You can work on one set of colors, switch to another and make adjustments, switch to another, and so on without having to click OK in between. For example, you can adjust the reds in the image and leave the blues untouched, or you can adjust the reds and then tweak the blues without having to exit the dialog box.

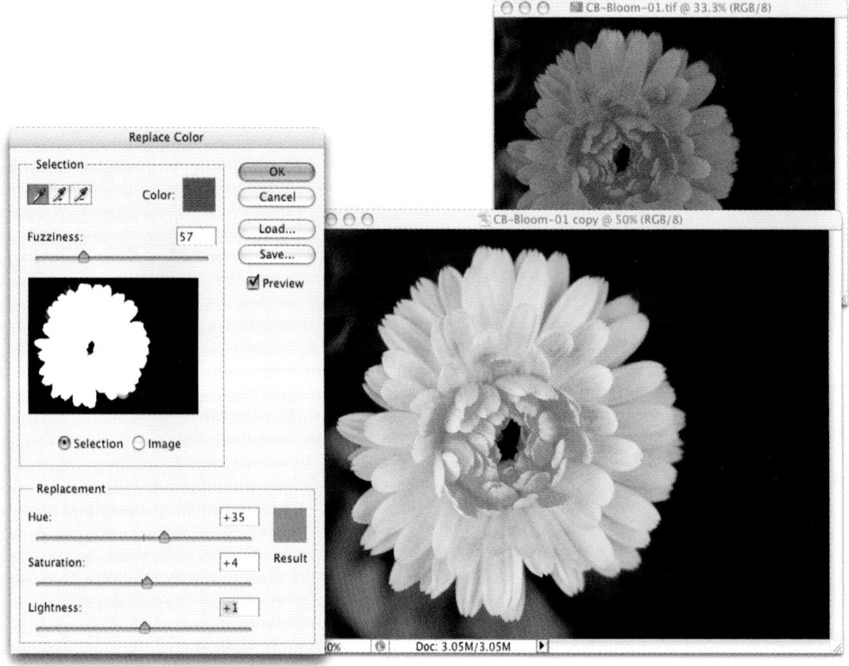


Figure 6-13: Make a selection, change the selection's hue, saturation, and lightness.

When you have reasonably small adjustments to make, select the Relative radio button at the bottom. If you've got substantial changes — rather radical alterations — select the Absolute radio button.

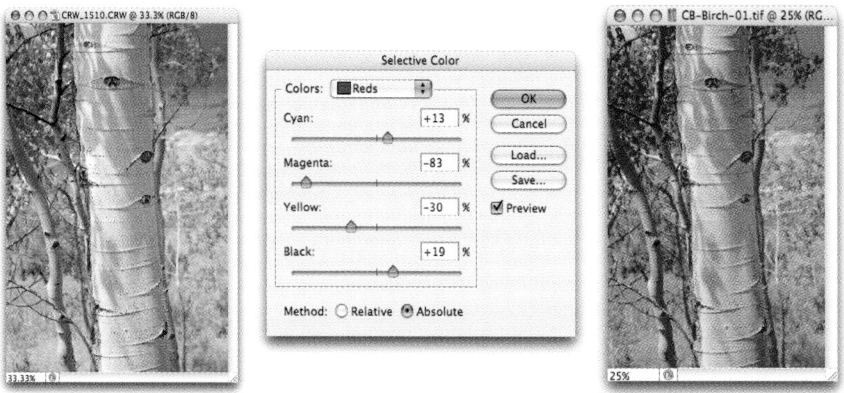


Figure 6-14: The excessive red is easily eliminated without changing anything else.

### Channel Mixer

Designed to repair a defective channel in an image, Channel Mixer lets you use sliders to replace some or all of the intensity of one color channel with content from the others. Should you come across an image with damage in one channel, you can certainly use the Channel Mixer adjustment to work on it (with some degree of success). You reduce the value of the target channel by dragging the slider to the left. You then drag one or both of the other sliders toward the right. Generally speaking, you want to add an amount (combined between the two other channels) just about equal to what you subtract from the target channel.

If you drag a slider to the left past 0 (zero), you invert the content of the channel. You can produce some incredible (and incredibly weird) effects with this technique, partially inverting one or two channels. When you get a chance, give it a try.

There is one thing that Channel Mixer does incredibly well, and it's even practical, too. You can create grayscale versions of your images in a variety of ways in Photoshop — by choosing Image➪Adjustments➪Desaturate or Image➪Mode➪Grayscale, for example, or by deleting channels, using the L channel of a Lab image, and so forth. But none of those techniques quite compares to creating grayscale with the Channel Mixer. Here's how you do it:

1. **Open the image in Photoshop and evaluate the color channels.**

   Start with a flattened 8-bit RGB image. Take a look at each channel individually by clicking it and hiding the other two color channels by clicking the eyeball icon to the left of each. See which channel holds detail information for which part of your image. Foliage, for example, will usually be most prominent in the Green channel.

   Make sure to click the RGB channel when you're done evaluating, or the Channel Mixer won't be available.

2. **Open the Channel Mixer.**

   Use the menu command Image➪Adjustments➪Channel Mixer. (The Channel Mixer is also available as an adjustment layer.)

3. **Select the Monochrome check box.**

   When you select the Monochrome option (lower-left corner of the dialog box), you're telling the Channel Mixer that you want one single channel when you're finished with the adjustment. (Although this discussion is about creating a tremendous grayscale image, that resulting channel could be used in a variety of ways in other images, perhaps as an alpha channel or a spot color channel.)

4. **Adjust the sliders to create a great grayscale image.**

   Start with the three channel sliders at +40 and the Constant slider at about –7. Now play with the sliders, keeping in mind your evaluation of the individual channels. Generally speaking, for a well-exposed original, the total value of the sliders' fields should be about 100. (Count the Constant slider at triple its value because it changes all three channels.) When your image looks great, click OK. In Figure 6-15, the emphasis is on the Green channel to maintain the detail in the trees.

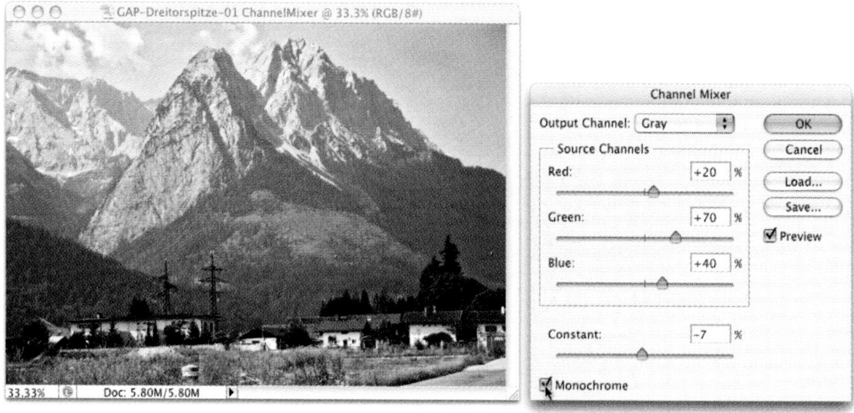


Figure 6-15: The Channel Mixer's Monochrome option lets you control your grayscale conversion.

5. **Save as Grayscale.**

   Use the Image➪Mode➪Grayscale command to convert to true grayscale (the Channel Mixer leaves the image in RGB mode), and then save. Make sure that you change the name or location so you don't overwrite your original image!

### Gradient Map

More creative than corrective, the Gradient Map feature re-creates your image by using a gradient. The left-most color stop (the anchor points where a gradient color is assigned) in the gradient is mapped to the shadows, the right-most to the highlights, and any color stops in between are appropriately assigned to the rest of the tonal range. In Figure 6-16, you can see how a two-color gradient (upper-left) lacks detail compared with the four-color gradient being created for the lower image.

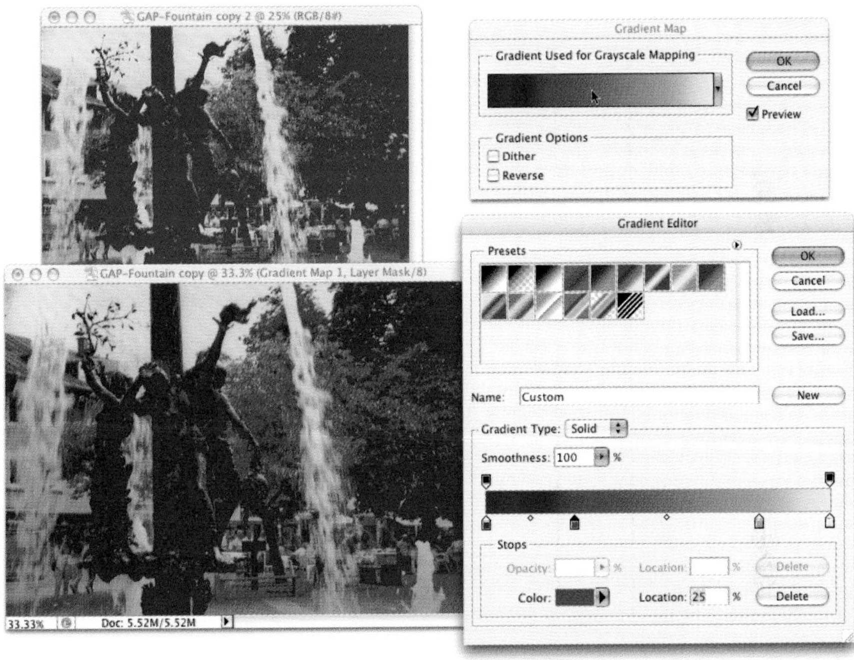


Figure 6-16: Using more colors in your gradient produces more detail.

Generally speaking, you use darker colors for the color stops on the left and lighter colors for the color stops on the right (although extremely interesting effects can be created by mixing things up). Using a black-to-white gradient produces a grayscale image.

To edit the gradient, simply click directly on the sample gradient in the Gradient Map dialog box. Click to add color stops, drag to move color stops, and click the color swatch near the bottom to change the color of the selected stop. (You can find more detailed information on creating and working with gradients in Chapter 14.)

### Photo Filter

Photoshop's Photo Filter is indeed an image adjustment rather than a filter. The filter in the name refers to those actual photographic filters that you screw onto the end of a lens. This adjustment is a great way to correct problems with *temperature* in an image — that perceived warmth or coldness of an image. When the camera takes a picture under unexpected lighting conditions, a color problem is apparent. (Say, for example, that the camera is set to Daylight when shooting indoors.) When an image is too blue, it's too *cool;* conversely, an image that's orangey is too *warm.* (Remember that these are the perceptual evaluations — blue light is technically hotter than yellow or red light.)

In Photo Filter, you select a preset filter from a pop-up menu or select a color of your choice. As you can see in Figure 6-17, both preset filters and custom colors can be effective in neutralizing a color cast. (You could, of course, also use these filters to add a color cast . . . if you wanted to, that is.)

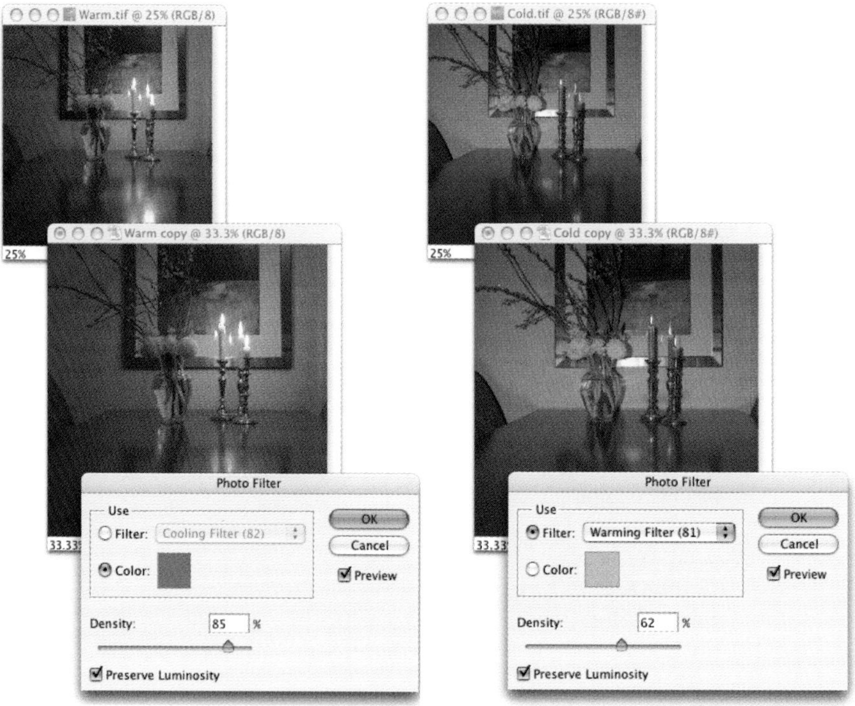


**Figure 6-17:** Neutralize a color cast with a filter of the opposite color in Photo Filter.

### Shadow/Highlight

The Shadow/Highlight adjustment is discussed at length in Chapter 5 as a tonal correction tool (the job for which it was designed). However, keep in mind that the Shadow/Highlight dialog box also includes the Color Correction slider. After you lighten shadows or tone down highlights, you can increase or decrease the saturation of the colors in the adjusted areas of your image with the Color Correction slider.

### Invert

Again, more creative than corrective, the Invert command (no dialog box) simply reverses the colors in your image or the selected area. Although inverting areas of an image (like desaturating) can draw attention to the subject of the image, it's an edgier technique and generally requires touch-up after inverting. You'll find that any *specular* highlight — a pure-white area (mainly reflections) — becomes a distracting black spot.

### Posterize

The Posterize command forces your image's broad range of colors into a few selected colors (as shown in Figure 6-18). You automatically get black and white, and then a limited number of additional colors, based on the content of the original. You pick the number of colors that you want to use, and Photoshop picks which colors to use. You can use as few as two colors (plus black and white) or as many as 255 (which pretty much gives you your original image). Posterize can create a rather pleasing rendering of a photo with very few colors.

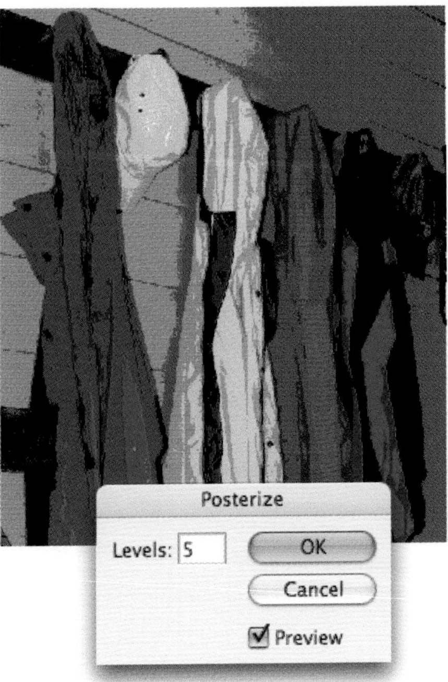


**Figure 6-18:** Reduce colors with Posterize for a special effect.

When experimenting with Posterize, click in the Levels field and use the up- and down-arrow keys on your keyboard to preview different numbers of colors. Start low and work your way up. If you see something that you like, you can stop or you can keep going and come back to that number later — the image will look exactly the same when you try that number again.

## Working with Variations

The Variations feature, which you find in the Image➪Adjustments menu, is a semi-automated way to make color and tonal adjustments to your images. You open the image, open Variations, and then click which version looks better. (See Figure 6-19).

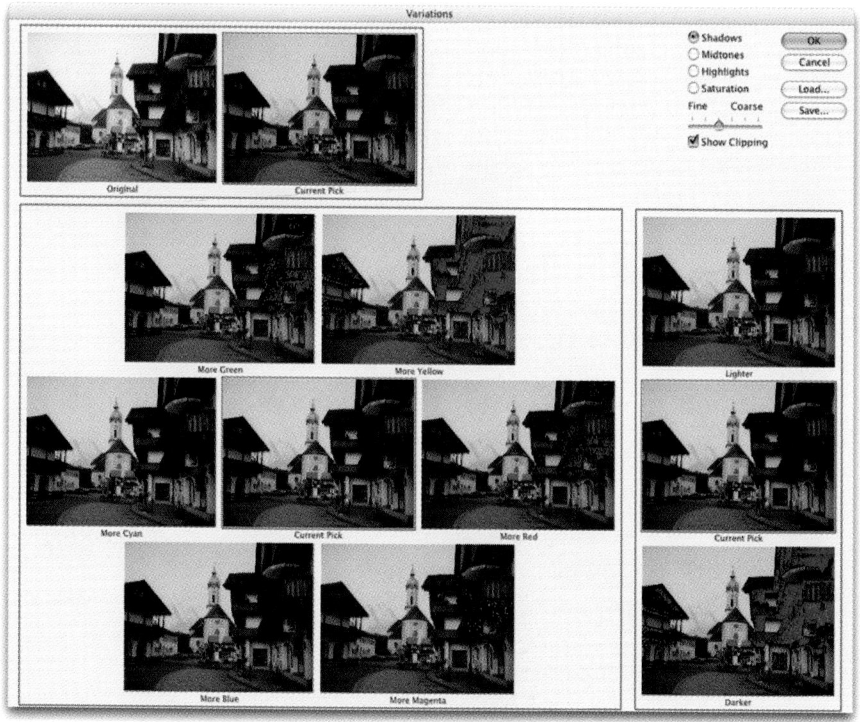


**Figure 6-19:** You use Variations to click your way to a perfect picture.

Much like getting new eyeglasses, using Variations is a matter of "Which looks better, *this* or *this?*" When you click one of the images, it moves to the Current Pick position, and a new set of variations is automatically generated. The blue areas that you see in some of the options in Figure 6-19 indicate areas where colors will be *clipped* — forced into black in the shadows or to white in the highlights — which results in a loss of detail in the image. You can disable that feature by clearing the Show Clipping check box in the upper right. Also note that you can adjust the shadows, midtones, and highlights independently, and you can also control (to some degree) the amount of variation from sample to sample.

Start with the Fine/Coarse slider set somewhere in the middle and get reasonably close to a great image, correcting midtones, shadows, highlights, and then saturation. Now drag that slider to the Fine setting and zero in on a perfect image.

## Manual corrections in individual channels

Sometimes different areas of an image require different corrections or adjustments. You can, for example, "paint" corrections into specific areas of a channel by using the toning tools in Photoshop's Toolbox. The image in Figure 6-20 has a distinct problem (okay, well, maybe a few problems). In the lower left is a light-green blob that needs to be eliminated if there's any chance of salvaging this photo. By using the Burn tool on one channel at a time, you can darken that specific area of each channel — each channel according to its needs.

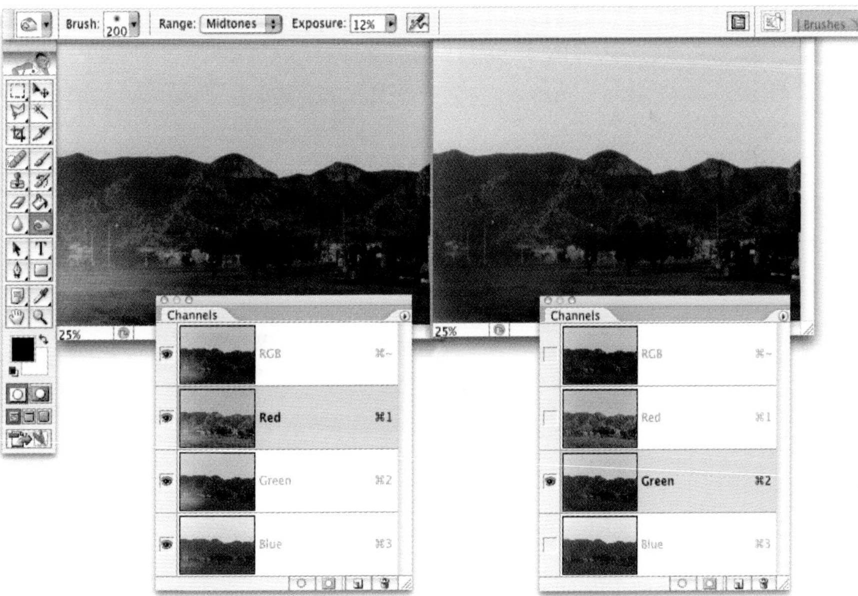


Figure 6-20: The problem is only in one area of each channel, but it can be fixed manually.

On the left, you can see the distinct light area in the thumbnail of each channel. On the right, after using the Burn tool, those lighter areas are gone, and so is the, the . . . what could it have been? Was it perhaps swamp gas? Ectoplasm? A UFO? Anyway, it's gone now, and the tabloids won't buy the photo for millions of dollars.

In addition to the Burn tool, you can use the Dodge, Blur, Sharpen, and Smudge tools. You can use the Brush tool and paint with black, white, or gray. You can use Levels or Curves on an individual channel or even a selection within one or more channels. When fine-tuning (or salvaging) an image, don't be afraid to work in one channel at a time, perfecting that channel's contribution to the overall image.

Take another look at the two Channels palettes shown in Figure 6-20. (Obviously that's a composite image because there's only one Channels palette in Photoshop, right?) On the right, the Green channel is active (you can tell because it's highlighted), and only the Green channel is visible (only it shows the eyeball icon to the left). The other channels are invisible, and you see only the grayscale representation from the Green channel in the image window. On the left, however, only the Red channel is active, but *all* the channels are visible. Any change I make to that image in that state is applied only to the Red channel. But because all channels are visible, I can see the overall impact on my image. Sometimes you want only one channel visible (when trying to balance the tonal range throughout the channel, for example), but most of the time, you want to see what's going on in the image as a whole. Click the one channel (or Shift-click two channels) in which you need to work. Then click in the left column next to the composite channel at the top to make all channels visible.

## The People Factor: Flesh Tone Formulas

One of the toughest (yet one of the most important) jobs in Photoshop is making sure that skin looks right. People come in a wide variety of colors and shades and tints, and each person varies in color in different places on their body and at different times of the year. (The top and bottom of your forearm are likely different colors, and the difference is generally much greater in summer than in winter.) There are even some exceptions to those broad generalities. Making skin tones look great is often a major challenge, yet often a critical challenge.

When you've got skin in your image, it's generally part of the focus of the image — the person whom you're photographing. And even when a person isn't the subject of the image, skin attracts attention in the image. The eye naturally goes to people in just about any image (perhaps not first, but eventually).

You'll also find that unnatural variations in skin color are *very* noticeable. Consider how often you think to yourself that someone looks a little pale, or flushed, or sunburned, or tanned, or just plain sick. You're making that judgment call based (at least to a large degree) on the appearance of the skin.

Keeping in mind that the numbers shown in Figure 6-21 are general guidelines and that real people vary quite a bit, I've prepared for you some target values for skin tones. Use these formulas loosely when using the techniques in this chapter to adjust the color in your images, keeping in mind the individual you photographed and the lighting at the time.

**Flesh Tone Formulas**

| | Pale Caucasian | Dark Caucasian | Afro-American | Asian |
|---|---|---|---|---|
| Highlights | C:4 - M:17 - Y:15 - K:0 | C:11 - M:35 - Y:42 - K:0 | C:5 - M:14 - Y:22 - K:0 | C:3 - M:11 - Y:13 - K:0 |
| Midtones | C:14 - M:35 - Y:35 - K:0 | C:14 - M:38 - Y:49 - K:0 | C:23 - M:50 - Y:63 - K:5 | C:12 - M:35 - Y:42 - K:0 |
| Shadows | C:31 - M:63 - Y:71 - K:31 | C:35 - M:64 - Y:73 - K:27 | C:35 - M:67 - Y:72 - K:52 | C:29 - M:60 - Y:56 - K:25 |

Figure 6-21: These are guidelines only, not absolute values!

Note that the numbers are CMYK, even for use with RGB images. Open the Info palette menu, choose Palette Options, and set the Second Color Readout to CMYK (see Figure 6-22). Remember, too, that you can use color samplers as placeholders in the image, monitoring the changes that you're making in the Info palette. Set the color sampler readings to CMYK in the Info palette itself by clicking the eyedropper symbol to the left of the color mode listed for each sampler.

Promise me that you'll keep in mind that these numbers are for reference only? Your individual image determines what the correct adjustment should be. You can use these numbers as a starting point, but trust your eyes and evaluate your image as you work.

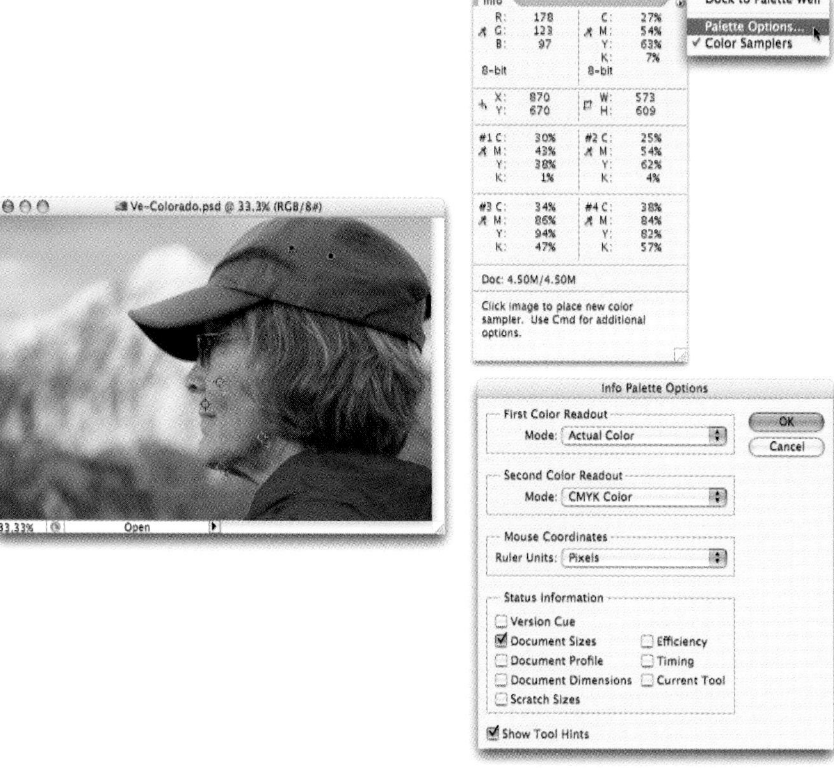


**Figure 6-22:** The Info palette options can be set to show you CMYK, even for an RGB image.

## Chapter 7

# Hur-RAW for the Home Team!

### *In This Chapter*

- Taking advantage of the Raw file format
- Evaluating your Raw capabilities
- Using the Camera Raw plug-in

There was a time, not so long ago in people years (but a couple of generations ago in computer years), when capturing digital photos in the Raw file format required you to spend tens of thousands of dollars. The wonderful thing about the Raw file format is that you use it to record images to save unprocessed image data, which gives you incredible control over the final appearance of your image. These days, however, cameras costing only a few hundred dollars can capture images "in the Raw." (And that's the naked truth!) If you don't have a Raw-capable camera now, after reading this chapter, you might decide that you *need* to have Raw capability.

In this chapter, I explain how Raw differs from other image file formats and why those differences can be important. I show you how to determine whether you have what you need to capture in Raw — and whether the Photoshop CS2 Camera Raw plug-in is capable of handling your camera's image files. Most of the rest of the chapter looks at the Camera Raw interface and what all those sliders do for you and for your image.

## Understanding the Raw Facts

The Raw file format at its heart is nothing but unprocessed image data. It comes in a number of variations — one or several for each camera manufacturer, it seems. Each has its own file extension (such as `.crw`, `.cr2`, or `.nef`), and many have their own special features that are totally incompatible with each other. And those camera manufacturers love to tinker with their proprietary formats, changing them regularly. But each of the formats, at the basic level, is Raw. (Check your camera's User Guide to see if it is capable of recording image data in a format other than JPEG or TIFF. If so, it's probably a variation of Raw.)

Thankfully, Adobe updates the Camera Raw plug-in for Photoshop (as shown in Figure 7-1) on a regular basis, adding the capability to work with the newest cameras shortly after they're available. (Plug-ins, like Camera Raw and most of Photoshop's filters, extend the program's capabilities. Updating your plug-ins regularly ensures you have the greatest capabilities.) Be warned, however, that purchasing a new model the day it comes on the market might mean using the camera's own software for a while until Camera Raw is updated.

Figure 7-1: The impressive Camera Raw window, explained fully in this chapter.

## What's the big deal about Raw?

Cameras that record images using the Raw format save unprocessed image data. When recording as TIFF or JPEG, the camera manipulates the image data, processing it in a variety of ways. So what's the big deal with preprocessing — Raw — image data? Assuming that you're as hungry for food as for knowledge, I'll use a cooking analogy.

Say you purchase frozen lasagna and heat it up in your microwave oven. It probably tastes good and fulfills your needs ("Food!"). However, the chef who designed this prepared meal and the good folks who churn it out use a specific recipe designed to appeal to a large number of people, hopefully offending very few. When you reheat your lasagna in the microwave, you have some choices. For example, you decide how warm to make it (generally following the package's reheating instructions). Or, you can add some salt and pepper to season to taste, or perhaps dump on the hot sauce.

What you *can't* do with that frozen lasagna is take out some of the salt (or fat) in it from the recipe designed by the chef and prepared by the good folks. You *can't* substitute olive oil for butter. You *can't* cut back on the garlic a bit (just in case your date goes well). You're pretty much restricted by what the original chef (and his good folks) prepared. Sure, you could pour a half-bottle of blue food coloring over it, creating a special effect, but you're not likely to turn that microwavable lasagna into a gourmet dinner.

And that's what Raw is all about! If you're just hungry and your demands are not too severe, no problem — shoot JPEG (the digital photo equivalent of a microwave meal). If, on the other hand, you consider yourself a gourmet chef, creating art from virtually nothing, Raw is the format for you. Avoid the limitations put on your image editing by preprocessing and dive right in with the greatest flexibility. (And you don't even have to go down to the Farmers' Market for fresh tomatoes.)

## Working in Raw

There's one critical difference between working with Raw images and working with JPEGs or TIFFs — you never actually make changes to the Raw file. Instead, you record your adjustments in the image's *metadata* (non-image data recorded with the image data) or in a *sidecar* file (a separate file in which Photoshop records any information that can't be recorded in the metadata). (Sidecar files have the same name as the image file, but use the `.xmp` file extension. Keep each sidecar file in the same folder as the image with which it is associated.) Because adjustments are recorded separately rather than applied to the images, the original image data remains unchanged, waiting for you to create again and again, all from the same unprocessed, undegraded image data.

Photoshop's Save As dialog box offers you the option of the Photoshop Raw file format. Photoshop Raw is *not* compatible with the Camera Raw plug-in and does not provide you with the benefits of using the Raw format with your digital camera. It is, however, necessary for certain high-end graphics and animation programs into which someone, somewhere, sometimes places images from Photoshop.

## The DNG file format

In late 2004, Adobe Systems, Inc. announced a new *open standard* (anybody can use it without licensing fees) for Raw photos. The DNG (digital negative) file format adheres to the basic Raw formulation but does allow for growth. The aim is to ensure that years from now, you'll still be able to open and process the images you shot yesterday. (Unfortunately, changes in camera-specific versions of Raw already make some early Raw photos inaccessible by today's software — and that's just the tip of the iceberg!) Adobe promises to continue support for backward-compatible DNG file processing in the future and makes the Adobe Digital Negative Converter software (as shown here) available for free. Although the hope is that camera manufacturers will adopt DNG as their cameras' own version of Raw, only time will tell. (Note that even if you convert copies of your images to DNG, Adobe recommends that you keep the original Raw files, just in case.)

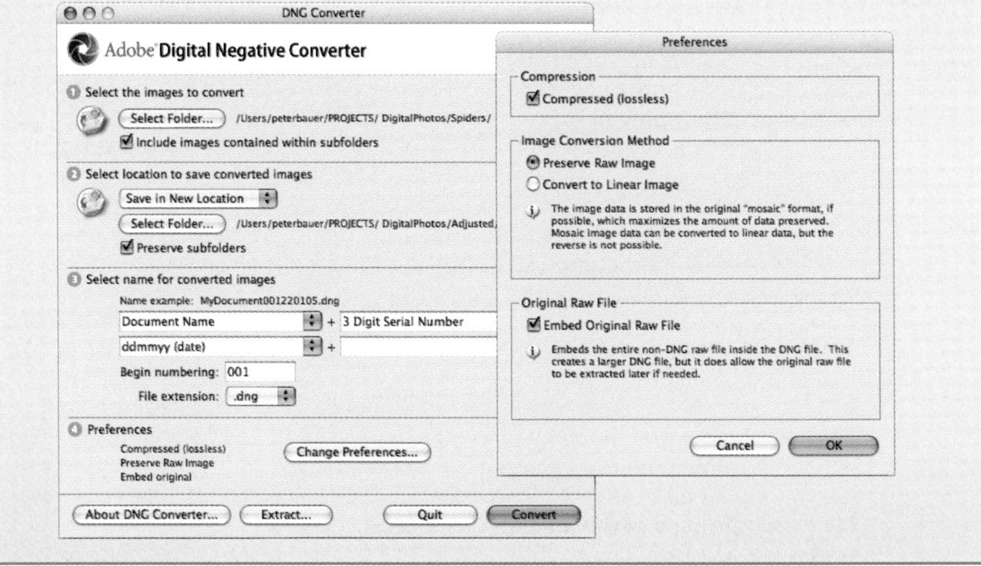

When capturing in Raw, you can basically ignore all the camera's settings other than aperture, shutter speed, ISO, and (of course) focus. Everything else can be adjusted in the Camera Raw plug-in. However, because Raw devotes significantly more resources to recording highlights than shadows, it's not a bad idea to concentrate on those highlights when shooting. When the highlights are great to start with, you can reallocate some of the image's tonal range to the deprived shadows, thus reducing unwanted digital noise and increasing detail.

Keep in mind that in addition to the Photoshop CS2 Camera Raw plug-in, you also have available the software that came with your camera. (And you might even have additional software packages available, depending on what camera make and model you have at your disposal.) Which package is best? As usual, *best* is a relative term. For example, Nikon's proprietary software does a great job with sharpness when processing `.nef` files, but it lacks some of Camera Raw's features. If sharpness is your overriding requirement, you might prefer the Nikon software. (Remember that your Raw file can't be processed by both the camera's software and then by Camera Raw, but you can process the data with either, and then further refine your image in Photoshop itself.)

# Do You Have What It Takes?

To capture images in the Raw format requires only a camera that shoots Raw. To work with those images in Photoshop, you need both a camera and software that can process the Raw files. To work with images in Photoshop CS2's Camera Raw plug-in, you need a camera on the supported cameras list for Camera Raw — and, of course, Photoshop with Camera Raw. Adobe updates the Camera Raw plug-in regularly to ensure compatibility with the latest cameras as well as with the latest nit-picky changes that camera manufacturers have made to their proprietary versions of Raw. (If we all get together and chant, "Dee-En-Gee" loud and long, do you think those camera companies might adopt the `.dng` file format?) Check for the latest Camera Raw update and list of supported cameras here (and don't forget to read the installation instructions):

```
www.adobe.com/products/photoshop/cameraraw.html
```

Working with images in the Raw format requires one other thing that you might not have: additional time. Opening the Camera Raw plug-in, making the necessary adjustments to your image, and then transferring the image into Photoshop all take time. Granted, making changes in Camera Raw eliminates the need for many of the adjustments that you'd be making in Photoshop, but working in Camera Raw could seem to be slower. (Actually, depending on your system, Camera Raw might speed things up because tonal adjustment, color correction, sharpening, and noise reduction are all in one place — there's no waiting for adjustments and filters to be applied and then for the next dialog box to open.)

# Working in the Camera Raw Plug-In

The cornerstone of Photoshop's Raw capability is the Camera Raw plug-in. Although you can open an image from Adobe Bridge, the file management program installed with Photoshop (see Chapter 4), directly into Photoshop, doing so assumes that you want to use the adjustments already recorded in the image's metadata. After an image is open in Photoshop itself, you manipulate the pixels directly, rather than manipulating the metadata. When you work in the Camera Raw plug-in, you never change the image itself, only the adjustments recorded in the file's metadata (or in a sidecar file).

As you can see in Figure 7-1, the Camera Raw window is filled with tools and sliders. Even though you might not work with all the Camera Raw features, here's the lowdown on the features there.

## Tools and preview options

In the upper-left corner of the Camera Raw window are several new tools at your command (as shown in Figure 7-2). In addition to the standard Zoom, Hand, and White Balance tools, Photoshop CS2 adds tools for cropping and straightening your images right in Camera Raw, giving you the capability of adding color samplers to track the adjustments as you're making them. You also find rotate buttons with the tools, which work in 90-degree increments.

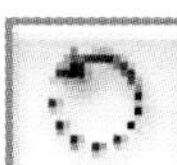

**Figure 7-2:** You find Camera Raw's tools in the upper-left corner of the window.

Drag the Crop tool to create a bounding box, which you can then adjust by dragging its anchor points. Position the tool just outside the bounding box and drag to rotate. The image is cropped when you click the Open button. If you drag the Straighten tool along a line in the image that should be horizontal or vertical, a crop bounding box is created with that alignment. If you don't need to rotate the image, use the Crop tool. If you do want to rotate your image, use either. (You will find that the Straighten tool is a great way to find the correct angle of rotation.)

When you add color samplers (a maximum of four) to the image preview area (click with the Color Sampler tool), their values are displayed below the tools. When you haven't added color samplers, that area is collapsed, leaving more room for the preview area. Color Samplers in Camera Raw function the same as they do in Photoshop (see Chapter 6).

Color samplers are great for making sure that you don't *blow out your highlights* (make them pure white) or *clog your shadows* (turn them pure black). Click with the Color Sampler tool to add a color sampler to both a highlight area and a shadow area, and then place your remaining two color samplers in strategic areas. (I like to place a color sampler in an area of the image that should be neutral, preferably mid-gray, and a color sampler in the most critical area of the image's subject.) Remember that you can drag a color sampler (with the Color Sampler tool) to move it and drag it out of the preview area to delete it. You can delete all color samplers with the Clear Samplers button.

To the right of the tools and rotate buttons are three preview check boxes. Check/uncheck the Preview box to gauge your progress as you make changes to the image's adjustments. Mark the Shadows and the Highlights check boxes to see *gamut warnings,* which are overlays that indicate when areas of your image are being forced to pure black or white. Those areas lose all detail, which you generally want to avoid. (I will readily admit that I often intentionally clog shadows and blow out highlights to produce special effects and to focus attention on the subject of my photos.)

## The histogram

Because of the unprocessed nature of Raw images, the histogram you see in the top-right corner of the Camera Raw window (also shown in Figure 7-3) is generally far more important that the Histogram palette in Photoshop itself. By keeping an eye on the histogram while you adjust sliders, you can ensure that you're not blowing out the highlights (when the very right end of the histogram starts crawling up the edge) or clogging the shadows (the left edge gets too tall). (The RGB values that you see just above the histogram represent the values of the pixel directly under the cursor when the cursor is in the preview area of the window.)

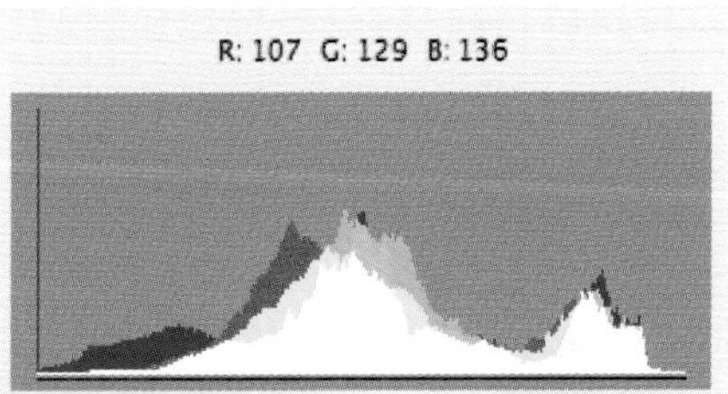


**Figure 7-3:** Use the histogram to make sure you don't wreck your highlights and shadows.

The histogram in Camera Raw shows you not only the distribution of tonal values but also the distribution by channel. In Figure 7-3, you can see that the Blue channel has a *lot* of dark pixels. (The blue column climbs the left edge of the histogram.) This could indicate any of a number of situations. However, because you also see a generally good distribution of blue throughout the histogram, you can be pretty sure that the column of blue to the left simply indicates a lot of yellow in the image. (Blue and yellow are color opposites in RGB.) As always, remember that what you see in the preview area — what your eyes tell you — trumps any information from a histogram.

## The preview area

As you can see in Figure 7-1, the bulk of the Camera Raw window is filled with the image preview, giving you the best possible view of your work. Remember that you can drag the lower-right corner of the Camera Raw window to resize it. The preview area benefits/suffers from the changes that you make as you enlarge/shrink the window. To the lower left are a pop-up menu with preset zoom factors as well as a pair of buttons to zoom in or out. (Don't forget about the Zoom tool!)

### Workflow options

Below the preview area is a check box that shows or hides the workflow options area (which is visible in Figure 7-4). The choices that you make in this part of the Camera Raw dialog box determine the pixel dimensions, color depth, resolution, and even the color profile of the image when opened in Photoshop.

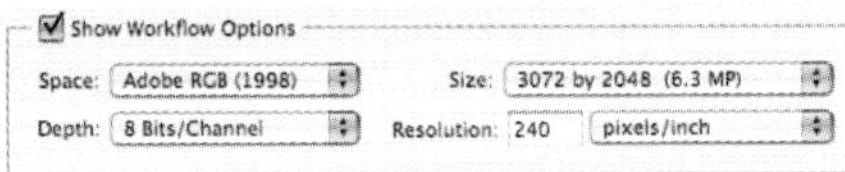


**Figure 7-4:** Make decisions about the processed image in the Workflow Options area.

After you make decisions and select options in the workflow area, you might want to clear the check box to increase the preview area. (That's generally more important with portrait-oriented images than with landscape images — when the image is taller than it is wide, you might want to maximize the preview area.)

Here are your options:

- **Space:** Camera Raw offers only four color spaces — Adobe RGB, ColorMatch RGB, ProPhoto RGB, and sRGB. Color spaces (read about them in Chapter 6) determine which colors are available in an image.

  Using the ProPhoto RGB color space gives you the widest *gamut* (the largest number of possible colors), which minimizes the chance of colors getting squished into each other as you work with your image. If your image has extreme colors, use ProPhoto (and 16-bit color) in Camera Raw, and then use Photoshop's Edit⇨Convert to Profile command to change your required profile (perhaps Adobe RGB or sRGB). Select Relative Colorimetric as the rending intent.

- **Size:** You can choose from among six pixel dimensions for your image in Camera Raw. The camera's native pixel dimensions for the image is the default, but you can also downsize to 50% or 67%, or upsize to 133%, 167%, or 200%. Camera Raw uses a variation of the Bicubic Sharper algorithm for *upsampling* (increasing the number of pixels in the image), so if you need to increase the image's size, you're generally better off opening the image at its native size and using Photoshop's Image Size command with Resample set to Bicubic Smoother.

- **Depth:** Because a greater color depth means more possible variations in color, generally you want to select 16-bit color and either keep the image in that color depth or switch to 8-bit color later in Photoshop (with the Image➪Mode➪8-Bits/Channel command). Use 8-bit color for any image that must be saved in JPEG format (including Web images), for CMYK (cyan/magenta/yellow/black) images, or when the file size overwhelms your printer. You might also opt for 8-bit color if storage space is limited. (Chapter 6 includes a detailed explanation of color depth.)
- **Resolution:** *Resolution* is simply an instruction to a printing device about what size to make each pixel. It can be assigned in Camera Raw or later in Photoshop's Image Size dialog box (with Resample unselected).

## The Settings pop-up and menu

Click the Settings pop-up menu — the menu to the left in Figure 7-5 — to select from among saved sets of adjustments and any recent image adjustments. Most of the time, you'll use these as a starting point — as soon as you make an adjustment to a slider, the Settings pop-up switches to Custom.

Use the menu shown to the right in Figure 7-5 to save sets of settings in Camera Raw for future use. If, for example, you shot a series of images under identical conditions with identical camera settings, you can adjust one of the images and save those adjustments for use with your other images.

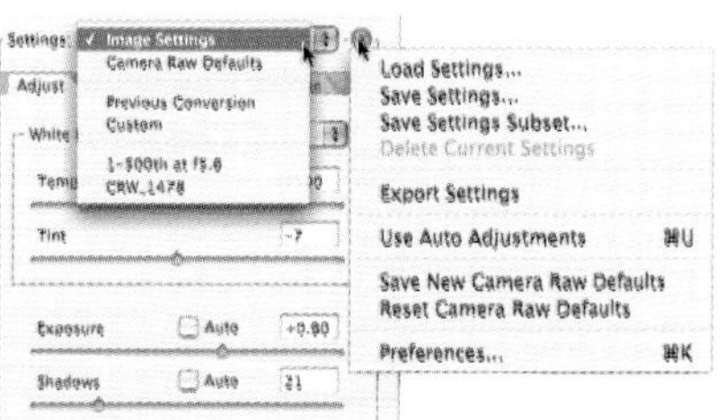


Figure 7-5: To the left are predefined adjustments; to the right you save and load settings.

Note, too, that you can access the Camera Raw Preferences through the same menu. In the Preferences tab, you can elect to save all the various image adjustments with the individual images in sidecar files or in a single database. (For most users, keeping the settings in a sidecar file is more practical.) You can also choose to apply any sharpening to the image preview or to the preview and the image itself. (Because you have more control over sharpening in Photoshop than you do in Camera Raw, I suggest that you don't do any sharpening in Camera Raw.) You can also increase the maximum size for the Camera Raw cache, which could be important if you process a huge number of images through the plug-in.

## The Adjust tab

Now *this* is the heart of Camera Raw! The Adjust tab (as shown in Figure 7-6) is where you make the most important adjustments to your image's appearance. Camera Raw generally does a very good job of combining its built-in knowledge of your specific camera model and its analysis of the individual image to provide you with a good starting point. You can then tweak the image (keeping an eye on the histogram) to bring out its best.

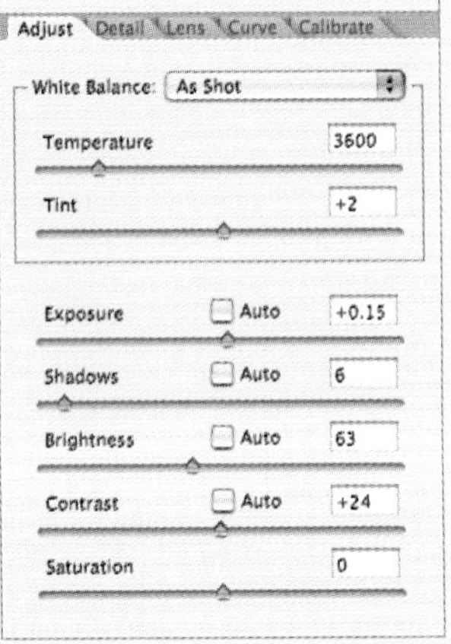


**Figure 7-6:** You make changes to tonality and color in the Adjust tab.

Generally, you adjust the white point (the Temperature and the Tint sliders) by clicking with the White Balance tool (which looks like the Eyedropper tool, seen here in the margin) in some area that should be neutral and close to white. Next, adjust the Exposure slider to spread the histogram across most of the space available. Work with the Shadows and the Brightness sliders to maximize the tonal range (without sending the histogram crawling up the left or right edges). The Contrast and the Saturation sliders, as you can guess, manage the contrast in the midtones and the saturation of the colors in your image.

As you work, the best adjustments are those that make the image look great to you and meet your creative goals.

When working with the Exposure and the Shadows sliders, you can press the Option (Mac)/Alt (Windows) key to see any pixels in your image that are being *clipped* (forced to the maximum value) in the shadows, highlights, or any color. Hold the Option/Alt key and drag the sliders. White pixels show where highlights are being clipped, black pixels show where shadows are being clipped, and colors indicate clipping in one or two color channels. Avoid clipping (except for special artistic effects) because your image loses detail when similar colors are forced to a single extreme value.

## The Detail tab

You have three sliders on the Detail tab to control sharpness and noise in your image. I suggest that as soon as you click the Detail tab, you zoom in to 200% (or even 400%) on an area of shadow in your image and drag the three sliders all the way to the left, setting them to 0 (zero). Leave the Sharpness slider at 0; do your sharpening in Photoshop's Smart Sharpen (or Unsharp Mask) filter, where you have a Radius slider to control how the sharpening is applied to the image.

Drag the Color Noise Reduction slider slowly to the right until all red/green/blue specks in the shadows disappear. Next, drag the Luminance Smoothing slider to the right until the bright specks in your shadows are reduced (but not so far to the right that detail in your image is damaged). Figure 7-7 shows a "before" and "after" comparison.

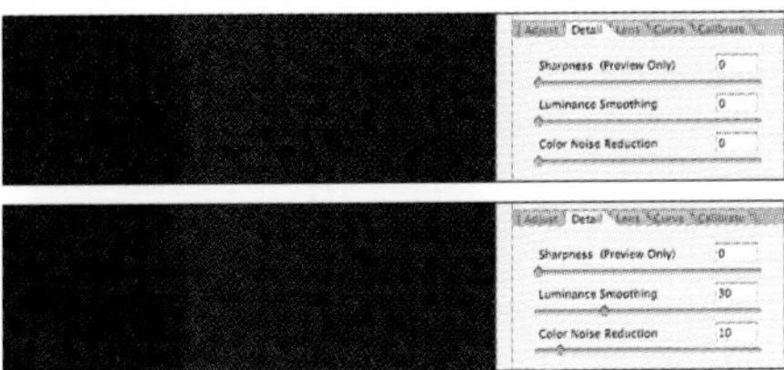


Figure 7-7: Reducing noise and smoothing luminance can greatly improve shadow areas.

## The Lens tab

Use the Lens tab's controls (as shown in Figure 7-8) to compensate for certain undesirable characteristics of your lens. Zoom in on an area of angled lines in an image — perhaps tree branches in front of a bright sky — and look for colorful halos or fringes along edges. Use the Chromatic Aberration sliders to minimize the fringe. Be patient and careful — often there will be one precise pair of settings that eliminates the problem.

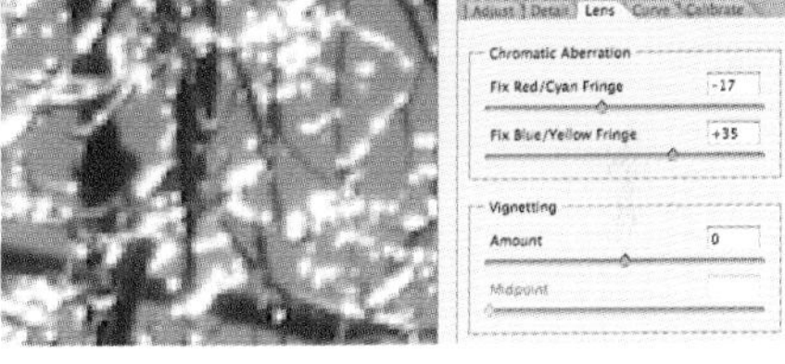


Figure 7-8: Minimize colored fringe with the Chromatic Aberration sliders.

Use the Vignetting sliders to eliminate darkness around the edges of the image or, perhaps, to introduce either darkness or lightness as a special effect. When the Amount slider has a value other than 0, the Midpoint slider is active, which lets you set the diameter of the vignette. In Figure 7-9, the original image is shown at the top. Below, you see what happens when you drag the Amount slider to the left for a dark effect and to the right to lighten the corners of the shot, smoothing the appearance of the sky.

Figure 7-9: Drag the Amount slider to the left to darken corners, to the right to lighten.

## The Curve tab

When you open the Curve tab in Camera Raw (see Figure 7-10), you can directly control the tonality of the image, just as you do in Photoshop's Curves dialog box. Keep in mind that this is *in addition to* changes that you make in the Adjust tab. The histogram you see ghosted behind the curve in Figure 7-10 represents the image's current settings in the Adjust tab.

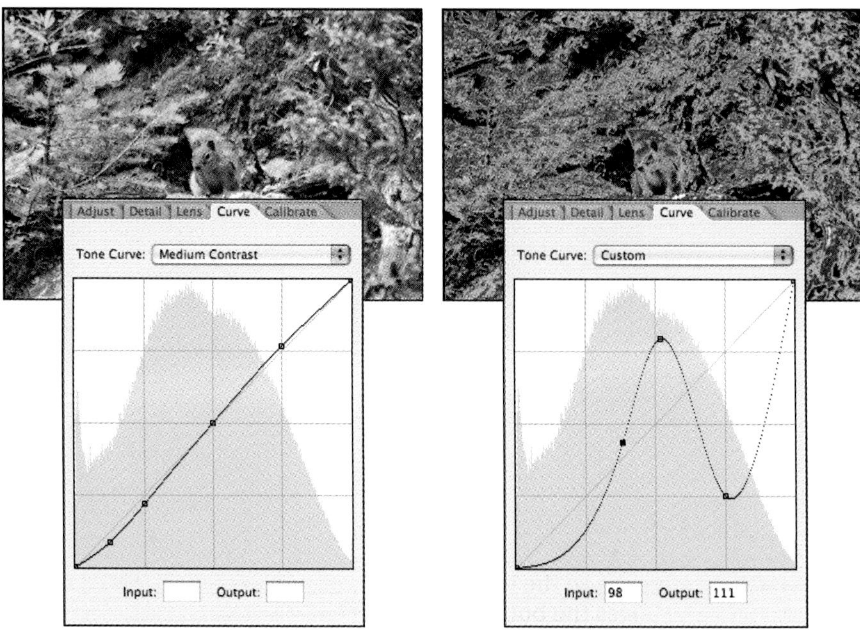


Figure 7-10: The Curve can be tweaked or jerked hard, depending on your artistic vision.

Manipulate the curve by dragging the existing six anchor points, or click and drag to create custom anchor points. You can use the Curve tab to very gently adjust the tonality of your image or to radically alter the image, creating very interesting color effects.

## The Calibrate tab

The Calibrate tab truly fine-tunes your adjustments. You might want to use it to adjust the camera default setting to compensate for what you perceive to be regular and consistent deviation in your camera's behavior. You might, under some circumstances, want to use the sliders in the Calibrate tab (see Figure 7-11) to reduce a *color cast,* an unwanted color tint in the image. (Use very small adjustments!) Generally, though, you'll skip the Calibrate tab completely.

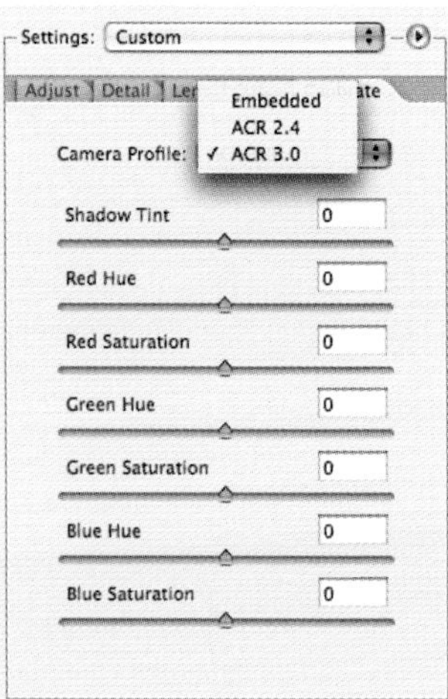


Figure 7-11: The Calibrate sliders might be useful for correcting a color cast.

## The Camera Raw buttons

In the lower-right corner of the dialog box are four buttons, three of which have hidden features that you access by pressing the Option/Alt key (as shown in Figure 7-12):

- **Save.../Save:** After making your adjustments, click the Save... button to open the DNG Converter dialog box and save a copy of the image as a DNG file. Option-click/Alt-click to bypass the DNG Options dialog box and simply save the image as a DNG file. When you close the Camera Raw window, the image is saved automatically. (For more on the DNG file format and the DNG Options dialog box, see the sidebar, "The DNG file format.")

Figure 7-12: Use the Option/Alt key to show the lower set of buttons.

- **Cancel/Reset:** Clicking Cancel closes the Camera Raw window without making any changes to the image's metadata. Holding down the Option/Alt key changes the button to Reset, which restores the settings seen when you first opened the image in Camera Raw.
- **Open/Open Copy:** After making your adjustments, click Open to update the file's metadata and open the image in Photoshop itself. Holding down Option/Alt changes the button to Open Copy, which opens the image without updating the metadata. You might use Open Copy when creating a second version of the image while preserving your exactingly precise original adjustments.
- **Done:** The Done button, with or without the Option/Alt key, simply updates the image's metadata with the adjustments you've made and closes Camera Raw without opening the image.

# Chapter 8

# Fine-Tuning Your Fixes

## In This Chapter

- Telling Photoshop where to work with selections
- Masking for both layer visibility and for protecting parts of your image
- Keeping your options open with adjustment layers

There you are, repainting the bedroom — all by yourself, saving money, being productive — and it's time to do the windows. Now, you probably don't want to paint over the glass, right? Just the frame, the sash, the sill, those little whatch-ya-call-its between the panes, right? There are several ways you can avoid painting the glass. You can use a little brush and paint *very* carefully. You can use a larger brush, paint faster, and scrape the excess from the glass afterward. You can grab the masking tape, protect the glass, and paint as sloppily as you like — when the tape comes off, the glass is paint-free.

Those are unbelievably similar to the choices that you have in Photoshop when you need to work on only a part of your image. You can zoom in and use tools, dragging the cursor over only those pixels that you want to change (just like using a tiny paintbrush). You can use the History Brush feature (which I introduce in Chapter 1) to restore parts of the image to the pre-change state (like scraping the glass). You can isolate the area of the image you want to change with a selection (much like protecting the rest of the image with tape).

In this chapter, you read about getting ready to make changes to your image rather than actually making those changes. You can isolate groups of pixels in your image in a variety of ways. For example, you can select pixels that are in the same part of the image (regardless of color), or you can select pixels that are the same color (regardless of location in the image). This is *power:* the capability to tell Photoshop exactly which pixels you want to alter. After you make that selection, you can manipulate the pixels in a variety of ways — everything from making color and tonal adjustments to working with Photoshop's creative filters to simply copying them so you can paste them into another image.

I discuss "taping the glass" first by making selections and then by using *masks* — channels that actually store selection information. After that, read about working with *adjustment layers,* which are special layers that help you apply certain color and tonal adjustments without actually changing any pixels in the image. An adjustment layer even lets you restrict the change to one or several layers in the image.

## What Is a Selection?

When you make a *selection* in your image, you're simply isolating some of the pixels, picking them (*selecting* them) so that you can do something to those pixels without doing it to all the pixels in your image. Photoshop shows you what part of the image is within the selection with a flashing dashed line. (Now that you're part of the Photoshop Inner Circle, you call that selection boundary the *marching ants.*)

Say, for example, that part of your image looks great, but part of the image looks, well, just plain wrong. Figure 8-1 is an excellent example.

**Figure 8-1:** Sometimes only part of the image needs changes.

By making a selection and applying an adjustment, I can make this image look much, much better. Of course, you might choose to make a different selection and apply a different adjustment, but you can see what I chose to do in the lower-left of Figure 8-2. By selecting the rails (in this case, with the Polygon Lasso tool, which I explain later in this chapter), I isolate those areas from the rest of the image, enabling me to change the color of those pixels without changing anything else.

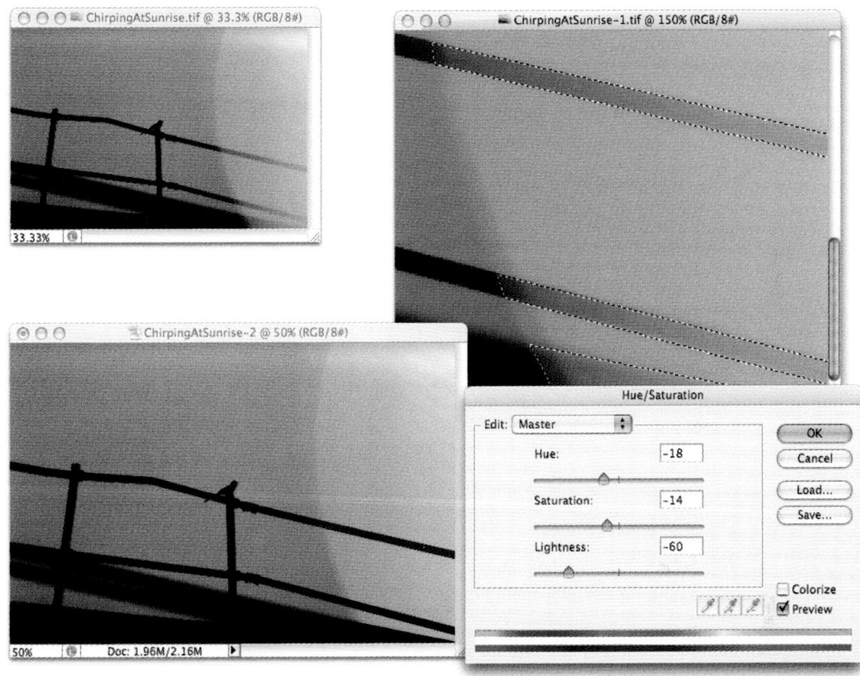


Figure 8-2: The selection (shown to the right) restricts the change to some parts of the image.

The tonal and color adjustments that I discuss in Chapters 5 and 6 are often applied to an image as a whole. You can, however, apply them to specific areas of an image. Much of the rest of the work that you do in Photoshop is not global in nature, but rather is done to only restricted areas of your image. You use selections to do that restricting.

You can also use selections for a variety of other jobs in Photoshop. One of the most common is copying from one image and pasting into another. You can see one example in Figure 8-3. The subject of one image (upper-left) is selected. (You can see a close-up of the selection to the right.) The menu command Edit⇨Copy copies the selected pixels to the computer's memory (the Clipboard). You can then switch to another image and use the Edit⇨Paste command to drop those pixels into a second image (lower-left). Adjust the lighting, size, and position. Perhaps add some shadows with the Brush tool. The job is ready for whatever nefarious purpose you might have in mind!

Figure 8-3: Make a selection, copy, switch to another image, and paste.

Any pixel in your image can be selected, unselected, or partially selected. For example, if you have a selection and fill it with red, the selected pixels turn red, the unselected pixels don't change, and the partially selected pixels get a red tint. How much tint depends on the level of selection. (Photoshop generally uses 8-bit grayscale for selections, so there are 256 different levels of "selected.")

# Feathering and Anti-aliasing

You need to keep in mind a couple of very important terms as you read about the various tools and commands with which you make selections. Both *feathering* and *anti-aliasing* make the edges of your selections softer by using partially transparent or differently colored pixels. That, in turn, helps blend whatever you're doing to that selection into the rest of the image.

Don't forget that all pixels in your image are square, aligned in neat, orderly rows and columns. (That's the *raster* in raster artwork.) When you create a curve or diagonal in your artwork, the corners of the pixels stick out. Feathering and anti-aliasing disguise that ragged edge. You can also use feathering to create larger, softer selections with a faded edge. Generally speaking, use anti-aliasing to keep edges looking neat and use feathering to create a soft, faded selection.

Nothing illustrates the power of feathering quite like a simple black-on-white demonstration, as you see in Figure 8-4. In the upper-left, I made an unfeathered selection and filled it with black. To the upper-right, the filled selection is exactly the same size but has a 2-pixel feather. Below, I used a 15-pixel feather when making the selection.

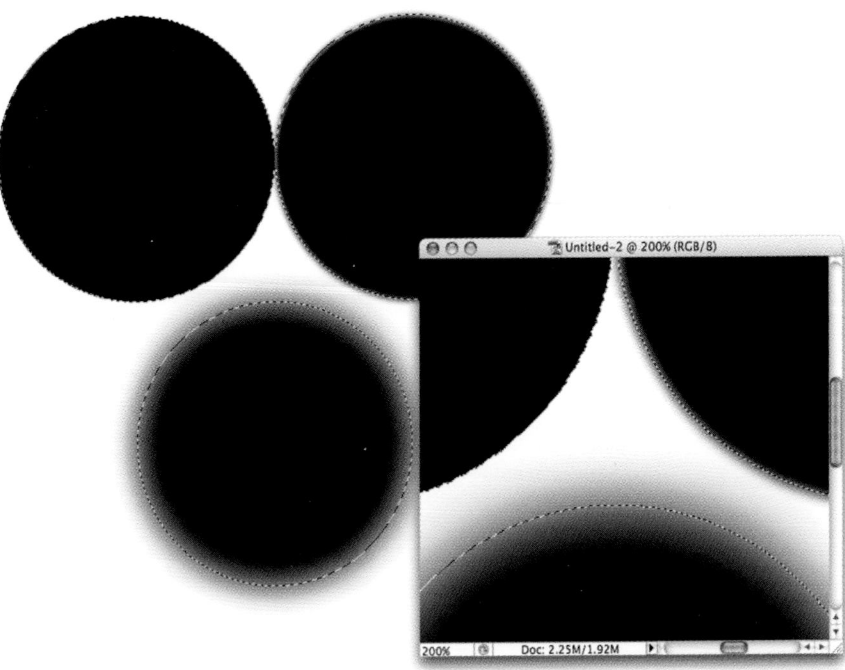


**Figure 8-4:** A close-up look at no feathering, feathering, and *lots* of feathering.

Note that there's feathering on both sides of the selection border. And don't be fooled by the amount that you enter in the Feather field on the Options bar — that's a general guideline, not a precise value. A 15-pixel feather for the Elliptical Marquee tool might give you 50 or 60 partially transparent pixels, half on either side of the selection border. Even a 1-pixel feather gives you a selection with several "soft" pixels on either side.

Anti-aliasing is similar to feathering in that it softens edges: It's designed to hide the corners of pixels along curves and in diagonal lines. You use anti-aliasing with type (as I explain in Chapter 13). You'll often find that anti-aliasing is all you need to keep the edges of your selections pretty; feathering isn't required. Anti-aliasing is a yes/no option, with no numeric field to worry about. Figure 8-5 compares a diagonal with no anti-aliasing, with anti-aliasing, and with a 1-pixel feather.

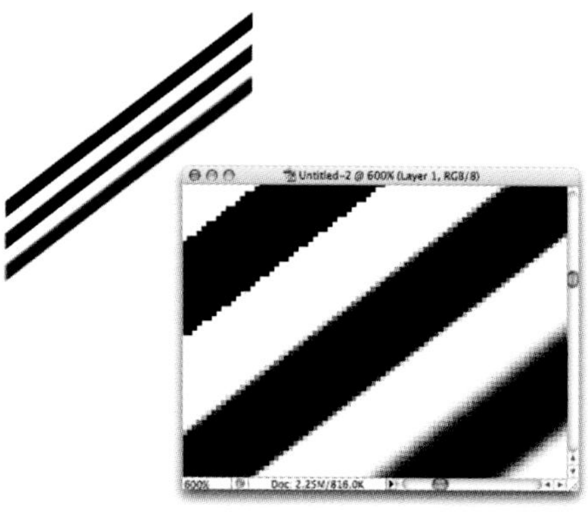

Figure 8-5: Anti-aliasing helps smooth the appearance of curves and diagonals.

At 100 percent zoom (to the upper left), the first line looks bumpy along the edges (has a case of the *jaggies*). The lower line looks soft and mushy, out of focus. And the middle line? To quote Goldilocks, "It's just right!" When zoomed to 600%, you can really see those jaggies and that softening. And in the middle, you see that the anti-aliasing uses light gray and mid-gray pixels interspersed along the edge among the black pixels. At 100% zoom (upper-left), your eye is fooled into seeing a straight black edge.

Generally speaking, use anti-aliasing with just about every selection (other than rectangular or square), and use feathering when you want to really soften the edges to create a special effect.

# Making Your Selections with Tools

Photoshop offers you eight tools whose whole purpose in life is to help you make selections. You also use those tools to alter your selections by adding to, subtracting from, and intersecting with an existing selection. The eight selection tools are divided into three groups:

- Four marquee tools
- Three lasso tools
- A single tool: the Magic Wand

## Marquee selection tools

You have four marquee selection tools although you'll generally use only two of them. Figure 8-6 shows the marquee selection tools, along with each tool's Options bar configuration.

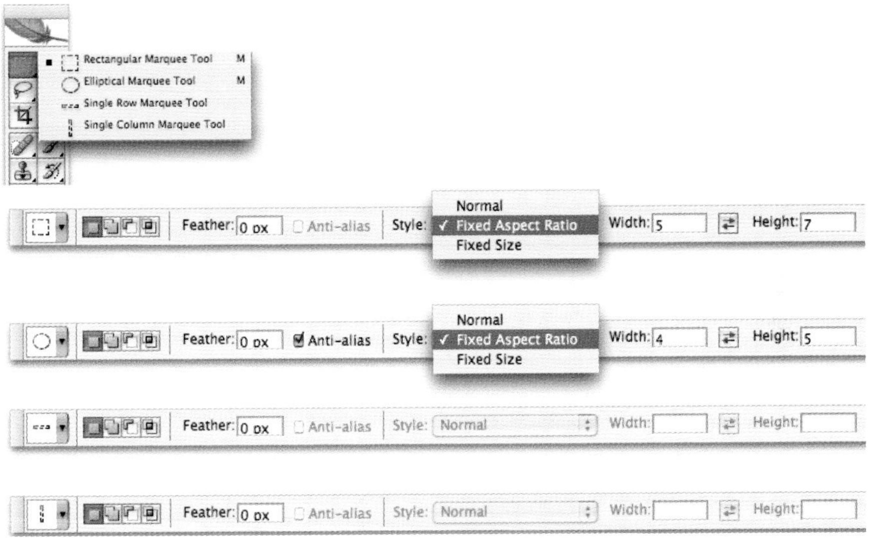


Figure 8-6: Marquee selection tools come in four flavors, two of which are tasty.

You drag the very-useful Rectangular Marquee and Elliptical Marquee tools to make selections. Click and drag in any direction to make your selection. After you start dragging, hold down the Shift key (while still dragging) to constrain proportions. When you constrain the proportions of a selection, you create a square or circle rather than a rectangle or an ellipse. If you start dragging a selection and press the Option (Mac)/Alt (Windows) key, the selection centers itself on the point where you click. The Shift and Option/Alt keys can be used together. Holding down the Shift key *before* you click and drag adds the selection to any existing selection. Holding down the Option/Alt key *before* dragging subtracts the new selection from any existing selection.

The Single Row Marquee and Single Column Marquee tools are simply clicked at the point where you want a 1-pixel selection, running from side-to-side or from top-to-bottom. These tools create selections that extend the full width or full height of your image. You might use these tools to create a grid-like selection that you can fill with color. Or you might never use them at all.

Take another glance at the Options bars in Figure 8-6. The four buttons to the left in the Options bar, which you can use with any of the tools, determine how the tool interacts with an existing selection.

- **New Selection:** When you select the first button, any selection that you make replaces an active selection (deselecting any previous selection). If, with a selection tool, you click inside an active selection when the first option is active, you can drag that selection in your image without moving any pixels. (When you haven't already made a selection, these tools always make a new selection, regardless of which button is active.)
- **Add To:** When you have an active selection and need to add to that selection, use the second button (or simply press and hold down the Shift key while dragging).
- **Subtract From:** When you have a selection and need to deselect part of it, use the third button. Say, for example, that you make a round selection and want to chop out the middle to make a donut shape. Click the third button, and then drag within the original selection to deselect the donut hole.
- **Intersect With:** You have a selection, but you want to keep only part of the selection. You could set your selection tool to subtract from the existing selection, or you could intersect with that original selection and deselect a number of areas at once.

Figure 8-7 presents a visual explanation of how all four buttons work. On the left, you see the selected option for the active marquee selection tool. Next is an original selection. In the third column, you see another selection being made (with the selection tool dragged from the lower-right to the upper-left). Finally, on the right, you see the result of combining the two selections.

In the bottom-most example, you could do a whole series of subtractions from the existing selection to chop off the "points," but using the intersect option takes care of the job with a single drag.

While you're dragging a selection with the Rectangular Marquee or the Elliptical Marquee tool, you can hold the mouse button down and press and hold the spacebar to reposition the marquee. When you've got it where you want it, release the spacebar and continue to drag.

## Lasso selection tools

You have three lasso selection tools available in Photoshop CS2. On the Options bar, all three of the lasso selection tools offer you the same basic features that you find in the marquee selection tools, as you can see in Figure 8-8. You can add to, subtract from, or intersect with an existing selection. You also have the feathering and anti-aliasing options available.

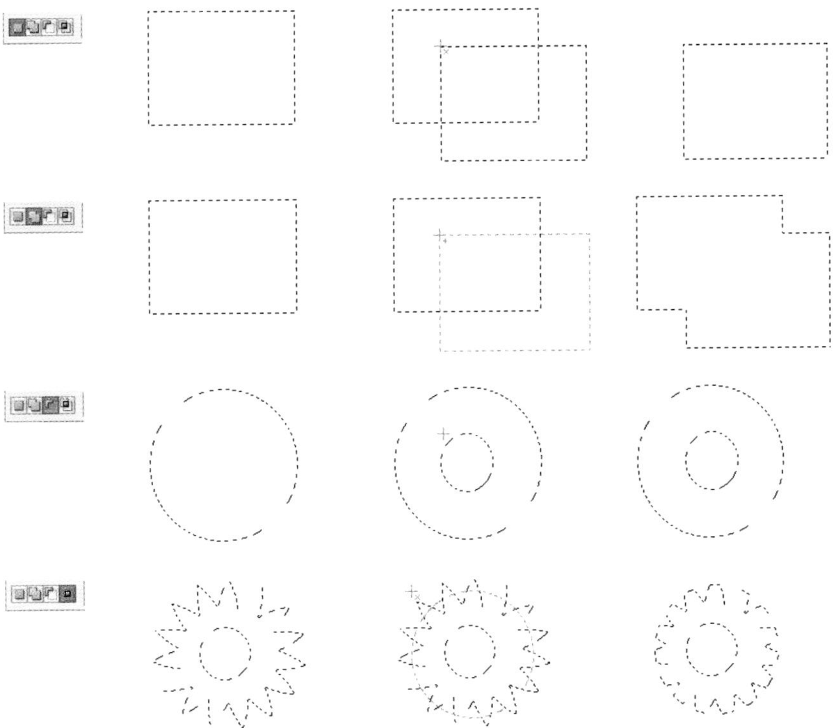

Figure 8-7: The buttons at the left on the Options bar control selection interaction.

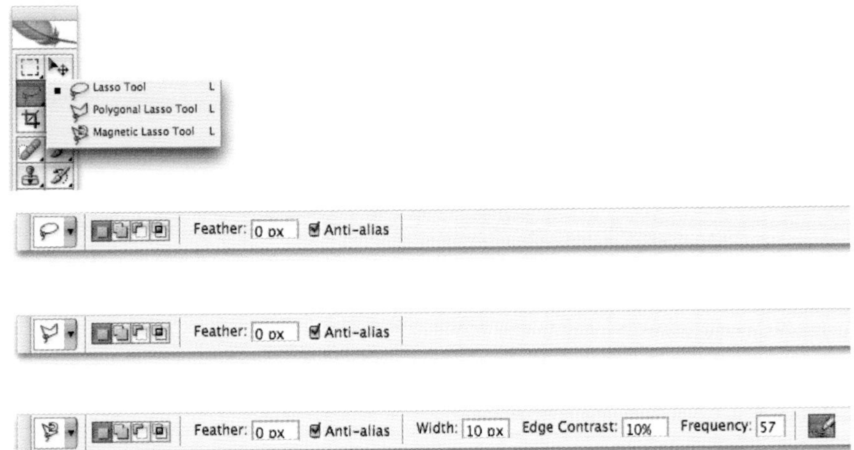


Figure 8-8: The basic options for the lasso selection tools match those for the marquee selection tools.

## Controlled selections

Lurking within the Options bar Style drop-down menu are two options worth noting: Fixed Aspect Ratio and Fixed Size. Using the Fixed Aspect Ratio option with the Rectangular Marquee or the Elliptical Marquee tool forces the selection to the height and width relationship that you specify in the Options bar. This is great for composing an image that you need at a specific size, say to fit in a standard picture frame. The selection tool won't resize the image for you, but you can make the selection and use the Image➪Crop command, and then use the Image➪Image Size command to resize to your required dimensions and resolution. (Read about resizing and cropping your images in Chapter 4.)

The Fixed Size option changes the behavior of the tools. After you enter an exact width and height in the Options bar, position the cursor in the upper-left corner of the area that you want to select and click once — the selection is created to the lower right of that point. Don't worry about being exact because you can drag the selection marquee into position afterward. (You'll want to have the left-most of the four buttons on the Options bar selected to reposition your selection.) And take a look at the button between the Width and Height fields on the Options bar: When you're using the Fixed Aspect Ratio or Fixed Size styles, click that button to swap the values in the two fields.

So what makes lasso tools different from a marquee tool? Read on to find out:

- **Lasso tool:** The Lasso tool is a true *freeform* tool; that is, you click and drag it wherever you want the selection to go. You can drag around and return to the starting point or you can release the mouse button anywhere, and your selection is finished along a straight line from that point to the spot where you start your selection. If you press and hold the Option/Alt key while dragging, you'll temporarily switch to the Polygon Lasso tool.
- **Polygon Lasso tool:** Rather than dragging, you click-click-click to make straight selection segments, at any angle, for any distance. When you position the cursor directly over your starting point, a little circle appears to the lower-right of the cursor to indicate that you're back to the start. Or simply double-click to finish the selection. If you press and hold the Option/Alt key while dragging, you'll temporarily switch to the regular Lasso tool, which lets you drag your selection any way you want. Using the Option/Alt key lets you switch back and forth between the freeform drag of the Lasso tool and the perfectly straight selection borders of the Polygon Lasso tool.
- **Magnetic Lasso tool:** When you need to select around a subject that has good contrast with its background, the Magnetic Lasso tool can do a great job. The perfect candidate for this tool is a simple object on a very plain background. You can, however, use it with just about any image where the edges of the area you want to select differ substantially from the rest of the image. Click and drag the tool along the edge of your

subject. If the tool misses the edge, back up and drag along the edge again. If the edge makes a sudden change in direction, click the mouse button to add an anchor point. If the tool places an anchor point in the wrong spot, back up and then press Delete/Backspace to remove the point. (By the way, if you have a Wacom pressure -sensitive tablet hooked up, you can set the Magnetic Lasso tool to vary its width according to pen pressure. Use the button just to the left of the Palette Well on the Options bar.)

The Magnetic Lasso tool works by identifying the difference in color along the edges, using all available color channels. From the Options bar, use the Width field to tell the tool how wide of an area it can look in to find an edge. The Edge Contrast field tells the tool how much the edge must differ while searching. Use the Frequency field to choose the number of anchor points the tool sets while outlining the selection.

## The Magic Wand tool

The Magic Wand tool selects pixels similar in color to the pixel on which you click with the tool. Like the other selection commands, you can add to, subtract from, or intersect with an existing selection, and you can select anti-aliasing. In Figure 8-9, you can see three additional options, unique among the selection tools. *Tolerance* determines how closely pixels must match your target color to be included in the selection. When you enable the Contiguous check box, only pixels connected to the spot that you click by pixels of the same color are selected. The Sample All Layers option lets you make a selection of similarly colored pixels on every visible layer in your image, not just the currently active layer.

In Figure 8-9, you can see the result of clicking the same spot, using four different Tolerance settings. In the upper left, the Magic Wand was set to Tolerance: 10; in the upper right, Tolerance: 20; in the lower left, Tolerance: 50; and in the lower right, Tolerance: 100. You can see that the higher the tolerance, the wider range of color selected. When you use a low Tolerance setting, you select only those pixels in the image that are very similar to the pixel on which you click. A high Tolerance setting gives you a much wider range of color, which might or might not be appropriate for the selection you're making.

Use a reasonably low Tolerance setting and Shift-click with the Magic Wand in different places to select a range of colors. In the photo in Figure 8-9, I would use a low Tolerance setting when Shift-clicking the highlights in the blooms to avoid selecting the highlights on the leaves and the fence.

Figure 8-9: The lower the Tolerance, the fewer pixels in the selection.

# Your Selection Commands

You have over a dozen menu commands at your service when selecting pixels in your artwork. Some, like those near the top of the Select menu, are rather simple and aptly named. See Figure 8-10 for a list of the Select commands.

## The primary selection commands

The commands near the top of the Select menu are features that you're likely to use regularly. (Okay, maybe not the Reselect command.) Memorizing their keyboard shortcuts is a timesaver.

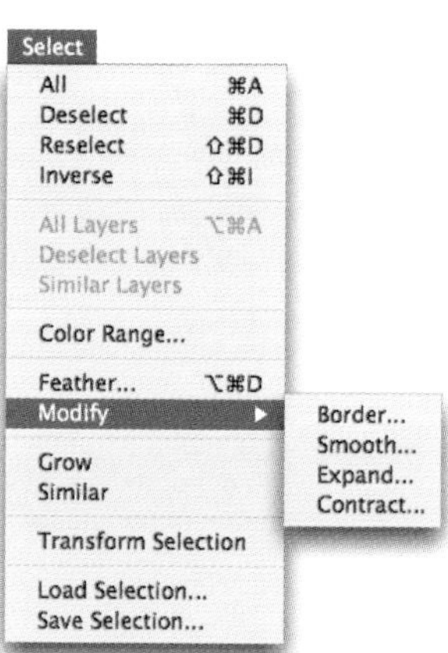


Figure 8-10: Photoshop's selection commands.

- **Select All (⌘+A/Ctrl+A):** Select All does exactly what the name implies — it makes a selection of all the pixels in your image on the active layer (or in an active layer mask).
- **Deselect (⌘+D/Ctrl+D):** Use the Deselect command to make sure that no pixels are selected. This is a handy command when it seems that a filter or adjustment command isn't working. There could be an unnoticed selection in the image, preventing the command from appearing how you expect.

- **Reselect (⌘+Shift+D/Ctrl+Shift+D):** This is a great little command for those times when you're making a complex selection, and a little slip accidentally deselects. Just use Reselect to restore the most recent selection.
- **Inverse (⌘+Shift+I/Ctrl+Shift+I):** The Inverse command reverses the selection. What was selected is deselected, and what wasn't selected becomes selected. (Don't forget to use the Shift key — without it, you invert the colors in your image rather than your selection!)

The second section of the Select menu contains three commands (All Layers, Deselect Layers, and Similar Layers) used not for pixels but rather with the layers in your image. Use these commands with multilayer images. (Read about using layers in your artwork in Chapter 10.)

## The Color Range command

In its own little group, right in the middle of the Select menu, is the incredibly powerful Color Range command. Check out those orange blooms from Figure 8-9. Rather than Shift-clicking with the Magic Wand, you can select the orange quickly and easily with the Color Range command. In Figure 8-11, I clicked and dragged through some orange areas in the image with the middle Eyedropper tool. (You can also click once with the left eyedropper and use the other eyedroppers to add and subtract colors from the selection.) The Fuzziness slider near the top determines how close a color must be to those through which you dragged to be included in the selection.

**Figure 8-11:** The Color Range feature selects by color.

Here are a couple of ways that you can get a better look at your selection as you create it. In Figure 8-12, you see the options (available from the Selection Preview menu). The Grayscale (upper left) and Black Matte (upper right) do a good job of showing that the background will be partially selected if you click OK. (Lower the Fuzziness or use the right-hand eyedropper to click in those areas of the fence that shouldn't be selected.) The White Matte (lower left) does an excellent job of showing that the tips of some leaves below the blooms will also be selected. (Ignore that and Option+drag/Alt+drag with the Lasso tool later to deselect that area.) Because of the color of this image's subject, the red Quick Mask preview (lower right) is almost worthless for this image (although it is often good with other images that don't have red and orange).

**Figure 8-12:** Color Range offers four ways to preview.

The pop-up menu at the top of the Color Range dialog box lets you pick among the RGB (red/green/blue) and CMY (cyan/magenta/yellow) colors, as well as the image's highlights, midtones, or shadows, and even any *out-of-gamut* colors in the image (colors that can't be reproduced within the selected color space). When you choose one of the presets from the top menu, the Fuzziness slider isn't available, limiting that feature's value.

## Selection modification commands

The next group of commands in the Select menu actually holds five separate commands (Feather and the four Modify commands), each with a one-field dialog box. Sneak a peek at Figure 8-13.

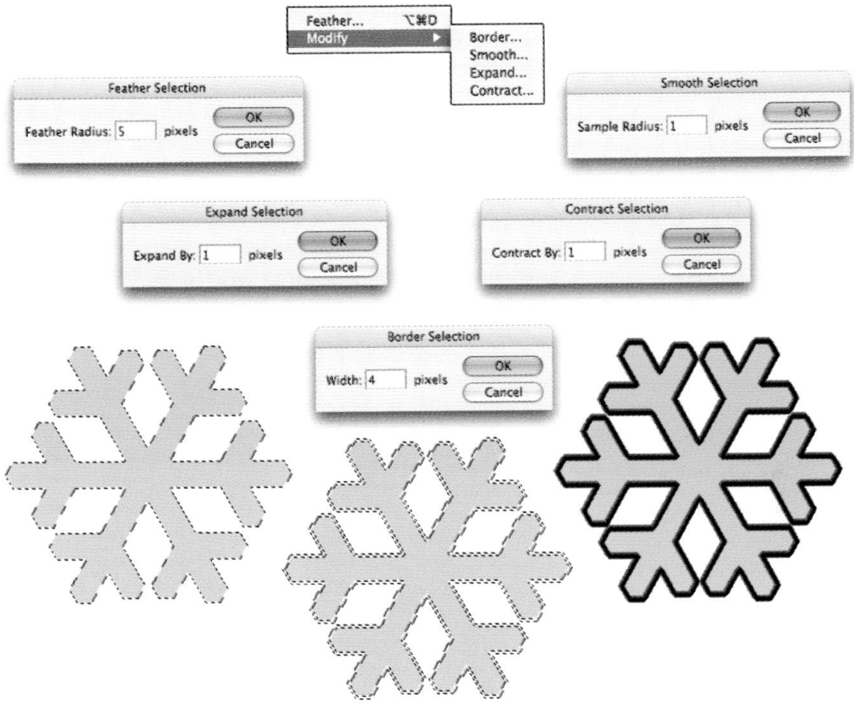


Figure 8-13: Each command presents you with a single option.

- **Feather:** *Feathering,* which I discuss earlier in this chapter, softens the edges of a selection. Normally when cutting and pasting a selection or moving a selection within an image, you want to feather a pixel or two. Feather can be used with any selection except when you use the Select All command.
- **Border:** Tucked away within the Modify submenu, the Border command creates a selection of your chosen width centered on the marching ants that you see as the original selection's edges. In Figure 8-13, you see the original selection (left), the 4-pixel border (center), and that border filled with black (right). Border is available with all selections (including Select All), but when the entire canvas is selected, you see only the border on the inside of the original selection.
- **Smooth:** It could happen that when you click with the Magic Wand to make a selection, you see all kinds of tiny 1- or 2-pixel areas within the selection that are not selected. Perhaps those few pixels were just a bit out of the Tolerance range for the tool. No worry! Use the Smooth command and a 1- or 2-pixel radius to snatch up those stray unselected pixels. Smooth can also eliminate jagged edges along the outside of your selection.

- **Expand:** The Expand command moves the selection border outward a specified number of pixels. Be careful, though, if your original selection includes sharp corners or points because using Expand rounds them off. (In the Paths palette, convert your selection to a path, scale the path, convert the path back to a selection. See Chapter 11 for info on paths.)
- **Contract:** The Contract command shrinks your selection by the amount specified.

If you make your way down the Select menu, you'll come across the Grow and the Similar commands, which are somewhat like the Magic Wand with Contiguous (Grow) and without Contiguous (Similar) selected on the Options bar. (In fact, they use the Magic Wand's Tolerance setting.) Grow adds to your selection any adjacent pixels of the appropriate color, and Similar looks throughout the entire image for similarly colored pixels. Use Grow and Similar when your initial selection consists primarily of a single color. Using these commands with a selection that contains lots of different colors generally results in most of your image being selected.

## Transforming the shape of selections

As you work with selections, you might find times when the selection capability doesn't match your need. For example, the Elliptical Marquee tool can certainly make oval selections, but those ovals are either vertical or horizontal. What if you need an oval selection at an angle, such as what you see in Figure 8-14? That's where the Select⇨Transform command comes into play. Make your initial selection, choose the Transform Selection command, and then manipulate the selection to fit your needs.

Figure 8-14: With Transform Selection, you can manipulate the selection itself.

In Figure 8-14, you see that the selection is not just rotated but is also skewed and distorted slightly. You can manipulate a selection any way you please with Transform Selection. (Okay, well, you *are* limited to two dimensions — you can't make the selection come forward out of the monitor onto your desk.) Consider Figure 8-15 to be your roadmap to transformations.

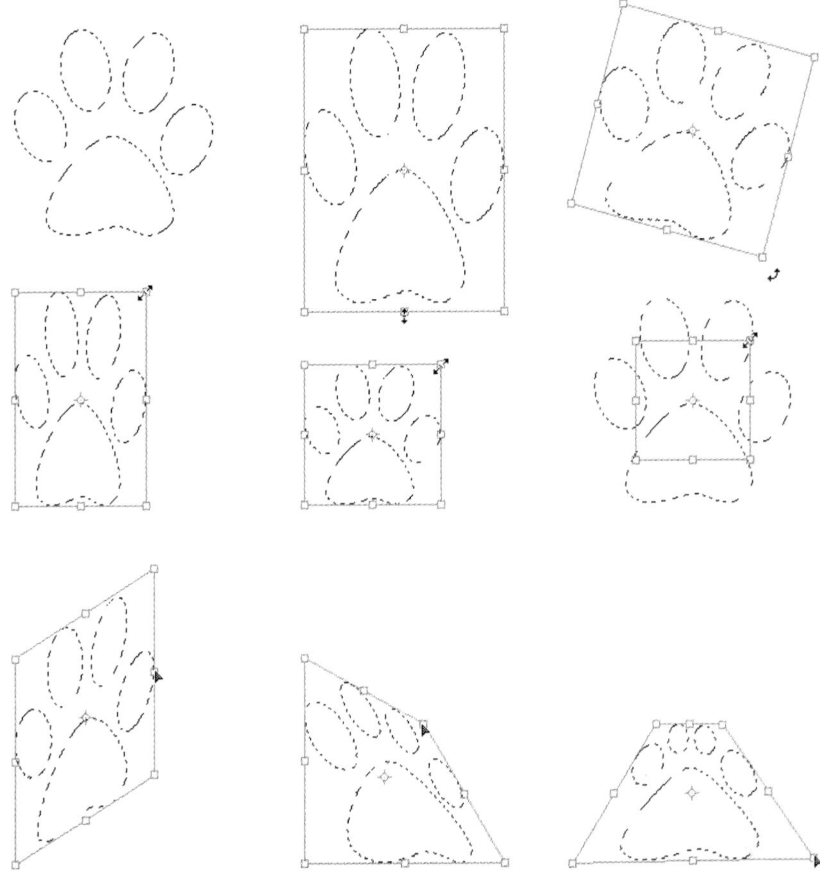

Figure 8-15: The many faces of transformations.

Here's what you see in Figure 8-15:

- **Top left:** This is the original selection.
- **Top center:** Click an anchor point on any side of the bounding box and drag to change the height or width of the selection.
- **Top right:** Position the cursor outside the bounding box and drag to rotate.
- **Middle left:** Drag any corner anchor point to manipulate the selection's width and height at the same time.

- **Middle center:** Hold down the Shift key while dragging a corner anchor point to avoid distorting the selection while changing size.
- **Middle right:** Hold down the Option/Alt key while dragging a corner anchor point, and you end up scaling the image based on that crosshair in the center of the bounding box. (You can drag that crosshair anywhere, even outside the bounding box, to change the point of transformation.) You can use the Shift key with Option/Alt, too.
- **Bottom left:** Hold down the ⌘/Ctrl key and drag any side anchor point to skew.
- **Bottom center:** Hold down the ⌘/Ctrl key and drag a corner anchor point to distort.
- **Bottom right:** If you ⌘/Ctrl-drag two or four corner anchor points, you can add perspective to the selection. I might, for example, fill this transformed selection with color, move the selection, scale it down a bit, fill again, and repeat a number of times to create a series of paw prints marching into the distance.

### The mask-related selection commands

At the bottom of the Select menu, you see a pair of commands that you use to store your selections for future use and to actually reuse them. When you save a selection, you create an alpha channel in the image. The *alpha channel,* like a color channel, is a grayscale representation of the image. White areas in the alpha channel represent areas that are selected when the channel is loaded as a selection. Black areas in the channel show you unselected areas. Gray represents feathering and other partially selected pixels.

I discuss channels in greater depth in the next section of this chapter. While discussing selection commands, the key points to remember are that you can use the Save Selection command to save any selection as an alpha channel, and then later use the Load Selection command to reactivate the selection without having to re-create it from scratch.

## Masks: Not Just for Halloween Anymore

In Photoshop, a *mask* is a channel (in the Channels palette) that stores information about a selection or about layer visibility. (When you talk about selections saved as masks, you can refer to them as *alpha channels.*) Any time you make a complex selection, consider saving it as an alpha channel, just in case. So what exactly counts as *complex?* That depends on how much time you have on your hands. If it takes me more than a minute or two to do *anything* in Photoshop, I want to save it. And what counts as *just in case?* You might need to return to the image at some later date to make changes, you might need to shut down for the day, or maybe you'll even (fingers crossed against!) have a crash. Save your selections, just in case. . . .

## Saving and loading selections

Creating an alpha channel from a selection is as simple as using the Select➪Save Selection command and choosing a name for the new channel. If you have more than one document *of exactly the same pixel dimensions* open in Photoshop, you can select any of the available documents for the new channel. If you already saved a selection as an alpha channel, you can elect to have the two selections interact in a single channel. As you see in Figure 8-16, the Operation choices parallel those that you find on the Options bar when working with selection tools: You can replace the selected channel, add to the existing channel, subtract from the existing channel, or intersect with that existing channel.

Figure 8-16: When you already have an alpha channel, the new selection can modify it.

When you need to work with a saved selection, choose Select➪Load Selection or simply ⌘-click/Ctrl-click the alpha channel's thumbnail in the Channels palette — either activates the selection.

The Load Selection dialog box offers the same key features that you see for Save Selection. (Refer to Figure 8-16.) When loading a selection, you can add to, subtract from, or intersect with an active selection. You can also invert a selection when loading by selecting the Invert check box. Using that check box produces the same result as loading the selection and choosing Select➪Inverse, but it's faster and easier.

## Editing an alpha channel

Alpha channels, like color channels, are grayscale representations. As such, you can edit them like you would any grayscale image. Click the channel in the Channels palette to make it active and visible. You see it in the image window as a grayscale (or black and white) representation of the saved selection. If you want to see the image while you work on the channel, click in the left column (the eyeball column) to the left of the RGB (or CMYK) channel. The alpha channel then appears as a red overlay on top of the image. Figure 8-17 shows you what the screen looks like with just the alpha channel visible (left) and how it appears when the alpha channel is active and the RGB channel is also visible. (And take a look at the difference in the Channels palette. See the eyeball column on the left?)

Figure 8-17: You can see just the alpha channel itself (left) or as a red overlay (right).

Here are some of the things that you might want to do to an active alpha channel:

- **Blur the alpha channel.** Blurring an alpha channel (Filter⇨Blur commands) is much like feathering a selection — it softens the edges. One of the big differences is that you can see a preview of the blur, which is much better than guessing how much feathering you need.
- **Sharpen the alpha channel.** Sharpening a saved selection (Filter⇨Sharpen commands) makes the edges cleaner and more precise.

- **Paint in the alpha channel.** Painting with the Brush tool using black, white, and gray in the channel changes the selection. Paint with white to add areas to the saved selection; paint with black to remove areas from the selection; paint with shades of gray to partially select areas of the image. You can edit an alpha channel with the Brush tool very precisely, adding and eliminating stray pixels, as well as creating precise edges. See Figure 8-18, upper left, for an example of a channel that needs some touch-up that's best done by hand.

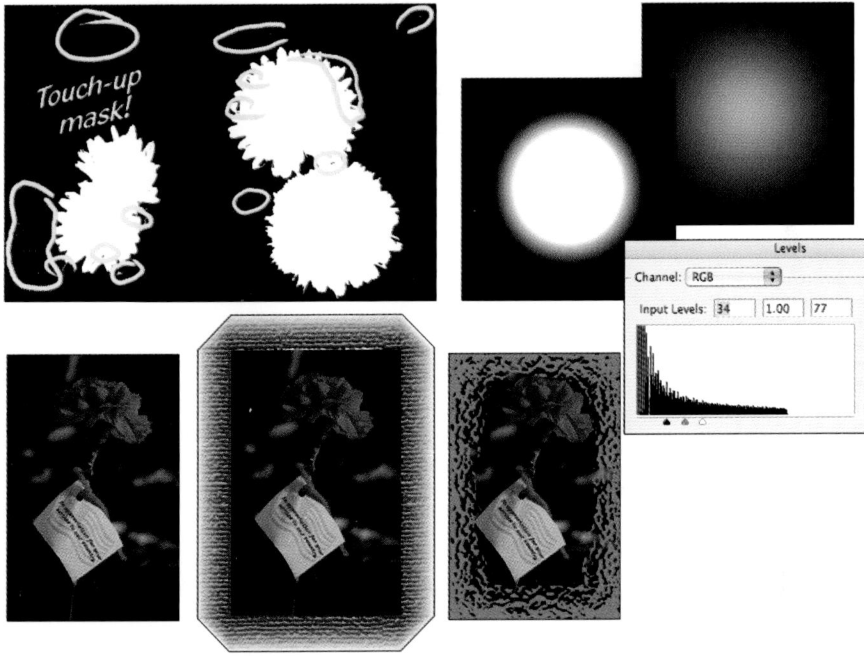


Figure 8-18: You have lots of ways — and reasons — to edit alpha channels.

- **Use levels or curves on the alpha channel.** If the saved selection has feathering or other areas of partial selection (grays in the alpha channel), you can manipulate them with a Levels or Curves adjustment (from the Image➪Adjustments menu). The Levels adjustment is particularly appropriate for controlling the feathering along an edge (as you can see in the upper right in Figure 8-18).
- **Apply one or more filters to an alpha channel.** Use artistic filters on a saved selection to create special effects, such as borders and frames. Take a look at the bottom of Figure 8-18. On the left is the original; to its right, you see a couple of samples. (This is one of those great places where you can let your imagination run free across the open plains of Photoshop!) Chapter 15 covers filters.

## Working in Quick Mask mode

Okay, so you want to make a selection, save it as an alpha channel, make the alpha channel active, click the eyeball column to make the RGB channel visible so you can see what you're doing, paint in and apply filters to the alpha channel, make the RGB channel active, load the alpha channel as a selection, and, well, do something creative with it. Whew! How about an easier way to do the same thing?

With Photoshop's Quick Mask mode, you make a basic selection, press Q on the keyboard to enter Quick Mask mode, edit the selection as if it were a mask, and then press Q again. Heck, you don't even have to start with a selection! In Quick Mask mode, your mask appears onscreen as a red overlay, just like an alpha channel appears when the RGB channel is visible (as you can see in Figure 8-17). Paint, apply filters or adjustments, or make selections — anything you can do to a grayscale image, you can do in Quick Mask mode.

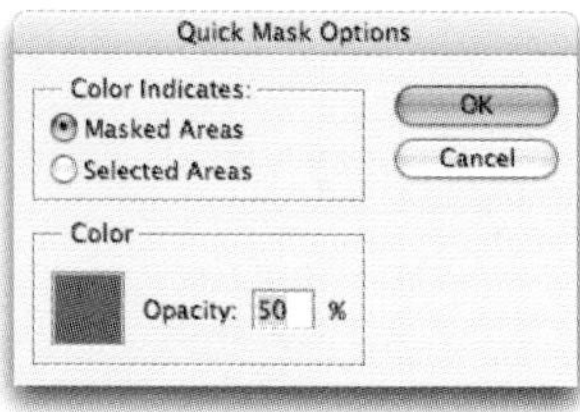


**Figure 8-19:** You can change the opacity and color of the Quick Mask overlay.

If you're more comfortable with the Brush tool than the Lasso tool, you might want to use Quick Mask mode to make all your selections. You may find it faster and easier to "paint" a selection in Quick Mask mode than to drag a selection with a lasso tool or use the selection commands. Enter Quick Mask mode, paint the mask, exit Quick Mask mode, and you have your selection. You can also enter and exit Quick Mask mode by clicking the buttons just below the color swatches in the Toolbox. Double-clicking either of those buttons opens the Quick Mask Options dialog box (as shown in Figure 8-19). You can reverse the behavior of the overlay, making it show selected areas instead of the unselected areas, and you can change the color and opacity of the overlay. (Hop back to Figure 8-12 to see how hard it is to see the edges of the orange blooms with the red overlay. Changing the overlay to, say, blue would solve that problem.)

By default, you paint with black in Quick Mask mode over areas that you don't want selected, paint with white over areas that you do want selected, and paint with shades of gray over areas that you want partially selected.

## Adding masks to layers

When your image has multiple layers (as I discuss in Chapter 10), you can partially hide layers with *layer masks.* Layer masks and alpha channels have much in common: Layer masks are selections saved as channels, you can paint in the layer mask, you can apply filters and adjustment to the layer mask, and so on. Just keep in mind that a layer mask appears in the Channels palette only when you select its layer in the Layers palette. (In the Layers palette, you'll see the layer mask thumbnail to the right of the layer's thumbnail.) To edit a layer mask, click its thumbnail in the Layers palette, and then edit it as you would an alpha channel. (Remember to click the layer thumbnail afterward to reactivate the layer itself.)

The easiest way to add a layer mask is to make a selection of the pixels that you want visible on that layer and then click the Add Layer Mask button at the bottom of the Layers palette (third button from the left). You can also make a selection and choose Layer➪Layer Mask➪Reveal Selection or Layer➪Add Layer Mask➪Hide Selection. That menu also offers Reveal All and Hide All as well as commands to *disable* (hide) or delete the layer mask. You can also *apply* the layer mask, which deletes any hidden pixels on that layer.

A layer named *Background* (in italics) in the Layers palette can't have any transparent areas, so you can't add a layer mask. Not a problem! Simply double-click the layer name in the Layers palette and rename the layer. That converts it to a regular layer, which would be more than happy to accept your layer mask.

In the Layers palette, a layer mask is *linked* to the layer — that is, if you drag the layer, the mask moves right along with it. You can unlink/relink the mask and layer by clicking the icon/space between their thumbnails in the Layers palette.

### Masking layers with vector paths

A layer can also be masked with a vector path. (Paths are explained in Chapter 11.) Vector masks have very precise edges, and you can edit them as a path with the Direct Selection tool. A layer (other than a Background layer) can have both a regular pixel-based layer mask and a vector mask. To show up in your artwork, pixels on that layer must be within both the layer mask and the vector mask. When a layer has both a layer mask and a vector mask, the vector mask thumbnail appears to the right in the Layers palette.

## Adjustment Layers: Controlling Changes

Photoshop's many commands for controlling the tonality and color of your image are presented in Chapters 5 and 6. Many of those commands are also available as adjustment layers. An *adjustment layer* applies the adjustment just as the comparable command would, but using an adjustment layer offers a few major advantages:

- **Adjustable adjustments:** You can reopen an adjustment layer's dialog box at any time to change the settings.
- **Reversible adjustments:** You can delete an adjustment layer, removing the change from your image.
- **Hidden adjustments:** Click the eyeball column to the left of the adjustment layer in the Layers palette to temporarily hide that change.
- **Tweakable adjustments:** You can change the opacity and blending mode of adjustment layers to fine-tune the effect.
- **Limitable adjustments:** You can add layer masks and vector masks to your adjustment layers to restrict their effect to only some of the pixels below. And you can later edit the masks as necessary.

Because of the added flexibility, you'll generally want to use adjustment layers rather than adjustment commands in your images. Of course, you still need the Image⇨Adjustments menu for those several commands that can't be added through an adjustment layer.

### Adding an adjustment layer

You can add an adjustment layer through the menu at the bottom of the Layers palette (click the fourth button from the left, and then move the cursor to the type of adjustment layer that you want to add) or through the Layer⇨New Adjustment Layer submenu. The choices are the same. When you select the particular adjustment that you want to add from the bottom of the Layers palette, that specific adjustment dialog box opens. Selecting the adjustment through the Layers menu presents you with the New Layer dialog box first. You can see all these various bits and pieces in Figure 8-20.

The top three options in the menu that you open from the Layers palette are *fill layers* — layers completely filled with a color, gradient, or pattern. You could add a new empty layer and use the Edit⇨Fill command to do the same thing, or add such a layer through the Layer⇨New Fill Layer menu.

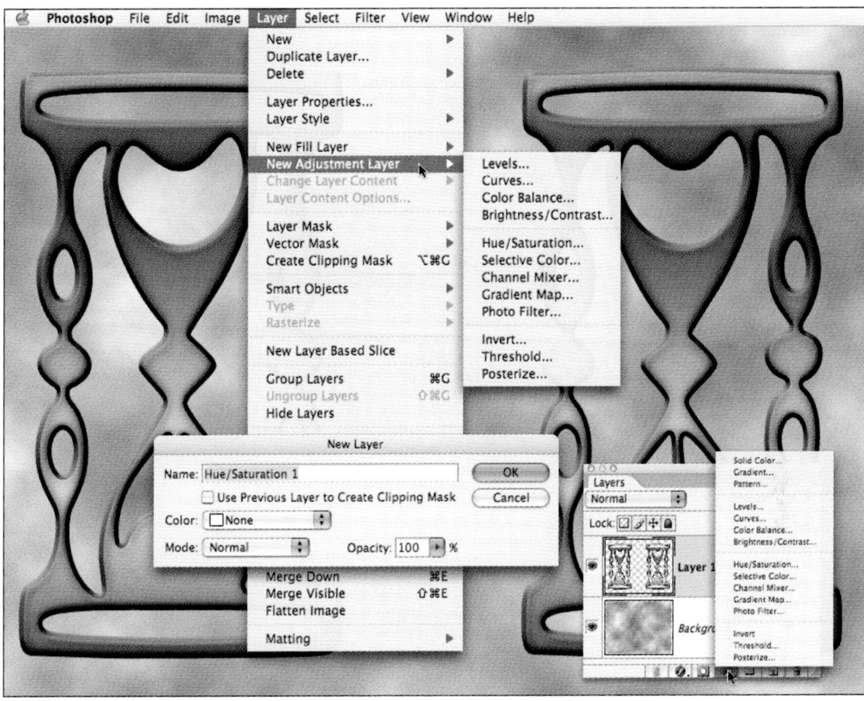


**Figure 8-20:** Adding adjustment layers from above and below.

## *Limiting your adjustments*

Take another look at the New Layer dialog box in Figure 8-20. Note the handy little Use Previous Layer to Create Clipping Mask check box. When you mark that check box to select the option, your new adjustment layer is *clipped* — restricted to the one layer immediately below it in the Layers palette. (That's the layer that is active when you add the adjustment layer.) Press and hold the Option/Alt key before selecting an adjustment from the bottom of the Layers palette to see this dialog box. And, not to worry — after adding an adjustment layer, you can clip it to the layer below by Option-clicking/Alt-clicking the line between the two layers in the Layers palette (which is also how you unclip a pair of layers). Figure 8-21 shows the difference between a clipped adjustment layer (left) and an unclipped adjustment layer (right). When unclipped, the adjustment is applied to all the layers below rather than to the one layer immediately below.

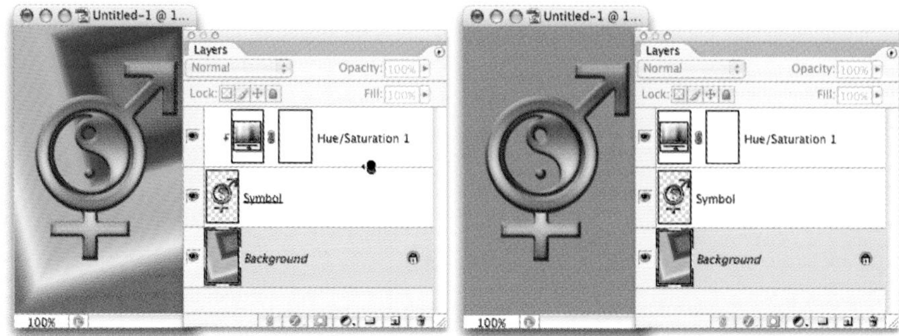


Figure 8-21: Restrict an adjustment to one layer by clipping it to the layer.

On the left side of Figure 8-21, the Hue/Saturation adjustment is applied only to the upper layer — the layer named Symbol. On the right, the adjustment layer isn't clipped, and so it changes both the Symbol layer and the *Background* layer. By the way, the thumbnail in the Layers palette shows the Symbol layer's original copper color prior to the addition of the Hue/ Saturation adjustment layer. Among the beauties of using adjustment layers is the joy you might feel when the client says, "Yup, you were right — let's go back to the original design."

In the Layers palette on the left in Figure 8-21, you can see the wedding rings icon between the adjustment layer and the layer Symbol immediately below. That's the icon that you see when Option-clicking/Alt-clicking to clip (or unclip) layers.

But what if you want an adjustment layer to change, say, three of the layers in your image? Create a layer group from the layers (click the New Group button at the bottom of the Layers palette, and drag the layers into the Group icon in the palette), add the adjustment layer within the group, and change the layer group's blending mode from Pass Through to Normal at the top of the Layers palette. The adjustment layer, within the layer group and at the top of the layer group, is applied to all your layers in the group and only the layers in that group.

Because they're layers, you can use a layer mask to apply the adjustment layer to only part of your layer. You'll find it easier to make a selection of the area where you want the adjustment before selecting the adjustment layer — the mask will be automatically created from the selection.

# Chapter 9

# Common Problems and Their Cures

### In This Chapter

- Perfecting portraits of people
- Hushing the noise in your images
- Editing your digital landscape

Sometimes you take perfect photos of imperfect people, and sometimes you take imperfect photos of, well, imperfect people. (Even the top models benefit from a little Photoshopping.) Although capturing absolute reality is the goal of some artists and most photojournalists, the people in your photos probably prefer to look as good as you (and Photoshop) can make them look.

In this chapter, I present you with some basic techniques for curing many of the most common problems that you encounter as a photographer. I show you how to remove that spooky *red-eye* effect that appears when your camera's flash reflects off the blood vessels in the back of a subject's eyes. I also show you tricks for removing wrinkles, whitening teeth, and tightening waistlines. Digital *noise* (those distracting red, green and blue pixels scattered in your image's shadows) is easy to minimize when you use the tricks here. At the end of the chapter, I cover how to remove some larger problems from images, such as distracting objects and ex-boyfriends. Throughout this chapter, I use real-world examples — the types of photos with which you're most likely to work. (After all, most of us don't get to shoot beautiful models *all* the time.)

# Making People Prettier

You can do lots of things in Photoshop to improve your images, but few are appreciated as much as fixing a person's photographed flaws (the appearance kind, not their bad habits). Whether it's a studio portrait or a snapshot, the people in your images generally can benefit from a little touching up.

Although you can theoretically make almost anyone look truly beautiful and glamorous using Photoshop, remember to balance *improving* with *reality*. Always work on a copy of your image. I also recommend saving separate copies at different stages during the editing process. The client might say that he wants the braces removed from his teeth, but after you present the finished product, he might just (gasp!) change his mind.

## Getting the red out . . . digitally

When a subject looks directly into the camera and the camera-mounted flash fires, the result is often red-eye. This is caused when light (such as a flash) bounces off the blood vessels at the back of an eye and gives the subject a spooky vampire look. Among the many ways to minimize this problem is with the Photoshop CS2 new Red Eye tool. Zoom in and click once with the tool to watch the red disappear, leaving the natural highlights and a perfect eye. As you see in Figure 9-1, the default settings are great even for severe cases of red-eye.

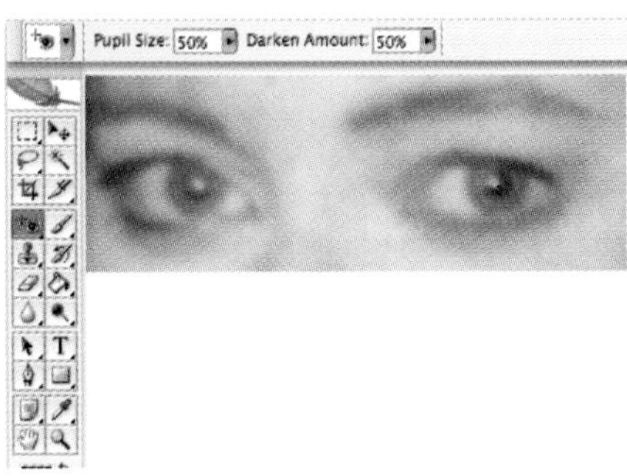


**Figure 9-1:** Click with the Red Eye tool to replace red with natural-looking black.

The Red Eye tool finds red and not green. For *green-eye* (in photos of animals) and too-bright white reflections from eyes, use the Brush tool (as you see in Figure 9-2). Set the foreground color to black; in the Options bar, select the Luminosity blending mode and an Opacity of about 50%. Use a brush diameter just slightly larger than the pupil and a brush hardness of about 75%. Click once and evaluate the result; if necessary, reduce the Opacity to 20% and click again. Here's one more red-eye/green-eye trick: The Sponge tool, set to Desaturate in the Options bar, does a great job with mild cases of red-eye.

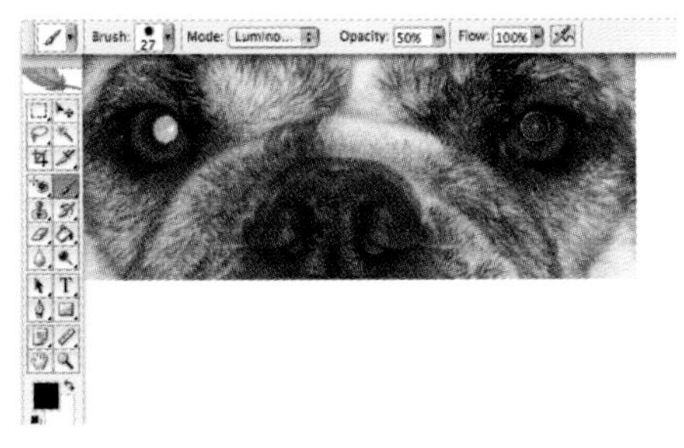


**Figure 9-2:** When the Red Eye tool won't work, use the Brush tool.

## The digital fountain of youth

At the end of Chapter 5, I show an example of using the Dodge tool to fade wrinkles without removing them completely. Photoshop, being that complex and capable animal we enjoy so much, has lots of other ways to minimize or eliminate wrinkles. Among the most powerful tools for this job are the Healing Brush, the Patch tool, and the Clone Stamp.

Both the Healing Brush and the Patch tool work by copying texture from one area to another. You can, for example, copy smooth skin onto a wrinkled area, smoothing the wrinkles while retaining the area's general tonality and color. To work with the Healing Brush, Option-click (Mac)/Alt-click (Windows) the area from which you wish to copy; then click and drag over the area that you're fixing. When you select the Aligned option from the Options bar, you maintain the relationship between the point from which you're healing and the area over which you drag. No matter where you move the cursor, the source point stays the same distance and direction. When repairing areas of a face, however, you might find it easier to clear the Aligned check box. Every time you release the mouse button, you start over from the same source point. By using short strokes, you can heal from the same source area to any area of your image.

To work with the Patch tool, make a selection (using any of Photoshop's selection techniques) and then drag with the Patch tool. Depending on which option you select from the Options bar, you can either select and drag the damaged area to a good area (select Source from the Options bar), or you can select a good area and drag to the damaged area (select Destination). You can use both the Healing Brush and the Patch tool to apply a predefined pattern, too. That can be handy for adding a texture where one doesn't already exist in your image.

Like the Healing Brush, you Option-click/Alt-click with the Clone Stamp to set the area from which you're copying and then paint over an area to make a change. The Healing Brush copies texture, but the Clone Stamp copies pixels, completely replacing the area over which you drag. (That is, of course, subject to the blending mode and opacity that you select from the Options bar.) Like the Healing Brush, the Clone Stamp offers the Aligned option. Figure 9-3 shows a comparison of wrinkle reduction using the Healing Brush and the Clone Stamp set to Normal and 100% opacity. (If you use the Clone Stamp to repair skin, reduce the opacity and make sure to select a source area that has similar skin color and lighting.)

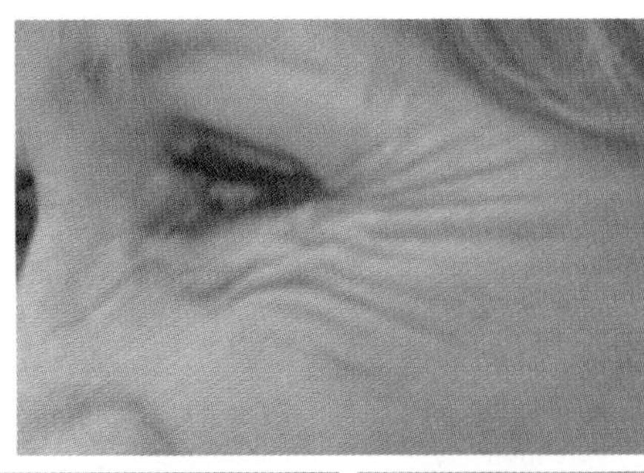

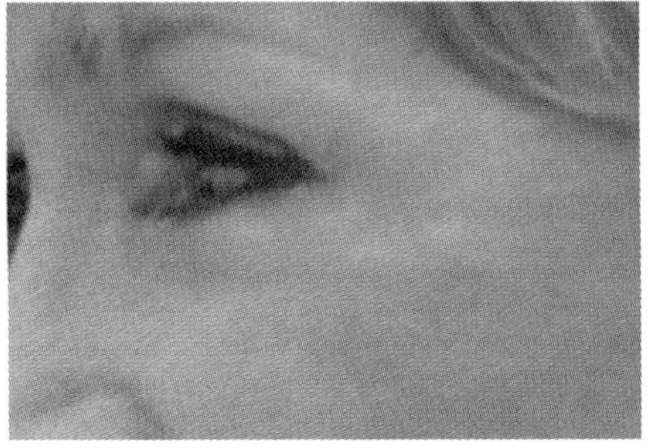

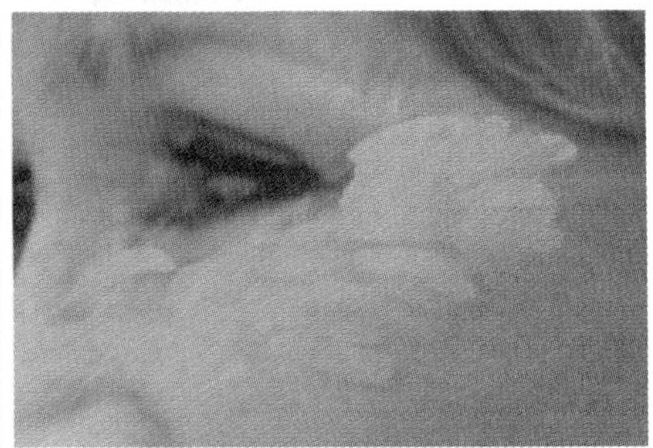



Figure 9-3: Use the Healing Brush (lower left) instead of the Clone Stamp (lower right) to minimize wrinkles.

## Dieting digitally

You can certainly use the Clone Stamp tool to reduce a bit of a bulge at the waistline or below an upper arm, but you might find it easier (and more natural looking) to make a selection and rotate the outer edge inward a bit. Take a look at Figure 9-4. Although this subject hardly has what you'd call a "spare tire," that bit of extra sticking out above her skirt isn't particularly flattering. Make a selection with the Lasso tool that includes some of the background and some skin (or shirt or dress). Press ⌘+T/Ctrl+T to enter Free Transform (or use the Edit⇨Transform⇨Rotate command). Drag

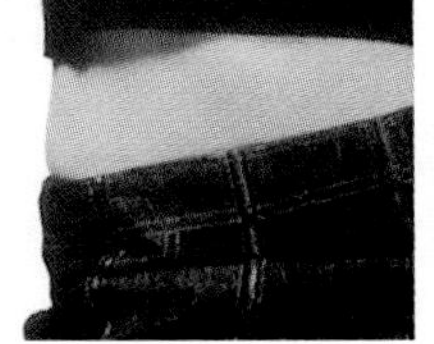

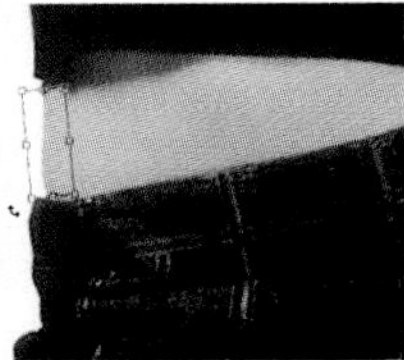

Figure 9-4: Rotate a selection to pinch in a waist.

the *point of rotation* (the little crosshair symbol in the middle of the bounding box) to the top of the bounding box, and then position the cursor slightly outside the bounding box and drag to rotate. When you're satisfied, press Return/Enter to accept the transformation. (With complex backgrounds, you might need to do a little cloning to even things out.)

When working with double chins, your best bet is usually to minimize rather than eliminate. Putting a skinny neck under a fleshy face looks unnatural. You can certainly tuck in the sides of the second chin a bit by using the rotate method, but rely on the Burn tool to darken. By darkening the excess flesh under the chin, you make it appear to be in shadow — and, therefore, under the actual chin (see Figure 9-5). Use the Dodge tool (if necessary) to hide any creases or wrinkles associated with the excess chin. Redefine a natural-looking jaw line and chin — but once again, remember that the result must not only look natural, but it must also be acceptable to the client.

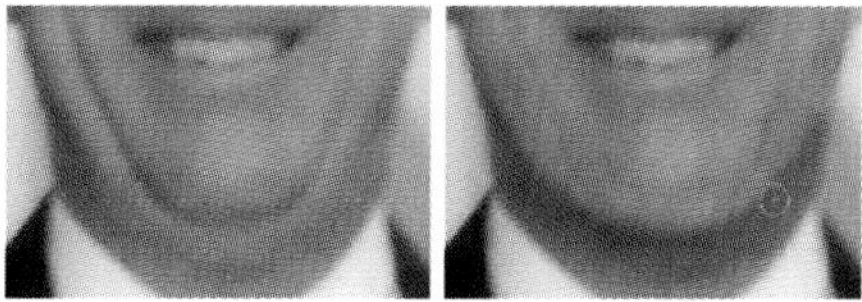

Figure 9-5: Burning and dodging can reduce even a very prominent double chin.

When working with the Burn and Dodge tools, don't forget to reduce the Exposure setting in the Options bar — 15%–20% is plenty strong for this type of work. You'll also want to juggle between Highlights and Midtones (the Range setting in the Options bar) when creating an artificial shadow on a double chin with the Burn tool. Zoom in when doing this sort of work, but also open a second window via Window➪Arrange➪New Window for [*filename*] to keep an eye on the overall impact of your changes.

You can use Photoshop's Filter➪Liquify feature to push, pull, twist, pucker, bloat, and otherwise manipulate pixels into the shape and position you need. There's really nothing more powerful when it comes to reconfiguring a figure. In Figure 9-6, you see how leveling off a beltline in Liquify is sometimes all that's needed to restore that trim-man-she-married look. And a little touch-up with the Dodge and Burn tools can eliminate the wrinkles in the shirt, helping improve the overall appearance of the image by reducing distraction. (Chapter 15 has full info on using Liquify.)

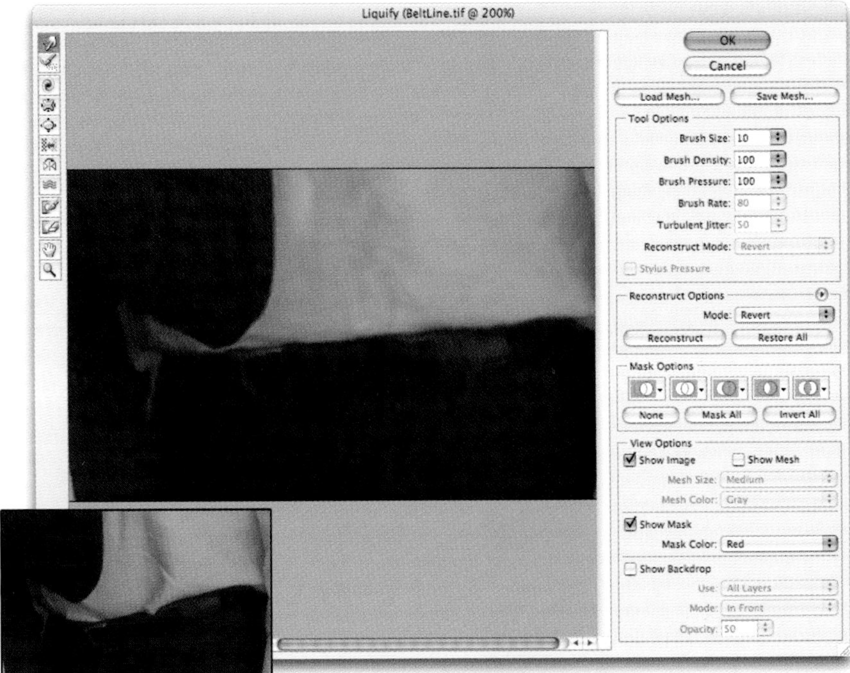


Figure 9-6: Use Liquify to make major adjustments to figures.

## De-glaring glasses

Although hindsight is usually 20/20, many of the rest of us need spectacles. Unfortunately, those eyeglasses can be a photographer's nightmare! The reflections off glass are usually *specular highlights* — that is, areas of pure white with absolutely no detail in them. To properly evaluate flash reflections in eyeglasses, open the Info palette and move the cursor through the area. If you see a noticeable variation among the RGB values in the Info palette, you might be able to restore the area with the Burn tool.

If the Info palette shows RGB values of 255/255/255 or close to it, the area has no detail. Use the Clone Stamp tool to copy over the area from another part of the image (or you can use another image as the source point for the Clone Stamp).

In severe cases, you might need to copy from another photo of the same person. When possible, say in a portrait sitting, try to take one shot of the subject without eyeglasses, just in case.

### Whitening teeth

Teeth generally are not truly white (unless somebody has spent a *lot* of time and money getting ready for a portfolio shoot). Instead, you see shades of ivory and yellow in teeth, but they don't necessarily have to be unattractive or distracting shades of yellow. Use the Dodge tool to lighten teeth. From the Options bar, set the tool to Midtones (*not* Highlights) and an Exposure of perhaps 30% for front teeth. Then switch to Shadows and lighten those molars visible in back. Don't overdo it — remember that folks who don't make their living in Hollywood or on TV generally don't have snow-white teeth. Figure 9-7 shows normal people teeth, "improved" normal people teeth, and Hollywood teeth. Balance your judgment with the client's needs.

**Figure 9-7:** Coffee, cigarettes, and caps; Dodge tool digital correction; show-biz-white teeth.

## Reducing Noise in Your Images

Moving from the darkroom to digital has saved thousands of dollars in film and processing costs (not to mention a reduction in environmental degradation) but has added a new set of challenges to the art and business of photography. Perhaps foremost among the problems presented by digital photography is *noise.* Those pesky red, green, and blue (or light and dark) specks in an image can ruin a digital photo. Noise is generally most prominent in shadow areas and against dark colors in your images.

If your camera lets you select an ISO setting, you can help minimize digital noise in your photos by using a low ISO. Sometimes you do need to shoot the equivalent of faster film, such as at sporting events. However, when you have a choice, use a low ISO to minimize noise. And using a tripod can help, too!

### Decreasing digital noise

Photoshop CS2 adds a new weapon to your arsenal in the war on noise. You find the new Reduce Noise filter under the Filter⇨Noise menu. As you see in Figure 9-8, it does a very good job of neutralizing the random red, green, and blue pixels while preserving detail in the image.

Notice that Reduce Noise also offers a Remove JPEG Artifact option. When saving in the JPEG file format, you compromise between image quality and smaller file size. The smaller the file, the greater the likelihood of compression damage to your image. That damage generally shows itself as visible lines between blocks of pixels measuring eight pixels square.

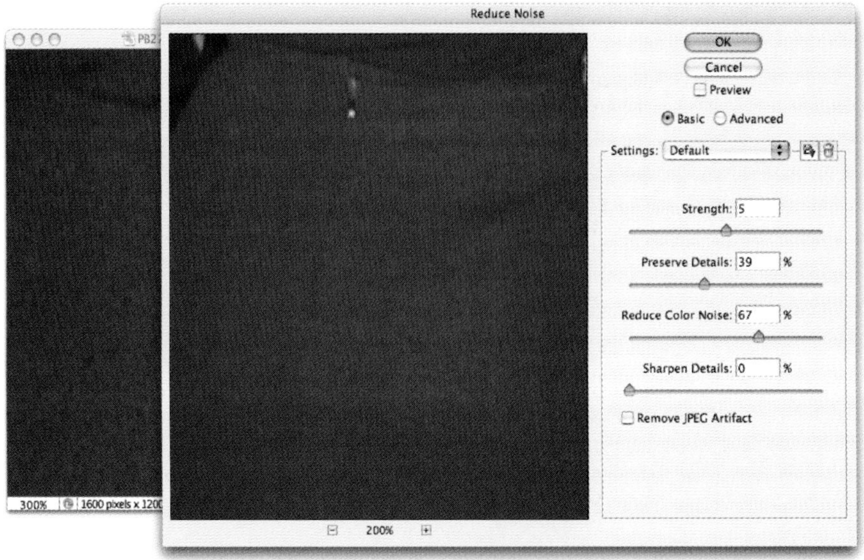


Figure 9-8: The Reduce Noise filter keeps your image sharp while eliminating RGB noise.

You'll also find the Color Replacement tool very handy for noise reduction, especially in areas of rather uniform color. Option-click/Alt-click right in the area to set the foreground color; then simply paint away the digital noise. As you move from area to area in your image, Option-click/Alt-click to pick up a new foreground color.

## Eliminating luminance noise

In addition to the red, green, and blue specks of digital noise, you might face *luminance noise,* which is the bright and dark specks sprinkled throughout your photo. The Photoshop CS2 new Surface Blur filter can handle luminance noise, but you have more control over the result when working with the Blur⇨Smart Blur filter. Unlike Surface Blur, Smart Blur lets you enter fractions for both the Radius and Threshold values (as shown in Figure 9-9). Sometimes the difference between a 1.5-pixel blur and a 2-pixel blur is the salvation of the fine detail in your image.

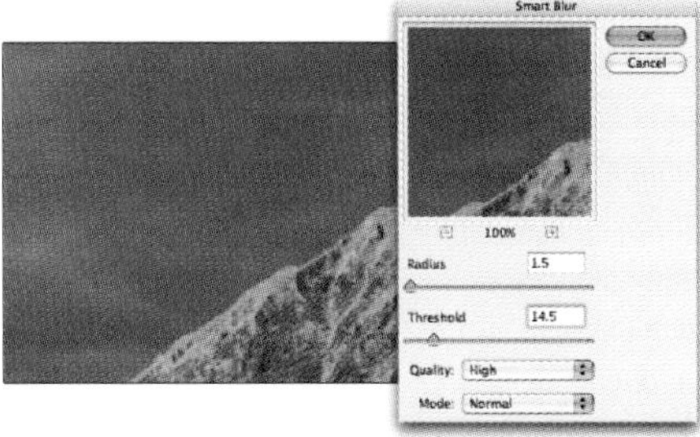


Figure 9-9: The Smart Blur filter is a good choice for luminance noise reduction.

# Fooling Around with Mother Nature

Sometimes a very nice photo has something in it that you want gone . . . a piece of litter, telephone lines in the distance, a building that distracts from the composition, or perhaps a person whose memory you'd like to erase. Other times, everything in the image is fine, but the image looks wrong because of the angle at which the image was taken. Photoshop offers you quite a variety of tools and techniques for cutting out, copying over, cleaning up, and even correcting perspective.

## Removing the unwanted from photos

Perhaps the easiest way to remove something from an image is to *crop* the photo: that is, cut off that part of the picture. This technique is easy enough if that piece of litter or whatever happens to be at the edge of the image and cropping won't ruin your composition. However, when you must cover up rather than crop out, consider both cloning and copy/paste.

One of the keys to using the Clone Stamp tool is keeping an eye on your work. Zoom in close so you can work precisely but use the Window➪Arrange➪New Window for [*filename*] command. Keep that second window zoomed out and off to the side so you can monitor your progress while you work. I also like to keep a copy of the original image open for reference. You can make a copy of the file with the Image➪Duplicate command or by clicking the left button at the bottom of the History palette. In Figure 9-10, you see the original image to the upper-left, the zoomed-in work image below, and a zoomed-out second window for the work image. (The Navigator palette shows you what part of the zoomed-in image is visible.)

Here are some tips for working effectively with the Clone Stamp tool:

- **Work on a separate layer.** Before cloning, click the New Layer button at the bottom of the Layers palette and click the Sample All Layers button on the Options bar. By cloning to the new layer, you protect yourself from irreversible errors (you can always erase part of the upper layer) and can show/hide your work layer to check progress. If the image already has multiple layers and you want to clone from only one, hide the other layers in the Layers palette by clicking the eyeball icons in the left column.
- **If color or pattern is uniform, clone near.** If, for example, you're removing a power line in a beautiful blue sky, clone from right above and below the power line so that you get the best possible color match. For delicate jobs or larger items, you can clone by halves — clone half from one side and the other half from the other side.

- **To avoid a recognizable pattern, clone far.** In Figure 9-10, I cloned over the bicycle handles in the lower-right corner of the image from a variety of places to avoid creating any recognizable replicas of nearby flowers or rocks. You should, however, try to clone from areas that are approximately the same distance from the lens as the area over which you're cloning. If you clone from the far distance into the foreground, you'll have a recognizable size mismatch and perhaps a focal difference as well.
- **To copy areas or objects, use Aligned.** In Figure 9-10, I copied patches of wildflowers, grass, and rock. By using the Aligned option, the relationship between the point from which I sampled and the point to which I cloned remained constant when I released the mouse button. To pick a new source point, I Option-clicked/Alt-clicked.
- **To repeat a pattern or texture, don't use Aligned.** If you have a specific object, texture, or pattern that you want to replicate in more than one area, you can clear the Aligned check box on the Options bar. Every time you release the mouse button, the source point returns to the exact spot where you Option-clicked/Alt-clicked. You can copy the same part of the image into as many different places as you choose.

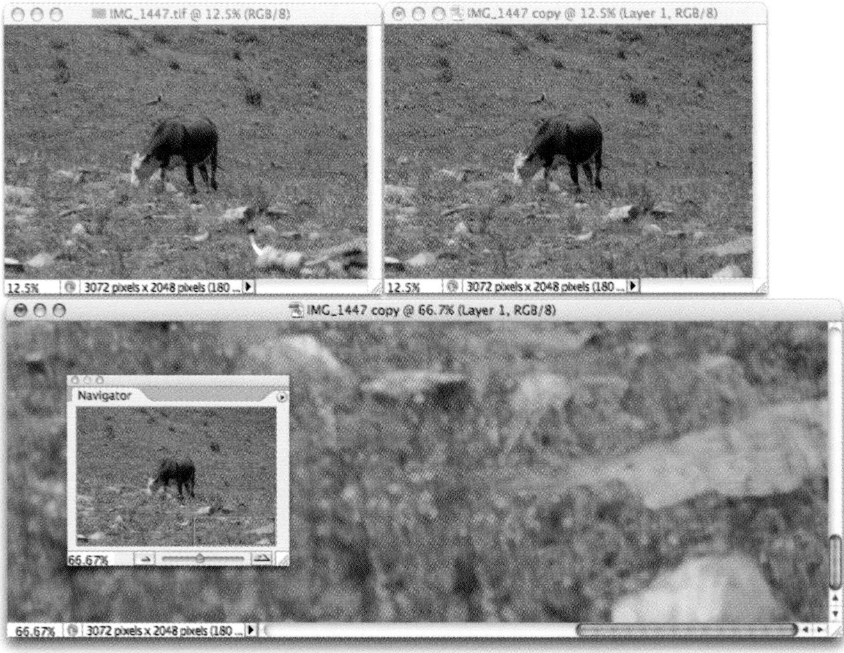


Figure 9-10: Use the Clone Stamp to remove unwanted bits and pieces.

- **You can vary the tool's opacity and blending mode.** Generally speaking, when you want to hide something in the image, use the Normal blending mode and 100% opacity. However, you can also clone with other blending modes and reduce opacity to subdue rather than hide and, of course, for fun special effects.
- **Adjust your brush size on the fly.** Pressing the left and right brackets keys (to the right of P on the standard English keyboard) decreases and increases the brush diameter without having to open the Brushes palette.
- **Check the brush's hardness and spacing settings.** To get the smoothest result for general cloning, reduce the brush's Hardness setting to about 25%, allowing edges to blend. There are times, however, when you'll need a more distinct edge to the brush, but you'll rarely need to clone with a brush set harder than perhaps 90%. In the full-size Brushes palette (found by default in the Palette Well), I generally set the Spacing (in Brush Tip Shape) to 1% for cloning to ensure the edge is as smooth as possible.

The Spot Healing Brush, new in Photoshop CS2, works much like the Healing Brush to repair and replace texture. However, instead of designating a source point by Option-clicking/Alt-clicking, the Spot Healing Brush samples from the immediate surrounding area, which makes it perfect for repairing little irregularities in an area of rather consistent texture. The Spot Healing Brush could, for example, do a fine job with individual flowers and small rocks in Figure 9-10, but it's not up to the task of hiding a bicycle or a steer.

Larger challenges sometime require more drastic measures, such as duplicate layers and layer masks. Take a look at Figure 9-11. At the top left, you see the "before" photo: at the top right, the "after" image. Below are images from three key steps in the process.

Here are the steps I took to remove the boy from the group photo:

1. **Decide what needs to go and how best to cover it.**

   In this case, the young man is no longer welcome in the group photo. The easiest way to remove him (without using scissors and leaving an empty hole) is to move the two young women at his right to the left.

2. **Make a selection of the area that you'll use to cover.**

   I used a large rectangular selection that included everything to the right of the young man.

3. **Copy to a new layer.**

   Use the keyboard shortcut ⌘+J/Ctrl+J to copy the selection to a new layer.

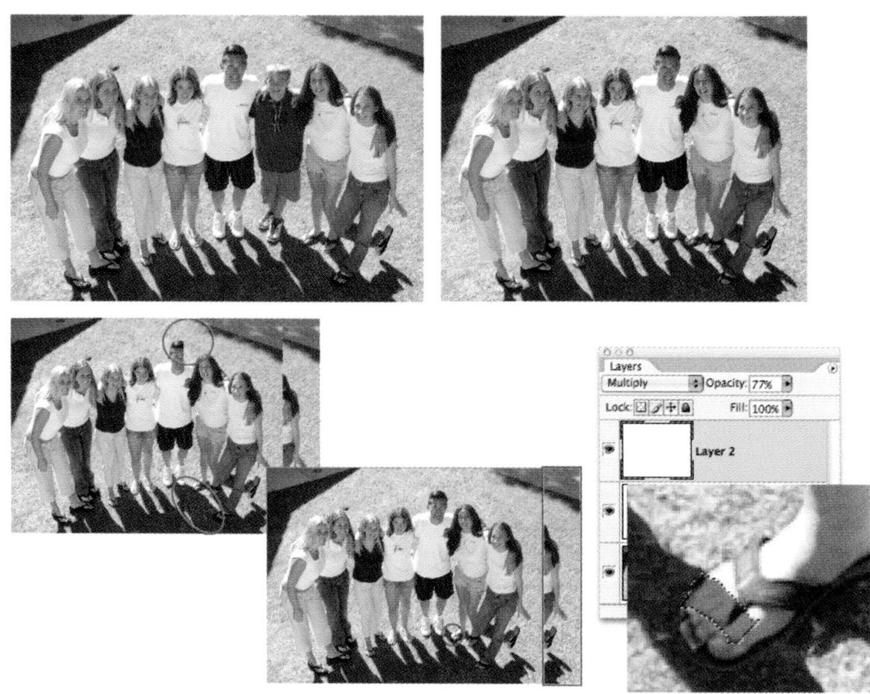




Figure 9-11: A new layer with a layer mask and — POOF — he's gone!

4. **Position the new layer.**

   Use the Move tool to slide the new layer over the top of the area you want to remove.

5. **Add a layer mask.**

   Click the Add Layer Mask button at the bottom of the Layers palette, and then paint with black in the layer mask to hide areas of the upper layer. As you can see in the lower-left in Figure 9-11, the upper layer covers areas of the lower layer that need to show (such as the man's head), creating an unnatural shadow pattern. The layer mask in the lower-center image exposes as much of the lower layer as possible, leaving the upper layer visible only where necessary to show the two young women and their shadows as well as to hide the people on the lower layer.

6. **Look for and adjust anomalies.**

   In the lower-center of Figure 9-11, you see that one woman's foot should be in the man's shadow. I added a new layer, made a selection of the area that should be in shadow, filled with the color of the toes that are already in shadow, and then used the Multiply blending mode and the Opacity slider to match the original shadow. (See the lower-right image in Figure 9-11.)

7. **Crop.**

   Glancing again at the lower-center image in Figure 9-11, you see the area that needs to be cropped, off to the right. Using a rectangular selection of everything I want to save and the Image➪Crop command, and the alteration is complete.

You can use a similar technique to move something in your image to a new location. As shown in Figure 9-12, copy the entire image, reposition it, use a layer mask to hide parts of the upper layer, and clone to remove anything not needed on the exposed areas of the lower layer. In Figure 9-12, the background layer is copied and moved upward (after using the Image➪Canvas Size command to expand the canvas), and a layer mask hides everything except the boy, his racket, and the ball. On the lower layer, the boy is cloned out. (The look of surprise from the boy in the red hat in the background is simply a fortuitous coincidence that seems to add creditability to the adjusted image.)

Figure 9-12: One small step for Photoshop, one giant leap for mankind!

## Eliminating the lean: Fixing perspective

When you take a photograph at an angle, perhaps shooting upward at a building, you get *foreshortening,* with the distant part of the subject shrinking. You can use Photoshop's Edit➪Transform➪Perspective command to fix the problem. Make a selection, choose the Perspective command, and then drag outward on a corner of the edge that's too small (or inward on the corner of an edge that's too large). When the vertical and horizontal lines in the image are straight, press the keyboard shortcut ⌘+T/Ctrl+T to enter Free Transform mode. Make the subject a little taller, too. As you see in Figure 9-13, fixing perspective properly also requires a height adjustment. Press Return/Enter when finished.

Figure 9-13: Squaring an image with Perspective usually also requires a height adjustment.

You can also use Photoshop's Crop tool to fix perspective. Mark the Perspective check box on the Options bar before dragging a bounding box. For best results, position the four corners of the bounding box on visible corners of something in the image that should be rectangular or square; then drag the side handles outward to expand the bounding box to encompass your image. Press Return/Enter when done. Figure 9-14 shows that the Crop tool does a good job of adjusting the height to fit the perspective.

**Figure 9-14:** The Crop tool's Perspective option does a great job of fixing perspective.

## Rotating images precisely

Buried under the Eyedropper in Photoshop's Toolbox is the little-known Measure tool. Generally, you use it in conjunction with the Info palette to find distances and angles in your image. You can also use it to make sure that you apply the exact amount of rotation needed for your image. Select the Measure tool, drag it along any line in your image that should be vertical or horizontal, and then choose Image⇨Rotate Canvas⇨Arbitrary. The angle of the Measure tool will already be waiting for you in the dialog box, so you need only click OK to precisely rotate your image.

One final thought for this chapter: When you come across an image that requires more fixing than you have time for, or one with such severe luminance noise that smoothing removes too much detail, or just a problem photo in general, head for the Filter Gallery. It's amazing how many flaws you can hide with a few artistic effects. Creating an artistic rendering of an image is often preferable to deleting a lousy photo. Blur away the noise and add a canvas texture with the Texturizer filter. Blown out highlights? Try the Colored Pencil filter. When faced with lemons, think of the Filter Gallery as your own personal lemonade stand.

# Part III
# Creating "Art" in Photoshop

"Are you sure that's the best way to apply a stroke to a path?"

## In this part . . .

Photoshop is far more than just a pixel-pushing image editor. More than merely perfecting excellent photography, you can create art in Photoshop. And Photoshop includes a very powerful painting engine. You need to understand the extremely complex Brushes palette and painting tools, all covered here.

Chapter 10 introduces you to *compositing* (combining images into a piece of artwork) and working with layers. You also see the powerful Extract feature, which is a great way to cut and paste from one image to another. Chapter 11 introduces you to Photoshop's *shape layers* and *vector paths,* which are illustration tools used to add specific elements.

In Chapter 12, I show you how to work with the Styles palette and how to create your own custom styles — and make sure you don't lose them by mistake! Chapter 13 looks at the many tools, palettes, and commands you have available in Photoshop to add text and type. Chapter 15 introduces you to those filters you need on a near-daily basis, and then shows you how to work in the Filter Gallery and in Liquify.

# Chapter 10

# Combining Images

### *In This Chapter*

- Putting pieces together with layers
- Integrating with blending modes and opacity
- Cutting it out with Extract
- Keeping it in perspective with Vanishing Point
- Automating with Photomerge and Merge to HDR

A pharaoh's head on a lion body. Lion claws on a dragon body. As we know from the Sphinx and the mythological griffin, compositing elements has been around a lot longer than Photoshop (but Photoshop certainly makes it easier!). Take part of one image, drop it onto another image, and sell the composite to the tabloids for thousands of dollars. (One of the more infamous misuses of Photoshop occurred during the 2004 U.S. Presidential campaign, with the publication of a fake photo of candidate John Kerry with actress and anti-war activist Jane Fonda.) Photoshop offers you incredible power — use it wisely!

In this chapter, I show you some basic techniques for *compositing* (combining two or more images into a single picture), how to use Extract to select part of an image for compositing, the new Vanishing Point feature, and then wrap up the chapter with a look at a couple of automated features for combining images.

## Compositing Images: 1 + 1 = 1

You make a selection in one image, copy, switch to another image, and paste. There you have it — the basic composite! Pretty simple, isn't it? Whether you're putting together two images or creating complex artwork involving dozens of elements, the trick is making the composited image look natural. The key techniques are blending the edges of your selections and matching color among the elements.

## Understanding layers

When you put together images, you work with *layers.* Think of layers in Photoshop as stackable elements, each of which holds part of your image. Where an upper layer is transparent, the lower layers show through. Where the upper layer has pixels that aren't transparent, those pixels either block or interact with pixels on the lower layer. (You control that interaction with blending modes and opacity, explained later in this chapter.)

Take a look at Figure 10-1 (which reveals how Figure 13-2 is created). The Layers palette shows the individual layers and their content. The individual elements come together to create a single image.

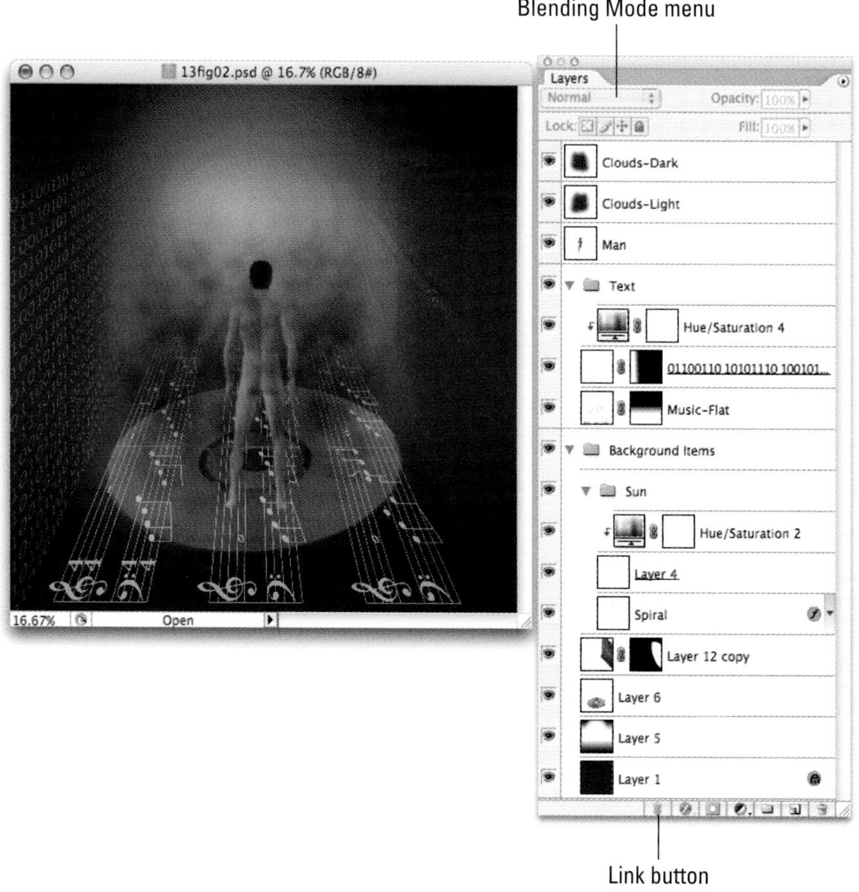


Figure 10-1: Elements on different layers form a single image.

You can manipulate the content of each layer independently — moving, resizing, erasing, painting, or adjusting color and tonality — to suit your needs and artistic vision. You can *link* two or more layers so that they maintain their positions relative to each other as you move them. (Shift-click to select the layers; then click the Link button at the bottom of the Layers palette — a Link symbol appears to the right of linked layers when active in the layers palette.) You might, for example, have a type layer that you want to remain centered in a rectangle. Link the two, and you can move the rectangle and type together without knocking them out of alignment.

The left column in the Layers palette, known as the *eyeball column* (for an obvious reason) allows you to hide a layer, making the content of the layer invisible. The pixels are still there; they're just not visible. Click the eyeball icon to hide the layer, and then click the empty space in the left column to make the layer visible again. You can hide and show adjustment layers, too, which lets you see their impact on the image. (Read about adjustment layers in Chapter 8.)

One key concept about layers is well illustrated in Figure 10-1. The higher a layer is in the *stacking order* (the order of layers in the Palette from the top down), the more "in front" it will be. The layers Clouds-Dark and Clouds-Light are on top of everything in the image. The layer Man is in front of everything except the clouds. Because of the stacking order, the man appears to be walking on top of the musical notes, and the notes appear to be on top of the compact disc.

You can also create *groups,* which are two or more layers packaged together in the Layers palette so that you can work with them together. (In prior versions of Photoshop, you had layer *sets.* Groups are, generally speaking, comparable to layer sets in form and function.) As you can see in the Layers palette in Figure 10-1, you can have *nested groups:* a group within a group. The group named Background Items includes another group, named Sun, as well as several layers that are not part of the Sun subgroup.

## Using the basic blending modes

The pop-up menu at the top-left corner of the Layers palette offers almost two dozen different *blending modes.* A layer's blending mode determines how the pixels on that layer interact with the visible pixels on the layers below.

Because a layer named *Background* can't have any layers below it, you can't change the blending mode of background layers. Convert a background layer to a regular layer by changing the layer's name in the Layers palette. Simply double-click a layer name in the layers palette and type to rename the layer.

In Figure 10-2, the black-white and rainbow gradients each use the blending mode shown by the text outline. (You can see the original gradients in the Normal stripe.) Normal, Multiply, Screen, Overlay, and Luminosity are the blending modes you're most likely to use regularly.

Figure 10-2: Blending modes control the interaction between the gradients and the photo.

When working with layer blending modes, always keep in mind that you can use the layer's Opacity and Fill sliders to help determine the layer's visibility and appearance.

The Layers palette blending mode pop-up menu is divided into six sections, based loosely on how the pixels on the upper layer affect the pixels on the lower layer. Here's a quick look at how you use the key layer blending modes:

- **Normal:** Photoshop picks Normal by default. Pixels on the upper layer completely hide the pixels on the lower layers (subject, of course, to the Opacity and the Fill settings). Use Normal to show the content of the layer without any interaction with lower layers.
- **Multiply:** The Multiply blending mode darkens where your upper layer is dark and ignores white. Use Multiply when you want the upper layer to darken but not obscure the lower layer and also for shadows and dark glow effects.
- **Screen:** The Screen blending mode — the opposite of Multiply — uses lighter pixels to lighten the pixels below. Use it for highlights and light-colored glows.

- **Overlay:** Overlay works like a combination of Multiply and Screen. Use it when you're working with an upper layer that includes both dark and light pixels that you want to interact with pixels on layers below.
- **Soft Light:** Soft Light is a subtle blending mode. Like Overlay, where your upper layer's pixels are dark, the lower layer is darkened; where they're light, the lower layer is lightened. Soft Light is like adding a diffused spotlight to the lower layer — useful for adding a little drama to the lower layer.
- **Hard Light:** The Hard Light blending mode is much like a more vivid version of Soft Light. Use it to add a *lot* more drama to the lower layer. Hard Light works well with colors that aren't overwhelmingly bright (see Figure 10-3).

*©1998 PhotoSpin, PhotoSpin image #0070069*

Figure 10-3: Use the Hard Light blending mode to add impact.

- **Difference:** Where the upper layer (using the Difference blending mode) and the lower layer are exactly the same, you see black. Where the two layers are different, you see brightness or color. For example, use Difference (temporarily) when trying to align two overlapping photos. Set the upper layer to Difference, move the upper layer until the areas of overlap show black, and then switch the upper layer's blending mode back to Normal.
- **Color:** When the upper layer is set to Color, the lower layer's brightness and saturation are retained, and the upper layer's color is used. If you want to create a color picture from a grayscale picture, convert the image to RGB (Image➪Mode➪RGB), add a new layer, change the upper layer's blending mode to Color, and paint on the upper layer (as shown in Figure 10-4).

*©2004 PhotoSpin, PhotoSpin image #1410053*

Figure 10-4: Paint on a layer set to Color to retain the detail of the layer below.

- **Luminosity:** When the upper layer is set to Luminosity, the color and saturation of the lower layer are retained, and the brightness (luminosity) of the upper layer is applied. Because the luminosity (dark and light) generally provides texture, use this blending mode to produce detail in the lower layer.

## Opacity, transparency, and layer masks

Blending modes help determine how pixels on an upper layer interact with pixels on a lower layer, but those upper pixels have to be *visible* before they can do any interacting at all. When looking at any pixel on a layer, you have to consider four factors about transparency:

- Whether the pixel has any color to start with
- The Opacity value
- The Fill value
- Whether there's a layer mask

When you add a layer and paint on it, for example, you color some of the pixels yet leave other pixels transparent. (Every layer in every image is completely filled with pixels, whether visible or not.) If nothing is done to color some pixels, they remain transparent, and the lower layers can be seen through that part of your upper layer. In Figure 10-5, the words *upper layer* are on a separate layer above the layer containing the words *Lower Layer.* Where the upper layer has transparent pixels, the lower layer shows through.

**Figure 10-5:** Where you see the lower layer, the upper layer is transparent.

A layer named *Background* in the Layers palette can have no transparent pixels.

Lowering the Opacity or the Fill slider in the Layers palette (or the Layer Style dialog box) makes all visible pixels on the layer partially transparent: The pixels on layers below can be seen through the upper layer's pixels. (The Opacity slider controls the pixels on the layer and any layer style; the Fill slider works only on the pixels, not the layer style. In Chapter 12, you can read about the Glass Type technique, which demonstrates the difference.)

Chapter 8 discusses layer masks and vector masks. Remember that any pixel inside the mask is visible, and any pixel outside the mask is transparent, regardless of whether it has color. But, as you can guess, any transparent pixels inside the mask remain transparent.

## Creating clipping groups

This being Photoshop, here is yet another way to restrict the visibility of pixels on an upper layer: clipping groups. *Clipping* an upper layer to the layer below, in effect, creates a mask on the upper layer. The opacity of the pixels on the lower layer is applied to the pixels on your upper layer. Where the lower layer is transparent, the upper layer (regardless of original content) becomes transparent. In the Layers palette, Option-click (Mac)/Alt-click (Windows) the line between two layers to clip the upper layer to the lower. (When you hold down the Option/Alt key, the cursor turns to the wedding rings icon.) Figure 10-6 shows how Figure 13-6 is created with a clipping group.

Figure 10-6: Option/Alt-click the line between two layers to clip the upper to the lower.

After Option/Alt-clicking the line between Layer 0 and the layer named GARDENS, the upper layer is visible only within the text on the lower layer. The upper layer is indented to the right in the Layers palette, with a downward-pointing arrow, to let you know that it's clipped to the layer below. Note that the upper layer's thumbnail in the Layers palette shows the entire layer, not just the visible area.

Photoshop CS2 lets you show the layer thumbnails in a new way. In the past, the entire layer, including all areas of transparency, showed in the thumbnail. Although that gives you a good indication of how large or small the particular layer's content is in the image, layers with little content have little to show in the thumbnail. By using the Palette Options (from the Layers palette menu) or Control-clicking/right-clicking the empty area at the bottom of the palette, you can elect to show a thumbnail that includes only non-transparent areas of the layer. Little things fill the thumbnail, but they also appear out of proportion to the other thumbnails. Your choice.

## Making composited elements look natural

One of the keys to compositing two images is a slight fade to the edges of the element you're adding to the original image. That fade, called *feathering,* makes the edges of the image appear to fall off into the distance very slightly rather than having a sharply defined edge that sticks out like a sore thumb. (See Chapter 8 for full information on feathering.) You have a number of ways to feather a selection, including the following:

- Use the Feathering field on the Options bar before you use a selection tool.
- Choose Select➪Feather after you make a selection.
- Apply a slight blur to a saved selection's alpha channel in the Layers palette (or to a layer mask).

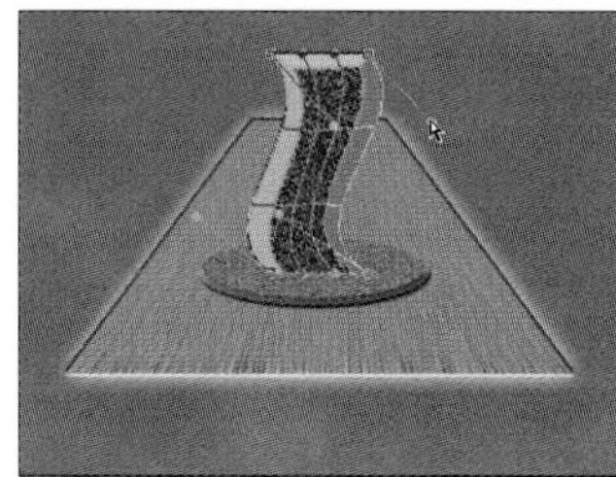

Figure 10-7: Drag anchor points to transform.

Matching color between two layers is also critical for a natural appearance. Take a look at Chapter 6 for full information on Match Color and Photoshop's other color adjustment capabilities.

You also need to be aware of *perspective* and *scale.* When an element in your composited image seems to be too large or too small, or when it seems to be facing the wrong way or standing on air, rely on the Edit➪Transform commands. Although the Scale and Rotate commands are self-explanatory, Figure 10-7 shows visually how you can use the other Transform commands, such as Skew, Perspective, and the new Warp command. Drag the bounding box anchor points to transform the selected pixels.

Figure 10-8: Use the Warp transformation to distort layers or selections.

The new Edit➪Transform➪Warp command adds a simple mesh over the content of the layer or selection. You click and drag the direction lines for the corners of the mesh and at the intersection of mesh lines to distort your artwork. As you see in Figure 10-8, the Warp distortion gives you the level of control previously offered only in Photoshop's Liquify feature (discussed in Chapter 15). You can also use Warp with paths and shape layers.

# Selecting with Extract

To copy something from one image to another, you must first make a selection. You read a lot about making selections and creating masks in Chapter 8, but one more Photoshop feature deserves attention: Filter⇨Extract. Extract is great for making tough selections, such as flyaway hair and various types of fringe. Here's how to use Extract:

1. **Use the Highlighter tool to trace along the edges you want to select.**

   Try to center the green highlighting on the edge, including all the fringe and individual hairs within the green streak.

2. **Click with the Fill tool (it looks like the Paint Bucket tool) inside the highlighted edge, identifying the part of the image you're extracting.**

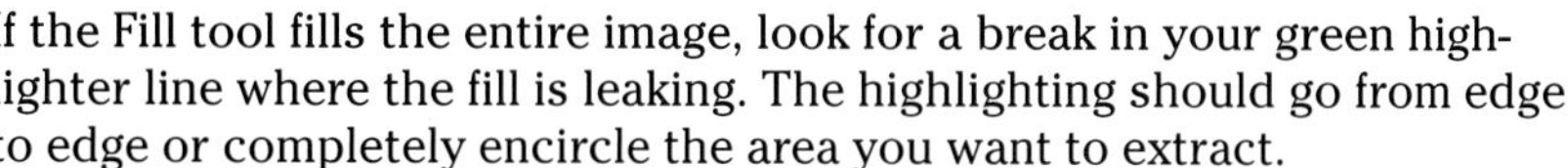

   If the Fill tool fills the entire image, look for a break in your green highlighter line where the fill is leaking. The highlighting should go from edge to edge or completely encircle the area you want to extract.

3. **Click OK.**

As you can see in Figure 10-9, Extract is also suitable for irregular horizons and other such situations in which you might need to extract your foreground to paste in front of a prettier background.

Figure 10-9: Identify what parts of the image to select, and let Extract do the work.

Here are a few tricks to clean up irregularities along the edge of your extracted image:

- **Duplicate the layer.** Drag the extracted layer to the New Layer button at the bottom of the Layers palette a few times to duplicate it. Any semi-transparent pixels along the edge become more opaque. When the edge looks good, use the Layers palette menu command Merge Visible to create a single layer.
- **Paint with the History Brush.** Use the History Brush to paint back areas that should not have become transparent.
- **Erase excess.** If Extract misses the edge in places, you can grab the Eraser tool and eliminate those areas manually.

# Vanishing Point!

When combining images to create a scene, you might find a need to add texture or a pattern along what is supposed to be a three-dimensional object. You might, for example, add a product box to a photo of a kitchen and need to add a logo to the front of the box. Or maybe you will create a room, perhaps in a castle high on a hill, and you'll need to add a realistic stone texture to the walls. Use the new Photoshop CS2 Vanishing Point feature to "map" a pattern to angled surfaces, such as walls, floors, buildings, and boxes. Vanishing Point, using information that you provide, automatically determines the correct angle, scale, and perspective. (Vanishing Point is rather complex, so for simple jobs, you might want to stick with the Paste and Edit➪Transform commands.)

To use Vanishing Point, you follow a specific sequence of steps:

1. **Copy your pattern.**

   Open whatever pattern file (or texture or color or logo or whatever) you're going to add to the walls or sides in your image, make a selection, and then choose Edit➪Copy. You can now close the pattern file.

2. **Make a selection in your working image.**

   Identify where you want the pattern to be applied. If you're working with walls, for example, make a selection that includes the walls but doesn't include windows and doors.

3. **Open Vanishing Point (Filter➪Vanishing Point).**

   The Vanishing Point window opens, displaying your image.

**4. Create planes on your image in the Vanishing Point window.**

   a. *Select the Create Plane tool (the second tool from the top on the left edge of the window).*

   b. *Click on your image where you want to place the three corners of your plane, and then move the cursor to the fourth corner.*

   You see the plane extending along the last two sides.

   c. *When the cursor is in position, click to create the plane.*

   If the plane is yellow or red rather than blue, it's not aligned properly. Drag the corners of the plane to realign them, using the Edit Plane tool (the top tool on the left). Drag the side anchor points outward to expand the plane's mesh to cover the whole wall or side.

   d. *Create perpendicular planes by holding down the ⌘/Ctrl key and dragging the side anchor point at the point where the two planes should meet.*

   If the second plane's angle is off a little, drag one of the corner anchor points to adjust it. In Figure 10-10, you see two perpendicular planes.

**Figure 10-10:** Use the Create Planes tool to identify surfaces.

5. **Paste your pattern.**

   a. *Press ⌘+V/Ctrl+V to paste your pattern into Vanishing Point.*

      Your pattern is pasted into the upper-left corner of the Vanishing Point window.

   b. *Select the Marquee tool (third from the top) and drag the pattern into your plane.*

      The pattern automatically adopts the orientation of the plane. If necessary, press T on your keyboard, and then rotate and scale the pattern.

6. **Replicate the pattern.**

   Unless your pattern is an exact fit, you need to replicate it to fill the plane. With the Marquee tool selected, hold down the Option/Alt key. Then click and drag in your pattern to replicate it. Repeat as necessary to fill the plane. As you see in Figure 10-11, you can replicate a relatively small pattern to fill a large area.

Figure 10-11: Option/Alt-drag with the Marquee tool to copy your pasted selection.

If the lighting in your original image varies, set the Healing pop-up menu (at the top of the window, only with the Marquee tool active) to Luminance. That helps maintain the original lighting on the new pattern or texture.

7. **Click OK to exit Vanishing Point and apply the pattern or texture to your image.**

   After exiting Vanishing Point, you might need to do some touch-up work on your image with the Clone Stamp tool (depending on how precise you were when dragging). You might also, depending on the original image, need to add a layer and paint some shadows or highlights to reproduce the original lighting in the scene.

Here are some tips for working with Vanishing Point:

- **Create accurate planes; then drag.** Click in four corners of any identifiable area of your plane — perhaps a window — and drag the side anchor points outward (or inward) to identify the whole plane.
- **Use the X key to zoom.** Pressing and holding the X key on your keyboard makes the preview area zoom to show the area where you're working. Release the X key to zoom back out.
- **Press T to transform.** After pasting your pattern, you can press T on your keyboard and then scale and rotate your pasted pattern.
- **Use the Shift key to drag in alignment.** Hold down the Shift key while Option/Alt-dragging to replicate your pattern. That keeps the new part aligned to the old.
- **Duplicate elements in the image.** Make a selection with the Marquee tool and ⌘+Option-drag/Ctrl+Alt-drag to the area where you want to place the copy.
- **Paste over objects in Vanishing Point.** Create your plane. Use the Marquee tool to select an area that you want to replace, and then hold down the ⌘/Ctrl key and drag to an area that you want to paste into the marquee selection.
- **Clone in Vanishing Point.** Define your plane, select the Stamp tool, and Option/Alt-click at the source point. Release the Option/Alt key and move the cursor to the point where you want to start cloning. When the preview is properly aligned, click and drag to clone.
- **Paint in perspective.** With a plane identified, the Brush tool in Vanishing Point shrinks or grows in accordance with your perspective plane.
- **Work on an empty layer.** You can add an empty layer in the Layers palette before entering Vanishing Point. Your result is added to the new layer, which lets you work with blending modes and opacity to merge your pattern into the original.

# Putting Together Images Automatically

You have a couple of features in Photoshop CS2 that automatically combine two or more images into a single image. You can combine overlapping images into a panorama, or you can combine multiple exposures of the same shot into a single well-exposed image. You'll find both Photomerge (for panoramas) and Merge to HDR (for high dynamic range combined exposure images) in Photoshop's File➪Automate menu.

## Creating panoramas with Photomerge

Sometimes a snapshot doesn't adequately portray a scene. (It's hard to capture the majesty of the Grand Canyon in a single frame.) For those situations, take a series of images and combine them into one large panorama with Photomerge.

The first step in using Photomerge successfully is taking appropriate photos. Here are some tips:

- **Use a properly leveled tripod.** Use a tripod, making sure that the tripod is steady and level so the individual photos align properly.
- **Turn off auto-exposure.** If you use your camera's auto-exposure feature, each image is actually exposed differently because of the lighting in that frame. Instead, expose for the center (or most important) photo and use the same settings for all shots.
- **Don't use auto-focus with zoom lenses.** Auto-focus can change the zoom factor of the lens. Instead, set the lens to manual focus after using auto-focus on your most important shot.
- **Overlap by 25 percent.** One-quarter of each shot (on each side) should overlap so that Photomerge has enough similarity between neighboring images.

When working with images that are properly exposed and have suitable overlap, Photomerge is fully automated. You open Photomerge, select the images you want to use, click OK, sit back, and watch the magic as the elements are put into order, aligned, and blended. Okay, well, sometimes Photomerge asks for a little help, and you need to drag pieces into position. (Put the images into the proper order in the bin at the top before dragging them into the main window for alignment.) Photomerge then attempts to generate a single unified whole. In Figure 10-12, three photos are merged.

Use the Save Composition As button in the top right of the Photomerge window to save the panorama as a work in progress, to which you can return at a later date to finish or to make changes. And pay particular attention to the Keep as Layers check box in the lower right. Enabling this is always a good idea so you can later realign as necessary and use adjustments (or adjustment layers) to fine-tune the blending.

When creating a panorama of a room or some other scene that has a definite this-point-is-farthest-from-the-camera vanishing point, use the Perspective option. By default, the *vanishing point* (that farthest point) is assumed to be in the center. If it's not, select the Set Vanishing Point tool (third from the top on the left) and click the correct image. When you use the Perspective option, your panorama might appear to be pinched in the middle. Enabling the Cylindrical Mapping option evens out the top and bottom and the perceived distance (see Figure 10-13).

**Figure 10-12:** Photomerge aligns and blends your elements automatically.

Figure 10-13: Photomerge using Perspective, with cylindrical mapping (top) and without.

## Combining exposures for HDR images

A rather specialized feature, the new Photoshop CS2 Merge to HDR command creates a composite image of two or more exposures of the same shot, taking the best-exposed parts of each. You might, for example, take two shots of a room, one exposed for the room itself and another exposed to capture the detail of the scene outside the window(s). Merge to HDR takes the best of both images and creates a single image. Here's how:

1. **Choose the File➪Automate➪Merge to HDR command.**

   The Merge to HDR dialog box makes an appearance.

2. **Select the images to use.**

   Make sure the Attempt to Automatically Align Source Images check box is marked (as shown in Figure 10-14).

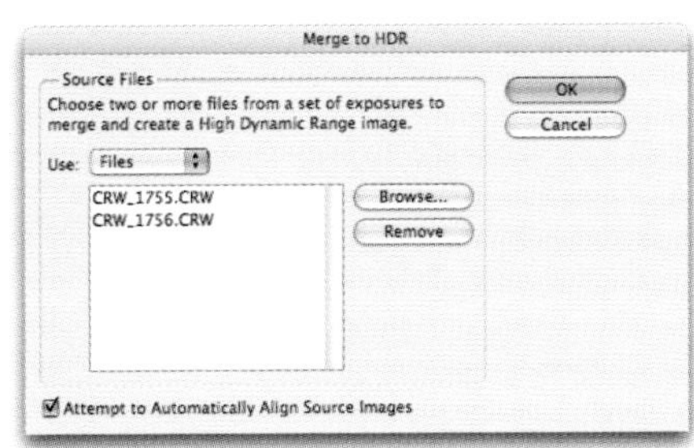


Figure 10-14: Select the images to merge, and let Merge to HDR try to align them.

3. **Click OK to open Merge to HDR.**

   In the upper-right corner of the Merge to HDR window is the Bit Depth option of creating a more common 16-bit image or even a highly usable 8-bit image rather than the 32-bits/channel HDR default. You can also adjust the image by dragging the Set White Point Preview slider. Generally speaking, the slider belongs under the right edge of the histogram, just where the histogram begins to rise.

   In Figure 10-15, you see the two source images to the upper-left. The merged image on the right uses the toned-down highlights of the upper source figure and the brightened shadows of the lower source figure to produce as much detail as possible throughout the image.

   The image is generated.

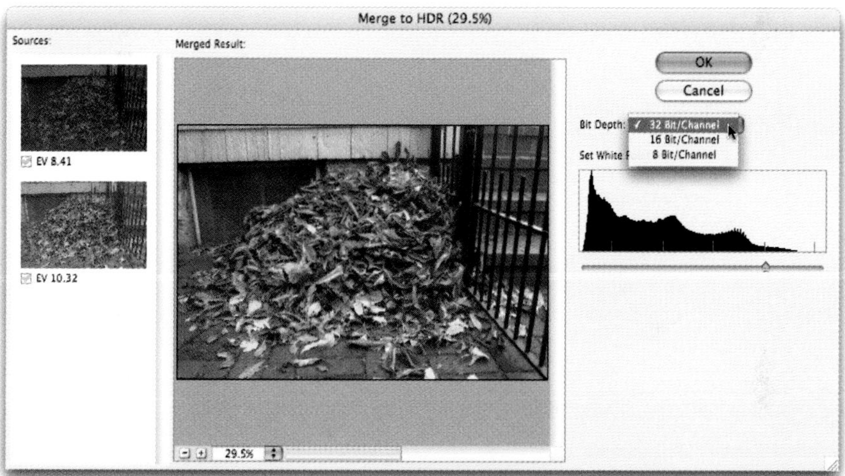


Figure 10-15: Merge to HDR creates a single image from multiple exposures.

If you choose to use the 32-bits/channel option, you can save your image in one of three file formats:

- PSD (Photoshop)
- PSB (Photoshop's Large Document format, if activated in Photoshop's Preferences)
- TIFF

Keep in mind that not a lot of programs use 32-bit/channel images, and even your editing capabilities within Photoshop are limited. But ain't it great to know the capability is there, just in case someday you need it? Or even if you never need it?

## Chapter 11

# Precision Edges with Vector Paths

### In This Chapter

- Understanding vector artwork
- Creating objects with shape layers
- Making a new path
- Changing the shape of an existing path
- Editing the shapes of type characters

Most of the images with which you work in Photoshop — digital photos and scanned artwork, layers on which you paint, and filled selections — are created with pixels. There's also another type of artwork — *vector art* — which you create by defining a *path* (an outline) and adding color within that path. That path has a very precise edge, enabling vectors (when printed appropriately) to give you very crisp, clean lines in your artwork.

Typically, vector art consists of specific elements (objects) that are uniform in color (although vector art can also include gradients). You might have, for example, a red triangle, a blue square, and a green circle as your logo (boring!). These three solid-color objects are best defined as *vector artwork.* Vectors, however, are not appropriate for photographic images and other such imagery that includes subtle transitions among colors.

In Photoshop, you have tools that create predefined shapes; you have tools that create freeform shapes; you have tools to edit the paths that define those shapes. You've also got a palette and a bunch of menu commands. You can even bring in shapes from Adobe Illustrator and create your own shapes, too. After reading this chapter, you'll have a solid understanding of all these bits and pieces. I even tell you where to find dozens, or even hundreds, of custom shapes already on your computer — absolutely free!

## Pixels, Paths, and You

The vast majority of the artwork with which you work (or play) in Photoshop is raster artwork. *Raster imagery* consists of uniformly sized squares of color *(pixels),* placed in rows and columns (the *raster*). Digital photos, scanned images, and just about anything that you put on a layer in Photoshop consists of pixels. While you edit the image, you're changing the color of the individual pixels, sometimes in subtle ways and sometimes in dramatic ways.

Vector artwork is a horse of another color. Rather than pixels, *vector art* consists of a mathematically defined path to which you add color. In a dedicated vector art program, such as Adobe Illustrator, the path produces the shape of the object, and you add color along the path *(stroke)* or within the path *(fill)* or both to make the shape become an object. Photoshop simulates vector artwork using vector paths on *shape layers* to hide parts of a layer, so you can fill the "shape" but not add a stroke to the path. (A shape layer is filled with a specific color, gradient, or pattern; and a vector mask determines what part of the layer is visible.) Remember that you can use layer styles in conjunction with shape layers to simulate strokes and other effects.

*©PhotoSpin, PhotoSpin image #PI009008*

**Figure 11-1:** Each element in vector art has a single specific color.

Figure 11-1 shows a fine example of vector artwork. Observe that each element in the image consists of a single color. Each section of the image is easily identifiable as an individual object, consisting of a specific color. (Remember, though, that vector objects can be filled with gradients rather than color.)

Each element in the artwork is defined by its path, which consists of a number of path segments. In Figure 11-2, you see the path that defines the woman's hair. (You read about the anatomy of a path later in this chapter, in the section "Understanding paths.")

**Figure 11-2:** Paths define the outline of an object — the woman's hair in this case.

When artwork is defined by pixels, the little square corners of the individual pixels can be noticeable along curves and diagonal lines. With vector artwork, the path is sharp, and the edges are well defined. However, to truly get the best appearance from vector art or vector type, the artwork must be printed to a PostScript-capable device, such as a laser printer. *PostScript* is a page-description language that takes advantage of the mathematical descriptions of vector art. When you print to an inkjet printer, the vector art is converted to pixels. If you print to such a non-PostScript device, use a high image resolution for best output — 300 pixels per inch (ppi) is usually good.

A vector path can be *scaled* (changed in size) almost infinitely without losing its appearance. A vector logo can be used for both a business card and a billboard without loss of quality because the path is mathematically scaled before the stroke or fill is added. Raster art, on the other hand, can be severely degraded by scaling. For a simple demonstration of the difference between scaling raster art and scaling vector art, see Figure 11-3.

Raster, from small to large

Raster, from small to large

Raster, from large to small

Raster, from large to small

Vector, from small to large

Vector, from small to large

Vector, from large to small

Vector, from large to small

**Figure 11-3:** Using text as an example shows the advantage of vector artwork when scaling.

Type in Photoshop is vector-based: That is, it's created with paths. Objects in Photoshop, such as circles and squares that you create with vector paths, can also be scaled as vector artwork. The paths are recalculated to their new size and retain their crisp, sharp edges.

# Easy Vectors: Using Shape Layers

If you made it through the preceding section, you're officially an expert on the theory of vector graphics. It's time to see how you can actually create these little devils in your artwork. Keep in mind that a vector shape in Photoshop actually consists of a shape layer with a path that defines what part of the layer is visible and what part is hidden. The content of the layer — be it solid color, pattern, or gradient — is visible within the path and hidden outside the path. The easiest way to create a shape layer in Photoshop is with the aptly named *shape tools,* which are tools that automatically create a color-filled layer with a vector path that shows/hides the layer according to the shape selected. Could you have it any easier? Just drag a tool and create a vector-based object!

## Your basic shape tools

Rectangles, rectangles with rounded corners *(rounded rectangles),* circles and ovals, multi-sided polygons, straight lines and arrows, and a whole boatload of special custom shapes are all at your command with a simple click-drag. Select the appropriate tool in the Toolbox, select the appropriate foreground color, and click-drag to create your object. (The various shape tools are nested in the Toolbox, as shown in Figure 11-4.) Sounds simple, right? It is — no tricks. Here are some additional features to make things even easier for you:

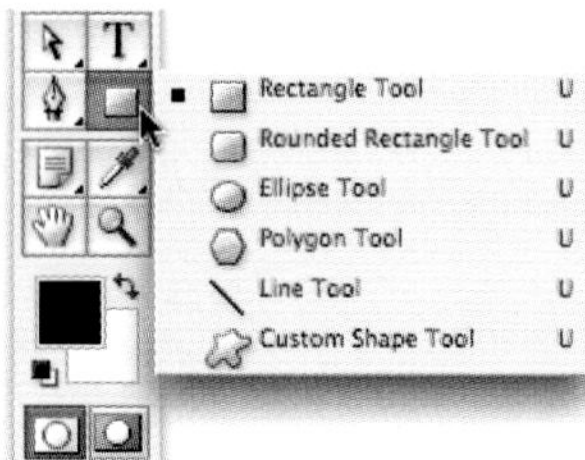


**Figure 11-4:** The shape tools are collected in one spot in Photoshop's Toolbox.

- **Use the Shift key.** Pressing the Shift key (both Mac and Windows) *constrains proportions* (maintains the width-to-height ratio) while you drag. With the Shift key, the Rectangle tool creates squares; the Ellipse tool creates circles; the Polygon tool creates proportional polygons; the Line tool creates horizontal or vertical lines (or lines at 45° angles). When using custom shapes, pressing the Shift key ensures that the shape retains the width-to-height ratio with which it was originally defined.
- **Use the Option (Mac) or Alt (Windows) key.** The Option/Alt key creates the object centered on the point at which you click. Without the Option/Alt key, the object is created in whichever direction you drag.
- **Use the Shift and Option/Alt key.** Pressing the Shift and Option/Alt together helps you create a proportionally constrained object, centered on the point at which you click.

- **Use the spacebar.** While you're dragging a shape, keep the mouse button down and press the spacebar on the keyboard. You can then drag to reposition the object while you create it. Still keeping the mouse button down, release the spacebar and finish dragging the object.
- **Check the Options bar.** When you switch from shape tool to shape tool, the Options bar changes to fit your needs. For example, with the Rounded Rectangle tool active, you choose the radius of the rounded corners. The Polygon tool offers a simple field in which you choose the number of sides for the shape. When you're using the Line tool, choose the thickness *(weight)* of the line in the Options bar. And click the triangle to the right of the shape tool icons in the Options bar to add arrowheads to the lines.
- **Change the layer content.** After you create a shape layer, you can change the color of the layer to another color, to a gradient, or even to a pattern. Use the menu command Layer⇨Change Layer Content.
- **Edit the vector path.** As you can see later in this chapter ("Adding, deleting, and moving anchor points"), you can use the Direct Selection tool to change the course of the path, altering the appearance of the shape layer and, therefore, the shape of the object on the shape layer.

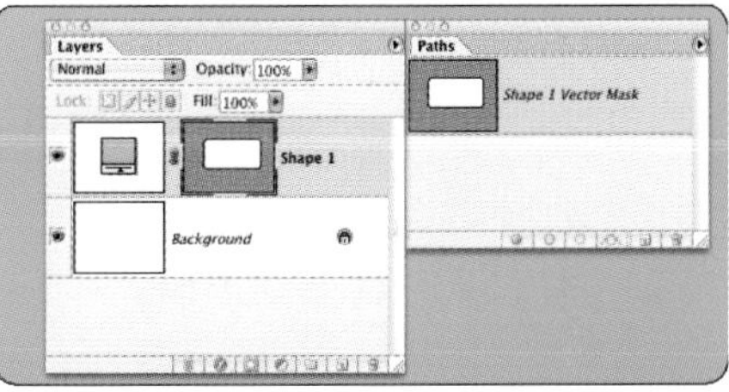


Figure 11-5: Dragging a shape tool creates a color-filler layer with a path to define a shape.

You can easily spot a shape layer in the Layers palette — especially when the default layer name starts with the word `Shape`. (You can, of course, change the layer name by double-clicking it in the Layers palette.) You can see in the Layers palette shown in Figure 11-5 that the shape layer consists of a color-filled layer (the thumbnail on the left) and a vector layer mask (the thumbnail on the right). That vector mask (a rounded rectangle path, in this case) is also visible in the Paths palette when the shape layer is selected in the Layers palette. If you click the *Background* layer in the Layers palette, the *Shape 1 Vector Mask* in the Paths palette is hidden.

## The Custom Shape tool

Although the basic shape tools are great for circles and squares and lines and arrows, you'll probably get the most use out of the Custom Shape tool. With this tool selected, you click the triangle to the right of the sample shape in the Options bar to open the Custom Shape Picker, as shown in Figure 11-6. The Custom Shape Picker offers a number of ready-to-use shapes. When you click the triangle in the upper-right corner, you can choose from a variety of other sets of shapes listed at the bottom of the Custom Shape Picker menu.

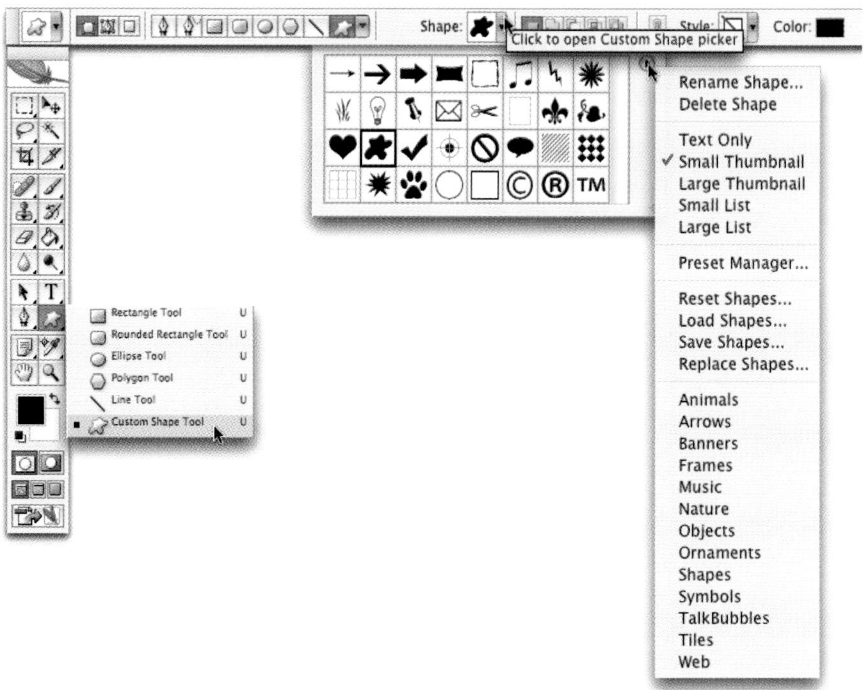


Figure 11-6: Load additional sets of custom shapes from the list at the bottom of the menu.

When you select a set of custom shapes from the menu (or use the Load Shapes command to add a set of shapes not in the menu), you are asked whether you want to add the new shapes to the current content of the palette (Append), replace the current shapes (OK), or not add the shapes after all (Cancel). When you load all the custom shape sets that come with Photoshop CS2, you've got a pretty impressive group from which to choose!

## Defining your own custom shapes

Photoshop's 300+ predefined custom shapes cover a wide range, but they might not fill all your needs. You can purchase commercial collections of custom shapes from a couple of sources. You can create custom paths and define shapes from them, too. But you've already got bunches of custom shapes on your computer already, just waiting for you to use them. Select

Photoshop's Type tool and take a look in your Font menu. Check out the fonts already there with names like *Wingdings, Webdings, Symbol,* and *Dingbats.* These are all examples of *symbol fonts,* which are fonts that have shapes and symbols rather than letters and numbers. Many more typical fonts also have special characters available when you use the Option/Alt key.

Here's how you can define a custom shape from a symbol:

1. **Choose File➪New to open a new document.**

   The document can be virtually any size and can be either grayscale or color.

2. **Select the Type tool and pick a font.**

   With the Type tool active, choose a symbol font from either the Options bar or the Character palette. The font size doesn't matter much because you're creating a vector-based shape that can be easily scaled.

3. **Type a single symbol and then end the editing session.**

   Click the check mark button to the right in the Options bar, switch tools in the Toolbox, or press ⌘+Return (Mac) or Ctrl+Enter (Windows) to end the editing session.

4. **Convert the type character to a shape layer.**

   With the type layer active in the Layers palette, use the menu command Layer➪Type➪Convert to Shape.

5. **Define a custom shape.**

   Choose Edit➪Define Custom Shape, give your new shape a name in the Shape Name dialog box (shown in Figure 11-7), and save it. Your new shape is added to the Custom Shape palette, ready to use.

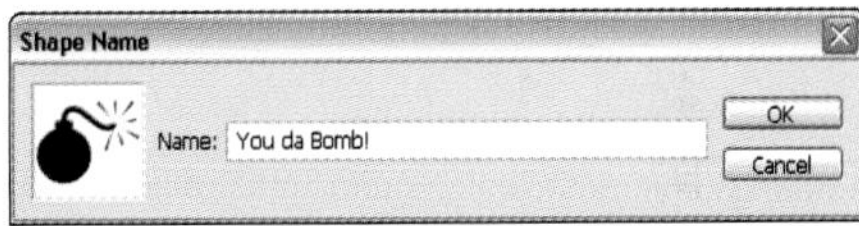


Figure 11-7: Name your new shape and click OK.

Later in this chapter, after you master using the Pen tool, remember this section. You can also define a custom shape from paths that you create with the Pen tool — any shape at all!

Remember that your custom shapes are not truly saved until you use the Custom Shape picker menu command Save Shapes (to save all the shapes in the palette as a single set) or the Edit⇨Preset Manager command (to save a set of selected shapes). In the Preset Manager dialog box, ⌘-click/Ctrl-click each of your custom shapes and then click the Save Set button to save them as a set (see Figure 11-8). Until you take this step, the shapes exist only in Photoshop's Preferences file. If the Preferences become corrupt, you could lose all your custom shapes. This holds true, too, for custom brushes, layer styles, swatches, and the like — use the Preset Manager to save all your custom items.

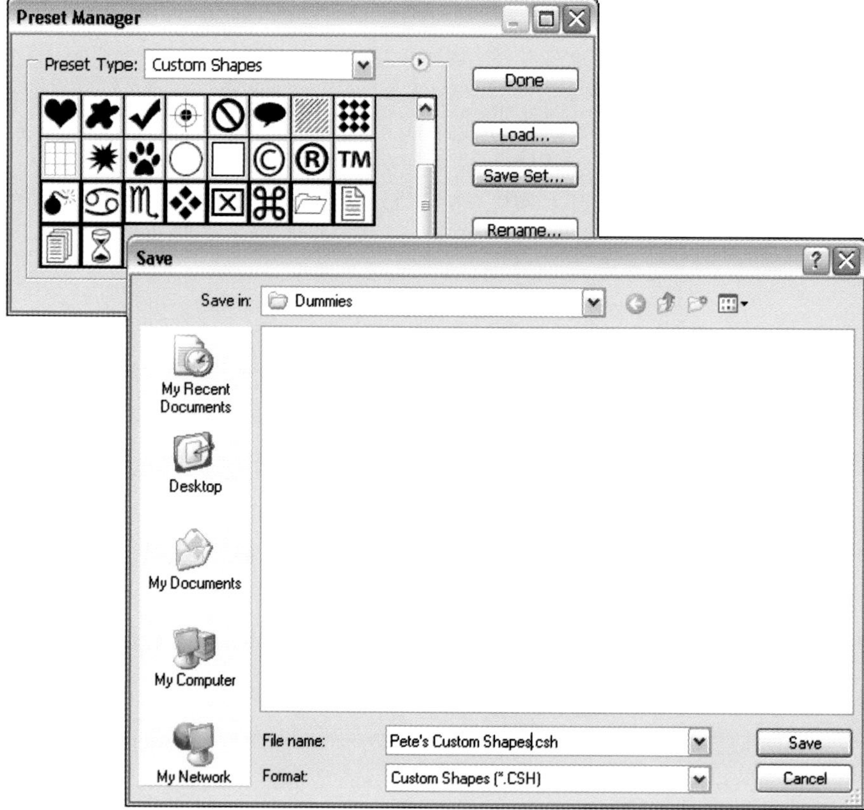


Figure 11-8: Use the Preset Manager to save sets of your custom shapes.

When saving custom shapes (or layer styles or brushes or any of your other custom bits and pieces) with the Preset Manager, save them in a folder outside the Photoshop folder. That prevents accidental loss should you ever need to (gasp!) reinstall Photoshop.

## Changing the appearance of the shape layer

After you use any one of the numerous shape tools in the Photoshop arsenal to add a shape layer to your artwork, you have a number of ways that you can enhance, adjust, and simply change its appearance:

- **Add a layer style.** Layer styles, such as bevels, glows, and shadows (applied through the Layer⇨Layer Style menu), can certainly spice up a shape layer. Compare, for example, the pair of shapes in Figure 11-9. (Layer styles are presented in Chapter 12.)

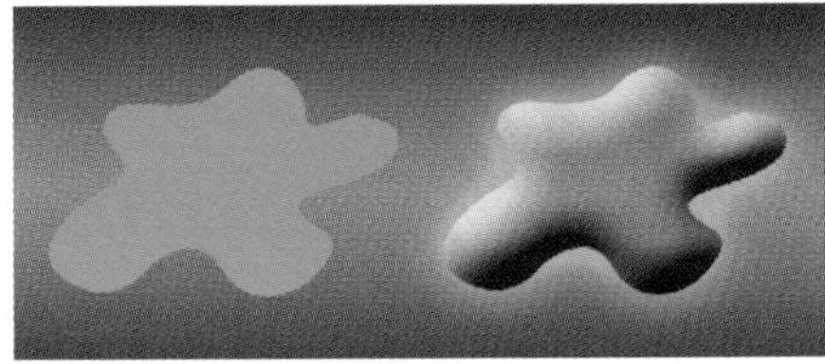

Figure 11-9: A simple layer style makes your shape jump off the page.

- **Change the layer content.** Via the menu command Layer⇨Change Layer Content, you can select a different color, a gradient, or even a pattern to fill the shape.
- **Edit the path shape.** Click a path with the Direct Selection tool and drag to change the path's shape. (This is discussed in more detail later in this chapter.)
- **Change the layer blending mode or opacity.** By default, your shape layer's blending mode is Normal, and the Opacity is set to 100%. Your shape layer blocks and hides the content of every layer below. By changing the blending mode or opacity, you can make your shape layer interact with the layers below in interesting ways. Experiment with different blending modes to find one that suits your artistic vision. (Blending modes are covered in more detail in Chapter 10.)

## Simulating a multicolor shape layer

Shape layers are typically filled with a single solid color although you can use a gradient or a pattern. Sometimes, however, you are better served with a multicolor shape. Take a look at Figure 11-10 and compare the pair of shape layers to the left with the same shapes to the right.

In addition to the layer styles applied, *layer masks* hide parts of the more elaborate pair of shapes on the right. Like the vector path that hides parts of a shape layer, a layer mask determines what areas of the layer are visible. You can use layer masks and vector masks together on a single layer, as you can see for three of the four layers in Figure 11-11.

Figure 11-10: Dressing up the shapes can make a world of difference.

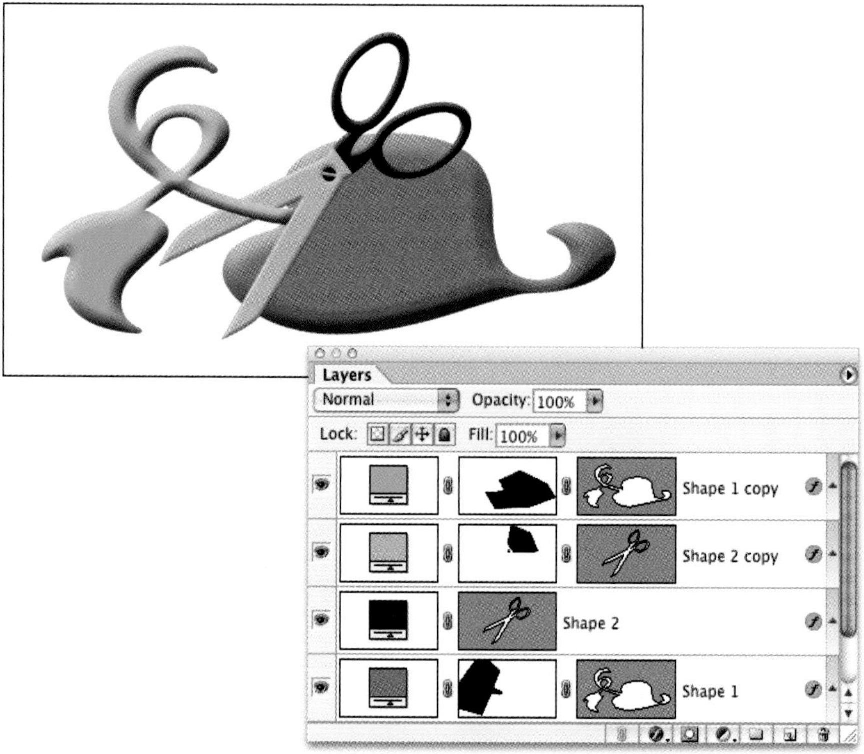


Figure 11-11: Layer masks and vector masks work together to determine layer visibility.

Here's what you're looking at in the Layers palette of Figure 11-11:

- **Layer Shape 1 copy:** This is the top layer and would normally hide everything on the layers below. The layer, as you can tell from the left-most thumbnail in the Layers palette, is filled with green. The right-most thumbnail is the vector mask created by the Custom Shape tool. You can see the shape's path in that thumbnail. The middle thumbnail is the layer mask. By painting with black in the layer mask, you can hide parts of the layer. In this case, the right part of the shape layer is hidden.
- **Layer Shape 2 copy:** Again, a pair of masks are used together. You can see that the vector shape is an entire pair of scissors. The middle thumbnail shows where the layer is hidden by a layer mask, leaving only the blades of the scissors visible on the gray-filled layer.
- **Layer Shape 2:** This layer requires only the vector path shape. The gray layer just above hides what would be black scissors blades.
- **Layer Shape 1:** The layers above partially hide the red shape layer. Notice how because of the order of the layers in the Layers palette, the blades of the scissors appear to be in front of the red part of the object and behind the green part of the object.

Adding a layer mask to your shape layer is as easy as clicking the Add Layer Mask button at the bottom of the Layers palette (third button from the left), and then painting with black to hide, white to show, and gray to partially hide. You can also make a selection in your image and use the Layer⇨Layer Mask menu commands. You can add layer masks to any layer except those named *Background.* (You can't have transparent areas on a background layer, but you can rename a background layer to convert it to a regular layer.)

# Using Your Pen Tool to Create Paths

Even with all the custom shapes available, you might need to create a path that is unique to a specific image. For that, Photoshop offers the Pen tool and its associated tools. Before you start creating paths willy-nilly, you probably will benefit from a little bit of background information about paths.

## Understanding paths

As you click and click-drag, you place *anchor points,* which connect the *path segments* that create your path. Path segments can be straight or curved. You control those curves not with diet and exercise but rather with *direction lines* and their *control points.* A straight path segment is bordered on either end by *corner anchor points,* and a curved path segment is bordered by two *smooth anchor points* or one of each type. As you can see in Figure 11-12, Photoshop helps you differentiate between path segments and direction lines by using squares (hollow and filled) for anchor points and diamond shapes for control points.

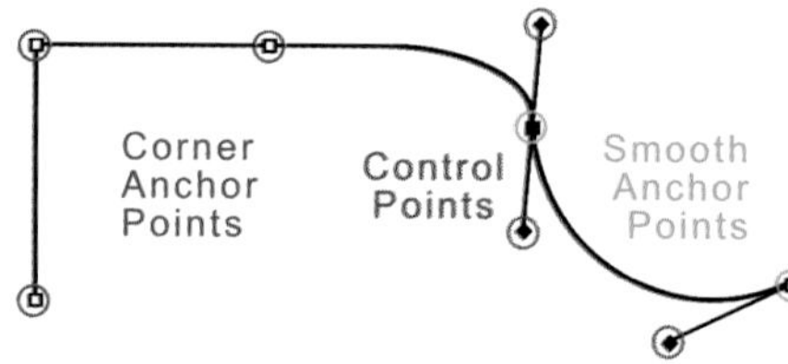


Figure 11-12: Paths have square anchor points and diamond-shaped control points.

Only smooth anchor points have direction lines and control points. The angle and length of the direct-ion line determine the shape of the curve. When you create a curved path segment between a corner anchor point and a smooth anchor point, only the smooth point's direction lines adjust the curve. When you create a curved path segment between two smooth anchor points, both points' direction lines affect the curve.

REMEMBER

Here's another important way to classify paths in Photoshop — open and closed:

- An *open path* has two distinct and visible endpoints; think of it as a pencil line or piece of string.
- A *closed path* has no beginning or end — like a circle or an unbroken rubber band.

When you use a shape tool, you're creating closed paths. When you click-click-click with the Pen tool, you create an open path — unless, that is, your final click is back on the very first anchor point.

## Clicking and dragging your way down the path of knowledge

All that theory about how paths work is fine, but you'll get a better understanding by playing around with the Pen tool. Open a new document (any size, resolution, and color mode will do) and select the Pen tool. On the Options bar, click the middle of the three buttons to the left (as shown in Figure 11-13) so that the tool creates work paths rather than shape layers, and then start clicking around. Randomly click in various places in the image, adding new straight path segments as you go.

Figure 11-13: Select the left button to create a shape layer, the middle button to create a work path.

Use the middle of the three buttons to the left in the Options bar when you want to create a path. Use the left-most of the three buttons when you need a shape layer. The button on the right, for adding pixels to the current layer, is used only with shape tools.

I'm sure Picasso would be proud, but it's time to let go of your new artwork and move on — press Delete (Mac) or Backspace (Windows) twice. The first time deletes the most recent anchor point; the second time deletes the rest of the path.

Now, in that same canvas, start click-dragging to create curved path segments. Watch how the distance and direction in which you drag controls the segment's curve. Just because it's fun, try a click-drag and, with the mouse button held down, move the mouse around and around in a circle. "Path Jump Rope!" Press Delete/Backspace twice to delete the path.

Now, to get a feel for how to control your curved path segments, try this:

1. **Choose File⇨New to open a new document.**
2. **Choose 800 x 600 from the Presets pop-up menu.**

   A reasonable size to work with, it should fit on your screen at 100% zoom.
3. **Show the Grid.**

   Press ⌘+' (apostrophe; Mac) or Ctrl+' (apostrophe; Windows) to show the Grid in the image. The Grid makes it easier to control the Pen tool as you drag. You can also show the Grid with the menu command View⇨Show⇨Grid.
4. **Select the Pen tool in the Toolbox.**
5. **Click and click-drag as shown in Figure 11-14.**

   Don't worry about precision — you won't be creating a work of art this time. Click on the dots; where you see a dashed line, click-drag in that direction for approximately that distance.

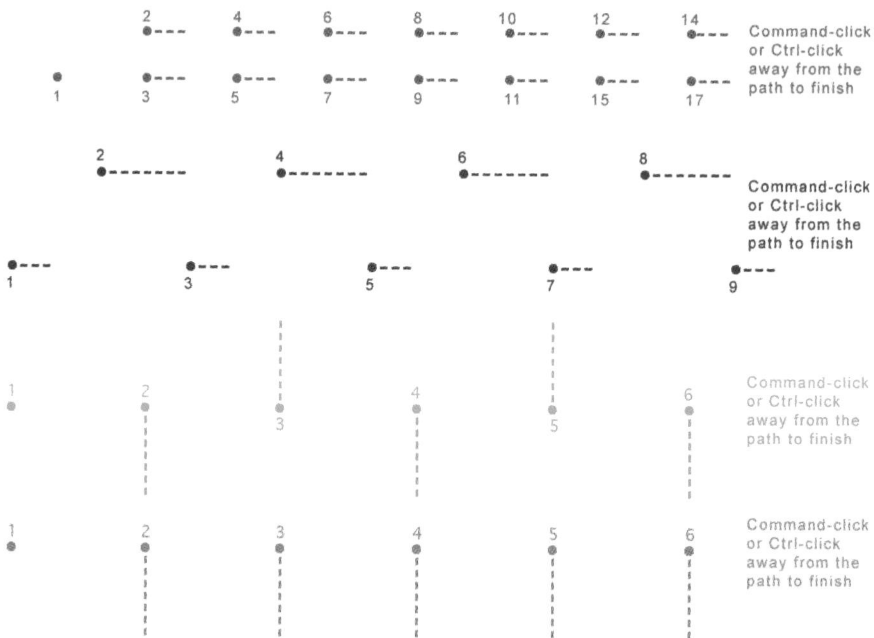


Figure 11-14: You don't need to be precise; just more or less follow the four patterns.

You've just created four of the more useful scallops and curve sets! These sorts of paths can be used in a variety of ways, including stroking, filling, and creating selections (all of which I discuss later in this chapter) to create decorative borders and artistic elements in your images.

You should know about a couple of other features of the Pen tool before you move on. With the Pen tool active, take a look at the Options bar (or look at Figure 11-15, which shows the Options bar).

Figure 11-15: The Pen tool has a couple of tricks up its sleeve!

When you have the Freeform Pen option selected in the Options Bar, you click and drag around your image, creating a path as you go. It's much like painting with the Brush tool or drawing lines with the Pencil tool — wherever you drag the tool, the path is created.

The Freeform Pen offers the Magnetic option, too. When you need to make a path (or selection) around the outside of something of uniform color in your image, using the Magnetic option forces the path to look for and follow edges. Take a look at Figure 11-16, which shows an example of an appropriate use for the Freeform Pen and the Magnetic option.

Figure 11-16: Tracing a uniformly colored object is a great job for the Freeform Pen using the Magnetic option.

## A closer look at the Paths palette

Paths are saved, duplicated, converted, stroked, filled, and deleted via the Paths palette (which, like all palettes, you can show and hide through the Window menu). You can even create a path from a selection by using the Paths palette. Without the Paths palette, your paths have no meaning or future and probably won't get into a good college.

### Pick a path, any path

The Paths palette can hold as many paths as you could possibly want to add to your artwork. You can also see the six buttons across the bottom of the palette that you use to quickly and easily work with your paths. You can classify paths in the five different ways shown in Figure 11-17.

You might not use them all, but it's good to know the five types of paths:

- **Clipping path:** *Clipping paths* are used primarily with page layout programs, such as Adobe PageMaker and QuarkXPress. Much like how a shape layer's vector path determines what parts of the layer are visible, a clipping path identifies what part of the image as a whole is visible. You won't need a clipping path when you work with Adobe InDesign — simply create your image on a transparent background and place that Photoshop file into an InDesign document. To create a clipping path, first make your path, give it a name in the Paths palette (to save it), and then use the Paths palette menu command Clipping Path (as shown in Figure 11-18).

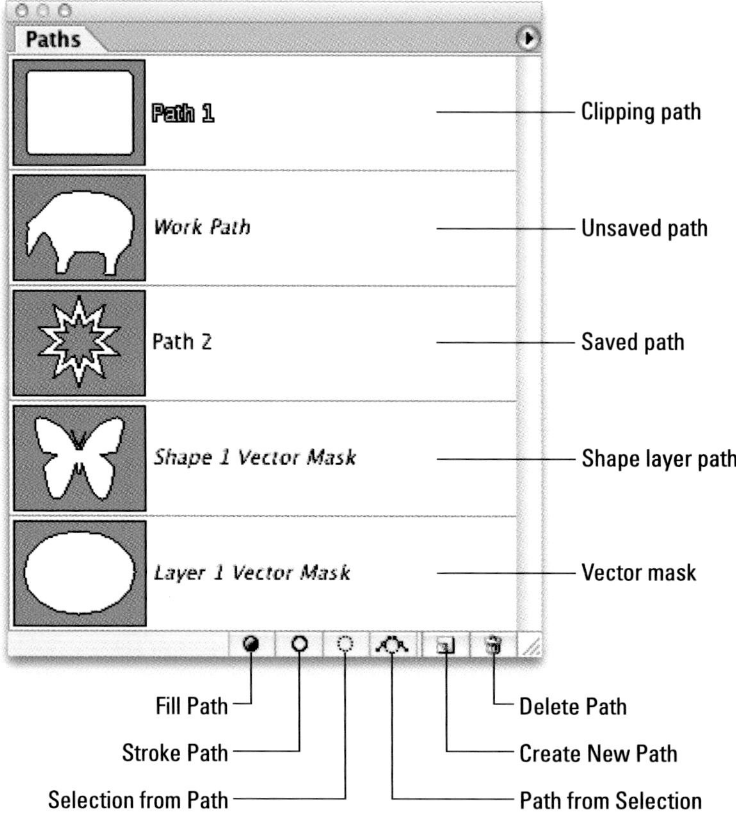


Figure 11-17: The Paths palette is your key to organizing and controlling vectors in your artwork.

Figure 11-18: Use the Clipping Mask command to create a clipping mask from a path.

- **Work path:** As you create a path, Photoshop generates a temporary work path. Unless you save your path, it is deleted as soon as you start to create another path or when you close the file. To save a work path, simply double-click the name field in the Paths palette and type a new name.
- **Saved path:** Much like working in the Layers palette, you can double-click the name of any path and rename it in the Paths palette. (You *must* rename a work path in order to save the path for later use.) After you give the path a name, it's safe from accidental deletion.
- **Shape layer path:** When a shape layer is active in the Layers palette, its vector mask path is visible in the Paths palette. If you want to customize a shape layer's path, you need to make the layer active first. When a shape layer path is visible, you can drag it to the New Path button at the bottom of the palette to create a duplicate. (It's the second button from the right.)
- **Vector mask:** When a regular layer has a vector mask assigned and that layer is visible in the Layers palette, the layer's mask path is visible in the Paths palette.

When creating a clipping path, leave the Flatness field (refer to Figure 11-18) completely empty unless your print shop specifically instructs you to use a specific value. The Flatness value overrides the output device's native setting for reproducing curves. Using the wrong value can lead to disastrous (and expensive!) mistakes.

To activate a path in the Paths palette, click it. You can then see (and edit) the path in the image window. With the exception of shape layer and vector mask paths, the paths in the Paths palette are independent of any layer. You could create a path with the Background layer active, and then later use that path as the basis for some artwork on, for example, Layer 3.

### The Paths palette buttons

The six buttons across the bottom of the Paths palette (refer to Figure 11-17) do more than just simple palette housekeeping. Use them to create artwork from a path and to convert back and forth between paths and selections.

- **Fill Path:** Click a path in the Paths palette and then use this button to fill the area inside the path with the foreground color. If you fill an open path (a path with two distinct endpoints), Photoshop pretends that there's a straight path segment between the endpoints. The fill is added to the active layer in the Layers palette. If a shape layer or a type layer is selected in the Layers palette, the Fill Path button is not available. You can see a filled path in Figure 11-19.

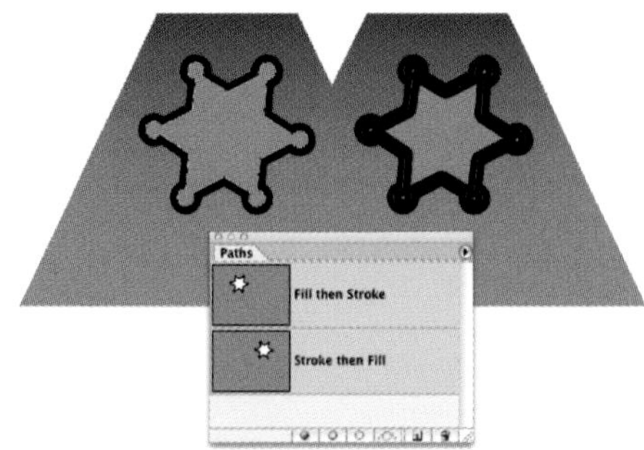


Figure 11-19: Think about whether you want to stroke first (left) or fill first (right).

- **Stroke Path:** Click a path in the Paths palette and then use this button to add a band of the foreground color along the course of the path. Most often, you can think of it as painting the path itself with the Brush tool. If you have a different brush-using tool active in the Toolbox (Clone Stamp, Healing Brush, Dodge, Burn, Eraser, and so on), the path is stroked with that tool. Like a fill, a stroke is added to the currently active layer in the Layers palette. You can't stroke a shape layer path. You can, however, duplicate such a path and stroke the copy on another layer. Take a look at Figure 11-19 to see how stroking and filling differ.
- **Selection from Path:** When you have a path selected in the Paths palette, you click this button, and *voilà!* An instant — and very precise — selection is at your disposal. You can create a selection from any path. If you want to add feathering to the selection, use the Paths palette menu command Make Selection rather than clicking the Selection from Path button.
- **Path from Selection:** You can create a work path from any selection simply by clicking this button. If the path isn't as accurate as you'd like, or if it's too complex because it's trying to follow the corner of every pixel, use the Paths palette menu command Make Work Path and adjust the Tolerance setting to suit your needs.
- **Create New Path:** You use this button primarily to duplicate an existing path. Drag any path to the button, and a copy is instantly available in the Paths palette. When you click this button, you're not creating (or replacing) a work path but rather starting a new saved path.
- **Delete Path:** Drag a path to the Delete Path button, or click the path and then click the button. Either way, the path is eliminated from the palette and from your artwork.

The order in which you stroke and fill a path can make a huge difference in the appearance of your artwork. The stroke is centered on the path, half inside and half outside. The fill extends throughout the interior of the path. If you stroke a path and then add a fill, the fill covers that part of your stroke that's inside the path. As you can see in Figure 11-19, that's not always a bad thing. (Both paths are visible for comparison purposes — normally only one path is active at a time.)

Keep in mind that Photoshop doesn't really create vector objects. If you stroke or fill a path and then edit the path itself, the stroke and fill don't move with the path — they stay right where they are, as pixels on a layer. If you're used to working with vectors in Illustrator, this can be a nasty surprise.

Sometimes the easiest and fastest way to create a complex path is to make a selection and convert the selection to a path. You might, for example, click once with the Magic Wand, and then click the Selection from Path button at the bottom of the Paths palette. Remember to rename the path to save it!

# Customizing Any Path

Photoshop gives you a lot of control over your paths, not just when creating them but afterward as well. After a path is created, you can edit the path itself. While the path is active in the Paths palette, the Edit➪Transform Path commands are available, giving you control over size, rotation, perspective, skewing, and even distortion. But there's also much finer control at your fingertips. You can adjust anchor points, change curved path segments, add or delete anchor points, and even combine multiple paths into *compound paths,* in which one path cuts a hole in another. (Think *donut.*)

## Adding, deleting, and moving anchor points

Photoshop provides you with a number of tools with which to edit paths although you might never use a couple of them. Consider, for example, the Add Anchor Point and Delete Anchor Point tools shown in Figure 11-20. Now take a look at the Option bar's Auto Add/Delete option. With the Pen tool active, you automatically switch to the Delete Anchor Point tool when over an anchor point, and automatically switch to the Add Anchor Point tool when the cursor is over a path segment. Smart tool, eh? The Convert Point tool, on the other hand, can be invaluable . . . or valuable, at least. Click a smooth anchor point to convert it to a corner anchor point. Click-drag a corner anchor point to convert it to a smooth point.

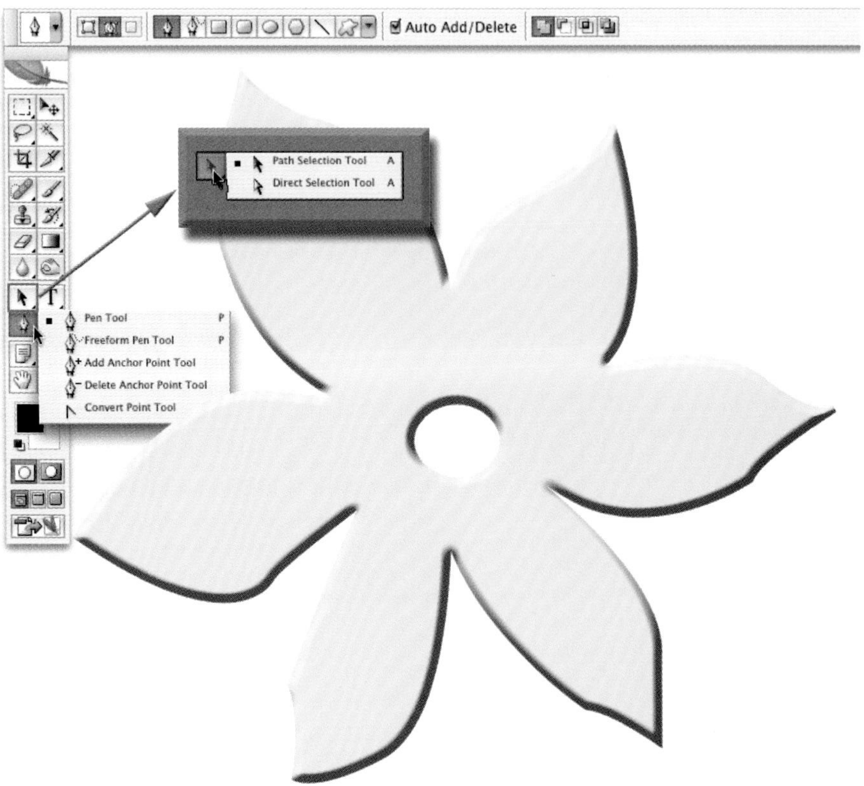


Figure 11-20: Photoshop gives you every tool you need to edit vector paths.

While looking at Figure 11-20, you might have noticed some red highlights. Okay, they were pretty hard to miss, pretty much on purpose. Although the Pen tool and the Convert Point tool have specific uses when you're editing a path, the true power is in the Direct Selection tool.

Nested in the Toolbox with the Path Selection tool (which you use to select and drag a path in its entirety), the Direct Selection tool lets you alter individual path segments, individual anchor points, and even the individual direction lines that control curved path segments.

When you click an anchor point with the Direct Selection tool, you can drag it into a new position, altering the shape of the path. If it's a smooth anchor point, clicking it with the Direct Selection tool makes the point's direction lines visible (as well as those of immediately neighboring smooth anchor points).

The Direct Selection tool has no user-definable options on the Options bar. It's a pretty straightforward, no-nonsense tool that follows a few simple rules of behavior (which you can see illustrated by pairs of "before" and "after" paths in Figure 11-21):

- **Drag a path segment.** Drag a path segment with two corner anchor points, and you drag those points along with you. If the path segment has one or two smooth points, you drag the segment (reshaping the curve), but the anchor points remain firmly in place. Note in Figure 11-21 (upper left) that when you drag a curved path segment, the adjoining direction lines change length, but they retain their original angles.

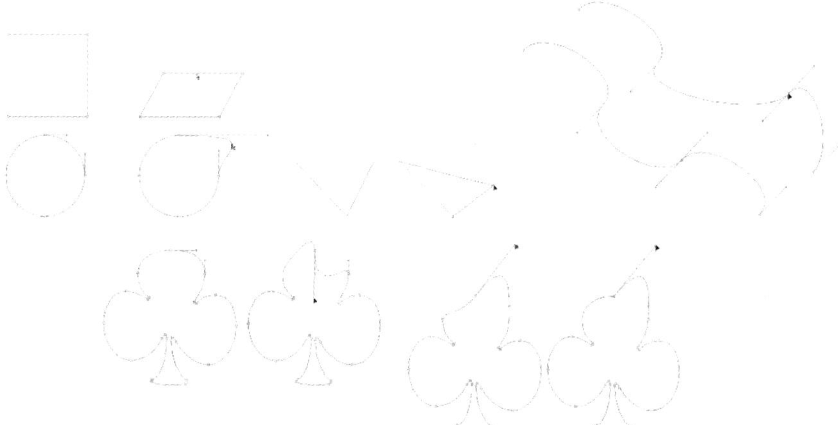

Figure 11-21: A number of ways to manipulate path segments and anchor points.

- **Drag a corner anchor point.** Click a corner anchor point and drag, and the Direct Selection tool pulls the two adjoining path segments along with it. As you can see in Figure 11-21 (upper center), the other two anchor points (and the path segment between them) are unchanged.
- **Drag a smooth anchor point.** When you drag a smooth anchor point, all four of the direction lines associated with the path segments on either side retain both their lengths and their angles. The direction lines don't change; only the curved path segments connected at the smooth anchor point are altered. In Figure 11-21 (upper right), the path continues to flow smoothly through the anchor point, even as the point moves.

- **Drag a smooth point's direction line.** Dragging a direction line changes the curves on either side of the anchor point so that the path still flows smoothly through the point. (Remember that you click the control point at the end of a direction line to drag it.) Figure 11-21 (lower left) illustrates how the path segments on either side of the smooth point adjust as the direction line is changed. However, paths don't always flow smoothly through a smooth anchor point — not if you used the following trick!
- **Option-drag/Alt-drag a direction line.** Hold down the Option/Alt key and drag a smooth anchor point's direction line, and you'll break the flow of the path through that point. With the Option/Alt key, you change only the path segment on that side of the anchor point, leaving the adjoining path segment unchanged. In Figure 11-21 (lower right), the direction line on the left is being dragged without the Option/Alt key. On the right, adding the modifier key preserves the appearance of the adjoining path segment.

You can use the Shift key with the Direct Selection tool to ensure that you're dragging in a straight line. You can also use the Shift key to select multiple anchor points before you drag.

## Combining paths

As you've probably noticed through the course of this chapter, some paths are very simple (like the paths in the preceding figure), and some paths are more complex (like the shapes shown earlier in Figure 11-11). Complex paths are often *compound paths:* that is, paths that contain two or more paths (called *subpaths*) that interact with each other. Think about a pair of circles, different sizes, centered on top of each other. What if the smaller circle cut a hole in the middle of the larger circle, creating a wheel (or, depending on how early you're reading this, a bagel)? Take a look at Figure 11-22.

There are several ways in which two (or more) paths can interact. Complete this sentence: *"The second path can* (fill in the blank) *the original path."*

- **Add to:** The areas within the two subpaths are combined, as if they were within a single path.
- **Subtract from:** The second path is used like a cookie cutter to delete an area from within the first path. (When you need to make a bagel, this is the option!)
- **Intersect with:** Only the areas where the two subpaths overlap is retained.
- **Exclude from:** All the area within both subpaths is retained *except* where the two paths overlap.

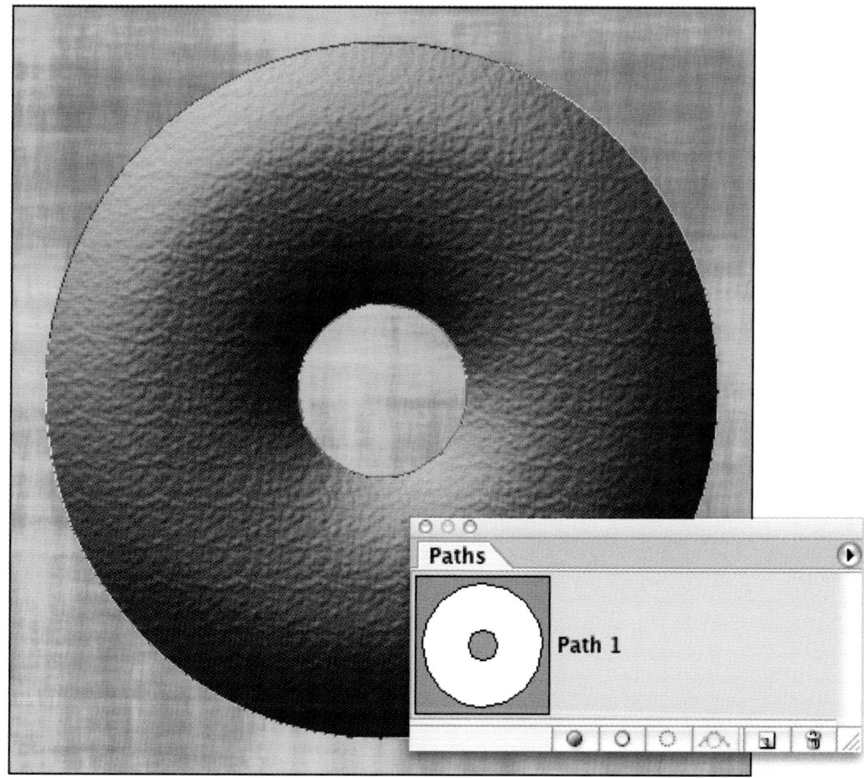


Figure 11-22: Two (or more) paths can interact with each other, creating a compound path, consisting of two or more subpaths.

When any shape tool or the Pen tool is active, the Options bar presents you with four buttons to determine the behavior of multiple paths. (The first path that you create will always be just a normal path. The buttons don't come into play until you add additional subpaths.) Figure 11-23 shows you the buttons, tells you which is which, and provides a simple graphic representation to demonstrate the interaction. The upper-left path is the original, with the lower-right path showing how each option controls the interaction between subpaths.

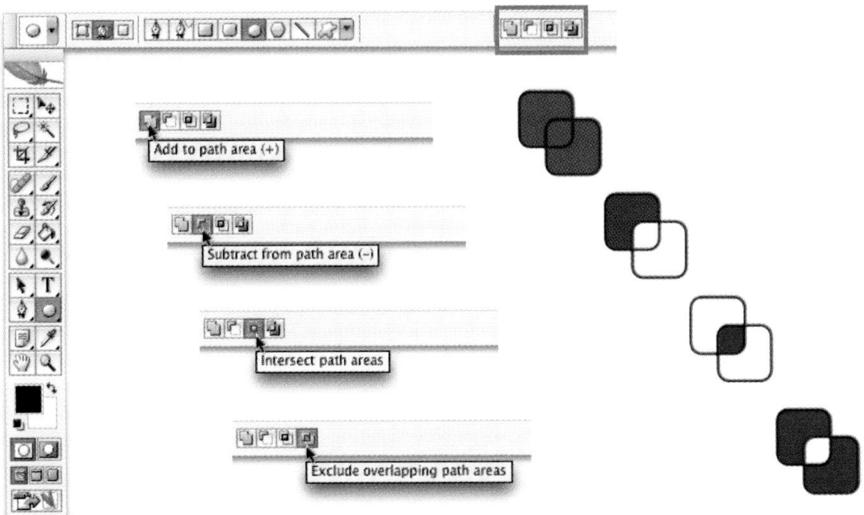


Figure 11-23: The buttons control how a second path (and any subsequent paths) interact with your original path.

## Tweaking type for a custom font

I want to show you one more little thing you can do with vectors in Photoshop, a last bit of fun before this chapter ends. Each individual character in a font consists of paths. You can convert the type to shape layers (or work paths) and change the appearance of the individual characters by editing their paths with the Direct Selection tool.

1. **Open a new document in Photoshop.**
2. **Select 800 x 600 from the Preset menu and then click OK.**
3. **Select the Horizontal Type tool in the Toolbox and set the font.**

   From the Options bar, choose Arial, set the font style to Bold, set the font size to 72, choose Sharp for anti-aliasing, left-align, and click near the center left of your document.

   Okay, in all honesty, you can use just about any settings you want — but if you use these settings, your image will look a lot like mine.
4. **Type the word** Billiards **in your image.**
5. **Press ⌘+Return/Ctrl+Enter to end the text editing session.**

6. **Choose Layer➪Type➪Convert to Shape.**

   This changes the type layer (editable text on its own layer) to a shape layer (a layer filled with color, with only those areas within the vector path visible in the artwork).

7. **Activate the Direct Selection tool.**

8. **Edit the shapes of the *L's* and the *D* to simulate billiard cues.**

   Drag the uppermost anchor points even farther upward to create cue sticks.

   See the result in Figure 11-24.

Figure 11-24: You can convert vector type to shape layers and edit the individual character shapes with the Direct Selection tool.

# Chapter 12

# Dressing Up Images with Layer Styles

### In This Chapter

- Understanding layer styles
- Applying layer styles with the Styles palette
- Creating your own styles
- Preserving your custom layer style

In artwork and photography, you use shadows and highlights in your image to produce the illusion of depth. Highlights and shadows lead the viewer to imagine that a light is falling on parts of a 3-D object. You can also use a shadow or glow to make it appear that some distance exists between one object in the image and another object behind it. Photoshop's built-in layer styles help you add shadows, glows, and other effects almost instantly.

In this chapter, I explain how transparent areas on layers enable lower layers to show through and let your layer styles appear on those lower layers. You get a good look at the Styles palette and how you use it to store and apply layer styles, including your very own custom styles. I then present the all-important (for layer styles) Layer Style dialog box and the various effects that you can add with it. I also show you how to save (and protect) your custom layer styles.

## What Are Layer Styles?

A *layer style* comprises one or more effects that surround or are applied to all the pixels on your layer. Effects that surround pixels include strokes (thin or thick outlines of color), shadows (just like the one this book is casting right now on your desk or lap), and glows (outlines of semitransparent color). Effects that are applied to pixels include overlays of color, patterns, or even gradients. But Photoshop offers even more, including the ever-popular Bevel and Emboss effect, which does a great job of giving the content of your layer a 3-D look. (And, of course, effects can be used in combination. Check out Figure 12-1 for some examples.) You can add effects to layers several ways, including through the Layer Style menu at the bottom of the Layers palette (as shown in Figure 12-2). I explain each of the effects individually later in this chapter in the section on creating your own custom layer styles.

Figure 12-1: Strokes, shadows, overlays, and bevels are just some of the effects available.

Just so everyone is on the same sheet of music, when you refer to a drop shadow or an outer glow or a color overlay or any of the other items shown in the menu in Figure 12-2, call it a *layer effect* or simply an *effect.*

After an effect is applied to a layer or saved in the Styles palette (which I discuss a bit later in this chapter), it becomes a *layer style.* A layer style can include one effect or several effects. The individual layer effects are built into Photoshop, but you can add or delete layer styles and even create your own. By the way, Blending Options at the top of the list in Figure 12-2 is not actually a layer effect but rather governs how the colors of the pixels on the selected layer interact with pixels on layers below.

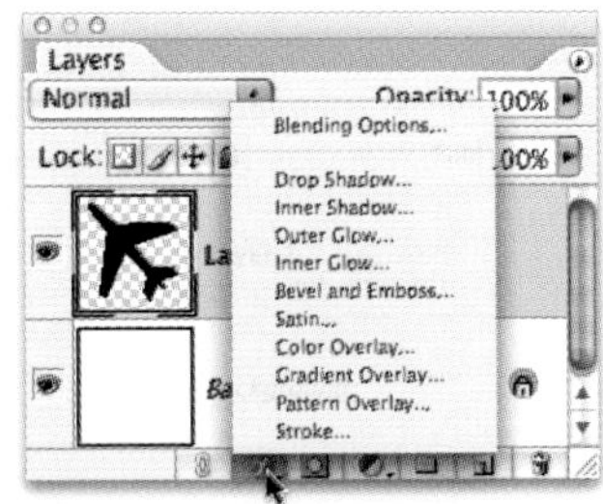


Figure 12-2: One way to add a layer style is through the Layers palette.

Some layer effects, such as drop shadows and outer glows, appear outside the content of the layer. For those effects to be visible in your artwork, the layer must have at least some area of transparent pixels. If the layer is filled edge to edge, the effect has no place within the image to appear because the glow or shadow would logically be outside the image's canvas. Take a look at a couple of layer style examples in Figure 12-3.

In both cases, if the layer is completely filled with color, the shadow can't be seen falling on the layer below. In the sample on the left, you can imagine that the shadow logically also appears to the lower right of the object as a whole, but that's outside the image's canvas, so that part of the shadow doesn't appear in the artwork.

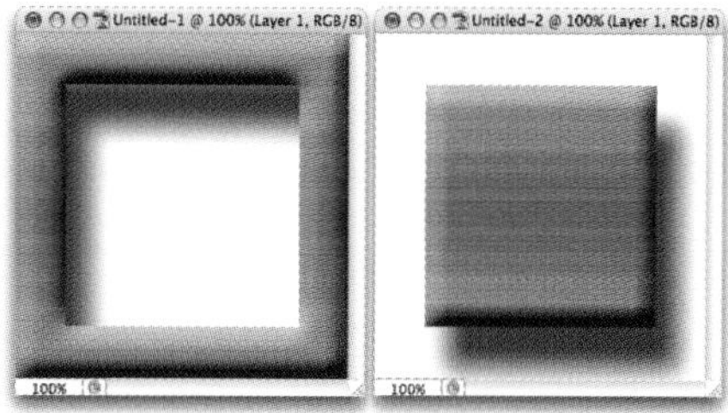

Figure 12-3: Some layer effects need transparent areas on the layer, or they won't appear.

Keep in mind that every layer in an image has the same number of pixels — but some of those pixels can be transparent. When a layer has areas of transparency, layers below in the image can show through. In the two examples in Figure 12-3, the white background layer is visible, giving the upper layers' shadows a place to fall. (And remember that a layer named *Background* can't have areas of transparency. Convert it to a regular layer by double-clicking the layer name in the Layers palette and renaming it.) Chapter 10 is full of information on working with layers.

## Using the Styles Palette

The Styles palette is, by default, nested with the Color palette and Swatches palette. If it's not there, use the Window➪Styles command to make it visible. This palette, which you see with its menu open in Figure 12-4, is where you find and store layer styles and is the easiest way to apply a layer style to your active layer.

To apply a layer style via the Styles palette, make the target layer active by clicking it in the Layers palette; then click the style that you want to apply. It's truly that simple! To remove a layer style from the active layer, click the leftmost button at the bottom of the Styles palette. You click the middle button to save a custom layer style (which I explain later in this chapter), and you drag a layer style to the Trash icon on the right to delete it from the palette.

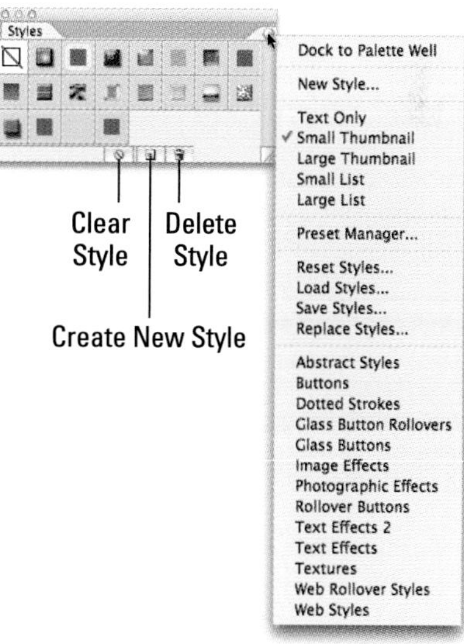


Figure 12-4: The Styles palette holds your preset and saved layer styles.

Take a look at the Styles palette menu, starting from the top and making your way down to the bottom. The first command lets you know that, like all palettes, you can add the Styles palette to the Palette Well (at the right end of the Options bar). You can select the New Style command from the menu to save a layer style although it's easier to click the middle button at the bottom of the palette. (Refer to Figure 12-4.)

Making your way further down the menu, you can choose from five different ways to view the content of the Styles palette. The Text Only, Small List, and Large List options might come in handy after you create a bunch of custom styles with names you recognize, but until you become familiar with the styles in the palette, their names are pretty much meaningless. The Large Thumbnail option gives you a better view of the effects in the style, but you see fewer styles at a time in the palette than you can with the default Small Thumbnails view.

The Styles palette Preset Manager command opens the same Preset Manager that you access through the Edit menu. Use the Preset Manager (discussed at the end of this chapter) to save custom styles in sets on your hard drive to protect them from accidental loss.

The next four commands in the Styles palette menu are what I call "housekeeping commands" because you use them to control the content of the palette:

- **Reset Styles:** The Reset Styles command returns the content of the palette to its default. You have the option of adding the selected set to the current palette content with the Append button or replacing the current content with the selected set by clicking OK.
- **Load Styles:** Use the Load Styles command to add custom styles from your hard drive (or another location.) You can even purchase prepared sets of layer styles on CD. The set is added to the current content of the palette automatically.
- **Save Styles:** The Save Styles command lets you save the current content of the palette as a set of styles. All the layer styles in the palette at the time are saved in the set.
- **Replace Styles:** Use the Replace Styles command to remove the current content and then add the selected set.

At the bottom of the Styles palette menu, you find a list of all the layer style sets saved in Photoshop's Presets⇨Styles folder. Select a set from that list, and you have the option once again of appending or replacing the current content of the palette. (The list in your Styles palette menu might differ from that shown in Figure 12-4.)

# Creating Custom Layer Styles

You create a custom layer style by applying one or more layer effects to your active layer. (Once again, remember that you can't apply layer effects or layer styles to a layer named *Background*.) When you have the effects looking just the way you want them, you can add that new style to the Styles palette and even save it for sharing with friends and colleagues. Combining multiple layer effects lets you create complex and beautiful layer styles that change simple shapes and text into art.

## Exploring the Layer Style menu

In addition to the pop-up menu at the bottom of the Layers palette (refer to Figure 12-2), you can apply layer effects through the Layer➪Layer Style menu. As you can see in Figure 12-5, a few more commands are on that menu than in the list of effects that you find at the bottom of the Layers palette.

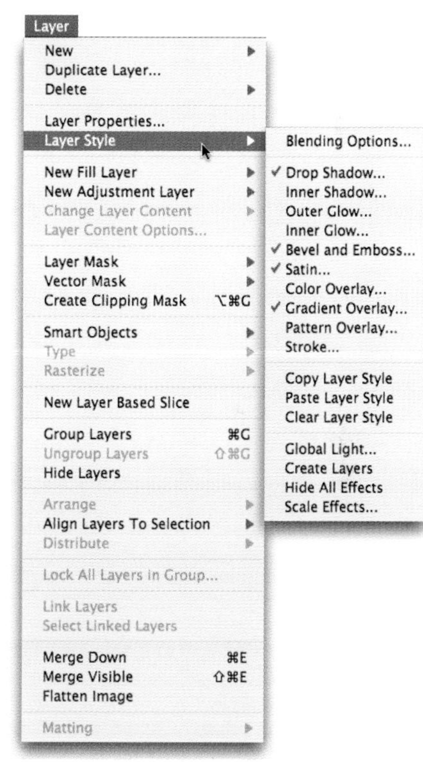


**Figure 12-5:** You can use the Layer Style menu to apply layer effects and more.

The ten items in the Layer Style menu below Blending Options are the actual layer effects. A check mark to the left of the effect indicates that it's currently applied to the active layer. The Copy Layer Style and Paste Layer Style commands come in handy, but if you're more mouse-oriented than menu-oriented, you'll find it easier to add the style to the Styles palette and click the style to apply it to other layers. Clear Layer Style is the equivalent of using the left-most button at the bottom of the Styles palette — it removes all layer effects from the target layer. The four commands at the bottom of the menu are worthy of a little special attention:

- **Global Light:** A number of layer effects are applied at an angle. *Drop shadows,* for example, simulate light coming from a specific angle (which, of course, determines where in your artwork that shadow falls). You use the Global Light command to set the default angle at which your effects are applied. Generally speaking, you want the angle to be consistent from effect to effect and from layer to layer in your artwork. There are exceptions, however, such as the situation shown in Figure 12-6. In that artwork, the two type layers have shadows receding at different angles to simulate a light source positioned immediately in front of and close to the image. (As you can read in the next section of this chapter, when you use layer effects that are applied at an angle, you have the option of using/not using the angle in Global Light.)

Figure 12-6: Sometimes shadows in your artwork shouldn't all use the Global Light setting.

- **Create Layers:** Sometimes you need to edit a layer effect — say, to control where a drop shadow falls on the lower layers in the image. The Create Layers command rasterizes each layer effect (adds it to the image as a separate layer or layers containing pixels). You can then erase portions of the new layers, apply artistic filters, or otherwise customize each effect layer. Remember that after a layer style is rasterized with this command, you can no longer edit it through the Layer Style dialog box, but the original style (if you added it to the Styles palette) is still available.

- **Hide All Effects:** You can temporarily hide a layer style with the Hide All Effects command. Alternatively (and more conveniently), you can click the eyeball icon next to the layer style in the Layers palette to hide the effects.
- **Scale Effects:** Use the Scale Effects command to uniformly make the layer style larger or smaller.

## Exploring the Layer Style dialog box

The first step in creating custom layer styles is to become familiar with the individual layer effects. Each of the ten effects available in the Layer Style dialog box (see Figure 12-7) has its own set of options. The basic default values are very good starting points: You might need to change only a color or perhaps adjust a Size, Distance, or Opacity slider. You can, of course, do lots and lots of customizing for some of the effects.

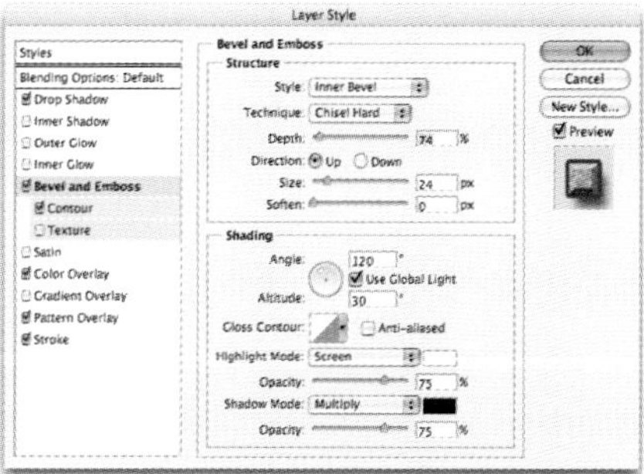


Figure 12-7: The Layer Style dialog box has separate options for each layer effect.

In the column to the left in the Layer Style dialog box, you can mark a check box to apply the effect, but you need to click the name of the effect to open that effect's options pane. In Figure 12-7, the check marks show that this particular layer style includes a drop shadow, bevel, color overlay, pattern overlay, and stroke. The options pane for Bevel and Emboss is visible, as you can tell by the highlighting in the left column (not to mention the subtle *Bevel and Emboss* in bold at the top-center of the dialog box). And in the far right of the Layer Style dialog box, note the Preview check box (upper right, which shows what the layer style will look like) and the small sample just below. That sample shows how your style will look when applied to a square about 150 x 150 pixels.

As you read the descriptions of the various sets of options, keep in mind some generalities about a few key options that you'll see a number of times:

- **Color Selection:** When you see a color swatch — a small rectangle or square, usually near the Blending Mode option — you can click it to open the Color Picker and select a different color.
- **Noise:** When you see the Noise slider, you can add a speckling effect to help diffuse a glow or shadow.

- **Contour:** Glows, shadows, and the like can be applied linearly, with a steady fade from visible to not visible. Or you can elect to have that transition vary with a nonlinear contour. Generally speaking, nonlinear contours can be great for bevels, but linear is usually best for shadows and glows.
- **Angle/Use Global Light:** You can change the angle for several layer effects by entering a specific angle in the numeric field or by dragging in the circular Angle controller. If the Use Global Light check box is marked, you change *all* the angles for that layer style.

## Layer effects basics

In this section, I explain the basics of each of the ten layer effects, showing the options available the Layer Style dialog box for that effect in an insert, as well as one or more examples. And don't forget to take a look at the sidebar, "The key blending modes." Later in this chapter, you can read about the Opacity and the Fill sliders as well as some other advanced blending options.

### Drop Shadow

A drop shadow is a great way to separate the content of one layer from the rest of the image, as you can see by comparing the large and small versions of the artwork in Figure 12-8. In effect, the content of the target layer is copied, converted to black, and placed behind your layer. The blending mode and opacity determine how the shadow interacts with the layers below. You decide how much to offset and blur the duplicate with the sliders. (Remember that this is a layer style, so no second layer is actually added to your image.) You'll generally want to leave the Contour option of your drop shadows set to the linear default. Drop shadows are great with type layers!

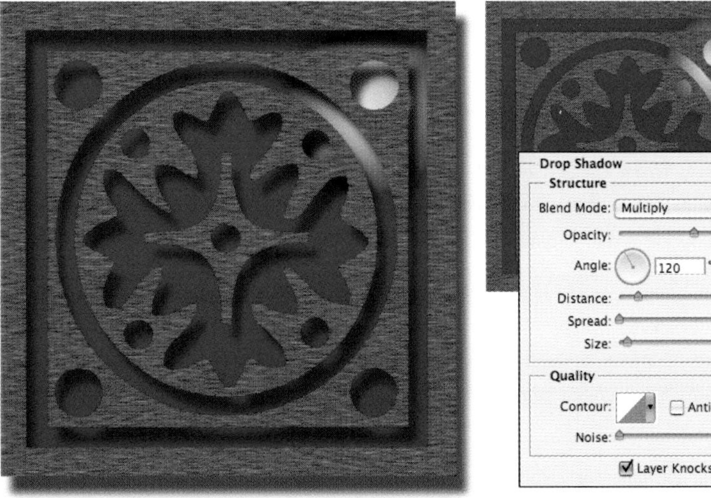


Figure 12-8: Drop shadows can separate the upper layer from the lower layer.

### Inner Shadow

You can do a couple of things with the Inner Shadow layer effect, as you can see in Figure 12-9. Compare the two sets of options. On the left, a soft, light-colored inner shadow using the Screen blending mode softens edges. On the right, a hard inner shadow, using a dark color and the Multiply blending mode, produces a totally different look. The layer effect is applied to the red shape on the *upper* layer.

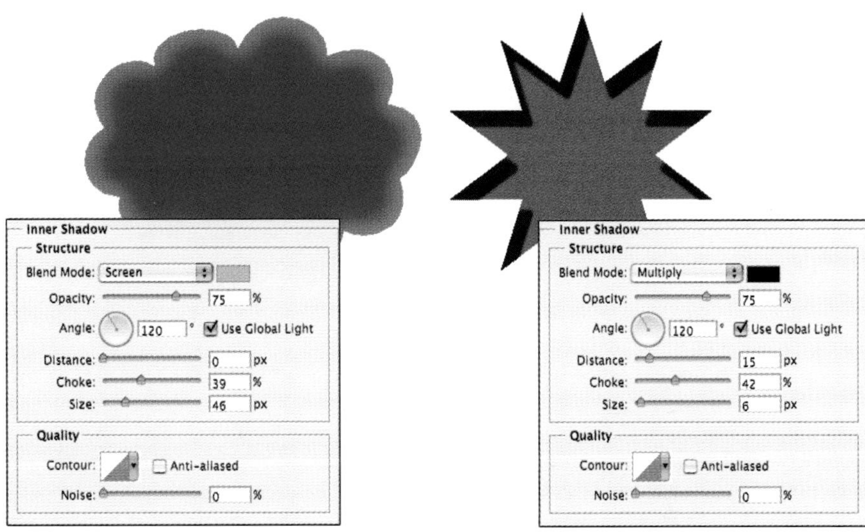


**Figure 12-9:** Inner shadows can be soft or hard, light or dark.

## The key blending modes

Photoshop offers over two dozen different blending modes, many of which you see in the Layer Style dialog box. You really need only a few on a regular basis although it's always fun to experiment with the others, just in case one of them gives you a cool effect.

The *Multiply blending mode* generally darkens. When working with dark shadows or glows, choose the Multiply blending mode so that the layer effect darkens (but doesn't hide completely) the pixels on the layers below. The *Screen blending mode* lightens. Use Screen with light glows and other such effects. The *Overlay blending mode* is a mix of Multiply and Screen. When working with patterns that contain both dark and light colors, you might opt for Overlay as the blending mode.

Of course you should remember the *Normal blending mode,* too! If you want a glow or shadow to completely block whatever lies below, choose Normal at 100% opacity. You might also want to use Normal with a somewhat lower opacity for a uniform coverage over both dark and light pixels. And don't be afraid to experiment — run through the blending modes (and opacity settings) to see whether you can't tweak that custom style just a little more.

### Outer Glow

The Outer Glow layer effect is much like a nondirectional shadow when applied using a dark color. However, you'll also find that it has a variety of uses when used with a light color and the Screen blending mode. As you can see in Figure 12-10, it has practical uses and whimsical uses. (Please remember that in real life, stars do *not* appear between the horns of a crescent moon!)

In the upper area of the Outer Glow options (Structure), you select the blending mode and opacity, add noise if desired, and select between a color (click the swatch to open the Color Picker) or a gradient (click the sample to open the Gradient Editor). You define the size and fade of the glow in the middle section (Elements). The Technique pop-up menu offers both Softer and Precise — try them both. And don't overlook the options at the bottom (Quality). Although you use Jitter only with gradients (to add some randomness), the Range slider is an excellent way to control the distance at which your glow is offset. And when you get a chance, play with different contours for an Outer Glow effect.

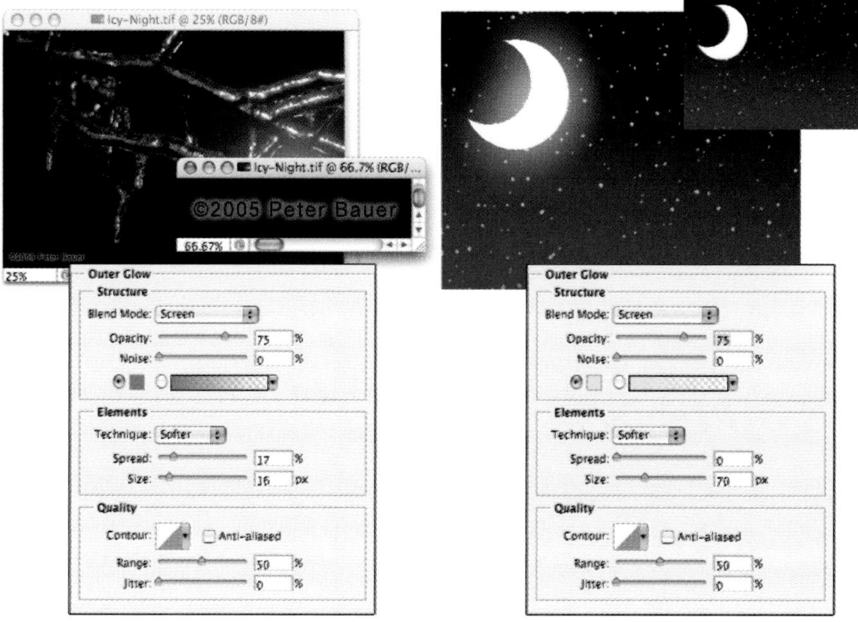


**Figure 12-10:** An Outer Glow layer effect is a multipurpose layer effect.

### Inner Glow

The Inner Glow effect offers you the same control as an Outer Glow, with the impact of an Inner Shadow. As you can see in Figure 12-11, an Inner Glow can be the base for a neon glow style. (Add an Outer Glow effect, perhaps a Stroke effect, and there you go!)

Figure 12-11: Inner Glow offers more control than Inner Shadow.

You can also develop some rather amazing styles by using the Inner Glow and the Inner Shadow in combination. Using similar Size settings and varying the colors and blending modes let you overlay a pair of effects in combination. And when you play with Inner Glow and Inner Shadow in combination, don't overlook the Contour variations.

### Bevel and Emboss

Perhaps the most fun of all the Photoshop layer effects, Bevel and Emboss is a quick and easy way to add a 3-D look to your artwork. You can apply a Bevel and Emboss layer effect to text, to buttons for your Web site, and to create more complex elements in your artwork, examples of which you can see in Figure 12-12.

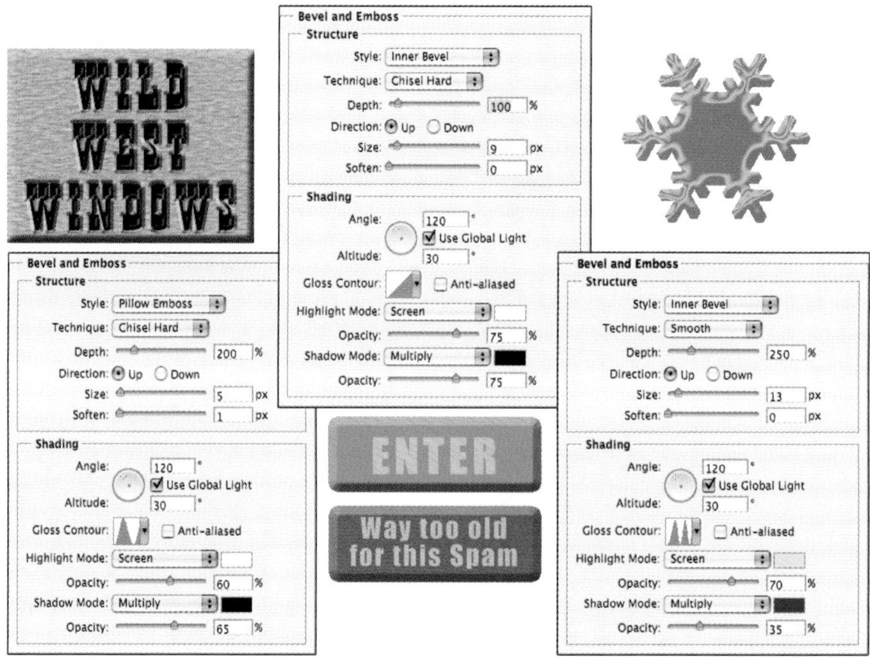


Figure 12-12: The Bevel and Emboss layer effect is very versatile.

When you feel the need (and have the time) to let your imagination frolic through the fertile fields of Photoshop fun, filters are first, but Bevel and Emboss follows fruitfully. Let me suggest that you take the time to play with the various settings in the Bevel and Emboss pane of the Layer Style dialog box to see what they do. Add a new layer, create a simple shape (perhaps with one of the shape tools), select Bevel and Emboss from the pop-up menu at the bottom of the Layers palette, and experiment — that's a far more efficient way to learn this effect than reading technical explanations of each of the options. (One caveat: You won't see any change in your layer with the Stroke Emboss style unless you are also using the Stroke layer effect.)

As you read this book, keep an eye out for the Bevel and Emboss layer effect. When you come across a bevel or emboss effect, such as those shown in Figure 12-13, you might want to take a moment to remember your experimentation and think about what settings might have been used.

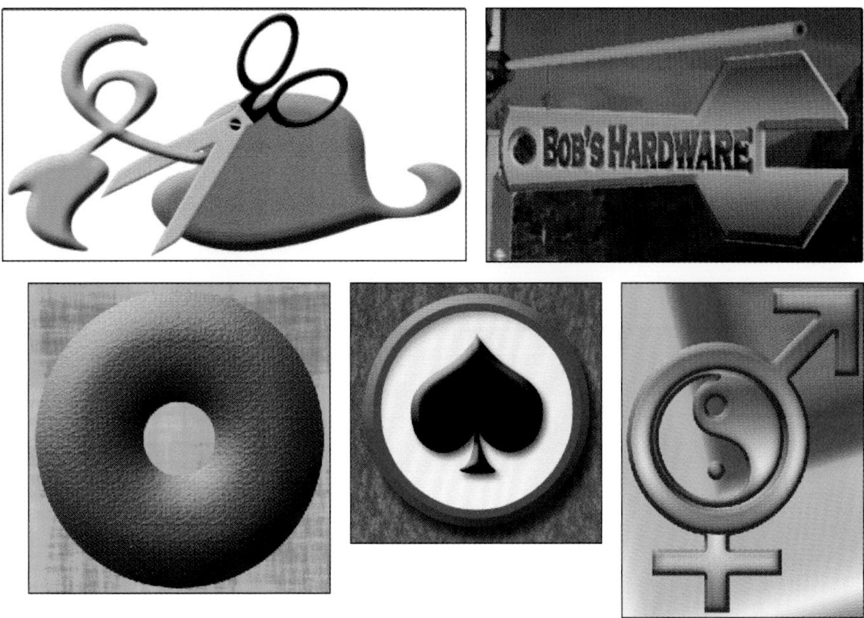


Figure 12-13: Many illustrations in this book use the Bevel and Emboss layer effect.

### Satin

The Satin layer effect uses the shape of the object to produce a wave-like overlay. As you can see in Figure 12-14, it's more effective with type and complex shapes than it is with large plain shapes.

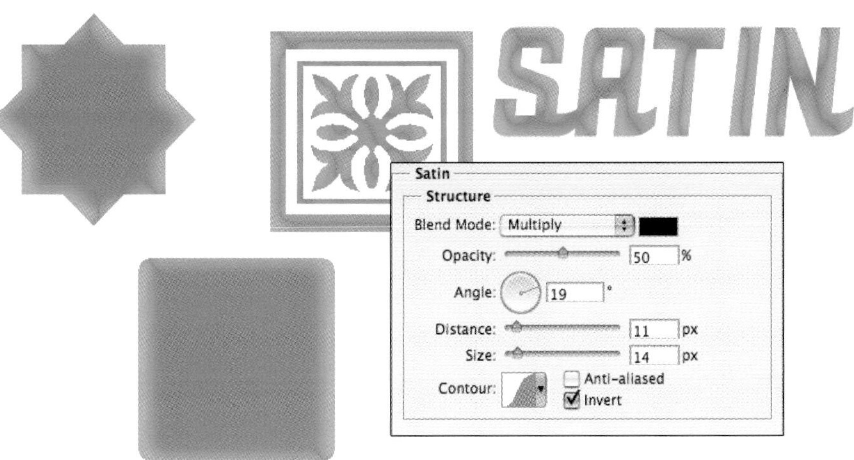


Figure 12-14: The Satin layer effect is very effective with complex shapes.

### Color Overlay

The key to using the Color Overlay layer effect is the blending mode. (See the sidebar, "The key blending modes.") When you use Normal, in effect, you paint all the pixels on the layer with the selected color. To blend the color with the original artwork or other effects (such as pattern overlays), choose an appropriate blending mode — Multiply with dark colors, Screen with light colors — or simply experiment with blending modes. However, using the Color Overlay layer effect with the Normal blending mode in a custom layer style is a good way to ensure consistency in artwork, such as buttons and banners for a Web site.

Although you'll generally find Color Overlay most useful for simple shapes in artwork and on Web pages, you can certainly use it for more exciting effects, such as those that you see in Figure 12-15. The original is in the upper left, and each example shows the color and blending mode selected. Remember that when you use a layer effect, you can later return and alter or remove that change from your image.

Figure 12-15: Color Overlay can produce subtle or dramatic changes in your artwork.

### Gradient Overlay

Unlike the Gradient Map adjustment (see Chapter 6), which applies a gradient to your image according to the tonality of the original, the Gradient Overlay effect simply slaps a gradient over the top of your artwork, using the blending mode and opacity that you select. You also control the shape of the gradient, the angle at which it's applied, and the gradient's scale (see Figure 12-16).

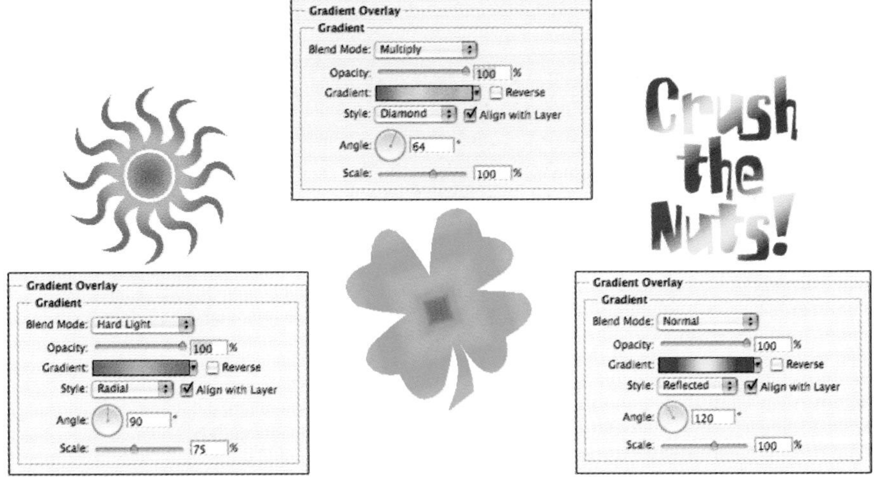


Figure 12-16: In keeping with its name, the Gradient Overlay effect overlays a gradient.

When working with gradients, you click the triangle to the right of the gradient sample to open the Gradient palette. You directly click the gradient sample itself to open the Gradient Editor.

### Pattern Overlay

Like the Color Overlay layer effect, Pattern Overlay relies on the blending mode and opacity settings to determine how the artwork (pattern) that it overlays interacts with your original artwork. As you see in Figure 12-17, you can scale the pattern, align it to the upper-left corner of your image (with the Snap to Origin button), and link the pattern to your layer so that the appearance of your artwork doesn't change as you drag the layer into position. Click the triangle to the right of the sample pattern to open the Pattern palette and then select a pattern.

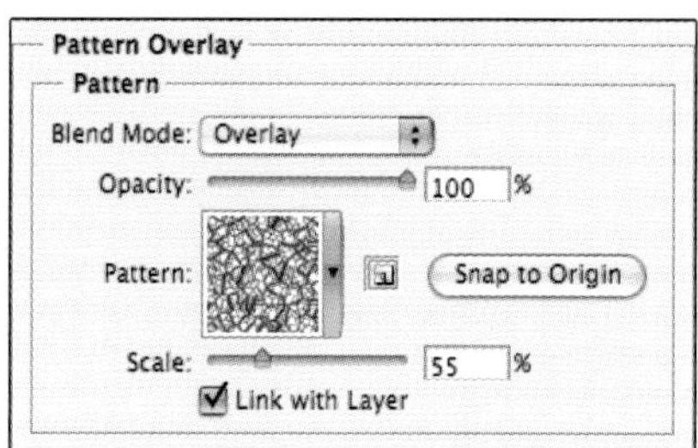

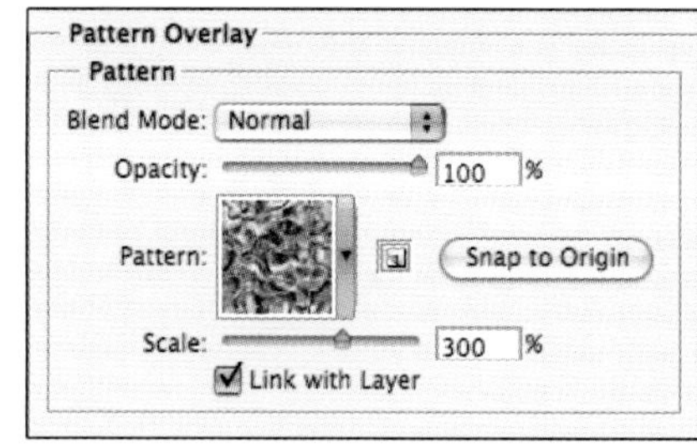


Figure 12-17: The Pattern Overlay layer effect adds texture to your layer's artwork.

### *Stroke*

If you've read this chapter to this point, you've seen the Stroke layer effect for several pages now. Each of the insets from the Layer Style dialog box in the preceding figures has a one-pixel black Stroke layer effect applied. Adding that tiny stroke helps set off the dialog box from the background.

You'll find that not only is Stroke a handy and practical production tool, but it's a wonderful creative effect, too, especially when you use it in conjunction with other layer effects. For example, a stroke of a contrasting color is a great way to redefine the edge of your object when working with an outer glow and an inner shadow. (In the Stroke effect's options, remember that you click the color swatch to open the Color Picker.) A simple stroke can convert even the plainest text into an eye-catching statement. And don't forget that without the Stroke effect, the Bevel and Emboss effect's Stroke Emboss option does nothing for your artwork. Figure 12-18 has a few examples.

Figure 12-18: The Stroke effect can stand alone or be used with other layer effects.

## Opacity, fill, and advanced blending

In the Blending Options area of the Layer Style dialog box and the upper-right corner of the Layers palette, you see a pair of adjustments named Opacity and Fill, as shown in Figure 12-19. Both have an impact on the visibility of the content of your layer.

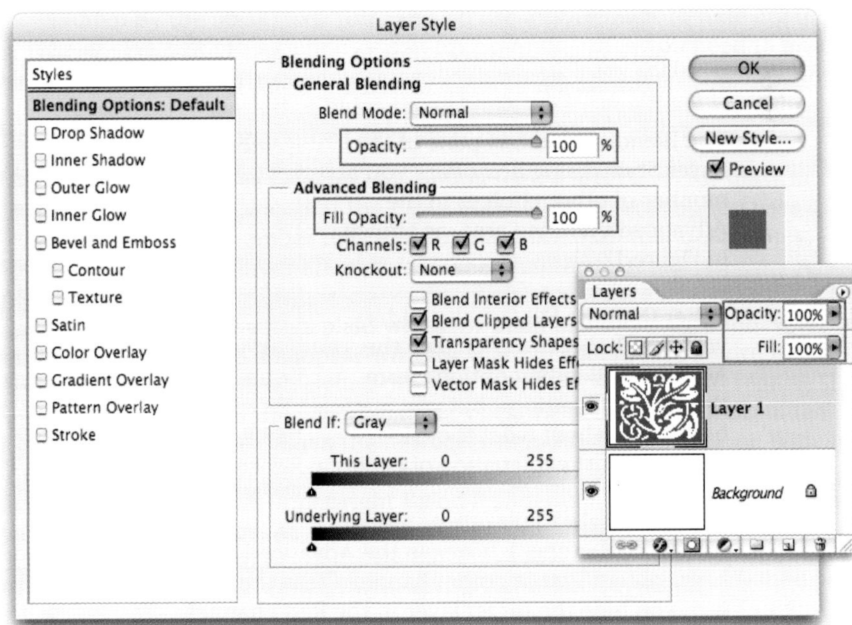


Figure 12-19: The Opacity and Fill sliders control visibility of a layer.

- **Warp type and type on a path** are typically single lines of type that are bent, curved, or otherwise distorted as a special effect. Use the Option bar's Warp Text feature or click with a type tool on a path.

In this chapter, I discuss the tools and palettes that you use to add text to an image, how to add paragraphs and columns of text (as you might use in a brochure or booklet), and even how to make your type bend and twist along paths.

# Making a Word Worth a Thousand Pixels

Photoshop offers you four tools, the Options bar, and a pair of palettes (Character and Paragraph) to control your work with text. By default, the Character and Paragraph palettes are hidden; because you can make the major type-related decisions (such as font style and alignment) right from the Options bar, that's generally fine. You might need to show the palettes if you're doing some fine-tuning of the text appearance. When you do need the palettes, you can show them by choosing Window➪Character or Window➪Paragraph, respectively, from the menu bar or (with the Type tool active) by clicking the Palettes button toward the right end of the Options bar, as shown in Figure 13-1.

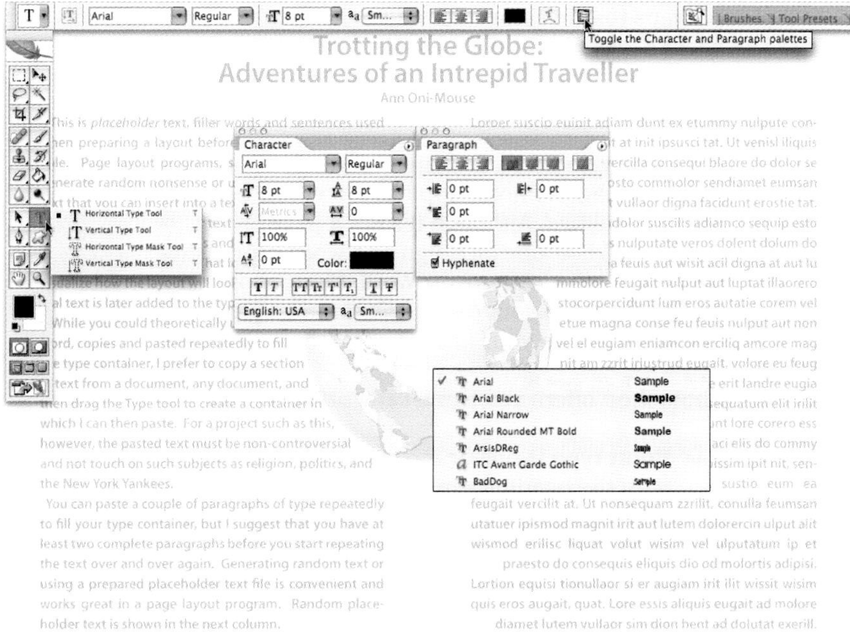


Figure 13-1: Photoshop gives you lots of tools for working with text.

Figure 12-18: The Stroke effect can stand alone or be used with other layer effects.

## *Opacity, fill, and advanced blending*

In the Blending Options area of the Layer Style dialog box and the upper-right corner of the Layers palette, you see a pair of adjustments named Opacity and Fill, as shown in Figure 12-19. Both have an impact on the visibility of the content of your layer.

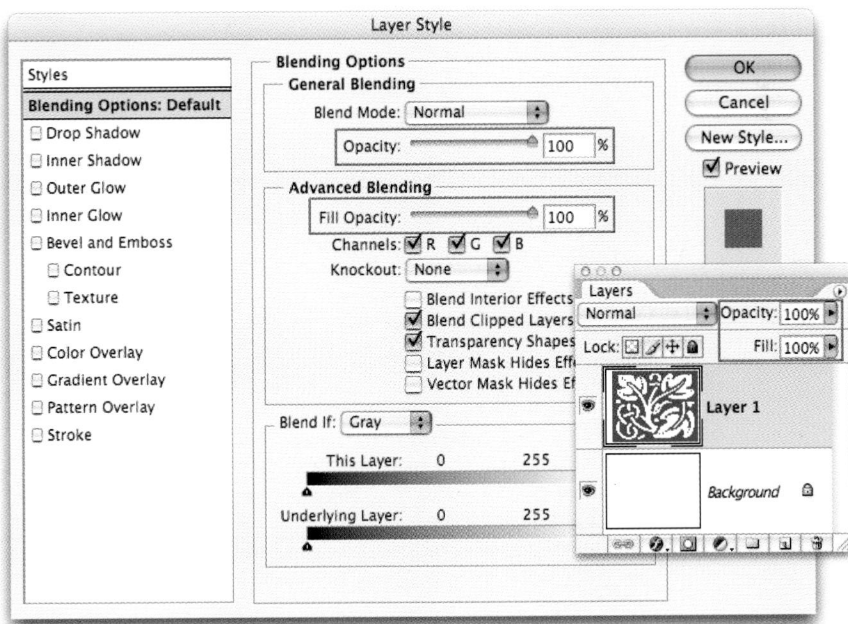


Figure 12-19: The Opacity and Fill sliders control visibility of a layer.

When you reduce the Opacity setting for the layer, you make the layer content and any layer style partially or completely transparent. Reducing the Fill slider changes the opacity of the pixels on the layer but leaves any layer effects fully visible. When might you want to use the Fill slider? The first thing that comes to mind is the ever-popular *Glass Type technique,* which produces see-through text perfect for your copyright notice on any image:

1. **Add some text to an image.**

   This is a wonderful trick for adding your copyright information to sample images because everyone can see the image, but no one can use it without your permission. Start by adding your copyright information or perhaps the word *Sample.*

2. **Apply a layer style to the type layer.**

   A bevel, a thin black stroke, and perhaps an inner shadow make an excellent combination.

3. **Reduce the Fill slider to 0%.**

   You can click and type in the Fill field, click the arrow to the right of the field and drag the slider, or simply click the word *Fill* and drag to the left. The type layer disappears, but the layer effect remains.

   You can see all three steps in Figure 12-20.

Figure 12-20: Add a type layer, apply a layer style, and then reduce the Fill setting to 0%.

The Blending Options pane of the Layer Style dialog box offers you a number of other choices in the Advanced Blending area, as shown in Figure 12-21.

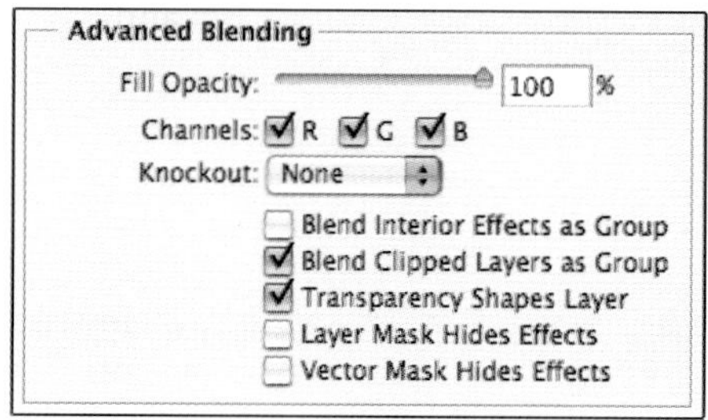


Figure 12-21: You find Advanced Blending options in Blending Options of the Layer Style dialog box.

Other than the Fill Opacity slider, you'll probably never change the Advanced Blending options from their default settings, but you may be curious about what they do. Here's a short explanation of each:

- **Channels:** Clear one or more of the color check boxes in the Advanced Blending area to hide the layer's content in that color channel. Clear the R check box, for example, and you hide the target layer in the Red channel.

- **Knockout:** You can use the content on the target layer to create transparency on lower layers. The top layer becomes transparent as do the layers below every place that the upper layer had visible pixels. (I think of it as a "cookie cutter" effect.) If you want to restrict the effect, use the Shallow option, and the knockout extends only to the lowest layer in your layer group. The Deep option knocks out to the *Background* layer (or to transparency if your image doesn't have a background layer).
- **Blend Interior Effects as Group:** You can blend the Inner Glow, Satin, and your overlay effects before the layer as a whole is blended with lower layers. Use this option if it seems your layer effect's blending mode is being canceled out by the layer's own blending mode.
- **Blend Clipped Layers as Group:** If you have layers clipped together (see Chapter 10), you can elect to use the base layer's blending mode for all the layers or let each layer interact independently. You generally want to leave this check box marked.
- **Transparency Shapes Layer:** Another option that you'll almost always want active, Transparency Shapes Layer restricts the layer style to the visible pixels on the target layer. If, for example, you're working with a small rounded rectangle and a Color Overlay layer effect, clearing the check box fills the entire layer — not just the rounded rectangle — with color.
- **Layer Mask Hides Effects:** If the target layer's visibility is controlled with a layer mask (see Chapter 8), you can opt to have the layer style hidden by the mask, too. You can also use a layer mask to hide *just* the layer style with this option — say, for example, when you need to make sure that your drop shadow doesn't fall where it shouldn't. Simply create a layer mask that hides those areas where you don't want the style visible and mark the Layer Mask Hides Effects check box.
- **Vector Mask Hides Effects:** This option uses a layer's vector mask in exactly the same way that the Layer Mask Hides Effects option uses a layer mask. (Remember that a *vector mask* is a path that determines which areas of a layer are visible — see Chapter 11.)

If you've got an image with a plain white (or plain black) background, you can make that background disappear with the Blend If sliders (see Figure 12-22). In the Layers palette, double-click the layer name *Background* and rename the layer. At the bottom of the Layers palette, click the second button from the right to add a new layer. Move the new layer below the original layer. With the original layer active, open the Blending Options pane of the Layer Style dialog box and drag the upper-right Blend If slider control to the left until the background disappears. As the white background disappears, the checkerboard *transparency grid* becomes visible. Press ⌘+E (Mac)/Ctrl+E (Windows) to merge the layers and retain the now-transparent background.

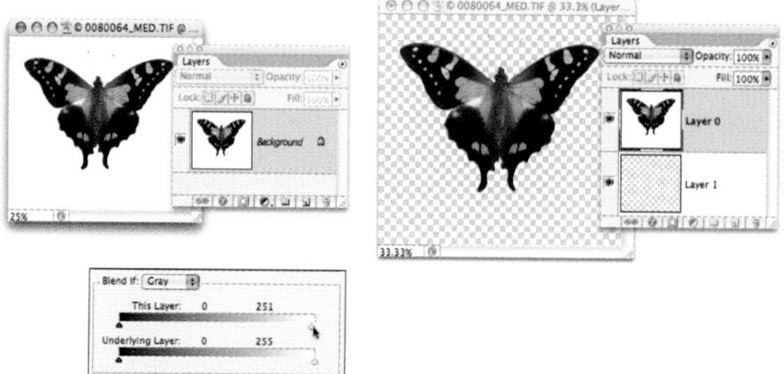


©1998 PhotoSpin, PhotoSpin image #0080064

**Figure 12-22:** Make a white background disappear with the Blend If sliders.

# Saving Your Layer Styles

Creating custom styles takes some time and effort. Saving the styles means that you don't have to spend time re-creating the style again. Save your styles not only in the Styles palette but also on your hard drive.

## Adding styles to the Style palette

After you have your layer style looking just right, you can add it to the Styles palette. From the Styles palette, you can apply your custom style to any layer (except, of course, layers named *Background*) in any image with a single click. You simply make the target layer active in the Layers palette by clicking it; then click your custom style in the Styles palette.

**Figure 12-23:** Click the button at the bottom of the Styles palette to save your custom style.

To add your style to the Styles palette, you must first create it. Select a layer in the Layers palette, open the Layer Style dialog box, and select the layer effects and options. After clicking OK in the Layer Style dialog box, click the middle button at the bottom of the Styles palette (see Figure 12-23). Then, in the New Style dialog box that appears, assign your custom style a name and click OK. If desired, you can also elect to save the target layer's blending mode as part of the layer style.

## Preserving your layer styles

Adding your custom styles to the Styles palette makes them available day in and day out as you work with Photoshop. However, should you ever need to replace Photoshop's Preferences file (see Chapter 3) or reinstall the program, all your custom styles are wiped from the Styles palette. To make sure that you don't accidentally lose your custom styles, create and save a set of styles, which you can then reload into the palette whenever necessary.

The Styles palette menu offers the Save Styles command (refer to Figure 12-4), which lets you save all the styles currently in the palette as a set. However, for more control — to actually select which styles you want in your set — use Photoshop's Preset Manager (see Figure 12-24). You can open the Preset Manager from either the Styles palette menu or through the Edit menu. (Make sure that you retain the `.asl` extension in the filename so that Photoshop recognizes the file as a set of styles!)

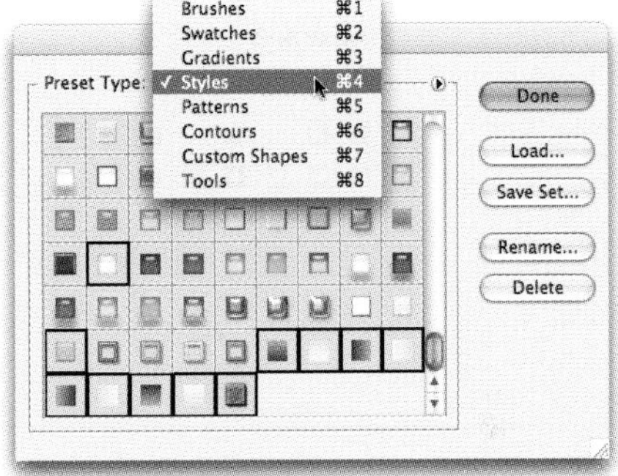


Figure 12-24: Use the Preset Manager to make sure your custom styles are safe.

As you can see in Figure 12-24, you use Preset Manager to save many kinds of custom bits and pieces. And use it you should! Shift-click to select a series of items or ⌘-click/Ctrl-click to select individual items; then click the Save Set button. Give the set a name (again, with the `.asl` file extension), pick a location, and click OK.

Saving sets of styles, brushes, custom shapes, and the like in Photoshop's Presets folder adds those sets to the various palettes' menus. That makes it quite easy to load the set into the palette: Just choose the set from the palette menu. However, you should also save a copy of the set someplace safe, outside the Photoshop folder, so it doesn't accidentally get deleted when you upgrade or (horror!) reinstall.

## Chapter 13

# Giving Your Images a Text Message

### In This Chapter

- A word says a thousand pixels
- Creating paragraphs with type containers
- Shaping up with Warp Text and type on a path

*Un croquis vaut mieux qu'un long discours.* Or, as we often paraphrase Napoleon, "A picture is worth a thousand words." But sometimes in your Photoshop artwork, nothing says Bob's Hardware quite like the very words *Bob's Hardware.* A picture of a hammer and a picture of a nail — perhaps toss in some nuts and bolts — all are great symbols for your client's logo. But you also need to give Bob's customers a name and an address so they can actually spend some money, which goes a long way toward helping Bob pay you.

For a program that's designed to work with photographic images, Photoshop has incredibly powerful text capabilities. Although it's not a page layout program like Adobe InDesign or a word processing program such as Microsoft Word, Photoshop can certainly enable you to add lines or even paragraphs of text to your images.

Photoshop offers you three categories of text:

- **Point type** is one or more lines of text, comparable with the headlines in a newspaper or the text that you add to, say, a Bob's Hardware advertisement. Click with a type tool to add point type.
- **Paragraph type** consists of multiple lines of text. Like in a word processing program, each new line is added whenever your typing reaches the margin. Drag a type tool to create paragraph type.

- **Warp type and type on a path** are typically single lines of type that are bent, curved, or otherwise distorted as a special effect. Use the Option bar's Warp Text feature or click with a type tool on a path.

In this chapter, I discuss the tools and palettes that you use to add text to an image, how to add paragraphs and columns of text (as you might use in a brochure or booklet), and even how to make your type bend and twist along paths.

# Making a Word Worth a Thousand Pixels

Photoshop offers you four tools, the Options bar, and a pair of palettes (Character and Paragraph) to control your work with text. By default, the Character and Paragraph palettes are hidden; because you can make the major type-related decisions (such as font style and alignment) right from the Options bar, that's generally fine. You might need to show the palettes if you're doing some fine-tuning of the text appearance. When you do need the palettes, you can show them by choosing Window➪Character or Window➪Paragraph, respectively, from the menu bar or (with the Type tool active) by clicking the Palettes button toward the right end of the Options bar, as shown in Figure 13-1.

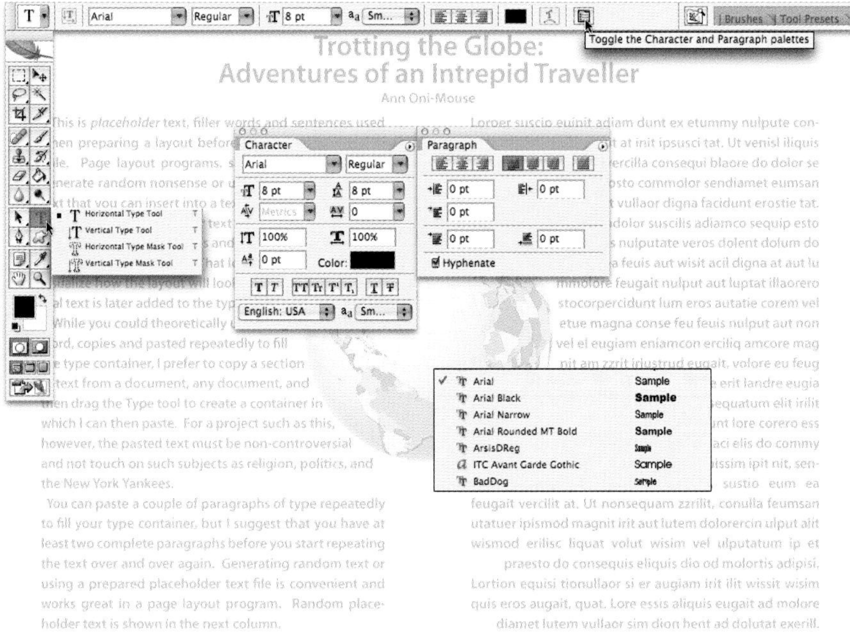


Figure 13-1: Photoshop gives you lots of tools for working with text.

Photoshop CS2 adds one of the most requested type-related features in the history of the program. For the first time, as you can see in the inset to the lower right in Figure 13-1, Photoshop's Font menu actually shows a preview sample of the font styles so that you don't need to memorize the appearance of all your various type faces. And you can choose Preferences➪Type to select from three different sizes for the font preview.

Type can be informative or decorative or both. You can use the type tools to add paragraphs of text or a single character as an element of your artwork. The text can be plain and unadorned or elaborately dressed up with *layer styles,* such as drop shadows, glows, bevel effects, and other effects that you apply to make the layer content fancier. However you use it, text can be a powerful element of both communication and symbolism. Take a look at Figure 13-2, in which I use the Type tool to add the binary code to the left and even the musical notes below.

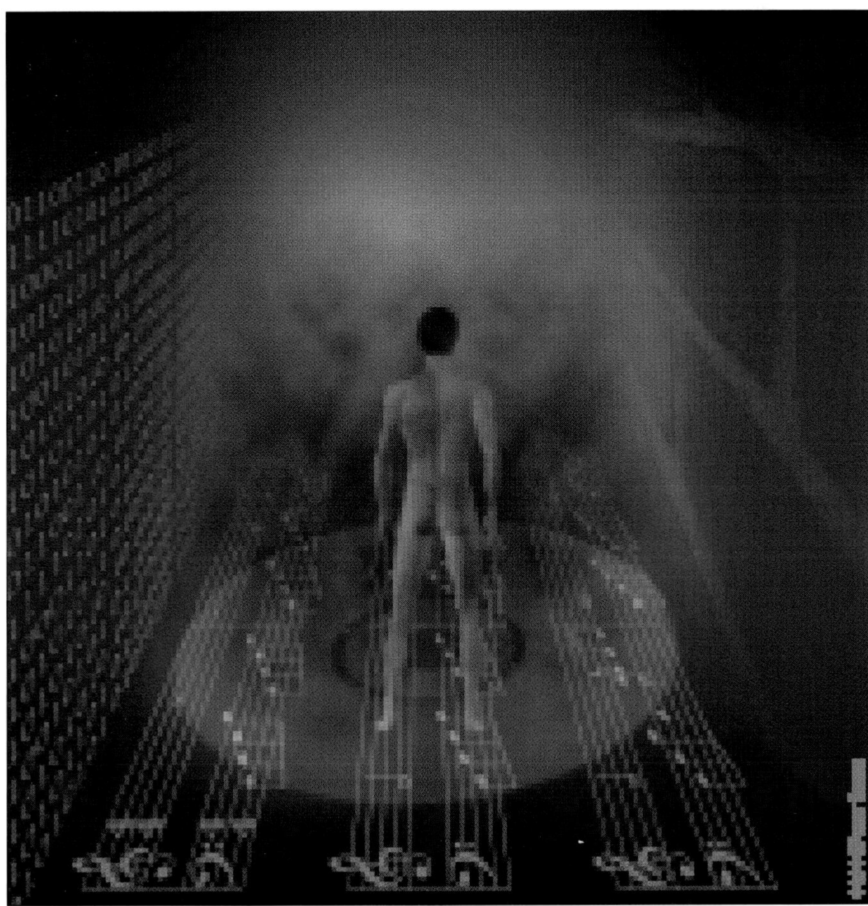

**Figure 13-2:** You can also use Photoshop's type as symbolic or decorative elements.

But before you add any text to your artwork, you need to have a good handle on the various type tools, palettes, menus, and options available to you. I start with an introduction to Photoshop's type tools.

### A type tool for every season, or reason

Photoshop offers four type tools — or, perhaps more accurately, two pairs of type tools — that assist you with adding text to your images. The Horizontal Type tool and the Vertical Type tool (the first pair) create *type layers,* which show up as special layers in the Layers palette that enable you to later re-edit the text that you put there. The Horizontal Type Mask tool and the Vertical Type Mask tool (the second pair) make selections on the active layer, just as if you had used the Rectangular Marquee or Lasso tools (as I describe in Chapter 8).

In addition to that glorious advantage of being able to easily correct accidental misspellings, creating and using type layers offer a number of other advantages. You can

- **Apply layer styles to type layers to fancy them up.** For example, try a simple Inner Bevel or Drop Shadow effect to make the words leap from the background.
- **Adjust type layer blending modes and opacity.** Doing this can help you achieve a unique integration with the artwork's other elements or background.
- **Produce extraordinarily crisp and clean type on the page.** When printing with a laser printer (or other PostScript device), the text on type layers prints beautifully.

Until the image is flattened or the type layer is merged or *rasterized* (converted to pixels), you can change any type attribute, such as the spelling, font, layer styles, opacity, and blending modes as I show in Figure 13-3.

You automatically gain the advantage of using type layers when you use the Horizontal Type or Vertical Type tools to add text to your images in Photoshop. (You can spot a type layer in the Layers palette easily. The layer shows a T instead of a preview for the layer thumbnail.)

When adding type to your image — whether a simple © Peter Bauer (yeah, okay, use your own name if you want) or a couple of columns of text to a brochure — you'll generally use the Horizontal Type or Vertical Type tools. But when, you might ask, would you ever need to use the type mask tools? Perhaps never. If you ever need a selection in the shape of your text, though, you can manage that trick by adding a type layer and then ⌘-clicking (Mac) or Ctrl-clicking (Windows) the type layer's thumbnail in the Layers palette. *Voilà!* You are presented with a text-shaped selection, *and* you still have an editable type layer that you can hide and save, just in case.

Figure 13-3: When you have type layer, you have the flexibility to make changes.

That, of course, doesn't answer the questions of why you might want a text-shaped selection in the first place, why type mask tools even exist, or why the sky is blue. Although the third question is probably better answered in a book named *Skies For Dummies,* here are a number of reasons to use a type mask tool:

- **Stroke:** You can *stroke* a selection, which adds a line of color along the path of the selection. With a type-shaped selection, this gives you a type-shaped line of color. Stroke a selection with the menu command Edit⇨Stroke.
- **Fill:** You can fill that selection with color, a gradient, or even a pattern with the Edit⇨Fill command.
- **Delete:** You can delete that selection from an existing area of color, creating a type-shaped hole in the color or layer. I chopped the words in Figure 13-4 from the key-shaped sign with a text-shaped selection made with the Horizontal Type Mask tool.

Figure 13-4: Use type mask tools to quickly and easily make text-shaped selections.

Whether working with type layers or creating type masks, you have the option of using either horizontal or vertical type. The difference between type that is set vertically and the more common horizontal type rotated 90 degrees is illustrated in Figure 13-5. The figure also shows that when you add text with a type mask tool, you see the characters cut out of a red overlay (top right in figure); when done, you see the traditional marching ants selection border (bottom right). Chapter 8 gives you more information on working with selections.

Figure 13-5: Vertical type stacks the individual characters. You can rotate horizontal type for a different look.

You can select type options before adding text to the image, or you can change your options afterward. When you make the type layer active in the Layers palette — but haven't yet selected any text in your image — any changes that you make are applied to all the text on the layer. You can also click and drag to select some of the text on the layer and make changes to only those characters or words.

When done adding or editing text, you can end the editing session in any of a number of ways:

- Click the check mark button (or the Cancel button) on the Options bar.
- Switch to a different tool in the Toolbox.
- On the keyboard, press ⌘+Return or Ctrl+Enter.
- ⌘+Shift-click or Ctrl+Shift-click to finish that type layer and start a new type layer.

## What are all those options?

Here you are, the proud owner of the world's state-of-the-art image editor, and now you're adding text, setting type, and pecking away on the keyboard. You're faced with a lot of variables. Which options are you going to need now and then? Which ones are you going to need all the time? Which ones can you ignore altogether? Read on as I introduce you to the various text and type variables, and toss in a few general guidelines on which options are most (and least) frequently required.

Take a look at Figure13-6, in which you can see (in all their glory) the most commonly used text attributes, all of which are available to you from the Options bar whenever a type tool is active.

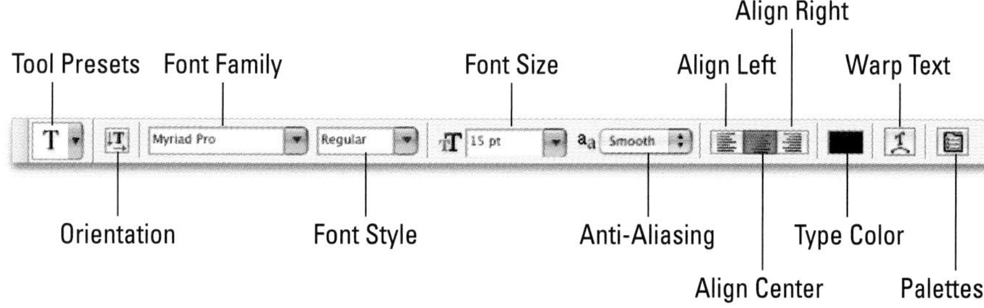


**Figure 13-6:** Use the Options bar to quickly and easily change the primary attributes of your text.

You can change the following text attributes via the Options bar, which is usually available at the top of your screen:

- **Tool Presets:** The Tool Presets palette enables you to select a predefined set of options that you've already saved. Say, for example, that you always use the same appearance for headlines in a recurring project and a different appearance for the body type. Set each up as a preset, and then activate all the options with a single click. (See Chapter 3 for more detailed information on tool presets.)
- **Orientation:** The Orientation button toggles existing type layers between horizontal and vertical. Regardless of what type is selected, the entire type layer is flipped when you click this button. (The button is grayed out when no type layer is active in the Layers palette.)
- **Font menu:** Click the triangle to the right of the Font Family field to open the Font menu, showing all your installed fonts in alphabetical order. You can also click in the field itself and use the arrow keys on your keyboard to switch fonts. If you select some type with a type tool first (as shown in Figure 13-7), using the arrow key automatically applies the change to the selected characters. If no characters are selected, you change the entire type layer.

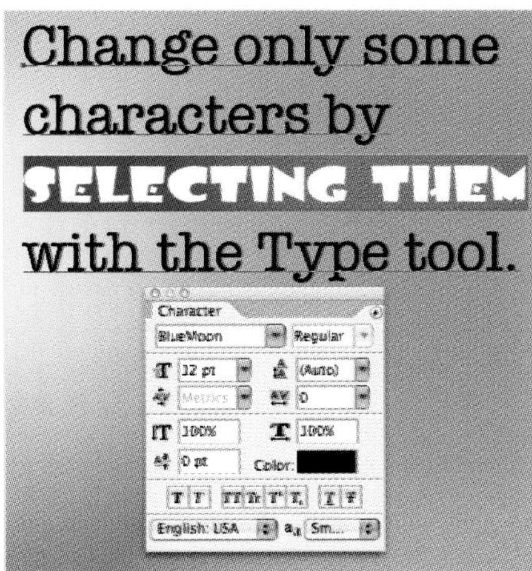


Figure 13-7: Select specific characters to change or make no selection to change all.

- **Font Style:** When a font has multiple styles built in, you can choose a variation of the font from the Font Style menu. Styles include Regular (or Roman), Bold, Semibold, Italic, Condensed, Light, and combinations thereof (as you see in Figure 13-8). Many fonts, however, have no built-in styles.

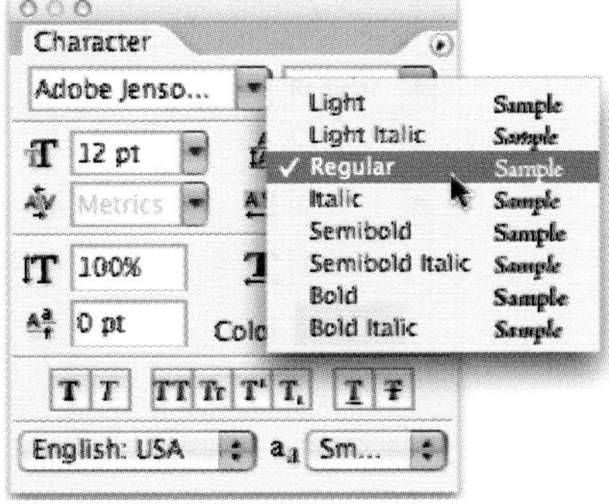


Figure 13-8: Some fonts have many styles available.

- **Font Size:** You can select a font size by typing a number in the Font Size field, by clicking the triangle to the right of the field and selecting a font size from the pop-up menu that appears, or by clicking the icon to the left of the Font Size field and then dragging left or right to change the value in the field. Font size is generally measured in *points* (1 point = 1/72 inch), but you can elect to use pixels or millimeters. Make the units change in Photoshop's Preferences (choose Preferences⇨Units & Rulers).

- **Anti-Aliasing:** *Anti-aliasing* softens the edges of each character so that it appears smooth onscreen. As part of this process, anti-aliasing hides the corners of the individual pixels with which the text is created. When outputting to a laser printer or other PostScript device, anti-aliasing isn't required. It is, however, critical when printing to an inkjet or when producing Web graphics. Generally, the choices here have little difference among them (other than None, of course). Smooth is a good choice unless your text begins to look blurry, in which case you should switch to Crisp. Use the Strong option with very large type when the individual character width must be preserved.
- **Alignment:** The three alignment choices on the Options bar determine how lines of type are positioned relative to each other. The buttons do a rather eloquent job of expressing themselves, wouldn't you say? ***Note:*** Don't confuse the term *alignment* with *justification,* which straightens both the left and right margins (and is selected in the Paragraph palette).
- **Type Color:** Click the color swatch on the Options bar to open the Color Picker and select a type color. You can select a color before adding text, or you can change the color of the text later. If you start by selecting a type layer from the Layers palette, you'll change all the characters on that layer when you select a new color in the Color Picker. Alternatively, use a type tool to select one or more characters for a color change, as you can see in Figure 13-9.
- **Warp Text:** Warp Text, which I discuss later in this chapter, bends the line of type according to any number of preset shapes, each of which can be customized with sliders. (The text in Figure 13-9 uses the Arc Lower warp style.) Keep in mind, however, that the Warp Text feature is not available when the Faux Bold style is applied through the Character palette. (I talk about faux styles later in this chapter.)

Each character in a type layer can have its own attributes. Click and drag over one or more characters with a type tool and then use the Options bar or Character palette to change the text attributes. Color, font, style — just about any attribute can be assigned.

Like many word processing programs, you can select an entire word in Photoshop by double-clicking (with a type tool) the word. Triple-click to select the entire sentence. Quadruple-click to select the entire paragraph. Click fives times very fast to select all the text.

Figure 13-9: Select any individual character and change its font, color, size, or any other attribute.

## Taking control of your text with palettes

For incredible control over the appearance of your text, use the Character and Paragraph palettes. In addition to all the text attributes available on the Options bar, the palettes provide a wide range of choices. With them, you can customize the general appearance of the text or apply sophisticated typographic styling.

The Character and Paragraph palettes can be shown and hidden by using the Palettes button on the Options bar or through Photoshop's Window menu. By default, the two palettes are nested together, so choosing Window⇨Character or Window⇨Paragraph makes both palettes available.

You can use the Character palette to edit a single selected character, a series of selected characters, or the entire content of a type layer. Figure 13-10 shows what you face when "building character" using this palette.

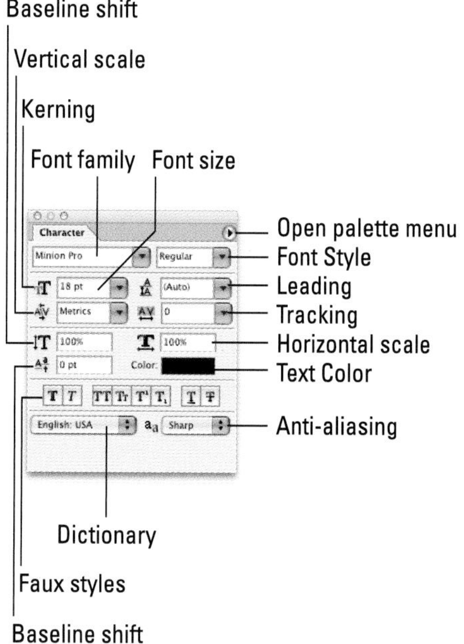


Figure 13-10: More choices than the Options bar!

Unless you're a fontographer, a number of the fields in the Character palette might require explanation:

- **Leading:** Leading (pronounced *LED-ding* — which refers to the lead [rather than *leed*] strips of metal that typesetters used to place between lines of type) is the vertical space between lines of text. Generally, you'll leave Leading set to Auto. However, you can select one or more lines of text (select the whole line) and change the spacing. Adding more space gives the text an airy, light appearance. Reducing the leading tightens up the text, which enables you to fit more lines in the same area.
- **Kerning:** The space between two characters is determined by the *kerning* built into a font. You can, however, override that spacing. Click with a type tool between two letters and then change the setting in the Kerning field to change the distance between the letters. You might, for example, want to reduce the kerning between a capital *P* and a lowercase *o* to tuck the second character protectively under the overhang of the taller letter. This can produce a cleaner and better-connected relationship between the two characters.
- **Scaling:** Vertical and horizontal scaling modifies the height and/or width of the selected character(s). You'll find this useful primarily for customizing short bits of type rather than long chunks of text.
- **Baseline Shift:** Produce subscript and superscript characters, such as those used in $H_2O$ and $e = mc^2$, with the Baseline Shift field. The Character palette's Baseline Shift option is best used in conjunction with a slight reduction in the font size for the specific character(s).

- **Faux Styles:** Use faux styles to apply the appearance of a character style, even when they're not built into the font. From the left, as the buttons show, the available faux styles are Bold, Italic, All Caps, Small Caps, Superscript, Subscript, Underline, and Strikethrough. Generally speaking, if a font offers a specific style in the Font Style menu, you'll use the font's built-in style rather than the faux style.
- **Dictionary:** Photoshop CS2 has almost two-dozen dictionaries built in. And, wonderfully or confusingly (depending on your personal linguistic talents), dictionaries can be assigned on a word-by-word (or even character-by-character) basis. You could, for example, insert a *bon mot* into the middle of your text (in the language of your choice), assign the appropriate language dictionary, and not have that phrase trigger an alert when you run a spell check (Edit⇨Check Spelling).

Type warping isn't available when Faux Bold is applied to any of the selected characters. As warped as it might sound, that's the only faux style that interferes with Warp Text.

You'll probably find yourself using certain sets of options pretty regularly in Photoshop. Luckily for you, you don't need to make changes on the Options bar and Character palette every time you want (for example) Arial Bold, 24 pt, Sharp anti-aliasing, 22 pt leading, and tracking +10. Set up the options once, and then click the Create New Toolset Preset button in the palette at the left end of the Options bar, as shown in Figure 13-11. The next time that you want those specific text attributes, select the preset from that palette, and you're ready to type!

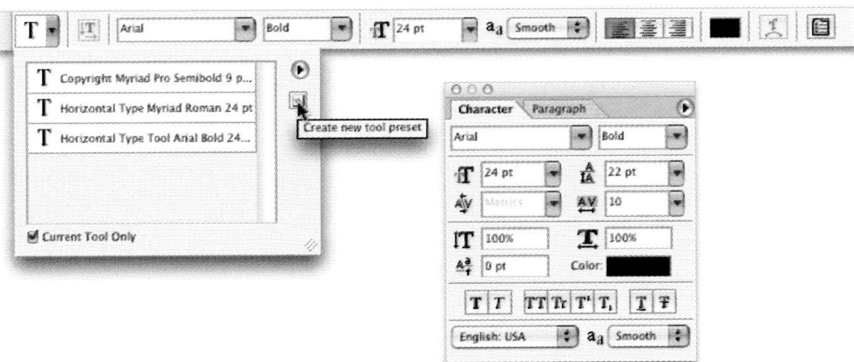


Figure 13-11: Tool presets can save you lots of time.

Photoshop's Paragraph palette is used, not surprisingly, with paragraph type. The alignment options that you see in the upper left of the Paragraph palette in Figure 13-12 can be applied to both point type and type on a path, but you can usually access your alignment options much more easily from the Options bar.

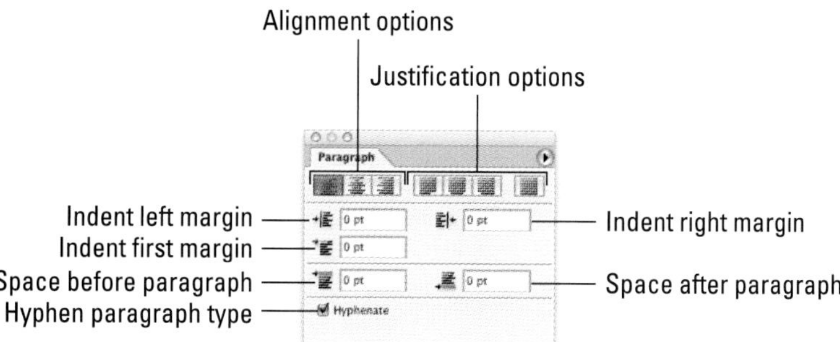


Figure 13-12: Most of this palette is only for paragraph type.

You'll see the term *type container* when I start discussing the Paragraph palette and paragraph type. Think of it as a rectangular column of text, with the words flowing from line to line, just as they do when you compose e-mail or use a word processor. You drag a type tool to create the rectangle, and then type inside that rectangle. In contrast, when you simply click a type tool and start typing, you need to press the Return (Mac) or Enter (Windows) key at the end of each line.

You'll find specific information about some of these options later in the chapter (when I discuss paragraph type), but here's a quick look at the other choices in the Paragraph palette:

- **Justification:** Unlike *alignment,* which balances lines of type based on a point of origin (left, center, or right), *justification* equalizes both the left and right margins of a paragraph of type. As you can see by the icons, the difference among the four options is the last line in the paragraph. That last line can be aligned left, centered, aligned right, or stretched to fit from left to right (called *full justification*).
- **Indent Margins:** Paragraphs of text can be indented from the left margin or from the right. Even if you have only a single word selected, the entire paragraph is indented. Harkening back to that last term paper you wrote (whenever that might have been), think in terms of a block quote. You can also use negative numbers in the Indent Margin fields, which extends the paragraph beyond the margin.

- **Indent First Line:** You can indent the first line of your paragraphs (or extend the first line to the left past the margin with a negative value) without having to press the Tab key. The option can be set before you start adding text and is applied to each paragraph.
- **Space Before/After:** When your type container includes multiple paragraphs, you can specify the distance that's automatically added between them. Rather than pressing the Return/Enter key an extra time between paragraphs, set the spacing in the Paragraph palette.
- **Hyphenation:** If you're using justification rather than alignment, I recommend keeping the Hyphenate check box marked. When words at the ends of lines of justified type are not hyphenated, the spacing within the lines can get rather messy. If you don't like the look of hyphens along the right margin and you don't like words that wrap from line to line, clear Hyphenate and don't justify your text.

Keep in mind that after you drag a type tool to create a type container, you can have as many paragraphs as fit. When you reach the end of a paragraph, press Return or Enter. A new paragraph is created within the type container. Consider the type container to be a column of text, such as you'd see in a newspaper, magazine, or newsletter.

## The palette menus — even more options

Like most of Photoshop's palettes, clicking the triangle in the upper-right corner of the Character or Paragraph palette opens the Palette menu, which holds a cornucopia of options you probably never need to see. (Consider this: If it truly were a *really* important option, it would be easier to get to, wouldn't it?)

As you can see in Figure 13-13, not all menu options are available for all fonts. Some of the options are merely command forms of the palette menus (such as the faux styles), and other options are specific to Japanese fonts. A number of the options apply only to *OpenType fonts,* which include a much larger selection of *glyphs* (characters) than do other fonts.

**Figure 13-13:** Not all options are used with all fonts.

Here are a couple of palette menu options with which you should be familiar:

- **Fractional Widths:** When selected, Photoshop uses this option to adjust the spacing between letters on an individual basis. Will you or I spot the difference? Not with large type, but if you're creating small text (especially for the Web), clear this option. How small is small? Generally 10 pt or smaller.
- **System Layout:** Unless you need to match the appearance of text in Mac's TextEdit or Windows Notepad, leave this option deselected. When might you need it? When designing interface items for a program or game.
- **No Break:** When working with paragraph type, you can select one or more words and choose No Break to prevent them from being hyphenated. You might want to do this with words that are difficult to recognize when split between two lines.
- **Roman Hanging Punctuation:** Found on the Paragraph palette menu, this option permits the smaller punctuation marks located at the left and right margins of justified text to hang out past the margins. When quotation marks and the like are outside the margin, the margin itself has a cleaner look. Don't use this option if your layout can't handle text that extends past the edges of your column.
- **Adobe Composer:** This choice is actually quite simple: Single-Line Composer looks at one line of type to determine hyphenation. Every-Line Composer looks at the entire block of text, generally producing a more pleasing appearance.
- **Reset (palette name):** If you're seeing some strange behavior from your type tools, you might want to invoke the Reset Character and Reset Paragraph commands. Each restores the settings in the palette to their defaults, eliminating any errant setting that might be causing the problem.

## Putting a picture in your text

Enough of that heavy stuff for now — time to take a look at one of the coolest things that you can do with text. Here's an easy way to create a text-shaped picture, one that's fully editable.

1. **Using File⇨Open, Adobe Bridge, or by double-clicking an image file, open a photo in Photoshop.**
2. **If the Layers palette has a layer named *Background,* double-click the layer name and rename the layer (as shown in Figure 13-14). If the image has multiple layers, choose Layer⇨Merge Visible from the main menu.**

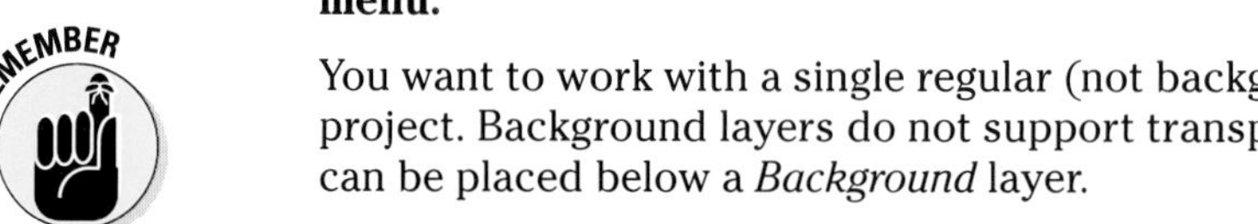

You want to work with a single regular (not background) layer for this project. Background layers do not support transparency, and no layers can be placed below a *Background* layer.

Figure 13-14: Renaming a background layer converts it to a regular layer.

3. **Add your type with the Horizontal Type tool.**
4. **Click the type layer in the Layers palette and drag it below the image layer.**
5. **In the Layers palette, Option-click (Mac) or Alt-click (Windows) on the line between the two layers.**

   The two layers are joined together, as shown in Figure 13-15. When you clip two layers, the lower layer serves as a *mask* for the upper layer. The upper layer is visible only where the lower layer has pixels and adopts the opacity of those lower-layer pixels.
6. **Finish the image with a layer style (applied to the lower layer) and any other artwork that the project requires.**

   You can click the lower layer in the Layers palette and then click a favorite layer style in the Styles palette. Or, of course, you can create a custom layer style by choosing the Layer⇨Layer Style command. In Figure 13-16, you see a stroke, a bevel, and a slight outer glow applied to the GARDENS layer.

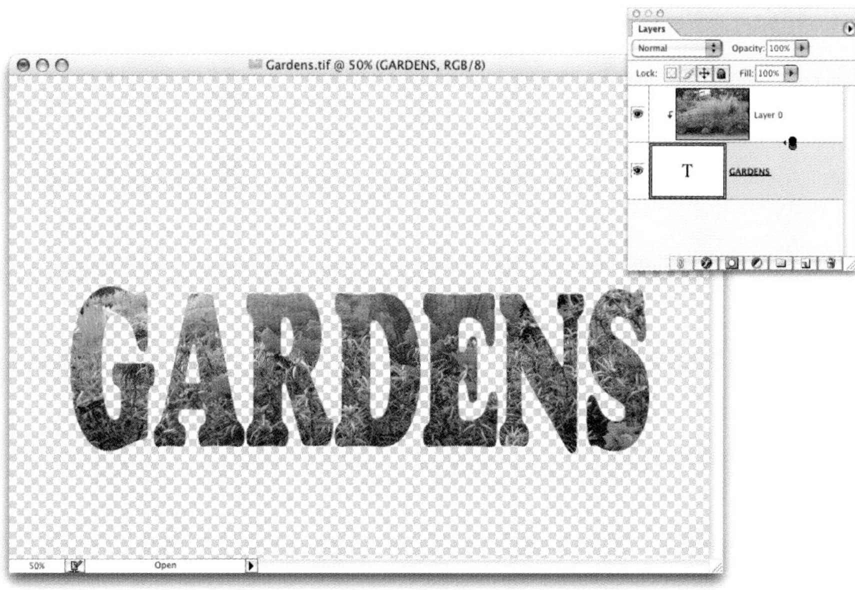


Figure 13-15: "Clip" the upper layer to the lower layer.

Figure 13-16: Add layer styles to the lower layer so that the effects are visible.

# Creating Paragraphs with Type Containers

Although the vast majority of the text that you add to Photoshop artwork is *point* type — that is, type that exists on just one or a couple of lines — you'll certainly find situations in which you need to use paragraph type in a type container. The primary advantage of using a type container is *word wrap*. While you type, the text automatically starts a new line every time it reaches the margin.

"Why is that a big deal?" you might ask. "I don't mind pressing the Return or Enter key at the end of each line." Ah, but consider the ever-present (when you type like me) typographical error! What if the very first sentence of your manual-Return paragraph is missing a word? To insert that word and maintain a visually pleasing right margin, you'd need to go back and redo every line of type. With paragraph type, the content of each line automatically adjusts as you insert that forgotten word.

The difference between point type to create a column of type and paragraph type is comparable with the difference between a typewriter and a word processor. (If you're old enough to remember Wite-Out and Liquid Paper, raise your hand, but not for very long — I don't want to tire you out.)

Adding a type container is simple. Click and drag with the Horizontal Type tool (or, in some rare cases, you might want to use the Vertical Type tool), and then start typing. The type automatically starts the next line as soon as you press enough keys to reach the far margin. You can keep typing until you fill the type container. Press Return or Enter whenever you want to start a new paragraph within your type container.

You can also copy/paste text from a word processing or text editing program. You can, for example, open a Microsoft Word document in Word, select the text that you want by clicking and dragging, and then choose Word's Edit⇨Copy command to place the text into the computer's memory (on the *Clipboard*). Switch to your Photoshop document; select a font, font size, and other attributes; drag a type container; and then choose Edit⇨Paste (or the comparable keyboard shortcut) to place your text inside the container. When the text you need already exists, you not only save time by using copy/paste, but you also eliminate the possibility of introducing typos.

But what if you have more text than fits in the type container? Unlike Illustrator and InDesign, you can't *link* two type containers, enabling the excess text to automatically move to the next container. Photoshop does, however, remind you that your text doesn't fit by showing you a symbol in the lower-right corner of the type container's *bounding box* — the dashed line surrounding the type container. As you can see in Figure 13-17, the lower-right anchor point of the bounding box has a plus sign in it.

When you have more text than the type container can hold, you have a number of options:

- **Enlarge the type container.** Click one of the bounding box's anchor points and drag to increase the size of the type container. Making a type container a little bit wider often gives you an extra line or two of text at the bottom.
- **Shrink the font.** Select the text with a keyboard shortcut (⌘+A/Ctrl+A) and select a smaller font size on the Options bar.
- **Decrease the space between lines.** Select the text and decrease the *leading* — the amount of space between lines of type — in the Leading field found in the upper right of the Character palette. By default (the Auto setting in the Leading field), Photoshop uses an amount equal to 120 percent of the font size. You can often reduce the leading to 1 or 2 pt larger than the font size before you start overlapping lowercase letters with descenders (*g, j, p, q,* and *y*) and uppercase letters on the line below.
- **Edit the text.** Rephrase the text, using fewer words to convey the same message. If you're not the author, however, this option might not be available.

This is *placeholder* text, filler words and sentences used when preparing a layout before the actual text is available. Page layout programs, such as Adobe InDesign, generate random nonsense or use prepared placeholder text that you can insert into a text frame. It doesn't really matter what the placholder text is about, as long as it uses normal-length words and sentences so that is looks like real text. That lets you better visualize how the layout will look when the real text is later added to the type container.

While you could theoretically use a single word, copies and pasted repeatedly to fill the type container, I prefer to copy a section of text from a document, any document, and then drag the Type tool to create a container in which I can then paste. For a project such as this, however, the pasted text must be non-controversial and not touch on such subjects as religion, politics, and the New York Yankees.

You can paste a couple of paragraphs of type repeatedly to fill your type container, but I suggest that you have at least two complete paragraphs before you start repeating the text over and over again. Generating random text or using a prepared placeholder text file is convenient and works great in a page layout program. Random text generated by InDesign may appear to be in a foreign language, but is actually just nonsense, strings of random letters, in random lengths, with periods at the ends of the "sentences" and line breaks at the end of "paragraphs." If you look closely at random place

line breaks at the
at random place

Figure 13-17: A plus sign in the lower-right anchor point warns you that text doesn't fit in the type container.

## Selecting alignment or justification

Photoshop gives you several options for controlling the appearance of your margins. In the "Taking control of your text with palettes" section earlier in this chapter, I outline a number of options that you can find on the Paragraph palette menu. But let me go into more detail about a couple of options that you have when adding paragraph type.

Perhaps the most important decision (other than font and font size) that you make when preparing paragraph type is a choice of alignment or justification. When text is *aligned left,* the left margin is perfectly straight, and the right margin is *ragged,* with each line ending where it ends, without any relationship to the lines of type above and below. A column of text that's *aligned right* has a clean right margin and a ragged left margin. If you choose *center aligned,* the middle of each line of text is centered. Take a look at Figure 13-18 for a visual comparison.

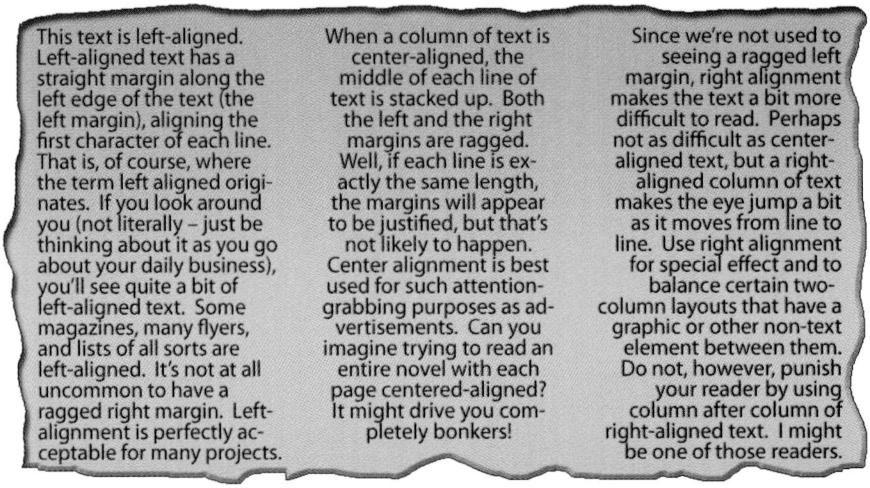

This text is left-aligned. Left-aligned text has a straight margin along the left edge of the text (the left margin), aligning the first character of each line. That is, of course, where the term left aligned originates. If you look around you (not literally – just be thinking about it as you go about your daily business), you'll see quite a bit of left-aligned text. Some magazines, many flyers, and lists of all sorts are left-aligned. It's not at all uncommon to have a ragged right margin. Left-alignment is perfectly acceptable for many projects.

When a column of text is center-aligned, the middle of each line of text is stacked up. Both the left and the right margins are ragged. Well, if each line is exactly the same length, the margins will appear to be justified, but that's not likely to happen. Center alignment is best used for such attention-grabbing purposes as advertisements. Can you imagine trying to read an entire novel with each page centered-aligned? It might drive you completely bonkers!

Since we're not used to seeing a ragged left margin, right alignment makes the text a bit more difficult to read. Perhaps not as difficult as center-aligned text, but a right-aligned column of text makes the eye jump a bit as it moves from line to line. Use right alignment for special effect and to balance certain two-column layouts that have a graphic or other non-text element between them. Do not, however, punish your reader by using column after column of right-aligned text. I might be one of those readers.

**Figure 13-18:** Compare the left and right margins of each column of text.

Unlike alignment, justification gives you straight margins on both sides of the column of text. The four justification options at the top of the Paragraph palette differ only in how they treat the last line of a paragraph. As you can see from the Paragraph palette buttons, the last line can be independently aligned left, center, or right; or it can be fully justified, spreading the last line from margin to margin. You shouldn't use the fourth option unless that last line (of every paragraph) is rather full because it looks rather strange when just a couple of words are stretched edge to edge.

### Ready, BREAK! Hyphenating your text

When a word is too long to fit on the current line of text, it can either be moved to the beginning of the next line (wrapped), or it can be broken into two parts: one finishing the upper line, and the other starting the next line (hyphenated).

The hyphenation options are for the truly geeky, *my-typography-is-my-life* types. The defaults are excellent and can suffice for all but the most precise layouts (which you should be doing in InDesign or perhaps Illustrator, anyway).

If you want to fine-tune how hyphenation is applied (or have far too much time on your hands), select Hyphenate from the Paragraph palette menu to open the options shown in Figure 13-19. The Hyphenation check box (upper left) activates/deactivates hyphenation. The top three fields govern which words to hyphenate and what limits to place on the hyphenation. (Think of the second and third fields as *Hyphenate or cram into the line without hyphenating.*) The lower two fields control the appearance of the opposite margin, limiting the number of consecutive lines that can be hyphenated and the maximum distance from that margin that a hyphen can be placed.

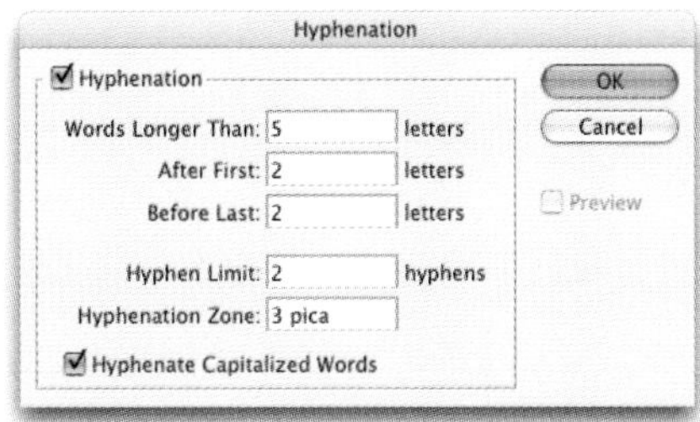


**Figure 13-19:** Default hyphenation values give you good results and a pleasing appearance.

## Shaping Up Your Language with Warp Text and Type on a Path

You can change the line along which your type flows by using either the Warp Text feature or by typing on a path. Type warping uses predefined shapes to which your type is formed (and can be used with both point and paragraph type), and typing on a path uses a custom path (and is used only with point type).

Warping type and placing type along a path are great ways to spice up your message as long as you don't overdo it and make the message illegible or distract from the overall appearance of your artwork. Warp Text is a quick and easy way to bend text, and placing type on a path is a more complex — and more controlled — technique.

## Applying the predefined warps

With a type layer active in the Layers palette and a type tool selected, click the button to the right of the color swatch on the Options bar. That opens the Warp Text dialog box, as shown in Figure 13-20, in which you choose both the distortion you want to apply as well as the settings.

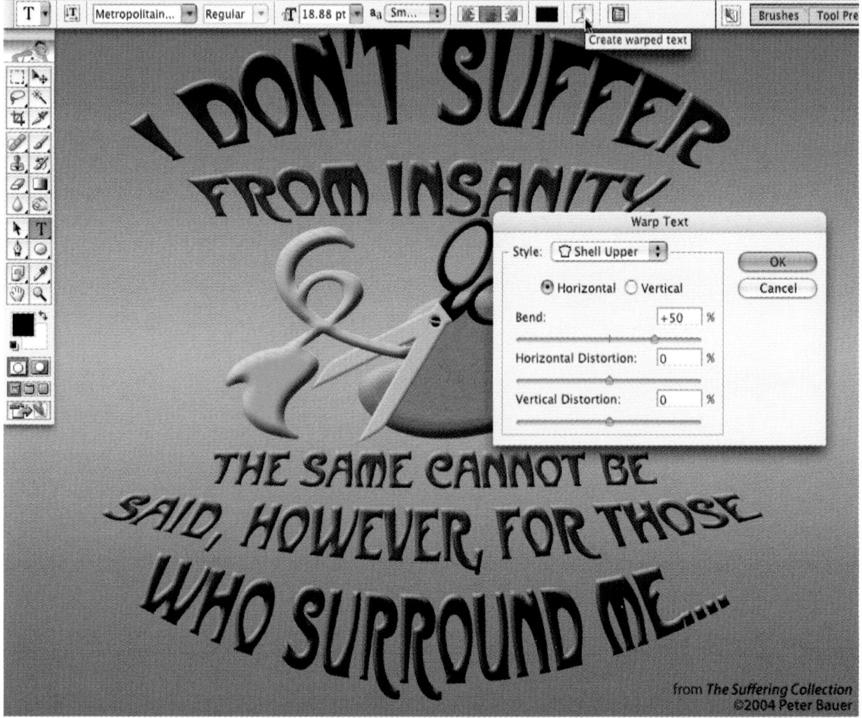


Figure 13-20: The illustration uses two separate type layers, each with its own Warp Text settings.

Photoshop CS2 offers 15 different Warp Text presets, each of which you can customize by dragging any of three sliders. As you can see in Figure 13-21, negative numbers can be used, too, reversing the warp. And note that the Horizontal and Vertical buttons are not available for some of the styles. Warp Text is one of Photoshop's truly fun features. The best way to become familiar with it is to open the dialog box and test-drive each of the variations. And don't forget to try the Horizontal and Vertical buttons when they're available!

Figure 13-21: Dragging the sliders back and forth in combination can produce some excellent results!

Keep in mind, too, that you can set the Bend slider to 0 and adjust the lower two sliders to create the appearance of depth or perspective for a type layer. Figure 13-22 shows both horizontal and vertical distortion to create a two-plane perspective change. And take a look at the Layers palette — when Warp Text is applied to a layer, the layer thumbnail changes to that feature's icon.

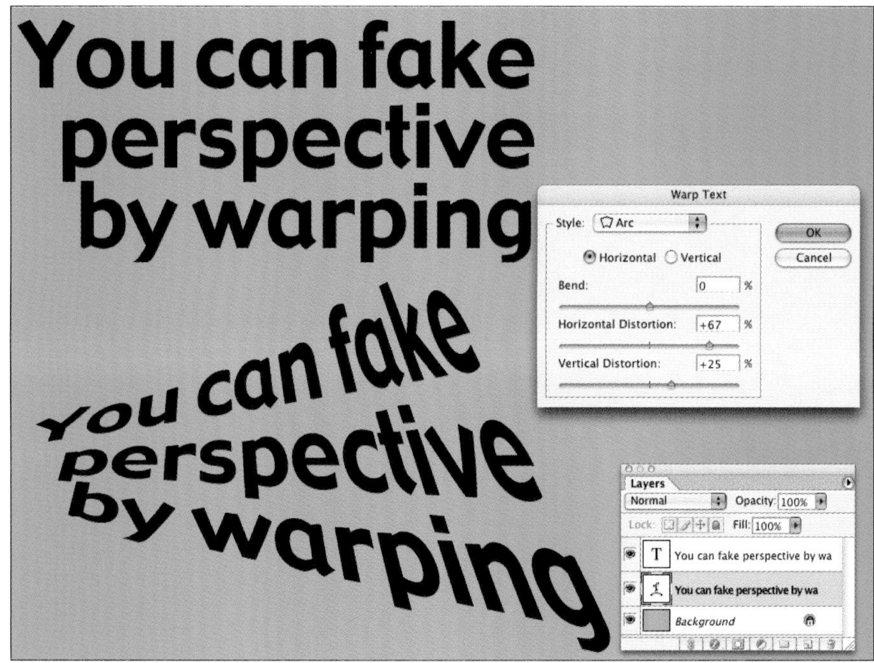


Figure 13-22: There's no formula for warping type. When the preview looks right to you, the settings are correct.

## Customizing the course with paths

You can use the shape tools or the Pen tool to create a custom path along which you add your text. (You find full information about paths and shape layers in Chapter 11.) To add type along a path, simply select the Horizontal Type or Vertical Type tool, click the path, and type. The flow of the type from the point on the path where you click is determined by the alignment option that you select from the Options bar or the Paragraph palette. If the text is left-aligned, characters are added to the right of the point where you click (called the *point of origin* for the type). Left alignment is great when adding type along an open path, such as the upper path in Figure 13-23. You might, however, want to choose center alignment when adding type along the top of an arc or circle, so you can click on the top of the arc and not worry about dragging the type later to center it.

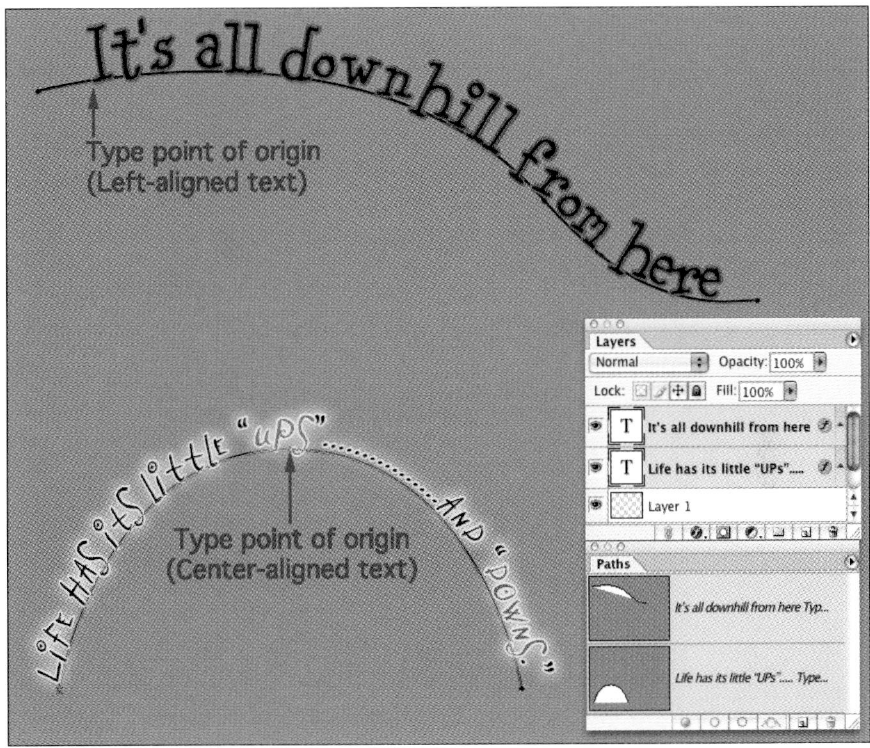


Figure 13-23: Text alignment determines where the text goes from the point where you click on the path.

If you want type to go in two different directions — say, pointed upward along both the top and the bottom of a circle — you need to create two separate paths and two separate type layers, as shown in Figure 13-24.

Figure 13-24: Sometimes you need to create two separate type layers, using two separate paths, to achieve your artistic goals.

After you add your type to the path, you can press the ⌘/Ctrl key and reposition the type along the path by dragging. When you press and hold ⌘/Ctrl, the type tool's cursor changes to an I-beam cursor with a heavy black arrow on either side, indicating which way you can drag the type. You see the type's point of origin as a hollow diamond on the path (not to be confused with the hollow squares that represent the path's anchor points). Take a look at Figure 13-25 for a zoomed-in look at the converted cursor and a comparison of the point of origin diamond and the anchor point square. Note, too, that not only can you drag type along a path, but you can also drag it *across* the path, flipping over the type.

After flipping type across a path, you might need to adjust the *tracking* (the space between characters), which is the second field from the top on the right in the Character palette. And don't be afraid to click in the type and press the spacebar a few times to adjust the placement of words along the path.

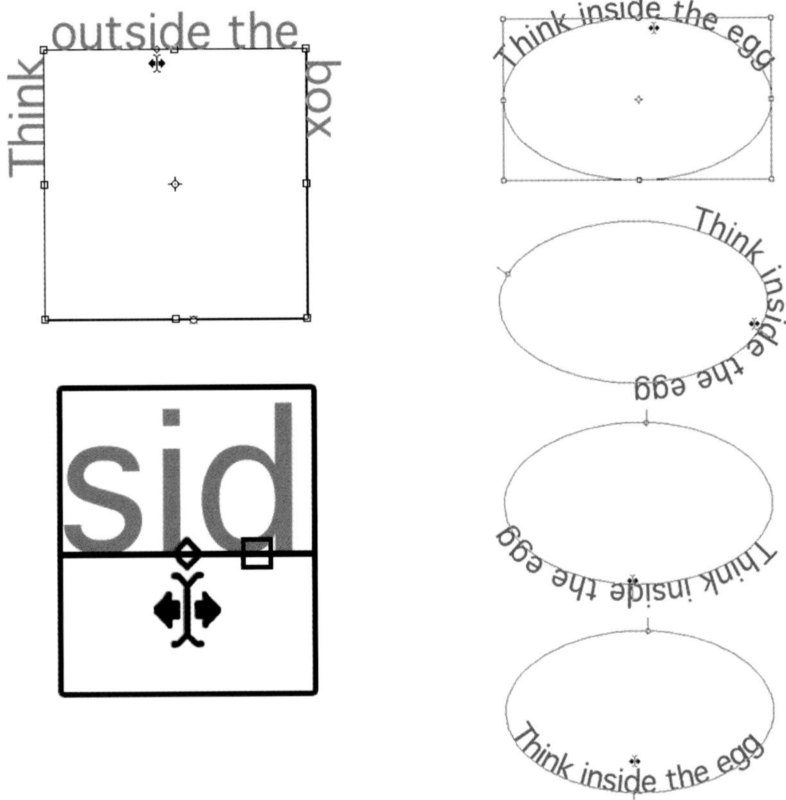


Figure 13-25: When you drag the cursor across the path a short distance, type flips over.

# Finding and Adding Fonts

You already have a nice selection of fonts installed on your computer. Some are installed with the operating system (Windows or Mac), a number of fonts are installed with Photoshop CS2, and other programs could have tossed more morsels into the stew. However, you might find that the more you work with text, the more you crave additional fonts.

## Downloading and purchasing fonts

You can find many places on the Web to download free fonts. I must warn you, though, that some free fonts are problematic and can cause instability. In addition, don't download any bitmap fonts, no matter how cool they look. Always stick with PostScript fonts (True Type, Type1, and OpenType). In a wholly nonpreferential, alphabetical order, here are a few of my favorite sites for downloading free fonts.

- www.1001fonts.com
- www.abstractfonts.com
- www.chank.com
- www.fonthead.com
- www.larabiefonts.com

A number of Web sites that don't specialize in fonts also offer them. Stock photo sites, clip art sites, and even general graphics-related sites often have free fonts available. Collections of commercial fonts can be purchased from a wide variety of sources, including my two favorite font sources:

- www.adobe.com/type
- www.fonts.com

Although having lots of fonts can stretch your options, too many fonts can lead to slowdowns and other problems. If you do find yourself someday with a massive collection of fonts, none of which you could bear to part with, use a font management utility. The Mac OS has the built-in Font Book, and Extensis (www.extensis.com) offers Suitcase (available online for about $100) for both platforms.

If you download fonts from a Web site, be aware that the files might be compressed. Compressing a downloadable file does several things:

- **Provides for a faster download:** The smaller the file, the less time it takes to travel through cyberspace from the Web server to your computer.
- **Reduces storage:** A compressed file takes up less space on the Web server's hard drive — and less space on yours, too! After installing the font, move the compressed file to a safe place to save as a backup. And consider burning your special font files to CD for security.
- **Allows for secure transmittal:** Files that are compressed are less likely to become corrupted in transit and are also less likely to set off alarm bells for your antivirus software.

How can you tell whether a file is compressed? Look at the file extension at the end of the filename. If you see .zip (both platforms) or .sit or .sea (Mac only), you have a compressed file. Simply double-click the file to launch the StuffIt (Mac) or WinZip (Windows) utility before attempting to install the font.

## Installing (and removing) fonts: Mac

To make a font available to all programs (and to all users in a multi-user environment), install it at the system level by copying the font file to the folder

[*harddrive*].Library.Fonts

To restrict the font to a single user, perhaps for licensing reasons, install the font into this folder:

```
[harddrive].Users.[username].Library.Fonts
```

Quit Photoshop (and any other font-using programs) before installing fonts.

To remove a font, quit all programs that use fonts, go to the appropriate Fonts folder, and drag the font to the Trash. Why would you ever delete a font? You might find that the font menu is too crowded, making it difficult to find the font you need. You might have accidentally installed multiple versions of a single font. The font itself might not work properly. Or, of course, it might just be a truly ugly and worthless font that was installed with a collection.

Remember, too, that some programs — our beloved Photoshop CS2 among them — install fonts into special folders so that they don't have to share them with all the other programs. But sharing is nice, don't you think? You can move many of the fonts from their secret hiding places into the main Fonts folder to make them available to all programs. Photoshop installs fonts into the folder

```
[harddrive].Library.Application Support.Adobe.Fonts
```

Do *not* move the fonts in the folder named Reqrd. (That's a secret Adobe code that means *required*.) If you move those fonts, Photoshop is likely to become very, very unhappy and not play with you at all.

### Installing (and removing) fonts: Windows

Certain fonts should *never* be moved, copied, deleted, or perhaps even thought about after the sun goes down. These fonts are critical for the performance of the operating system or a specific program. They can generally be recognized by location (in a hidden folder in Windows, or a folder named Required) or by an exceptionally cryptic filename with underscores and numbers. When in doubt, err on the side of caution.

## It's a family affair

Generally, folks toss off the term *font* incorrectly. To be precise, you should usually use the term *font family*. For example, Times is a font family. Arial is a font family. Myriad Pro is a font family. Comparatively, Times New Roman Bold 24 pt is a font, and Minion Pro Semibold Italic 24 pt is a font.

When does it actually matter? Well, you might want to recognize the difference when shopping for collections of fonts or perhaps for a laser printer. One collection (or printer) might advertise *2,500 Fonts!* while another offers only 100. You can be pretty sure that one is referring to fonts and the other to font families. But when you're just chatting, saying *font* is perfectly fine — now that we all understand the difference.

After you copy or download (and decompress, if necessary) your new font file, quit all programs that use fonts (including Photoshop). Choose Start⇨Control Panel and then double-click Fonts in the Control Panel window to access the Fonts dialog box. On the File menu, choose Install New Font. In the Add Fonts dialog box, shown in Figure 13-26, navigate to and select your new font file or files, and then click OK. The font is added to the Fonts folder and made available to all font-using programs.

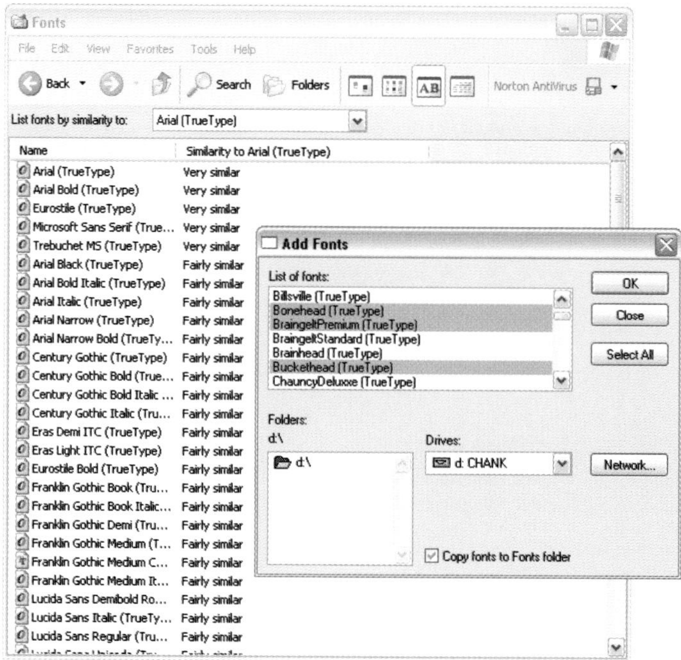

Figure 13-26: The three selected fonts are copied from their CD to the Fonts folder.

To remove one or more fonts, open the Fonts dialog box from the Control Panel, select the font(s), and choose Delete from the File menu. As when you add a new font, close all font-using software before deleting fonts.

When you're in the Fonts folder, take a look at the View menu. Try the List Fonts by Similarity option. Select a font and watch how Windows rearranges the content of the font list to show you which fonts are closest in appearance (and which are extremely different, too). Oh, and by the way, you can double-click any font in the list to open a preview of the font, which you can print to create your own font book.

# Chapter 14

# Painting in Photoshop

### In This Chapter

- Adding color manually for complete control
- Discovering tools with brushes and tools without
- Traversing that amazing Brushes palette
- Creating do-it-yourself brushes

*Painting.* The word evokes images of brushes and palettes and color being precisely applied to canvas. Or, perhaps, images of rollers and buckets, color being slopped on a wall and spread around. It doesn't generally bring to mind digital image editing. But painting certainly has a place in your arsenal of Photoshop skills, even if you never create an image from scratch.

In addition to painting landscapes and portraits (which you certainly can do in Photoshop, if you have the talent and training), you use Photoshop's painting tools for a variety of other tasks. For example, you can paint to create masks and layer masks, adjust tonality or sharpness in specific areas, repair blemishes and other damage in an image — even to create graphic elements and special effects.

In this chapter, I concentrate on those editing-related painting skills rather than fine art painting. I introduce you to the basic concepts of painting in Photoshop and also walk you through the basic brush-related tools and the Brushes palette, concentrating on those features that you most likely need (as well as a few of the other, more artistic features). To wrap up the chapter, I show you how to create custom brush tips and how to save them for future use.

## Discovering Photoshop's Painting Tools

Nothing in Photoshop gives you more precise control of color in your image than using the Pencil tool with a 1-pixel brush. Remember that your image consists of a whole lot of little colored squares (pixels) and that the color of those individual squares is what produces the appearance of a tree or a sunset or even good ol' Uncle Bob. If you zoom in really close on an image, you can paint pixel by pixel — you could even create an entire image, one pixel at a time!

Whether you're using a tiny brush with the Pencil tool or a larger one with the Brush tool, adding color to your image with the painting tools enables you create beautiful or whimsical imagery, such as that shown in Figure 14-1 (with acknowledgment to Picasso's *Woman with Pears*).

As you work in Photoshop, however, you'll find many very important roles for the brush-using tools other than creating imagery. From touching up dust and scratches in a scan to removing distant power lines from a photo to perhaps adding wispy hairs to soften the outline of a head, you have lots of reasons to paint in Photoshop (many of which you can read about in Chapters 9 and 10). When you're capable and confident using the Brush tool, you might even find it the best way to make selections in your image. Selections with the Brush tool? That's right — painting in an alpha channel creates or refines a saved selection. (You can read about alpha channels in Chapter 8.)

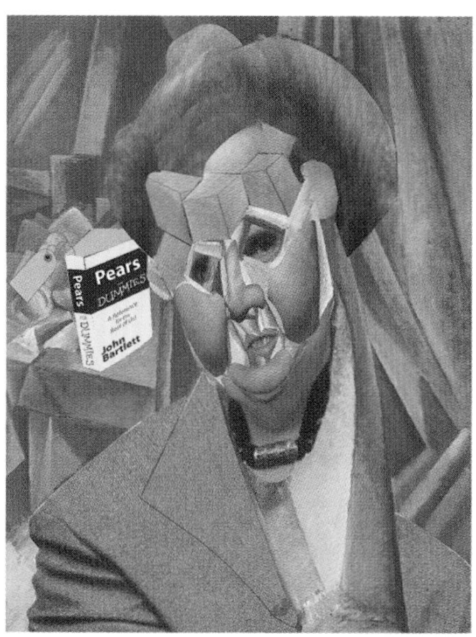


*Original artwork ©2005 Peter Bauer*

**Figure 14-1:** Painting with the Brush tool is yet another way to create in Photoshop.

You have 17 tools that use brushes available in Photoshop CS2. Here are just a few of the things that you can do with these tools:

- Add color (Brush, Pencil)
- Adjust tonality (Burn, Dodge)
- Sharpen, blur, and smear (Sharpen, Blur, Smudge)

- Correct color and texture (Healing Brush, Spot Healing Brush, Color Replacement)
- Copy/paste pixels (Clone Stamp)

In this section, I discuss the primary painting tools and introduce you to some of the other brush-using tools. (Check Chapter 9 for additional information on healing and cloning in your image.)

## Painting with the Brush tool

You control where the Brush tool works by selecting a brush tip of a particular size, shape, and *hardness* (the fuzziness, or lack thereof, along the edges of a round brush tip). Remember, too, that you can use the Brush and other painting tools to create subtle changes in existing colors. By selecting an appropriate blending mode and opacity, you can mix the painting color into the existing colors in your image. Make these basic decisions from the Options bar, shown for the Brush tool in Figure 14-2.

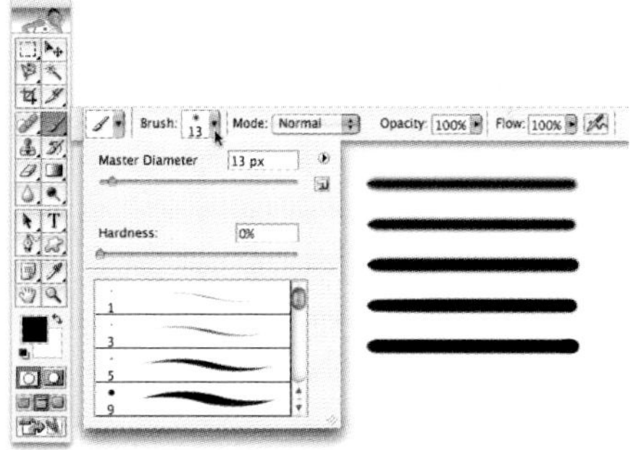


Figure 14-2: Make the primary decisions about painting tool behavior from the Options bar.

As you see in Figure 14-2, the Options bar gives you access to a mini-Brushes palette, from which you can pick a brush tip, change its size, and adjust the hardness of the brush's edges. (Only round brush tips use the Hardness adjustment.) The five sample lines to the right show Hardness, from 0% to 100% in 25% increments, all using a 13-pixel brush. The Brush tool can use any brush tip that you have in the Brushes palette — and, as you can read later in this chapter, you can customize the brush tip in a variety of ways.

You're actually ready to paint in Photoshop already! Select a foreground color, select the brush size that you want, decide how hard or fuzzy the edges should be, change the blending mode and opacity (if desired), and drag the tool in your image. (And, perhaps best of all, no turpentine needed for cleaning up — just switch tools in the Toolbox.)

As you work with the brush-using tools, always remember that the selected brush tip is applied as a series of individual impressions, called *instances.* Consider an instance to be a single impression of the brush tip, like tapping a pen once on a piece of paper — it leaves a single dot. Take a look at the outer borders in Figure 14-3. Changing the brush tip's Spacing value (in the main Brushes palette, found in the Option bar's Palette Well) shows how instances appear. In the upper left, the spacing is set to the default 25% and a continuous line results. To the upper right, Spacing is set to 67%, and the individual brush tip instances are visible as overlapping circles. To the lower left, Spacing is set to 133% — this is a setting that you might use for a dotted or dashed line — and each brush tip instance is visible individually.

Figure 14-3: Changing the Spacing makes the individual brush tip *instances* visible.

Here's one other option that you should know about before getting too far into the discussion of painting tools. In Photoshop's Preferences➪Display & Cursors menu, you have a couple of additional ways to show the cursor when a brush-using tool is active. As in prior versions of Photoshop, you can show the cursor as the active tool (although you can see that already in the Toolbox and the Options bar), as a tiny crosshair (for precision), or in the shape and size of the brush tip. New in Photoshop CS2, you can elect to show the cursor as *Full Size Brush Tip,* which uses the same shape and size with one difference. When you have a round brush tip with a Hardness setting of less than 100%, this new option uses a circle that encompasses every pixel to be changed. (The now-named Normal Brush Tip trims the circle back to a diameter enclosing pixels that will be *most* affected by the tool.) Here's one additional change in the Preferences: You now have the Show Crosshairs in Brush Tip check box available that adds the precise cursor's crosshairs in the middle of the Normal Brush Tip and Full Size Brush Tip cursors. Great for painting along edges!

If you know you have the cursor set to show the brush tip, but you're seeing the tiny little crosshairs instead, check the Caps Lock key on your keyboard. Caps Lock toggles between precise and brush-size cursors for the brush-using tools.

When you change the Brush tool's Opacity setting on the Options bar, you change the appearance of the stroke as a whole. Changing the Flow setting (also on the Options bar), on the other hand, changes the amount of color applied with each instance of the brush tip. When the flow is reduced and the spacing is set to less than 100%, the overlapping area of each brush instance appears darker (or lighter when painting with, for example, white on black). Back in Figure 14-3, a Flow of 50% for the stroke with Spacing set to 67% shows as a series of interlocked, overlapping gray circles, darker where they overlap. If, on the other hand, Flow were set to 100% and Opacity were set to 50%, you'd see the same stroke as Figure 14-3, just gray rather than black.

One last option for the Brush tool deserves a quick look. To the right of the Flow field is the Airbrush button. When the Airbrush is on (the button turns dark), the Flow value takes on more meaning. As you paint with the Brush in Airbrush mode with a reduced Flow setting, pausing the cursor with the mouse button down allows color to build up (become more opaque) as if you were using a real airbrush. You can use the Airbrush both as a traditional airbrush artist and to simulate spray paint. You can see both in Figure 14-4.

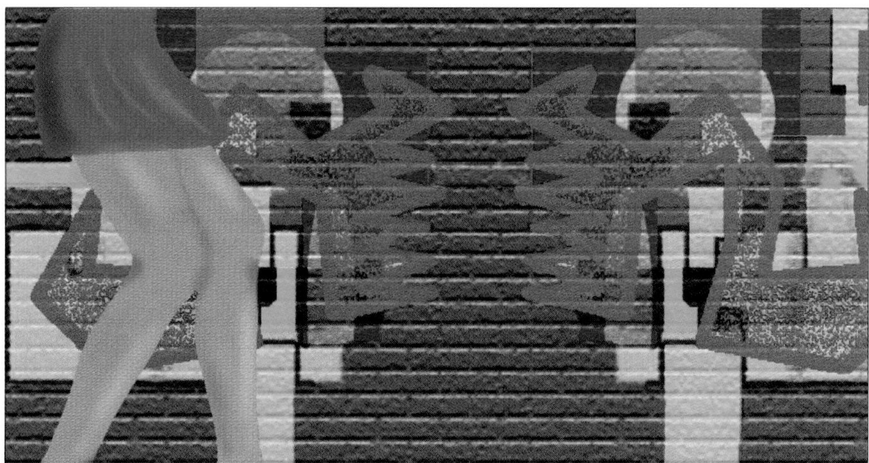

**Figure 14-4:** Airbrushing and spray painting with the Airbrush option for the Brush tool.

## Adding color with the Pencil tool

The Pencil tool differs from the Brush tool in one major respect: Regardless of the Hardness setting in the Brushes palette, the Pencil tool always uses a hardness value of 100%. With the Pencil tool active, the Options bar offers the mini-Brushes palette, choice of blending mode and opacity, and the somewhat-misnamed Auto Erase option. When selected, Auto Erase lets you paint over areas of the current foreground color using the current background color. Click an area of the foreground color, and the Pencil applies the background color. Click any color other than the foreground color, and the Pencil applies the foreground color. But remember, you're not erasing, just painting with the background color (even on layers with transparency).

## Removing color with the Eraser tool

The third of your primary painting tools is the Eraser. On a layer that supports transparency, the Eraser tool makes the pixels transparent. On a layer named *Background,* the Eraser paints with the background color. On the Options bar, the Eraser tool offers you the same options as the Brush tool (including Airbrush) and one more important choice: To the right of the Airbrush button, you'll find the Erase to History check box. When selected, the Eraser tool paints over the pixels like the History Brush (see the sidebar "Selective Undo: The History Brush"), restoring the pixels to their appearance at the selected state in the History palette.

You have a couple of variations on the Eraser tool tucked away with it in the Toolbox, too. The Background Eraser tool can, in fact, be used to remove a background from your image. However, it's not limited to something in your image that appears to be a background. Remember that digital images don't really have backgrounds and foregrounds or subjects — they just have collections of tiny, colored squares. What does this mean for using the Background Eraser? You can click and drag on any color in the image to erase areas of that color. You can also elect to erase only the current background color and designate the foreground color as protected so that it won't be erased even if you drag over it.

The Magic Eraser, like the Magic Wand selection tool (see Chapter 8), isn't a brush-using tool, but this is a logical place to tell you about it. Click a color with the Magic Eraser tool, and that color is erased, either in a contiguous area or throughout the image. And, like the Magic Wand, you can set the tool to work on the active layer or all layers, and you can also set a specific level of sensitivity (Tolerance). Here is the one difference between the two: The Magic Eraser is, in fact, a painting tool in that you can set an opacity percentage, which partially erases the selected pixels.

## Picking a color

If you want to apply a specific color to your image with a painting tool, you have to be able to select that color, right? Photoshop provides you with a number of ways to select a color:

- **Click a saved color swatch in the Swatches palette.**
- **Enter numeric values or drag sliders in the Color palette.**
- **Click a color swatch at the bottom of the Toolbox or in the Color palette to open the Color Picker.**
- **Select the Eyedropper tool and click any color already in your image.** Heck, click in your image with the Eyedropper tool, hold the mouse button down, and drag to any color *anywhere on your screen* — that color doesn't even have to be in Photoshop!

## Selective Undo: The History Brush

Photoshop's History Brush is a rather interesting tool — think of it as "Undo in a brush." When you use the Edit⇨Step Backward command or the oft-employed shortcut ⌘+Z (Mac)/ Ctrl+Z (Windows), you reverse everything you've just done. In contrast, Photoshop's History Brush lets you paint back *areas* of your image to a prior state, leaving the rest of the image just as it is.

For example, you can help the subject of an image stand out by blurring the background. One of the simplest of the many ways to do this is to blur the whole image and then paint back the subject with the History Brush. In the figure here, you see the original, all-sharp image in the upper left. Below that is the image after applying a two-pixel Gaussian Blur (about which you can read in Chapter 15). To the right, I use the History Brush to paint back the original sharp version of the image for the primary bloom, leaving the rest of the image blurred.

To select a *history state* to use with the History Brush — that is, a stage in the image's development to which the tool will restore it — click in the left column next to that state in the History palette. (In the figure here, the selected history state is named Open.) Remember that the History palette holds only a given number of states, but you can create a *snapshot,* stored in the upper portion of the palette, by clicking the middle button at the bottom of the History palette. The snapshots are retained as long as the image is open. ***Note:*** The snapshots are discarded when the image is closed, whether you save it or not.

If you get a message that the History Brush is not available, take a look at the History palette. Did you crop the image or use the Image Size command? Any change in the actual pixel dimensions of the image invalidates any prior history states for the History Brush. No worries! Simply select a snapshot or history state in the palette that comes *after* the change in image size.

In both the Toolbox and the Color palette, the foreground color is shown in the swatch to the upper left, and the background swatch is partially hidden behind it. Swap the foreground and background colors by pressing the X key on your keyboard. Reset them to the default black and white by pressing the D key.

In Chapter 6, I introduce the Color palette and the various ways you can define color with it. Now take a look at the Color palette's big brother, the Color Picker (see Figure 14-5). The best way to get a feel for the incredible versatility of the Color Picker is to open it (click a color swatch at the bottom of the Toolbox or in the Color palette) and click each of the buttons to the left of the numeric fields. Each option changes how the Color Picker appears as well as how it defines color.

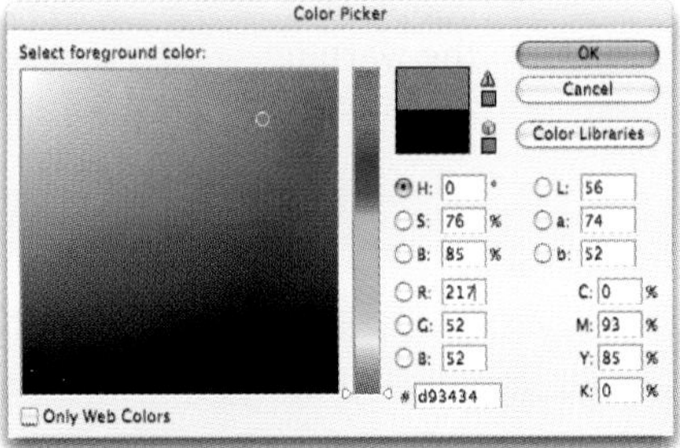


Figure 14-5: Use Photoshop's Color Picker to define colors with precision.

The default Color Picker configuration uses the radio button to the left of the H (Hue) field. It presents you with a vertical rainbow slider (the hue) and a square area that defines saturation (left-right) and brightness (up-down). Click or drag in the square area to the left and drag the slider up and down to pick a color. (Compare the two swatches to the left of the Cancel button to see the new color above the previously selected color.) If you click the button to the left of the S field, the slider shows saturation, and hue and brightness are defined in the square area to the left. Starting to see the pattern? Check out the configuration for Brightness (B) as well as the RGB and Lab options. And note that you can type numeric values to define a color as CMYK, but there are no buttons to the left to reconfigure the Color Picker. Likewise, you can type in the # (hexadecimal) field below the B field, but you can't use it to reconfigure the Color Picker. (Hexadecimal color definition is used with HyperText Markup Language [HTML] code in Web pages.)

Between the two color swatches in the top center and the buttons to the right are a pair of little icons that are not always visible. (You can see them in Figure 14-5 if they're not currently showing in your Color Picker.) The top warning triangle tells you that the current color can't be reproduced within your working CMYK color profile. Unless you're preparing artwork for commercial offset press, ignore it — it has nothing to do with your inkjet printer, for example. If, on the other hand, you *are* working on a press-destined project, click the swatch just below the warning triangle to jump to the nearest reproducible color.

The lower icon, a little cube symbol, lets you know that your current color is not Web-safe. *Web-safe colors* are the couple of hundred colors that are exactly the same in the base color scheme for both Mac and Windows. If visitors to your Web site have their monitors — or PDAs — set to show only 256 colors, everyone sees the same thing with Web-safe colors. Generally, you can safely ignore the warning because the variation isn't worth worrying about. (If you *do* want to work with Web-safe colors, click the swatch below the warning cube icon and then mark the Only Web Colors check box in the lower left.)

Also note the Color Libraries button, known in previous versions of Photoshop as the Custom button. Clicking that button swaps the Color Picker for the Color Libraries dialog box (as shown in Figure 14-6), in which you can select spot colors. *Spot colors,* which I explain in Chapter 6, are special premixed inks that can be specially requested when preparing a job for a commercial printing press. Adding a spot color ensures that the color will appear in the final product exactly as expected. However, because they generally require an extra pass through a press, adding spot colors increases the cost of your printing. Spot colors can be used to define colors for nonpress jobs, but the color is converted to your working color mode and printed with a mixture of your regular inks. Return to the Color Picker from Color Libraries by clicking the Picker button.

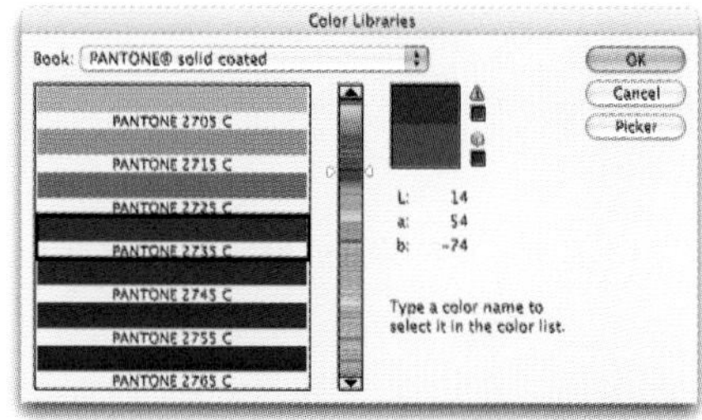


**Figure 14-6:** Choose custom spot colors in Color Libraries.

## Working with other brush-using tools

Photoshop has a double handful of additional tools that use brushes and the Brushes palette to make changes to your images. You can see the tools and their Options bar offerings in Figure 14-7.

These tools aren't used to paint color in your artwork. Rather, they're for fine-tuning details and repairing your images:

- **Healing tools:** The Healing Brush and Photoshop CS2's new Spot Healing Brush are designed to repair texture, like smoothing wrinkles or adding the appearance of canvas. With the Healing Brush, you designate a *source point* — an area from which you want to copy texture — and then drag over the target area. The Spot Healing Brush, on the other hand, automatically samples the texture around an area and makes the target area match its surroundings. Quite cool! (Nested with the Healing Brush and the Spot Healing Brush are the non-brush Patch tool and Red Eye tool. With the Patch tool, you use a selection to designate either the source or destination areas, and then you drag the selection to copy texture. The Red Eye tool is simply clicked in the red pupil of a subject's eye to darken it.)

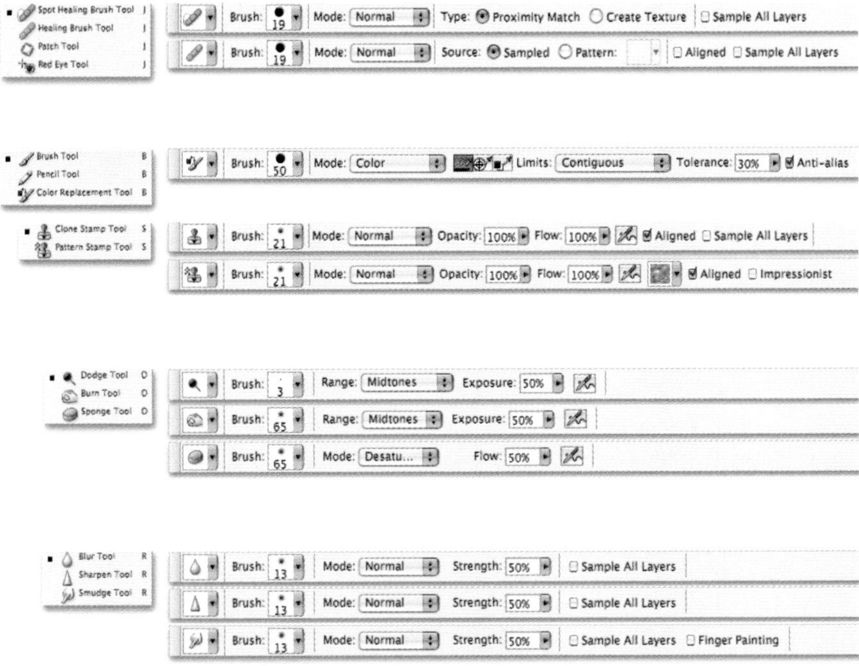


Figure 14-7: Photoshop has almost a dozen additional brush-using tools.

- **Color and clone tools:** The Color Replacement tool (now nested with the Brush and Pencil tools rather than the Healing Brush and Patch tools) replaces the color over which you drag with the foreground color. Remember that the Color Replacement tool alters only the color, not luminosity, so painting with black over pink gives you gray rather than black. From the Options bar, you can set the tool to change luminosity rather than color to darken or lighten, or choose to match hue or saturation. The Clone Stamp tool, unlike the Color Replacement tool or the Healing Brush, doesn't copy an attribute (such as color or texture) but actually copies pixels. It's like having copy/paste in a brush. Option/Alt-click a source area and then drag where you want to copy those pixels. Powerful! The Pattern Stamp tool paints with a selected pattern, using the blending mode and opacity that you designate in the Options bar. The Pattern Stamp tool is sometimes a good way to add texture selectively.
- **Toning tools:** The Dodge tool lightens, the Burn tool darkens — and if you use the defaults, they do it too much! When using these tools to adjust luminosity in your image, it's best to start with an Exposure setting of about 12% and paint carefully, perhaps repeatedly, rather than making a huge change with Exposure set to 50%. You'll find the Sponge tool nested with the Dodge and Burn tools. Use it to either increase or decrease saturation as you drag. (Decreasing saturation with the Sponge tool is a great way to create an image that's partially grayscale.)

- **Focus tools:** The Blur and Sharpen tools do just what their names say. Like the toning tools, you might find the 50% Strength default to be way too powerful for most jobs. Selective sharpening can help bring out details and direct attention in an image. Likewise, selective blurring can hide minor defects and help direct the viewer's eye toward areas of sharpness in the image. You can use the Luminosity blending mode with the Blur and Sharpen tools to minimize unwanted color artifacts while blurring or sharpening. Tucked in with the focus tools is the Smudge tool. Click and drag to smear pixels along the path. (I find the Smudge tool especially useful for dragging out wispy hairs from heads that appear perhaps too well-defined.)

## Filling, stroking, and dumping to add color

You have several more ways to add color to your artwork, all techniques that don't use brushes at all. You can, for example, make a selection and fill the selection with color via the Edit➪Fill command, or you can add a band of color along the edge of the selection with the Edit➪Stroke command (using the dialog boxes shown to the right in Figure 14-8). You can also "dump" color into your image with the Paint Bucket tool (nested below the Gradient tool in the Toolbox). Use the Paint Bucket to fill an empty selection with color or to replace the color on which you click with the foreground color.

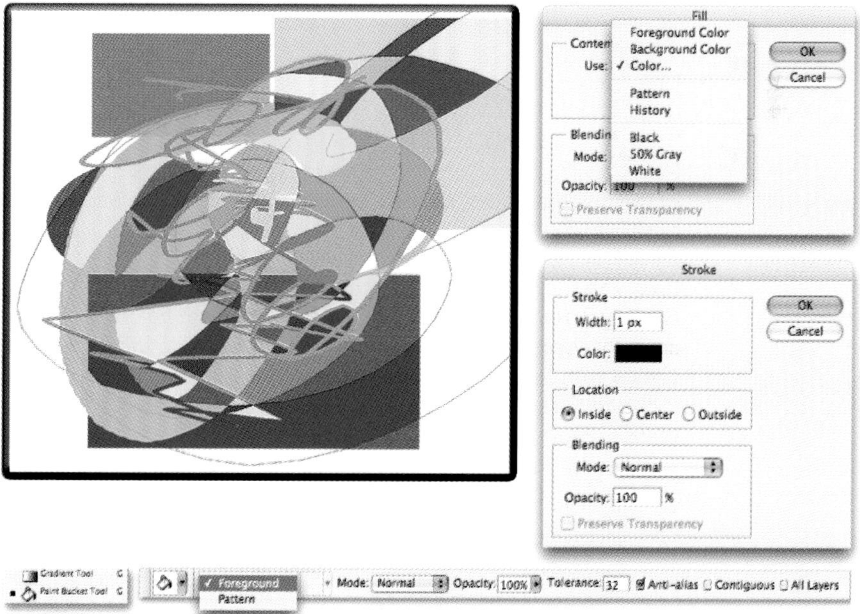


**Figure 14-8:** Photoshop offers several non-brush ways to add color to your images.

Don't forget shape layers, either! They're a great way to add perfectly defined areas of solid color to an image. (You can read about working with shape layers in Chapter 11.)

## Using gradients

You can add *gradients,* which are subtle blends of color, quite easily to your artwork:

1. **Make a selection.**

   Unless you make a selection first, the gradient fills your entire layer. If you want the gradient to fill the entire layer, don't make a selection first.

2. **Select the Gradient tool.**

   Click the Gradient tool in the Toolbox. If you don't see it, look for it nested with the Paint Bucket tool.

3. **Select a gradient.**

   You can open the Gradient palette by clicking the triangle to the right of the sample gradient on the Options bar (see Figure 14-9). You can also click the sample gradient directly to open the Gradient Editor.

4. **Choose a shape.**

   The five buttons to the right of the sample gradient on the Options bar show you the shapes available for the Gradient tool. (From the left, the buttons are Linear, Radial, Angle, Reflected, and Diamond.)

5. **Choose additional options.**

   You can pick a blending mode and opacity, flip the colors in the gradient with the Reverse option, choose Dither to help disguise the transitions between colors, and mark the Transparency check box to preserve any transparent areas on your layer.

6. **Drag the Gradient tool.**

   Where you start and in which direction you drag ultimately determine the appearance of the gradient.

The background gradient in Figure 14-9 uses the Angle Gradient option on the Options bar and the custom gradient that you see in the Gradient Editor. Notice in the Gradient Editor the *opacity stops* (above the sample being constructed) and *color stops* (below the sample). The *stops* — the squares with points positioned along the sample gradient — determine the color or opacity of the gradient at that particular point. By default, there's a smooth and even blend between neighboring stops, but you can adjust the blend by dragging the small diamonds you see on either side of the opacity and color stops. (***Hint:*** The active stops use filled triangles instead of hollow triangles with their little squares.)

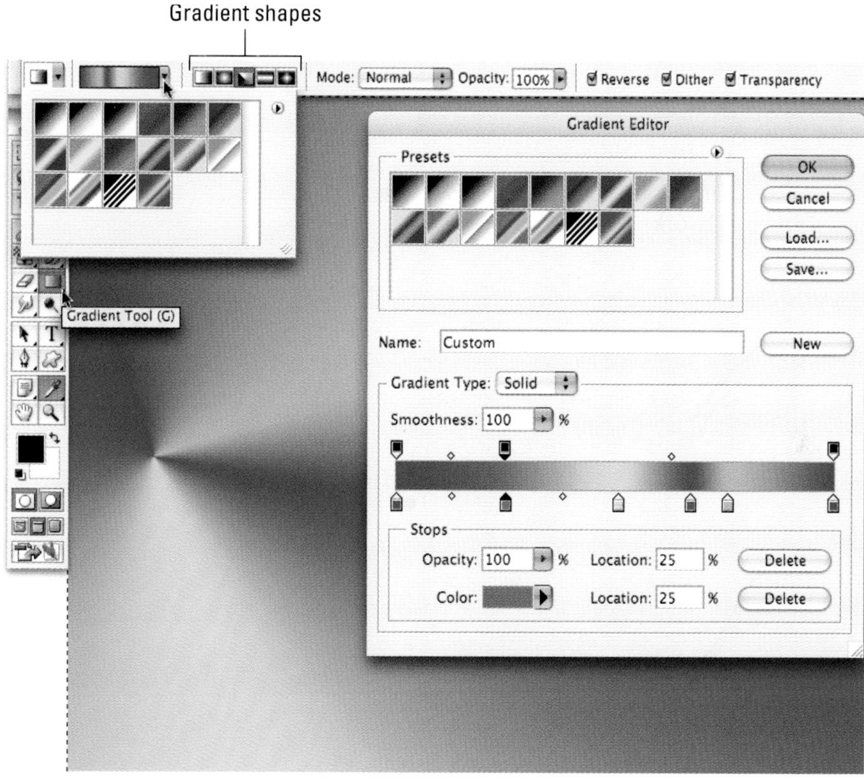


Figure 14-9: Control gradients with the Options bar, Gradient palette, and Gradient Editor.

Click anywhere along the top (opacity) or bottom (color) of the gradient to add a new stop. Drag stops to move them. Option/Alt-drag a stop to duplicate it. Change the attributes of the selected stop with the options just below in the Gradient Editor.

After designing your new gradient, remember to click the New button to add it to the Gradient palette. But keep in mind that custom gradients aren't really saved until you use the Save button or the Preset Manager to create sets on your hard drive. If you don't save your custom gradients, they'll be gone if you need to reset Photoshop's Preferences file (see Chapter 3).

# Browsing the Brushes Palette

Photoshop's Brushes palette provides a bewildering array of options, sure to confuse even the most diligent explorer. Thankfully, unless you intend to create fine art paintings digitally, you can safely ignore a whole bunch of options.

You must have a brush-using tool active to access the Brushes palette. If the active tool doesn't use brushes, the entire palette is grayed out and unavailable. If that's the case, simply press B on the keyboard to activate the Brush tool.

## An overview of options

The Brushes palette, like the Layer Style dialog box, has a column on the left that lists options. Like the Layer Style dialog box, you mark the check box to activate the feature, but you have to click the *name* to open that pane in the palette. As you can see in Figure 14-10, the Brushes palette menu offers a pretty normal selection of commands, including the variations in how to display the palette content, some housekeeping commands for resetting/loading/saving brushes, and a list of brush sets at the bottom of the menu.

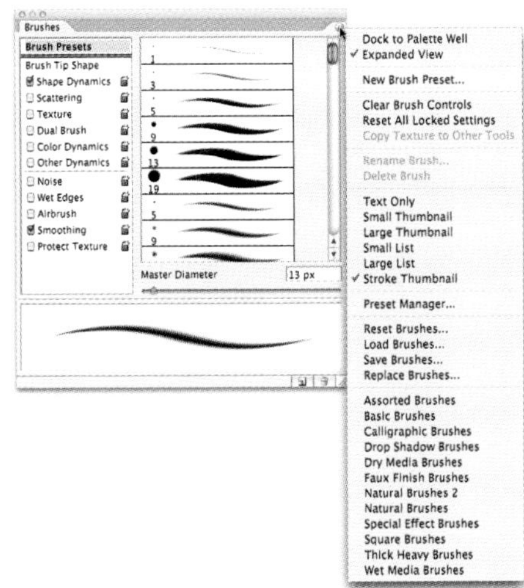


**Figure 14-10:** The Brushes palette and its menu — quite a handful!

And don't overlook those little lock icons to the right of the various pane names. Click the lock to preserve the settings in that pane while you switch among brush tip presets. Any unlocked attributes revert to those with which the brush tip was created. Locking, for example, Shape Dynamics retains those settings even if you switch to a totally different brush tip.

Here, in order, are the panes and the options in those panes to which you should pay attention:

- **Brush Presets:** Here's where you pick the basic brush tip shape from the brushes loaded in the palette. You can also resize the brush tip, but that's it. Note the lack of a check box in Figure 14-10. You don't activate/deactivate Brush Presets; you just pick a brush tip and size and then move on.
- **Brush Tip Shape:** Also without a check box, Brush Tip Shape is the pane in which you customize the selected brush tip. (Refer to the Brush Tip Shape pane in Figure 14-3.) This is perhaps the most important part of the Brushes palette. In this pane, you can select a brush tip, change its size, alter the angle at which it's applied, change the height-width relationship (Roundness) of the tip, and adjust the Spacing setting.

- **Shape Dynamics:** Dynamics in the Brushes palette add variation as you drag a tool. Say you're working with a round brush tip and choose Size Jitter. As you drag the brush tip, the brush tip instances (the individual marks left by the brush as you drag) will vary in diameter. The Shape Dynamics pane offers Size Jitter, Angle Jitter, and Roundness Jitter. Each of the "jitters" can be set to fade after a certain number of brush tip instances or can be controlled with the stylus that you use with a Wacom tablet. Angle can also be set to Direction, which forces the brush tip to adjust the direction that you drag or the direction of the selection or path you stroke. Use Shape Dynamics to add some variation and randomness to your painting, as shown in Figure 14-11.

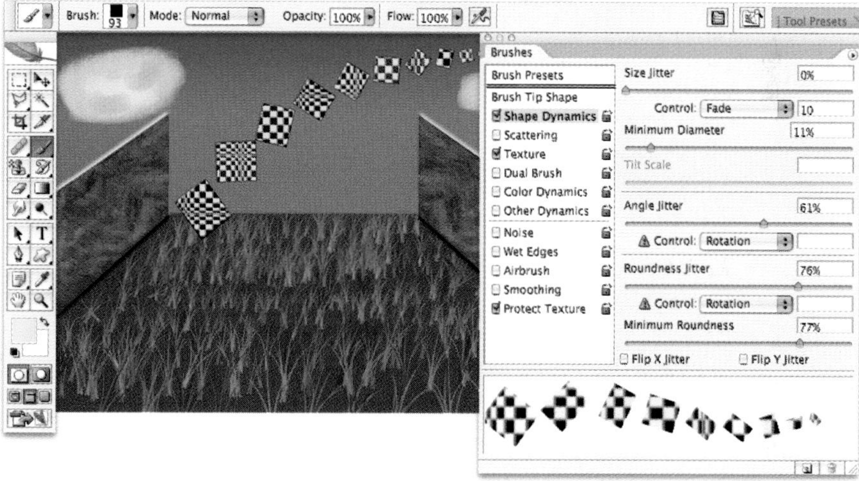


Figure 14-11: Use jitter to add variation to the application of your selected brush tip.

- **Scattering:** *Scattering* varies the number of brush tip instances as you drag as well as their placement along the path you drag. Like the shape dynamics, scattering can be set to fade or can be controlled with a Wacom tablet.
- **Texture:** Use the Texture pane to add a pattern to the brush tip. (It uses the same patterns that you use to fill a selection.) Texture is most evident when Spacing for the brush tip is set to at least 50%.

- **Dual Brush:** Using a blending mode you select, the Dual Brush option overlays a second brush tip. You could, for example, add an irregular scatter brush to a round brush tip to break up the outline as you paint.
- **Color Dynamics:** Using the Color Dynamics pane, you can vary the color of your stroke as you drag. This comes in most handy for painting images and scenes rather than, say, working on an alpha channel. Just as you might add jitter to the size, shape, and placement of a grass brush while creating a meadow, you might also want to add some differences in color as you drag. You could pick different shades of green for the foreground and background colors and then also add jitter to the hue, saturation, and brightness values as the foreground and background colors are mixed while you drag.
- **Other Dynamics:** Think of this pane as Opacity and Flow Jitter. You can add variation to the opacity and flow settings from the Options bar as you drag.
- **Other Options:** At the bottom of the left column are five brush options that don't have separate panes in the Brushes palette. They're take-it-or-leave-it options — either activated or not.
    - *Noise:* Adding Noise to the brush stroke helps produce some texture and breaks up solid areas of color in your stroke.
    - *Wet Edges:* Wet Edges simulates paint building up along the edges of your stroke.
    - *Airbrush:* The Airbrush check box simply duplicates the button on the Options bar.
    - *Smoothing:* Smoothing helps reduce sharp angles as you drag your mouse or stylus. If the stroke you're painting should indeed have jagged turns and angles, disable Smoothing.
    - *Protect Texture:* The Protect Texture option ensures that all the brushes with a defined texture use the *same* texture. Use this option when you want to simulate painting on canvas, for example.

When creating a dashed line or stroking a path with a non-round brush tip, go to the Shape Dynamics pane of the Brushes palette and set the Angle Jitter's Control pop-up menu to Direction. That enables the brush tip to rotate as necessary to follow the twists and turns of the selection or path that it's stroking. (You'll generally want to leave Angle Jitter set to 0% so that the stroke follows the selection or path precisely.)

## Creating and saving custom brush tips

You can use any artwork as a custom brush tip — you can even make a brush tip from your own face! With the artwork on a transparent or white background (you don't even need to make a selection), use the Edit➪Define Brush Preset command. Type a name (see Figure 14-12) and click OK. Your new custom brush is added to the Brushes palette. After you define a piece of artwork as a brush, you can add that image to any project with a single click or drag.

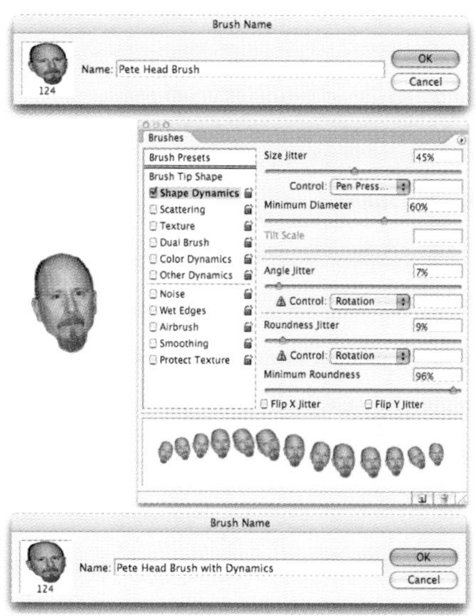


Figure 14-12: Define the new brush preset, set your options in the Brushes palette, and resave.

As soon as you define your custom brush, open the Brushes palette, select the new brush, and set Spacing and any other options that you'll generally want to use with the new brush. Then from the Brushes palette menu, choose the New Brush Preset command and resave your custom brush. Now when you select your custom brush, you have your preferred settings all ready to go!

Keep in mind these things when creating custom brushes:

- **All brushes are grayscale.** Regardless of the color in the artwork that you use to create your new brush, the brush itself is saved as a grayscale representation of the art.
- **Only one color is painted.** Again, the brush is grayscale: It applies the foreground color in tints to match the grays in the brush tip (unless, of course, you use the Color Dynamics option in the Brushes palette).
- **Your art might need more contrast.** You might want to convert a copy of your original to grayscale to see whether it wouldn't benefit from a Levels adjustment to boost the contrast. Higher contrast often makes for better brush tips.
- **Remember to save your custom brushes!** Once again (and you'll probably read this reminder a few more times elsewhere in this book), your custom brushes aren't really saved until you use the Brushes palette menu command Save Brushes (to make a new set of all the brushes currently in the palette) or Edit➪Preset Manager (to make a new set of only the brushes you select).

# Chapter 15

# Filters: The Fun Side of Photoshop

### In This Chapter

- Being productive with "fix it" filters
- Getting artsy with creative filters
- Adding wackiness (and precise correction) with Liquify
- Taking a quick look at the specialized filters

The Photoshop CS2 Filter menu includes over 100 commands that you can use to fix, flatter, finesse, and freak out your photos. You can use most of the filters on most of your artwork and some of the filters on some of your artwork, and you probably won't ever use a number of the filters.

In this chapter, I start you off with a look at what I call the "production" filters: namely, the key filters you use to improve or repair your images. Next, I show you the basics of two of the most fun features in all of Photoshop: the Filter Gallery and Liquify. Not only are they fun, but you can use them to do wondrous things to your artwork. I wrap up the chapter with a look at several other key filters.

## The Filters You Really Need

Photoshop has a number of filters that you can use on just about any image to improve or finesse it. Most photos, for example, benefit from at least a little bit of sharpening to improve the detail in the image. In some cases, you want to decrease the visible detail in an image in areas to hide defects, or perhaps you blur a background to draw more attention to the subject of your shot. And Photoshop CS2 has a couple of new filters that you'll find handy for correcting lens distortion and reducing *noise* (specks of red, green, and blue) in digital photos.

Some filters aren't available for images in CMYK (cyan/magenta/yellow/black) color mode, and some aren't available when you're working in 16-bit color. All the filters are available for 8-bit RGB and grayscale images. (No filters are available for GIF or PNG-8 images, which use Indexed Color mode.) And keep in mind that you can apply filters to specific areas of an image by making a selection first. (See Chapter 8 for info on selections and masks.)

You can instantly reapply the last used filter exactly as it was applied with the keyboard shortcut ⌘+F (Mac)/Ctrl+F (Windows). If you'd like to reopen that last-used filter's dialog box to change settings before reapplying, press Option+⌘+F/Alt+Ctrl+F.

## Sharpening to focus the eye

When looking at an image, the eye is naturally drawn to certain areas first. You generally look at bright areas before dark areas and areas of detail before smoother areas in the image. Compare, for example, the three photos in Figure 15-1 (which were taken using different focal lengths and lens apertures). Using Photoshop's sharpen filters enables you to improve the detail throughout your image or in specific areas to which you want to draw attention.

**Figure 15-1:** Blurry backgrounds help the subject stand out.

Photoshop offers five sharpen filters, three of which you can ignore. The Sharpen, Sharpen More, and Sharpen Edges filters have no user-definable settings and simply work in accordance with their names. Sure, they do a good job, but you don't have that all-important control over your images! Skip them in favor of the it-takes-some-work-but-it's-worth-it sharpening filters: Unsharp Mask and the new Smart Sharpen.

## Unsharp Mask

The Unsharp Mask filter is, indeed, a sharpening filter, despite the name (which comes from the blurry — *unsharp* — mask created from a copy of the image and used in the sharpening). As you can see in Figure 15-2, Unsharp Mask offers three sliders to adjust the appearance of your image.

Figure 15-2: Despite its name, Unsharp Mask actually sharpens your image.

In the upper left, you see the original image at 100% zoom. The middle image shows the sharpening at 100% zoom. To the right is a 300% zoom in the preview area of Unsharp Mask's dialog box.

Always evaluate your filters at 100% zoom even if you need to shrink the window to only a critical portion of the artwork. Zoomed in or zoomed out views might not accurately reflect the changes that you're making because the image isn't displayed with one screen pixel representing one image pixel. You can, of course, open a second view of the same image with the Window➪Arrange➪New Window for [*filename*] command.

Unsharp Mask works by identifying lines of strong contrast — the edges of elements within your image — and increases the contrast along those edges. Along the border of a dark area and a light area, Unsharp Mask uses a thin band of light and a thin band of dark to create a light and dark halo along the edges. That makes the edge appear much more defined. Here's how Unsharp Mask's sliders (as shown in Figure 15-3) work to control the effect.

- **Amount:** The Amount slider determines how much sharpening is actually applied by controlling the brightness and darkness of the halo. An amount of 50% is often suitable for small images that are already in pretty good shape. Use 100% for general photos. Use larger values, up to 500%, for special effects.

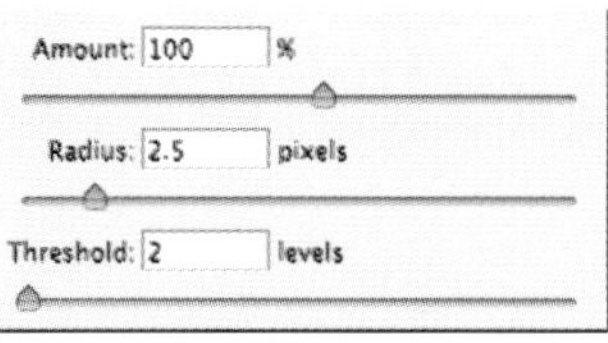

Figure 15-3: You adjust three sliders when sharpening with Unsharp Mask.

- **Radius:** Use the Radius slider to determine the width of the halo. You'll typically need a value as low as 1 pixel for small images and perhaps as high as 7 for larger images that don't have a lot of tiny detail.
- **Threshold:** The Threshold slider helps you avoid destroying your image by over-sharpening fine details. If the tiniest details in the image get wide, bright halos, they can look garish and unnatural. The higher the Threshold setting, the larger an area must be before sharpening is applied. Typical Threshold settings are 2 for a small image and 5 or 7 for a large image.

The new Photoshop CS2 Smart Sharpen filter provides you with an incredible amount of control over the sharpening process. Although it won't (quite) be able to give you a crisp image of that bank robber from the pixelated, blurry surveillance camera (that only happens on TV), it will help you improve just about any image. Those who photograph through microscopes and telescopes might find this filter particularly useful. However, remember that although you might improve an image, some blurs won't be removed by sharpening.

Figure 15-4 shows how well Smart Sharpen works with an appropriate image. In this image, the blurring is consistent throughout the subject of the shot, and there is a reasonable amount of blur. Note in Figure 15-4 that when you select the Advanced radio button, you get a pair of new tabs in the dialog box: namely, Shadow and Highlight. Use those tabs to control how strongly the effect is applied in the darker and lighter parts of the tonal range.

Smart Sharpen also enables you to specify any of three types of blurring that can be plaguing your image: Gaussian Blur (a uniform blur), Lens Blur (areas of blur beyond the focal distance of the lens), and Motion Blur (the subject or camera moving while the shot was taken). If you don't see distinct evidence of lens blur or motion blur, stick with Gaussian blur.

## The Edit⇨Fade command

Immediately after applying just about any filter or adjustment command, and after using many of Photoshop's tools, you can adjust the effect with the Fade command, found under the Edit menu. (Keep in mind that Fade is available only *immediately* after using a filter, adjustment, or tool. You can't even use the Save command in between.)

- With Fade, you can reduce the opacity of the previous command or tool, thus reducing its impact on your image. You can also change the *blending mode,* which alters how the command or tool interacts with pixel colors prior to your change.

  Say, for example, you paint a black stroke with the Brush tool set to Normal and 100% opacity. Immediately afterward, you go to the Edit menu and select the Fade Brush command. You can then pick a new blending mode and/or reduce the opacity setting, which changes the painted stroke to appear as if you'd selected the new settings in the Options bar before painting.

- You can also apply the Unsharp Mask filter and then select the Edit⇨Fade Unsharp Mask command, as shown in the figure here. (Yes, the Fade command changes names automatically!) In the Fade dialog box, changing the blending mode from Normal to Luminosity ensures that your Unsharp Mask filter doesn't alter the color of pixels along edges. Using the Fade command this way is the same as if you'd switched to Lab color mode and sharpened only the L channel — without having to switch color modes at all.

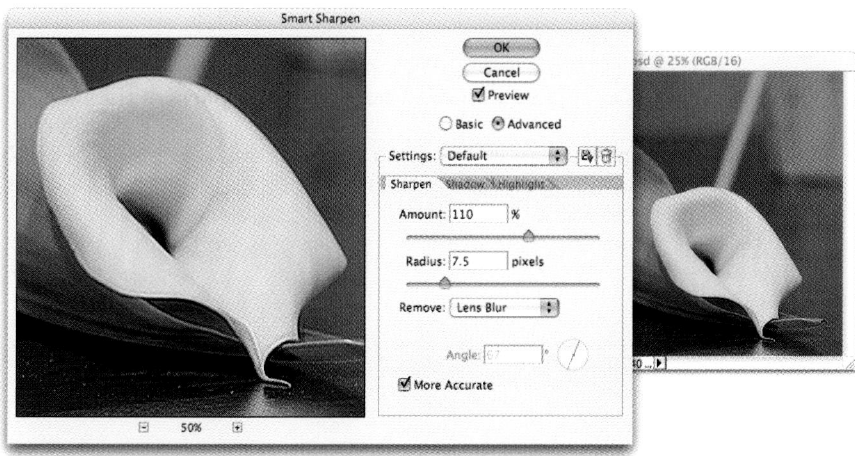


Figure 15-4: Smart Sharpen does a great job with appropriate images.

## Blurring images or selections

As you can see in Figure 15-1, blurred areas in an image attract less attention than do the sharper parts of the photo. By making a selection, you can selectively apply Photoshop's blur filters. You can also use the blur filters to hide flaws in an image, including dust, noise, and unwanted little bits and pieces in the picture. You might also want to blur all or part of an image prior to using some of the artistic filters available in the Filter Gallery (which I discuss later in this chapter).

Photoshop CS2 provides you with almost a dozen different blur filters, including three brand new blur filters. Although you'll eventually develop a special fondness for one or two blur filters, it's good to know how each of them works. Table 15-1 gives a quick overview of the available filters.

**Table 15-1 The Workings of Photoshop Filters**

| *Filter Name* | *What It Does* | *Tips on Using It* |
|---|---|---|
| Average | This filter looks at each of the pixels in the selection, determines the average color value, and then assigns that color to all the pixels in the selection, producing an area of solid color. | Changing the opacity or blending mode with the Edit⇨Fade Average command afterward softens the averaging to the point where it's more useful. |
| Blur | The Blur filter applies a slight blur throughout the image or selection. | Apply the Blur filter and then use the shortcut ⌘+F/Ctrl+F to reapply the filter numerous times to make the effect stronger. |
| Blur More | Blur More is simply a stronger version of the basic Blur filter. | |
| Box Blur | New in Photoshop CS2, this filter blurs the image vertically and horizontally; you see the effect most noticeably in small highlights that tend to bloom into squares. | In the Box Blur dialog box, you control the filter with a Radius slider. |
| Gaussian Blur | This filter produces a smoothly blurred version of your image without the distracting artifacts and lines you get by repeatedly applying the Blur More filter. | Get more control over the blurring effect by using a Radius slider that lets you control the amount of blurring. |

| Filter Name | What It Does | Tips on Using It |
|---|---|---|
| Lens Blur | This filter simulates the effect in which the camera's zoom and aperture create a sharp foreground and a blurry background. | Use an alpha channel (a saved selection) to determine where and how strongly the filter is applied. For a look at the Lens Blur filter in action, see Figure 15-5. |
| Motion Blur | This filter lets you choose any angle and a wide range of distances (measured in pixels) to suggest motion for all or part of an image. | Use it without a selection to produce the illusion that the camera (not the subject) was in motion. Make a selection and copy it to a new layer to blur just that part. |
| Radial Blur | An incredibly powerful, yet incredibly flawed, tool that blurs in a spinning motion around a center point in your image or selection, or simulates zooming in on that point. | With no preview available, you have no idea what settings are appropriate for your image (and artistic vision) without trial and error. |
| Shape Blur | The Shape Blur filter (new in CS2) uses a Radius slider and one of the shapes from your Shapes palette as a pattern for the blur. | You can load additional shapes by using the small black triangle at the upper right of the shapes area. |
| Smart Blur | Controls the blur by recognizing edges (areas of extreme difference along a line of pixels) and blurring within those areas. | Use Smart Blur in Normal mode to eliminate all fine detail in your image, use it again in Edge Only mode to trace edges in the image, and then use the shortcut ⌘+I/Ctrl+I to invert the image, which produces a black-on-white sketch of your original. |
| Surface Blur | As another wonderful addition to Photoshop CS2, this filter goes beyond Smart Blur in preserving edges. Restrict the blur to large areas of similar color in the image, leaving the fine detail of the image unblurred. (See Figure 15-6.) | Much like working with the Unsharp Mask filter, you use a Radius slider to determine the amount of change and a Threshold slider to exempt some areas of the image from the change. |

Figure 15-5: Lens Blur can use an alpha channel (mask) to control the blur.

Figure 15-6: Surface Blur blurs areas of similar color, preserving fine detail in the image.

## Using the Lens Correction filter

The new Photoshop CS2 Lens Correction filter (find it in the Distort filters) does a wonderful job of cleaning up *pin cushioning* and *barrel distortion* (the outer edges of your image appear to bend inward or outward, respectively). You'll see pin cushioning when shooting with a telephoto lens at its max zoom and barrel distortion at the lens's lower magnification. Both are most obvious when the photo has what should be straight lines at the edges. You can also use Lens Correction to adjust the vertical or horizontal plane of an image. In Figure 15-7, you see the Lens Correction window, a rather complex working environment.

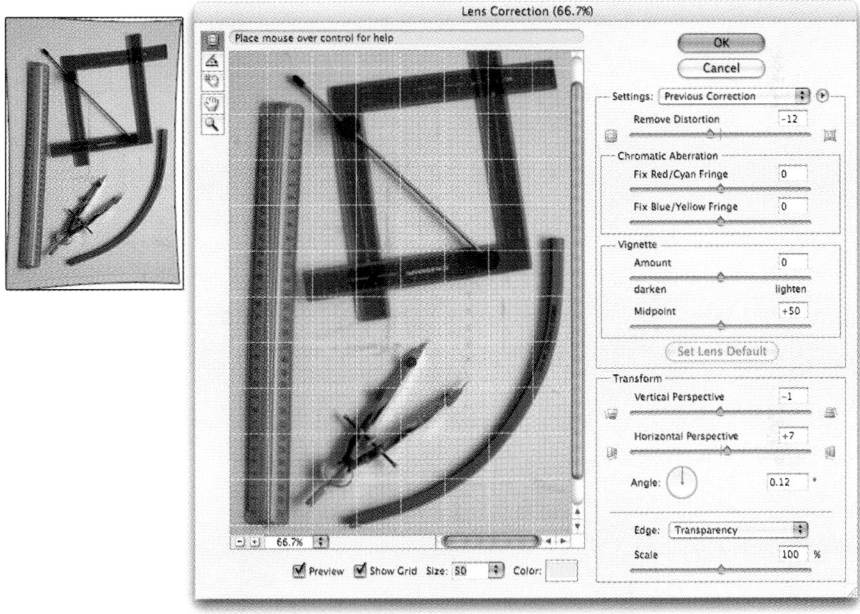


Figure 15-7: Fix barrel distortion, pin cushioning, and perspective with Lens Correction.

Here's what you have at your disposal in the Lens Correction window:

In the upper-left corner of the window are five tools:

- **Remove Distortion (top):** Select this tool to drag in the preview area to adjust the distortion factor.

- **Straighten (second):** This tool is simple: Click and drag along any line in the image that should be straight, and the image is straightened!

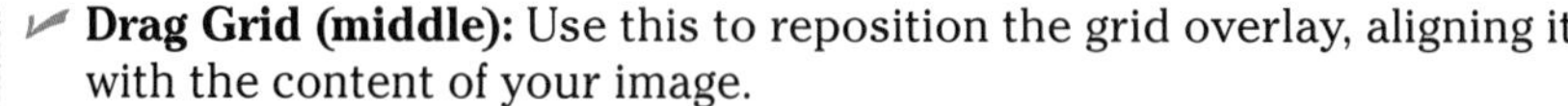

- **Drag Grid (middle):** Use this to reposition the grid overlay, aligning it with the content of your image.

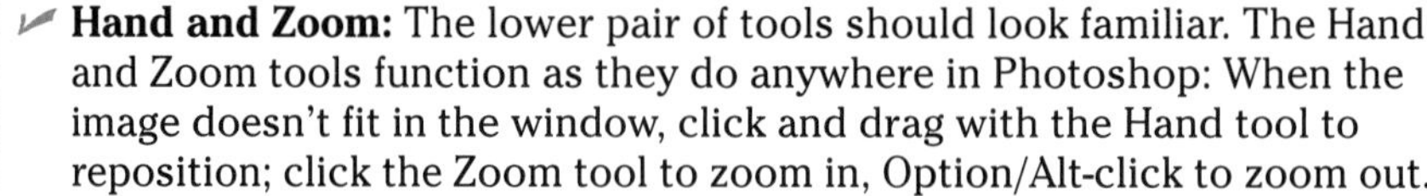

- **Hand and Zoom:** The lower pair of tools should look familiar. The Hand and Zoom tools function as they do anywhere in Photoshop: When the image doesn't fit in the window, click and drag with the Hand tool to reposition; click the Zoom tool to zoom in, Option/Alt-click to zoom out.

You'll also find

- **Remove Distortion slider:** The Remove Distortion slider is the heart of this filter. You use this to compensate for pin cushioning or barrel distortion in the image. Drag it back and forth until your image's vertical and horizontal lines are straight throughout the image.
- **Chromatic Aberration sliders:** Sometimes a photograph shows distorted color along fine angular lines, such as the branches of trees or latticework. You can minimize these colored halos or fringes with the Chromatic Aberration sliders. Generally speaking, you want to zoom in close on a specific area of detail to make the adjustment.
- **Vignette sliders:** Drag the Amount slider to the left to add a dark *vignette* (fading along the outer edges of the image) or to the right for a white vignette. The Midpoint slider increases and decreases the amount of shadowing or highlight along the edges.
- **Transform controls:** Use the Vertical Perspective and Horizontal Perspective sliders to make your image appear parallel to the viewer. Much like using the perspective crop option or the Edit⇨Transform⇨Perspective command, you're changing the perceived angle of the image to the viewer.
- **Zoom and grid:** Click the minus and plus buttons in the lower-left corner to zoom out and in, or choose a preset zoom factor from the pop-up menu. Click and drag on the Size field's label (the actual word *Size*) to resize the grid. Click the color swatch to change the color from the default gray. (I liked bright yellow for the image in Figure 15-7.)
- **Saving and loading settings:** From the Lens Correction window's menu (to the right of the Settings pop-up menu), you can save (and later load) settings. Because you can name the settings, you can save a set for each of your lenses, at each of their zoom factors, and apply the same correction easily, time after time.

Although Lens Correction is designed to fix images, there is no reason why you couldn't use it for special effects. For example, rather than using the Perspective command, you can use the Vertical Perspective and Horizontal Perspective sliders in Lens Correction, and perhaps add some barrel distortion as you would with the Distort⇨Pinch filter.

## Cleaning up with Reduce Noise

Digital *noise* — those annoying red, green, and blue specks in your image — can ruin an otherwise lovely picture. (To avoid noise, make sure that your camera is set to shoot at the lowest ISO setting possible.) Photoshop CS2 adds a new filter for reducing (not necessarily eliminating) digital noise in your images. Found under the Filter➪Noise menu, Reduce Noise can do an excellent job of minimizing the random red, green, and blue pixels in your image, as you can see in Figure 15-8.

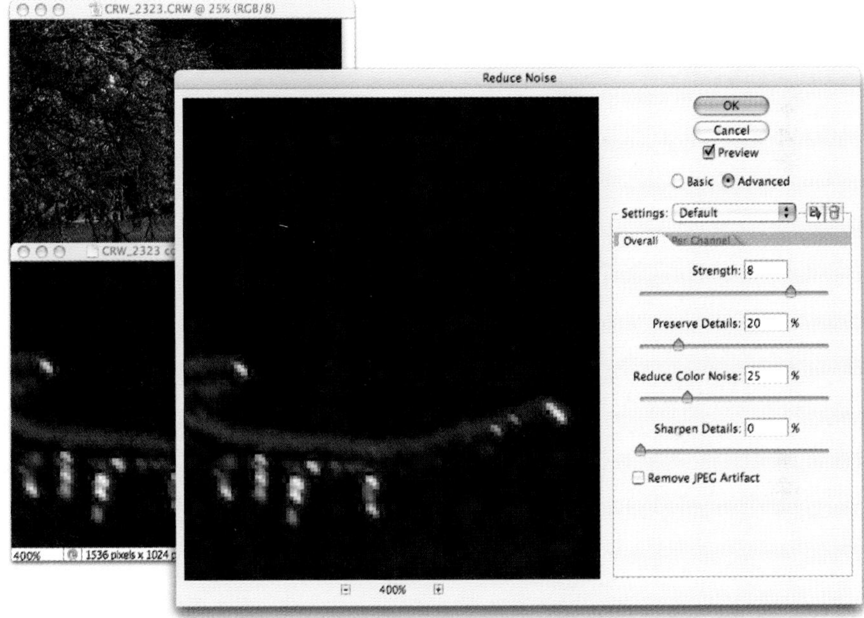


Figure 15-8: Reduce Noise neutralizes the red, green, and blue specks in a digital image.

When you work with Raw images, do all your noise correction in the Camera Raw plug-in (see Chapter 7). For images in formats other than Raw, use the Reduce Noise filter.

Here are the steps that I recommend when you use the Reduce Noise filter:

1. **Set the details sliders to 0 (zero).**

   In the Reduce Noise dialog box, drag the Preserve Details and Sharpen Details sliders all the way to the left. This eliminates any interference with the actual noise reduction.

2. **Reduce Color Noise.**

   Use the Reduce Color Noise slider to minimize the red, green, and blue specks in your image. Drag the slider slowly to the right until the color noise is gone.

3. **Adjust Sharpen Details.**

   Increase the Sharpen Details slider 1% at a time until the color noise returns; then back off 1%.

4. **Adjust Preserve Details.**

   Drag the Preserve Details slider to the right until you have a good balance between image detail and any luminance noise (bright and dark specks) in the image. In Figure 15-8, the distant trees are unlighted, yet some of their detail can be retained with Preserve Details.

If you see noise of one color considerably longer than the others when dragging the Reduce Color Noise slider, click the Advanced button near the top of the dialog box and work with each channel individually, according to its needs. Also note the Remove JPEG Artifact check box at the bottom of the window. If your image is suffering from JPEG compression problems, selecting that check box might help relieve the effects. (JPEG compression often results in visible borders between 8 x 8 pixels squares within your image.) Remember, too, that you can use the button to the right of the Settings pop-up menu to save your correction for future use — it will be added to the Setting menu.

## Getting Creative with the Filter Gallery

You can apply and combine many (but not all) of Photoshop's creative filters by using Filter⇨Filter Gallery. This integrated window lets you use multiple filters at the same time rather than guessing which settings will look good with another filter applied later. Each filter remains *live* (you can change the settings) until you click OK. Check out Figure 15-9.

The basic workflow goes like this: Adjust a filter, add a new filter to the stack, select the new filter in the middle pane, adjust the settings to the right, add a new filter to the stack, and so on. If you adjust your first filter settings and then click another filter in the middle column before adding another effect, you replace the first filter rather than adding to it. Here's my step-by-step strategy for working in the Filter Gallery window:

1. **Prepare your image before entering the Filter Gallery.**

   Many of Photoshop's creative filters work best when you prepare the image (or parts of the image) first. You've got a couple of key filters that don't appear in Filter Gallery — some to smooth fine detail, and one to add some detail.

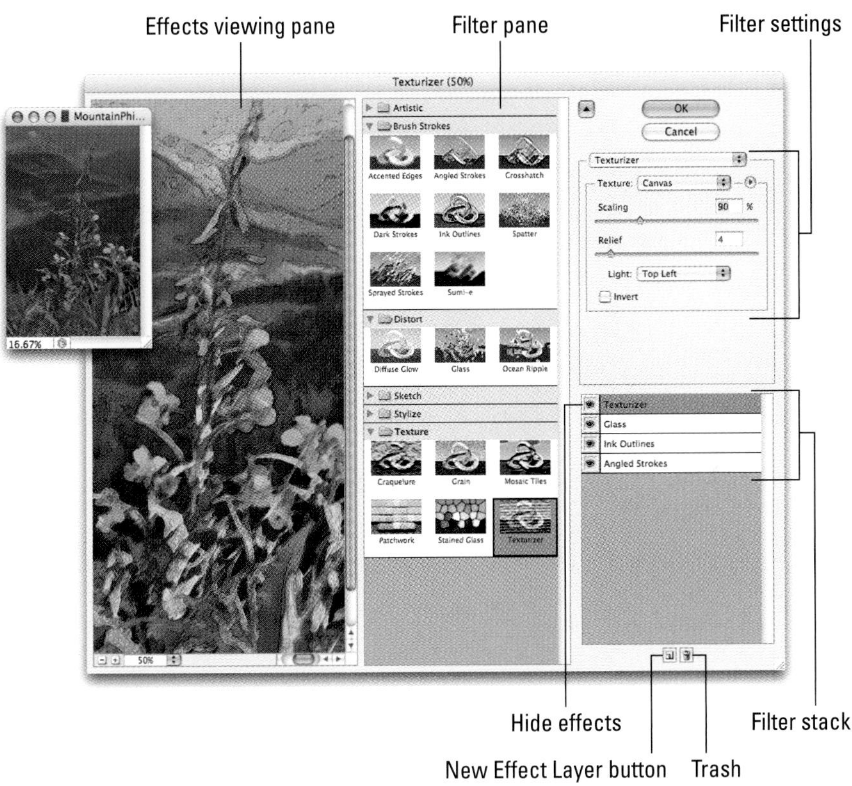


Figure 15-9: The expansive Filter Gallery interface.

- *Smoothing detail:* Because Photoshop's art-related filters can concentrate on details in your image, too much fine detail can make your filter effects crowded and cruddy. Before working with Ink Outlines, for example, try eliminating the tiny little bits in your image. You could try either Smart Blur or Surface Blur.
- *Adding detail:* Many of Photoshop's filters don't do anything if the target area doesn't have some texture or detail with which to work. That's where the Add Noise filter comes in handy, adding dark and light specks to the smooth area. Use the Monochromatic and Gaussian options, with an Amount setting from 10–15%. After adding noise to the too-smooth area, consider using the Blur➪Motion Blur filter or the Pixelate➪Crystallize filter (to make small specks bigger).

2. **Don't forget layers and blending modes.**

   Make a copy of your layer before entering the Filter Gallery so you can later mess around with layer blending modes and opacity to combine the filtered version with the original, which can soften or even enhance the effects you've applied.

3. **Add to the stack before selecting filters.**

   You make your initial filter selection and adjustment. Then before you switch to a different filter in the middle pane of the window, you need to add a filter to the stack by clicking the New Effect Layer button in the lower-right corner (to the left of the Trash icon)

4. **Play with the stacking order.**

   Drag filters up and down in the stack at the lower right to change their order.

   The order in which the filters are applied often makes a huge difference in the final appearance of your image.

5. **Use the eyeball column.**

   It's a good idea sometimes to hide one or more effects in the stack while you fine-tune a filter's settings.

   REMEMBER

   Filters are *cumulative* — changes that you make to one filter can themselves be changed by other filters in the stack.

Not all creative filters are available in the Filter Gallery. Remember that Photoshop has dozens of filters that are available only through the Filter menu, not through Filter Gallery. And don't forget that many filters can be used only with 8-bit RGB (red/green/blue) images. If you see a lot of grayed-out filters in the menu (or if Filter Gallery itself is grayed out in the Filter menu), head to the Image⇨Mode menu and make sure that you're working in 8-bit color and the RGB color mode.

## Push, Pull, and Twist with Liquify

Although the Lens Correction filter has added another powerful correction tool to your arsenal, you still want to sometimes fix a photograph's perspective or barrel distortion with Liquify. Perhaps. But with Lens Correction now available, Liquify can concentrate on its fun side.

I know of nothing in Photoshop that can bring a smile faster and more easily than creating some strange creature from a friend or loved one in Liquify. I will readily admit that the glow produced by the praise of an art critic is gratifying, but does it compare to, "More, Uncle Pete! Give me *bigger* ears!"? It would certainly be a disservice to the Liquify feature to overlook its powerful image-correction capabilities, so please remember that almost anything you can do to emphasize or enhance an attribute can be done in reverse to minimize that aspect of the image. Make someone short and wide? You can also make them tall and thin. Creating a bulging nose? Create a slim and pert nose. It's all possible with Liquify.

That having been said, examine Figure 15-10, which shows some rather dramatic changes. (But it should give you some idea of how useful Liquify can be for more subtle tasks, like trimming tummies, toning arms and legs, thinning noses, and other such work.)

Figure 15-10: Liquify gives you unbelievable control over the pixels in your image.

Take a look at the tools arrayed along the left edge of the Liquify window. Here's what they do, starting at the top:

- **Forward Warp tool:** Much like Photoshop's Smudge tool, you click and drag the Forward Warp tool to push the pixels around.

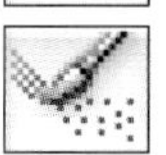

- **Reconstruct tool:** Use the Reconstruct tool as your "undo." (When in Liquify, you can use ⌘+Z/Ctrl+Z, but it goes back only one step.) Drag over areas that you want to restore to their original appearance.

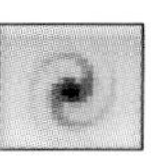

- **Twirl Clockwise tool:** Click and hold the mouse button down or drag in a circle to spin the pixels within the brush diameter. And if you want to twirl counterclockwise, simply add the Option/Alt key.

- **Pucker tool:** The Pucker tools sucks pixels into the center of the brush. You can click and hold or drag the Pucker tool. Holding down the Option/Alt button toggles you to the Bloat tool.

- **Bloat tool:** The opposite of the Pucker tool, the Bloat tool pushes pixels out from the center. Option/Alt switches you to the Pucker tool.

- **Push Left tool:** As you drag the Push Left tool, pixels are shifted to the left of the path along which you drag (not necessarily to *your* left). If you drag up, the pixels are shifted to the left on the screen; drag down, and the pixels are shifted to the right on the screen. Use the Option/Alt key to reverse the behavior and push pixels to the right of the path.

- **Mirror tool:** As you drag the Mirror tool, whatever pixels are immediately to the left of the cursor as you drag are flipped and pasted into the brush along the path you drag. When dragging left to right, whatever is directly above the cursor as you drag is flipped and copied into the brush. For best results, use the Freeze Mask tool (see the upcoming bullet) on the pixels that you want to copy before using the Mirror tool. The Option/Alt key reverses the behavior, copying the pixels to the right of the path as you drag.

- **Turbulence tool:** The Turbulence tool is great for adding smooth distortion along the path you drag. Think of it as making waves along the path. The Option/Alt key switches the Turbulence tool to the Reconstruct tool.

- **Freeze Mask tool:** One of the most important tools, the Freeze Mask tool lets you protect areas of your image from change. Paint over an area (you'll see a red mask) to *freeze* it — to keep it from changing.

- **Thaw Mask tool:** Unprotect areas with the Thaw Mask tool. It removes the red overlay and lets you liquefy the area again.

- **Hand tool:** As always, the Hand tool lets you reposition an image in the window when it doesn't all fit. Just click and drag your image to move it in the preview window.

- **Zoom tool:** As you might suspect, the Zoom tool functions as it usually does. Click to zoom in, Option/Alt-click to zoom out, and click and drag to zoom in on a specific area.

To the right in the Liquify window are a number of variables and options. Brush Size is the tool brush diameter; Brush Density is comparable with feathering (lower is softer); and Brush Pressure controls the strength of the active tool.

The Reconstruct Options let you restore or partially restore your image to the original appearance. The Reconstruct button is less like Step Backward or Undo and more like Fade. Rather than reversing the liquification steps you've already applied, it weakens them. The Mode pop-up menu offers several ways to control how strictly the image is reconstructed. The mode that you select is also used with the Reconstruct tool. (Revert is the most precise mode.) The Restore All button returns your image to its pre-Liquify appearance.

If you're working on only one layer of your image and that layer has a layer mask or transparent areas, or if you make a selection before entering the Liquify feature, you can use the buttons in the Mask Options area to create frozen areas (areas that are protected from change).

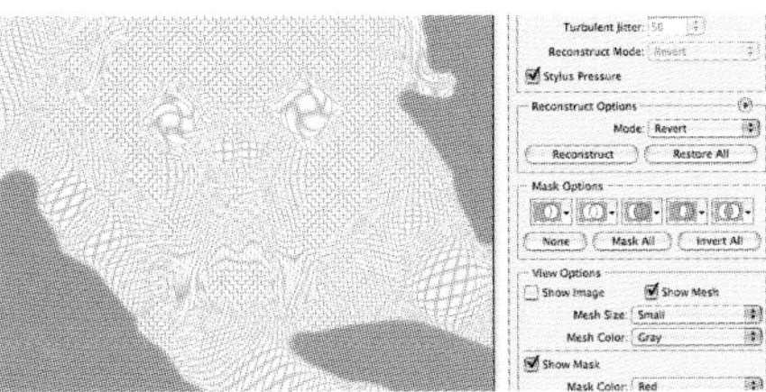


Figure 15-11: When the mesh is visible, you see precisely how you're distorting the image.

Near the bottom of the right side of the Liquify window (and in Figure 15-10), you can see the View Options, which let you show and hide the *mesh:* the actual distortion you're creating. (Figure 15-11 shows a portion of the mesh used in Figure 15-10.) Note the mesh size and color options.

# Do I Need Those Other Filters?

Photoshop has dozens of filters, creative and productive, that you access through the Filter menu rather than through the Filter Gallery. Some do strange and wonderful things to your selection or image, and some just do strange things that you might never need. You can find a description of each of Photoshop's filters in Photoshop's own Help, but a couple of them are worth a bit of attention here.

## Bending and bubbling

In the Filter⇨Distort menu, you find both the Shear and the Spherize filters, both of which are simpler alternatives to Liquify for many projects. Use the Shear filter to bend a selection back and forth, creating curves. Use Spherize to create a bulging, rounded image. Both Shear and Spherize are easiest to control when you make a selection of your target and copy it to a new layer. And, as you see in Figure 15-12, Shear works only vertically, so you might need to rotate your image before and after the filter.

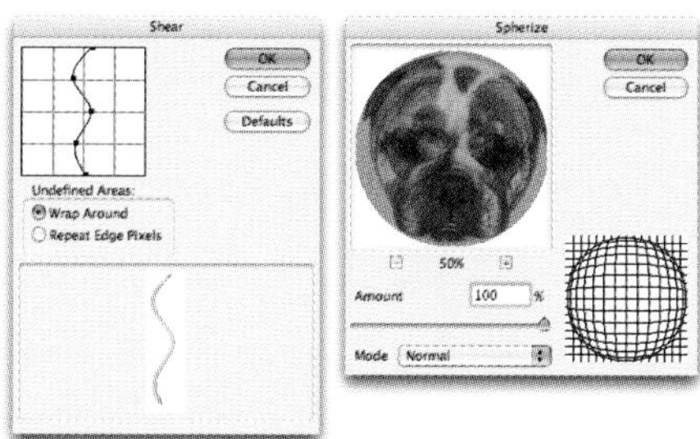

Figure 15-12: The Shear filter bends; the Spherize filter bulges and pinches.

## Creating clouds

Clouds make lovely, unobtrusive backgrounds (as you see in Figure 5-13), can be scaled and transformed to produce smoke or steam, and can even create marbling effects. In the Filter⇨Render menu, you'll find Clouds and Difference Clouds. Both use a mixture of the foreground and background colors to create a cloud pattern. The Clouds filter replaces the content of the selection or layer (if any), and Difference Clouds interacts with the existing pixels (you can't use it on an empty layer) pretty much like Clouds using the Difference blending mode. Apply Difference Clouds several times, perhaps as many as 20, to create abstract backgrounds and marble patterns, or perhaps to simulate microscope slides.

Figure 15-13: The Clouds filter produces pleasant backgrounds.

# Part IV
# Power Photoshop

"That's a lovely scanned image of your sister's portrait. Now take it off the body of that pit viper before she comes in the room."

## In this part . . .

This part is more specialized than the others in the book. These two chapters cover features of Photoshop that you might never need.

Chapter 16 shows you how to streamline some of your work with Photoshop's automation commands. You also read about recording Actions and get a quick look at using scripting to automate Photoshop. Keep in mind that Chapter 16 also includes information on printing multiple images on a single sheet of paper — saving both time and money!

If you never create graphics for the Web, you might skip Chapter 17. However, if spicing up your online presence (or making a few bucks helping someone else) sounds good, take a look. You see how to optimize images for faster download as well as how to create fancy rollover buttons and animations to add action to a Web page.

## Chapter 16

# Streamlining Your Work in Photoshop

### In This Chapter

- Taking advantage of Photoshop's built-in automation commands
- Working with Actions
- Using prerecorded scripts

A lot of the work that you do in Photoshop is fun — experimenting with filters, applying creative adjustments, cloning over former in-laws, that sort of thing. A bunch of your work, though, is likely to be repetitive, mundane, and even downright boring. That's where automation comes in. If a task isn't fun to do, if you need to speed things up, or if you need to ensure that the exact same steps are taken time after time, automation is for you.

I open the chapter with a look at some of Photoshop's major automation features — commands that help you quickly and easily create presentations and contact sheets. Next, I show you a couple of production-oriented commands that let you print multiple images on a single sheet of paper (and we know how much money *that* can save!) and how to save time by scanning multiple images in a single pass and then automatically separating them into individual files. After that, you see how to play Photoshop's Actions and even record your own. The chapter wraps up with a quick look at *scripts,* which are sort of little computer programs that you use to control your computer — Photoshop, other programs, your printer, or even an operating system itself.

# Running on Auto

Photoshop's File➪Automate submenu (as shown in Figure 16-1) contains a collection of some of the most useful features in the program. Chapter 10 shows you how to use a couple of the Automate commands: that is, those used for combining images. You'll find info there on both Photomerge (for creating panoramas) and the new Merge to HDR command (for combining multiple exposures). Chapter 4 introduces you to Web Photo Gallery (for creating simple yet elegant Web sites to display your images online). Here, I show you how to use some of the automation features to present your images — and one that speeds up bringing images into Photoshop.

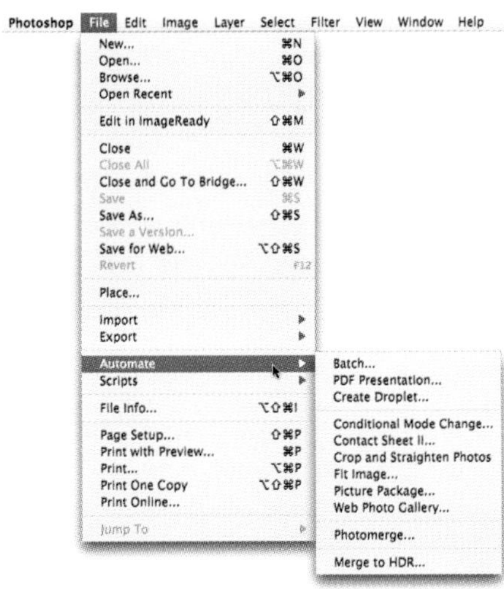


Figure 16- 1: Photoshop's Automate commands can make quick work of big jobs.

## Creating a PDF presentation

*Portable Document Format* (PDF), the native file format of Adobe Acrobat, has become an incredibly useful and near-universal format. It's hard to find a computer that doesn't have Adobe Reader (free software to open and view PDF files), and that helps make PDF a wonderful format for sharing or distributing your images.

You can use Photoshop's File➪Automate➪PDF Presentation (as shown in Figure 16-2) to quickly and easily create both onscreen presentations (complete with fancy transitions between images) and multipage PDF documents (suitable for distribution and printing).

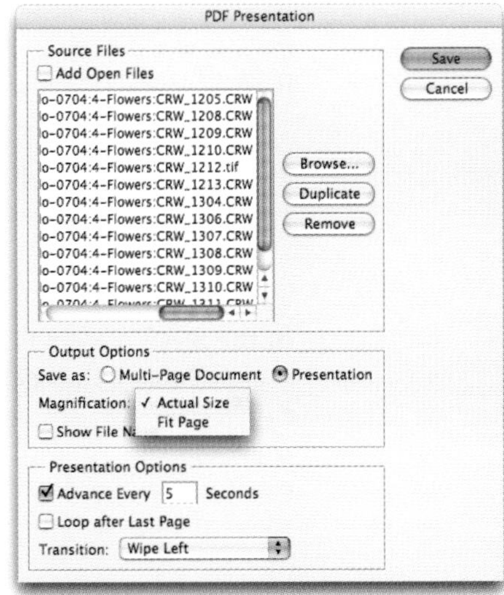


Figure 16-2: PDF is a great format for sharing images as presentations or as documents.

To create a PDF in Photoshop, take the following steps:

1. **If the files you want to use aren't already open in Photoshop, click the Browse button. You can click and then Shift-click to select a series of images or ⌘-click (Mac)/Ctrl-click (Windows) to select individual images.**

   ***Hint:*** You must select the images; you can't select only the folder.

   After you click the Open button, the filenames appear in the PDF Presentation window. Drag filenames up or down to reorder them.

2. **In the Output Options area, you can elect to create an onscreen presentation or a multipage document.**

   If you opt to use Fit Page for Magnification, the images are scaled as necessary to fill the screen or page. Using Actual Size shrinks images larger than the screen (or page) but does not enlarge smaller images. If you want, you can add the filename to each slide in the presentation or each page in the PDF. This is a good idea when sending images to someone who needs to know the image name, say, to order prints and give you cash.

3. **Select how you want the presentation to play.**

   You can have the presentation automatically switch images after a given number of seconds (or opt for manual slide advance), you can have the presentation automatically rewind and begin playing again *(loop),* or you can pick transitions between images. Do your audience a favor and pick a single transition and stick with it — preferably one simple transition, such as Wipe Left or Wipe Right. Those too-busy transitions are the 21st-century version of PowerPoint clip art — fun to play with, but distracting to your audience.

4. **Click the Save button.**

   You see the Save dialog box, from which you pick a location and a name and then click another Save button.

5. **In the Save Adobe PDF dialog box, make things simple for yourself and choose Smallest File Size or High Quality Print from the Adobe PDF Preset pop-up menu at the top.**

   If you're creating a presentation or want to create a multipage PDF from which the recipient can't print full-size images, choose Smallest File Size. For a multipage document from which you *do* want the client to print great images, use High Quality Print.

6. **The only other area of the dialog box that you really need to consider is Security.**

   You can assign a password to the file that the recipient needs to open and view the presentation or multipage PDF document. Alternatively, you can require no password to open the file but rather assign a password for printing or changing the file.

7. **Finally, at the end of the road, click the Save PDF button to actually generate the final file.**

Unlike the original PDF Presentation, the Photoshop CS2 version has *real* PDF security. When you password-protect your file, anyone attempting to open the PDF file or presentation in any program — Photoshop included — needs the password. (PDFs generated by the original PDF Presentation were password-protected for Acrobat but not Photoshop.)

## Collecting thumbnails in a contact sheet

In the old Dark(room) Ages, photographers regularly made a record of which images were on which film strips by exposing those strips on a piece of photographic paper, thus creating a *contact sheet.* The contact sheet serves the same purpose as thumbnails or previews in Bridge or the Open dialog box or thumbnail images on a Web page — they show which image is which. Hard copy contact sheets are useful to present to a client. Photoshop can automate the process for you with File➪Automate➪Contact Sheet II (see Figure 16-3).

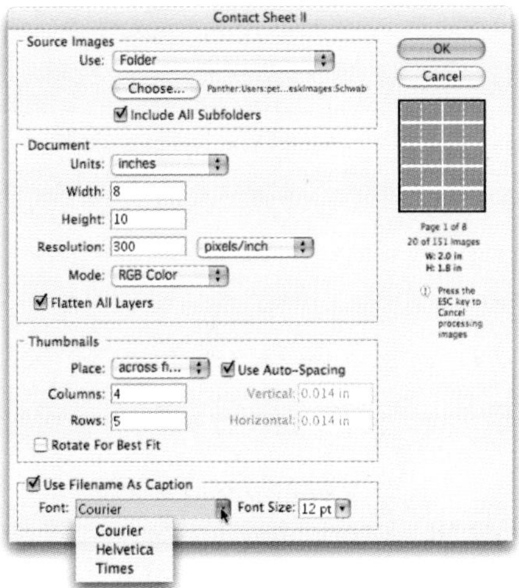


Figure 16-3: If you need a printed record of your images, consider Contact Sheet II.

1. **Select a source folder from the Use drop-down list in the Source Images area.**
2. **(Optional) If you want to include the images in any subfolders that might be within that folder, select the Include All Subfolders check box.**
3. **Using the Units, Width, and Height options in the Document area, describe your document, using the printable area of your page — not the paper size.**
4. **Select a resolution.**

   I recommend 300 pixels per inch (ppi) if printing and 72 ppi if you'll be slicing the image for your Web site.

5. **Use the Mode drop-down list box to choose a color mode (RGB unless printing to a color laser printer) and also decide whether you want to flatten layers (which makes a smaller but less versatile file).**

After all the external decisions are made, you need to make some choices about the layout and placement of the images on the page. Note in Figure 16-3 that you have some important information below the Cancel button. Contact Sheet II gives you a preview of the layout, tells you how many pages (and images) you're going to generate, and shows you how large each image will be on the page. Keep an eye on this area when making decisions in the Thumbnails section of the dialog box.

You can choose to have the images added to the page row by row (the second image is to the right of the first) or column by column (the second image is directly below the first). You also choose the number of rows and columns, which determines the size of each individual image. You then need to decide whether to use Auto-Spacing, to calculate the spacing between images, and to rotate images or not. If your source folder has a mixture of landscape and portrait images, rotating makes sure that each is exactly the same size — although some will be sideways. If image orientation is more important than having identical sizes, don't use the Rotate for Best Fit option. Take a look at the bottom row in Figure 16-4 to see how an unrotated image appears in a contact sheet.

Figure 16-4: To maintain image orientation, don't use the Rotate for Best Fit option.

If your folder is filled with portrait-oriented images, you can certainly have more columns than rows so that each image better fills the area allotted for it. For example, when printing 20 portrait images, using 5 columns and 4 rows produces larger printed images than using 4 columns and 5 rows.

Contact Sheet II also lets you add the filename as a caption below each image, which proves to be a very handy way of tracking your images. As you see in Figure 16-3, your font choices are rather limited. (Make sure you use a font size small enough to get the whole name within the width of the individual images.) By default, the filename is in black.

## Scanning multiple photos in one pass

You can often save a lot of time by placing multiple photos on the glass of your scanner and scanning them all at once. You don't need to reopen the scanner software or generate a new preview every time; rather, you just scan one big picture and make individual little pictures from it later in Photoshop. Photoshop's File➪Automate menu offers a neat timesaving featured named Crop and Straighten Photos, which generates a separate file for each photo it finds in the scan.

For best results, place the photos on the scanner's bed with a slight gap between them. I like to place a sheet of colored paper or plastic on top of the photos, between the backs of the photos and the scanner's lid (as you see in Figure 16-5). I use paper or plastic that is a very different color from any color found along the edges of the photos. This gives Photoshop a good idea about where each photo ends and the next begins.

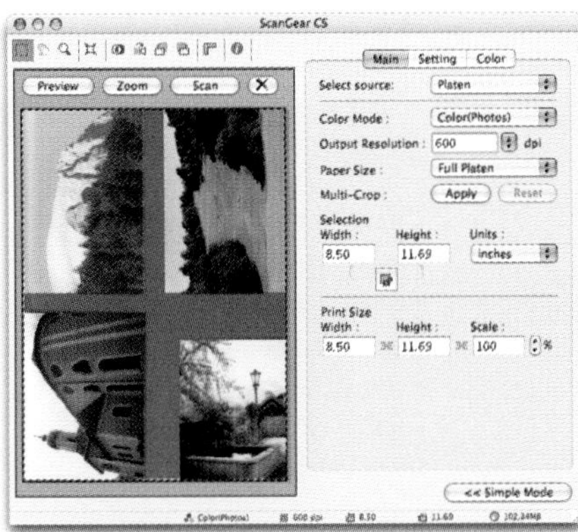


Figure 16-5: Use a contrasting background to help Crop and Straighten Photos find edges.

After the scan is complete and the image is open in Photoshop, use the File➪Automate➪Crop and Straighten Photos command. No dialog box, no submenus — just select the command and wait a few seconds while Photoshop identifies the individual scanned images and creates a separate file for each.

## Saving paper with Picture Package

Suppose you need to print a dozen images, each at 4 x 5 inches. Printing each on a separate sheet of paper takes 12 sheets (oh, the cost!) and 12 print cycles. Use the File➪Automate➪Picture Package command (as shown in Figure 16-6) to put four 4 x 5 images on a single page, and you use three sheets of paper and wait through only three print cycles. Um, let's see, which do you want to do. . . .

Figure 16-6: Multiple images on a single page with Picture Package.

Picture Package creates *zones* on a sheet of paper and places copies of the selected image, properly sized according the layout you select, in each zone. You can click each of the zones to select a different image or leave Picture Package set to print multiple copies of a single image.

Here are some tips for working efficiently with Picture Package:

- **Pick the Page Size first.** The layouts available are all based on the page size. The Layout pop-up menu shows only layouts designed for the selected dimensions.

  For Page Size, use the printable area of the page (the area within your printer's minimum margins), not the paper size.

- **Click each zone to add an image.** By default, Picture Package uses multiple copies of the same image in the Layout area. Click each of those images to change the photo assigned to that spot.

- **Create custom layouts.** Click the Edit Layout button to create custom arrangements to suit your needs. Click a zone and drag its bounding box to resize and move, or work numerically for precise zones.
- **Check your resolution.** If you intend to print your Picture Package page, you probably want a resolution of 300 ppi, or perhaps 240 ppi.
- **Decide whether to flatten.** If you don't select the Flatten All Layers check box, you can further manipulate the result, perhaps adding any necessary adjustment layers to fine-tune a specific image. Maintaining layers also lets you realign the images to make cutting them apart later much easier. As you can see in Figure 16-6, the edges of the two images on the left are not aligned, which will result in some extra work with the paper cutter or scissors.
- **Check your font size.** Make sure that if you add a label, you use an appropriate font size. If your label is too small, nobody can read it; conversely, if it's too large, you might disrupt the feel of the image.
- **Consider using Contact Sheet.** If you have a large number of images to process, you might be better off using Contact Sheet II because it automatically generates multiple pages from a single folder.

# Ready, Set, Action!

In Photoshop, an *Action* is simply a recorded series of steps that you can play back on another image to replicate an effect or technique. To choose a wild example, say that every image in your new book about Photoshop needs to be submitted at a size of exactly 1024 x 768 pixels at 300 ppi, regardless of content. Record an Action that uses the Image Size command to change resolution, and then use the Canvas Size command to expand the image to 1024 x 768 pixels. Use that Action (*play* the Action) on each image before submitting it. Better yet, wait until all the images for a chapter are ready and then use the Batch command to play the Action automatically on each of them!

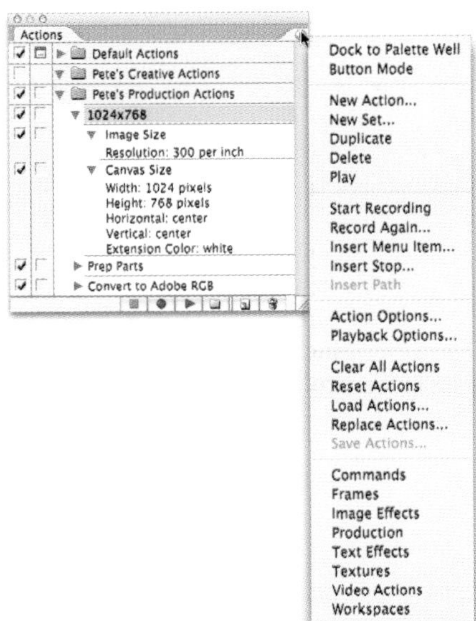


**Figure 16-7:** The Actions palette menu includes sets of Actions you can load into the palette.

Actions and the Batch command not only streamline repetitive tasks; they also ensure precision — that every one of those images will be *exactly* 1024 x 768 pixels, each and every time. But Actions also have a creative side to them. The lower part of the Action palette's menu (see Figure 16-7) contains Action sets that you can load into the palette to produce frame and border effects, text effects, and more. (The content of your Actions palette menu might differ from that shown in Figure 16-7.) You can also purchase collections of Actions from commercial sources.

To work with an Action, you open an image, select the Action in the Actions palette, and then click the Play button at the bottom of the palette. (As you can see in Figure 16-7, the three buttons to the left use the near-universal symbols for Stop, Record, and Play. The three to the right use the standard Adobe symbols indicating New Set, New Action, and Trash.)

Any step in the Actions palette that doesn't have a check mark in the left column is skipped when you play the Action. Any step that has a symbol visible in the second column (the modal control column) pauses when you play the Action. Click in the second column when you want the Action to wait for you to do something. Perhaps you'll click in that column next to a Crop step so that you can adjust the Crop tool's bounding box. You might click in the second column next to an Image Size step so that you can input a specific size or choose a resampling algorithm. After you make a change or input a value for that step, press Return/Enter to continue playing the Action.

Notice the grayed-out Save Actions command in the palette's menu in Figure 16-7. Remember that you have to select a set of Actions in the palette, not an individual Action, to use the Save Actions command. If you want to save only one Action, create a new set and Option/Alt-drag the Action to that set to copy it. You can also create a printable text file (`.txt`) of your Actions set by holding down the ⌘+Option/Ctrl+Alt keys when selecting Save Actions. Text versions of your Actions provide an easy reference for what each Action (and step) does to an image.

If you get hooked on Actions, you'll also want to try Button Mode in the Actions palette menu. Each Action appears in the palette as a color-coded button. You don't see the steps of the Action, so you don't know whether an individual step is being skipped and you can't change the modal control column, but you might like the color-coding to sort your Actions.

## Recording your own Actions

The real power of Actions comes to you when you record your own. Sure, the sets of Actions included with Photoshop are great, and those commercial packages of Actions have some good stuff too, but it's not *your* stuff. When you record your own Actions, you record the steps that work for your images, your workflow, and your artistic vision. (Remember, too, that Actions can be recorded in ImageReady.)

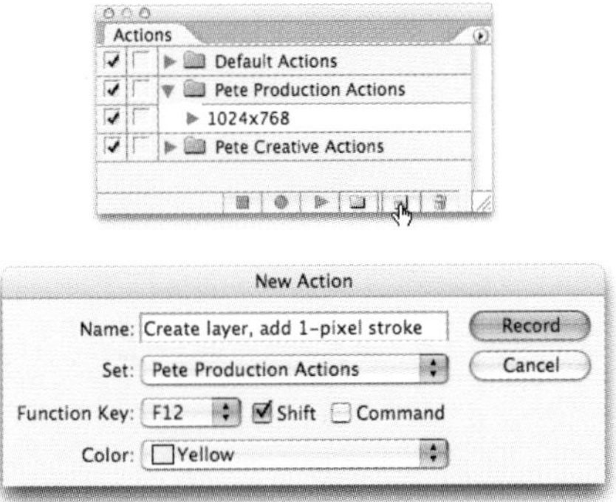


Figure 16-8: After you click the New Action button, you see the New Action dialog box.

Actions can't float free in Photoshop's Actions palette: Each Action must be part of a set of Actions. Before beginning to record your Action, you can select an existing set or click the fourth button at the bottom of the palette to create a new set. When you have a set selected, you can then click the New Action button (second from right). Then, in the New Action dialog box (as shown in Figure 16-8), assign a name (and color-code for Button Mode and perhaps assign an F-key combination) and click the Record button. From that point forward, just about everything you do in Photoshop is recorded as part of the Action until you click the Stop button at the bottom of the Actions palette. No worries, though — you can always delete unwanted steps after the Action is recorded by dragging them to the Trash icon at the bottom of the Actions palette. And if you want to change something in the Action, you can double-click a step and rerecord it.

You can record most of Photoshop's commands and tools in an Action, but you can't control anything outside of Photoshop. (For that you need *scripting*, introduced later in this chapter.) You can't, for example, use an Action to print (controlling the printer's own print driver), or copy a filename from the Mac Finder or Windows Explorer, or open Illustrator and select a path to add to your Photoshop document. Nor can you record the movement of the cursor in your Actions, which generally rules out recording painting tools.

Here are some tips about recording your own custom Actions:

- **Open a file first.** Open the file in which you're going to work *before* you start recording the Action. Otherwise, the Open command becomes part of the Action, and the Action will play on that specific file every time you use it. You can, however, record the Open command within an Action to open a second file — perhaps to copy something from that file.
- **Record the Close command after Save As.** When you record the Save As command in an Action, you're creating a new file on your hard drive. Follow the Save As command with the File➪Close command (and elect Don't Save when prompted). That closes the original image.
- **Use Percent as the unit of measure.** If you need an element in your artwork to be in the same spot regardless of file size or shape (like a copyright notice in the lower-right corner), change the unit of measure to Percent in Photoshop's Preferences before recording the Action.

- **Record/insert menu commands.** When you use a menu command while recording your Action, the actual values that you enter into the dialog box are recorded, too. If you'd rather select the values appropriate for each individual image (perhaps for the Unsharp Mask filter), insert the command rather than record it. When you reach that specific spot in your process, use the Actions palette menu command Insert Menu Item (refer to Figure 16-7). With the dialog box open, mouse to and select the appropriate menu command; then click OK to continue recording the Action. In Figure 16-9, you see the Insert Menu Item dialog box when first opened (before a command is selected) and after I used the mouse to select the Image Size command from Photoshop's Image menu.

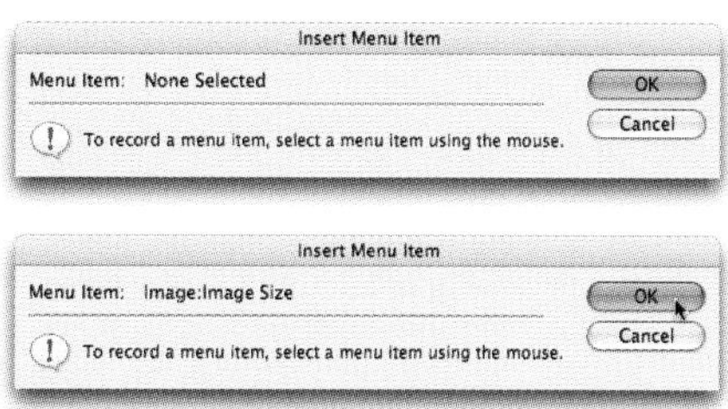


Figure 16-9: Using Insert Menu Item leaves a dialog box open when playing the Action.

- **Record multiple versions of a step, but activate one.** Say you want to record an Action that does a lot of stuff to an image, including changing the pixel dimensions with the Image Size command. However, you want to use this Action with a variety of images that require two or three different final sizes. You can record as many Image Size commands as you want in that one Action — just remember to clear (uncheck) the left column in the Actions palette next to each of the Image Size steps except the one you currently want to use. And you can record an Action within an Action, too. Just play the second Action while recording the first.

- **Insert a message or warning.** Use the Actions palette menu command Insert Stop to send a message to anyone who plays your Action. The message could be something like "You must have a type layer active in the Layers palette before playing this Action" with buttons for Stop and Continue. Or you could phrase it more specifically: "If you have not selected a type layer in the Layers palette, click Stop. If a type layer is active in the Layers palette, click Continue." The more precise the message, the less confusion later. In Figure 16-10, you see the Record Stop dialog box, where you type your message when recording the Action, as well as a look at how the message appears when the Action is played back later.

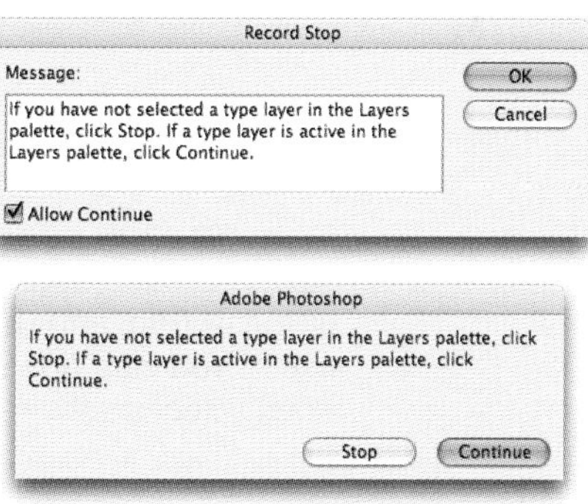


Figure 16-10: Insert a Stop to show a message when the Action is played.

- **Remember Conditional Mode Change and Fit Image.** These two commands in the Automate menu are designed to be recorded in an Action that you might later use on a wide variety of images.

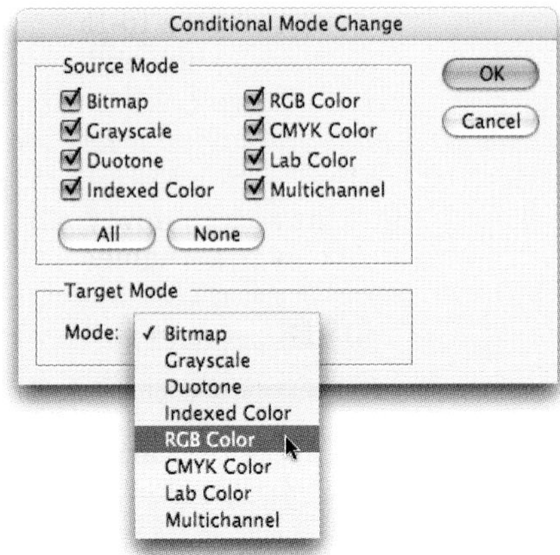


Figure 16-11: Conditional Mode Change converts every image to the target color mode.

  - *Conditional Mode Change* is very handy when your Action (or final result) depends on the image being in a specific color mode. When you record Conditional Mode Change in an Action, every image, regardless of its original color mode, is converted to the target color mode (see Figure 16-11). Say, for example, that you need to apply a certain filter in an Action, but that filter is available only for RGB images. Record Conditional Mode Change before the filter and the Action will play properly.
  - *Fit Image* specifies a maximum width and height that the image being processed must not exceed, regardless of size or shape — great for batch processing images for the Web. Fit Image maintains your images' aspect ratios (to avoid distortion) while ensuring that every image processed will fit within the parameters you specify (see Figure 16-12).

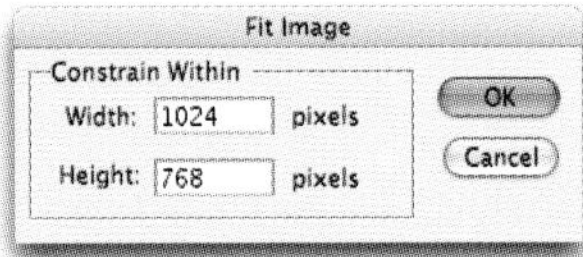


Figure 16-12: Fit Image scales all images to fit within the specified dimensions.

- **Always record an Action from a *copy* of your image.** Because the steps that you record in the Action are actually executed on the open file, record your Action using a copy of the original image. That way, if something goes wrong, your real image is protected.

## Working with the Batch command

Photoshop's File➪Automate➪Batch command plays back a single Action on a number of files. You select an Action to play and also a folder of image files to play it on; then you decide what you want to do with the files after the Action finishes with them. You can leave the images open in Photoshop, save and close them, or (much safer) save them to another folder, preserving the originals. Figure 16-13 shows the Batch dialog box and also the pop-up menu for the fields in the File Naming area. (When you select a new folder as the Destination in Batch, you must tell Photoshop how you want the new files to be named.)

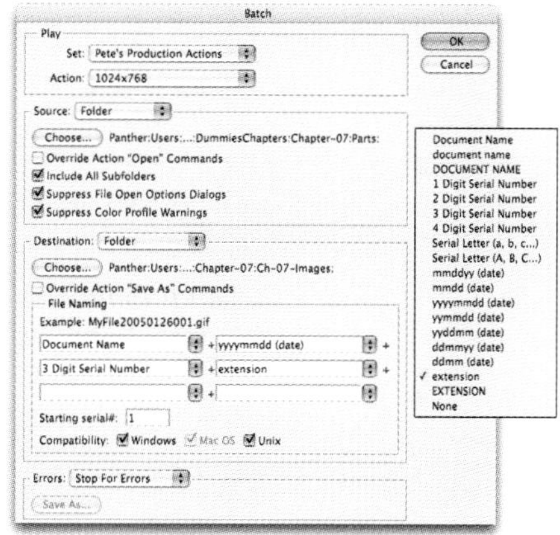


Figure 16-13: The Batch command is much simpler than it looks!

You must remember three things when assigning filenames:

- **Include a variable.** Something must change from filename to filename. Select one of the top nine items in the pop-up menu (some version of the document name or a serial number or a serial letter). It doesn't have to be in the first field, but one element of the filename must be different from file to file.
- **Don't use a period (.) in any field.** You can type in any of the fields (except the last one you use), but for compatibility, stick with letters, numbers, underscores (_), and hyphens (-).

***Absolutely*** do not use a period (.) in the filename. The only period that can be used in a filename is the one that's automatically added immediately before the file extension.

- **The last element *must* be the file extension.** In the last field you use, you must choose either EXTENSION or extension from the pop-up menu.

You have two other decisions of note in the Batch dialog box. When you elect to suppress any Open commands in the Action, you protect yourself from poorly recorded Actions that start by opening the image with which they were recorded. However, if the Action depends on the content of a second file, you do not want to override that Open command. Generally, you want to override any Save As commands recorded in the Action, relying instead on the decisions that you make in the Batch dialog box to determine the fate of the image.

Figure 16-14: Photoshop CS2 has a number of scripts already available.

## Sticking to the Script

You can use AppleScript (Mac), Visual Basic (Windows), and JavaScript (both) with Photoshop. Photoshop CS2 includes several very useful scripts in the File➪Scripts menu. (Your list of built-in scripts might differ from that shown in Figure 16-14.)

Among the prerecorded scripts are

- **Image Processor:** This converts Raw files to PSD, TIFF, or JPEG.
- **Export Layers to Files:** This creates a separate image file from each layer in your image.

You can find more scripts on the Internet, including some at `http://share.studio.adobe.com`. Select Scripts from the Adobe Photoshop Download pop-up menu.

Scripts are much more powerful than Photoshop's Actions because they can control elements outside of Photoshop itself. AppleScripts and Visual Basic scripts can even run multiple programs and play JavaScripts. If you're interested in scripting, go to the Photoshop folder on your hard drive and explore the content of the Scripting Guide folder. You'll find plenty of information to get you started!

# Chapter 17

# Spiffing Up Your Online Offerings

### In This Chapter

- Optimizing graphics for the Web
- Creating slices and image maps
- Adding button effects with rollovers
- Making motion with animation

Understand this one important point before reading further in this chapter: Photoshop and ImageReady are image-creation tools, *not* Web development tools. You use Photoshop and ImageReady to create graphic elements with which you construct a Web site in a dedicated Web design program, such as Adobe GoLive. Sure, you could design and create and slice and save an entire Web page using only Photoshop, and you could post that page on a Web server, creating a Web site. You could also pound nails with a screwdriver. Sure, it works (eventually), but it's not the most efficient way to go about your work. If you just need to put together a simple site to show off your photos, use Photoshop's Web Photo Gallery (see Chapter 4). If you want to create a full-fledged Web site or you want to become a professional Web designer, use GoLive.

That having been said, in this chapter, I show you how to optimize your Web graphics, making sure they load in a Web browser quickly and efficiently. You also see how to subdivide artwork into *slices* — sections of the image that can be optimized individually. This chapter is also the place to read how to create rollovers, buttons, and other images that change appearance interactively, as well as how to create animations, little mini-movies, or cartoons that play on your Web page.

Best Prices

# Integrating Photoshop and ImageReady

ImageReady is installed with Photoshop, right in the Photoshop folder. You can work with ImageReady as a separate program, launching it without Photoshop, or you can use it in conjunction with Photoshop. You can do your creative work in Photoshop and then — with a single click — transfer your image to ImageReady to slice, optimize, and otherwise juice it up for the Web. To open an image in ImageReady directly from Photoshop (to *jump* to ImageReady), click the Edit in ImageReady button at the very bottom of Photoshop's Toolbox (as shown in Figure 17-1). To return to Photoshop, click the Edit in Photoshop button at the bottom of the ImageReady toolbox. Or, if there's no need to return to Photoshop, simply save your image and close it.

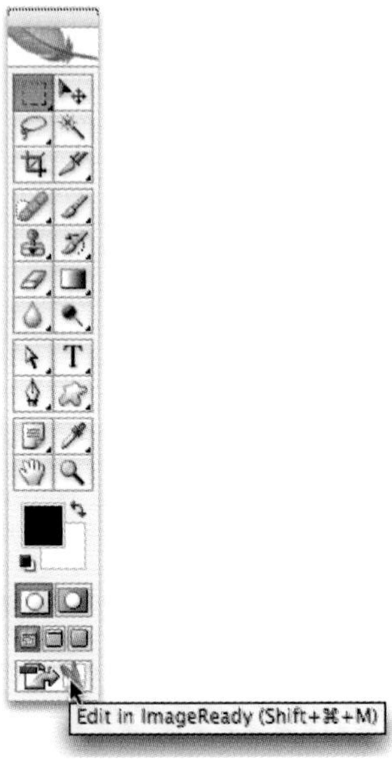


Figure 17-1: Easily move between Photoshop and ImageReady with Toolbox buttons.

# Compromising Quality for Speed

Although the days of slow dialup Internet connections seem to be fading in the rearview mirror rather rapidly, you should nonetheless be aware of the size of your graphics as you prepare them for use on a Web site. That person who visits your Web site through broadband connection from home or office might also find the need to visit while on the road, using a *hotspot* (public wireless connection) in some coffee joint, or maybe using a PDA (personal digital assistant) rather than a laptop. Because such connections might not be as efficient as a cable or DSL link, keeping your graphics file small (and therefore quick to display onscreen) helps keep your visitor happy. Keep in mind that smaller files not only download faster, but they also take up less space on your Web server.

## Optimizing with Save for Web

The process of optimizing an image file removes all non-image data to minimize file size. Using Photoshop's File➪Save for Web feature, you can fine-tune the file size by selecting a compression level (JPEG format) and also choose how the image appears as it downloads. When working in the Save for Web window, use the tabs in the upper-left corner to see the original or an optimized version, or you can compare the original image with one or three optimization alternatives, as shown in Figure 17-2.

Figure 17-2: Save for Web offers multiple view options, including 4-Up.

When working in the 4-Up configuration, you can compare four previews to see how different file formats and options affect not only the image's appearance but also the file size (shown below each preview).

To the upper right of the preview area is a small triangle that opens a menu from which you choose how to interpret the image's colors (I prefer Uncompensated Color) and a modem speed for estimating download time (with the file size under each preview). To the left of the preview area, you have four tools: Hand, Slice, Zoom, and Eyedropper. (They function in Save for Web as they do in Photoshop.) Directly below the preview area, you can change the zoom factor, keep track of the color under the cursor, and open the image in a Web browser to preview.

To the lower right of the preview area is something new in Save for Web. You can preview how the selected optimization settings will look for an animation. You can also click the button it below to close Save for Web and open the image in ImageReady. You make decisions about file format and format-specific options in the area to the right of the previews.

Save for Web works with only those image formats you can use on a Web page. You can't, for example, see a TIFF image in a Web browser, so Save for Web won't generate a TIFF file.

Here's a look at when to use each file format and which options to choose:

- **GIF:** Choose GIF for interface items that consist primarily of solid colors, without subtle or large gradients. Thumbnails of photographs (up to perhaps 100 pixels square) are fine as GIFs, too. However, don't use this format for full-size photos — each GIF file can contain a maximum of 256 different colors, which can greatly degrade the appearance of a photo.

  Generally you want to create the *color table,* which is the list of specific colors used in the image, with the Selective option (see Figure 17-3). The number of colors that you select in the Colors pop-up menu has a direct impact on the size of the file. Reduce the number of colors to shrink the file. Note, too, that you can edit the color table directly in the Color Table tab (which is used only with GIF and PNG-8).

  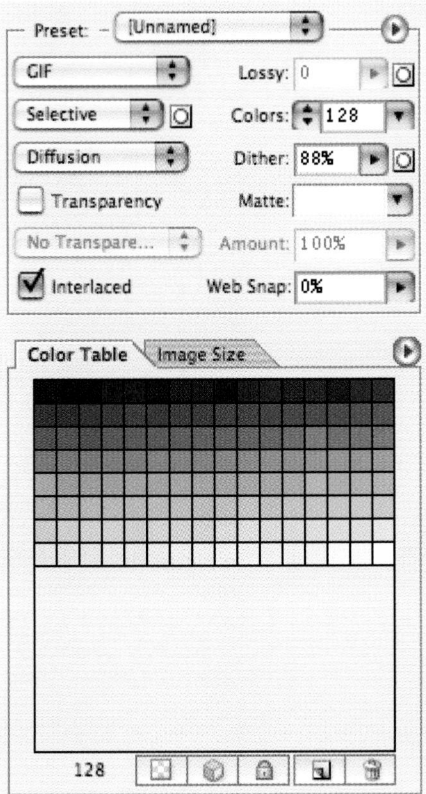


  Figure 17-3: You see these variables when saving as GIF.

  If the image includes transparent areas, select the Transparency check box. If there are shadows or glows over the transparency, choose Diffusion Transparency Dither; if there are distinct edges between opaque and transparent, consider using No Transparency Dither.

  Marking the Interlaced check box enables the Web browser to begin showing the image before it fully downloads, which gives your Web page's visitors the illusion of progress, even if the connection is slow. Although you have the option of using lossy compression to further reduce file size, using it will degrade the appearance of your image.

- **JPEG:** JPEG is your all-purpose file format for photographs and other artwork that includes subtle transitions between colors. The Quality setting determines the amount of compression applied to the image. The greater the compression, the smaller the file size. However, JPEG uses *lossy compression* (some image data is discarded to reduce file size, then "guesstimated" when the image is reopened). The greater the compression, the lower the image quality. Generally speaking, you'll reduce the Quality setting (as shown in Figure 17-4) a bit at a time until you reach an unacceptable level of image degradation.

  The Progressive option enables the image to display while it downloads. Save for Web also allows you to apply a little blurring to your images to further shrink file size (with the associated image degradation, of course). And although JPEG doesn't support transparency in an image, you can use the Matte pop-up menu to match the Web page's background color.

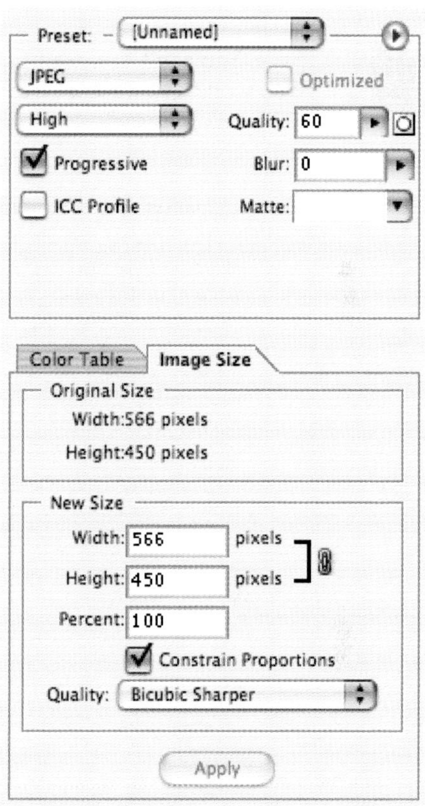


**Figure 17-4:** You balance file size with image quality when saving a JPEG image.

  In Figure 17-4, you also see the Image Size tab, which is available with all file formats. Use the Image Size tab the way you use Photoshop's Image➪Image Size command to change the pixel dimensions of an image. (There's no provision for changing the print dimensions or resolution, however, because this is a Web-oriented feature.)

- **PNG-8:** PNG-8 is an alternative to GIF and offers all the same options (as you see in Figure 17-5), with the exception of lossy compression. Use PNG-8 cautiously, however, because not all Web browsers support the format.

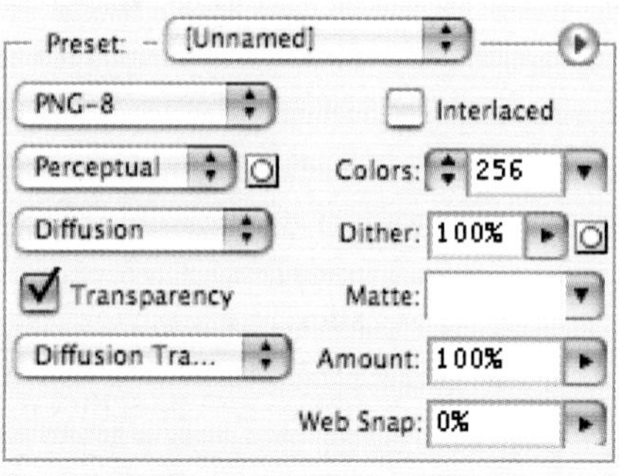


Figure 17-5: Except for lossy compression, you have the same options with PNG-8 and GIF.

- **PNG-24:** Developed as an alternative to JPEG, PNG-24 uses *lossless compression* (no image data is discarded). Also, unlike JPEG, PNG-24 does support transparency, but it's not supported by all Web browsers, and the file sizes are not as small as JPEG. As you see in Figure 17-6, you have few choices to make when saving an image in the PNG-24 file format. If the image includes transparency, select that option. The Interlaced option enables the image to appear in the Web browser while it's still downloading. Select a Matte color if you need the image to blend into the Web page's background along the edges.

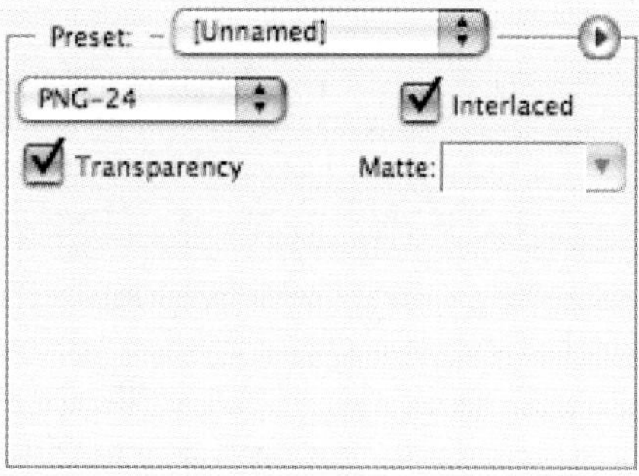


Figure 17-6: PGN-24 offers but a few simple options.

In addition to use on the Web, you can use PNG-24 when preparing images for PowerPoint presentations or for insertion into a Microsoft Word document.

- **WBMP:** The WBMP file format (see Figure 17-7) is used exclusively for wireless Internet devices that cannot display color or grayscale. Each pixel in a WBMP image is either black or white. Choose from diffusion, pattern, and noise dithering to best reproduce the image. Make your decision based entirely on appearance because there will be no difference in file size.

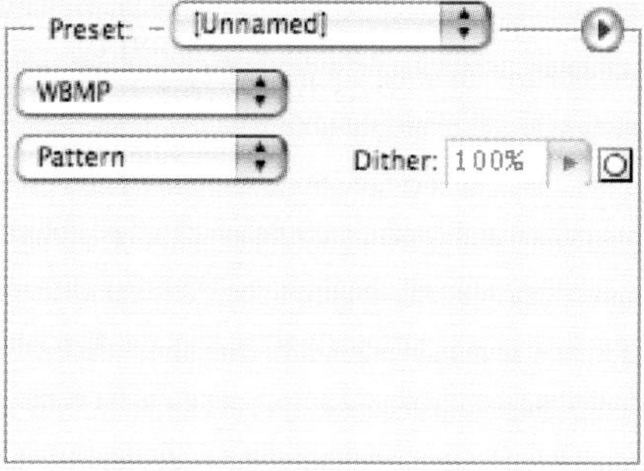


Figure 17-7: If you choose the Dither option, you select the amount of dithering.

To the right of the Preset pop-up menu in Save for Web is the little black triangle that indicates a menu. In the Save for Web menu, you'll find two very significant features:

- **Optimize to File Size:** This feature enables you to select a target file size and let Save For Web choose the options that best preserve image appearance while meeting the size requirement. When working with a sliced image, you can elect to optimize the currently selected slice, optimize each slice to the same target size, or optimize all the slices in the image to a specified total file size. (Read more about slices in the upcoming section, "Creating slices: How and why.")
- **Edit Output Settings:** This feature lets you monkey around with how Save for Web generates slice names, tables for sliced images, and other HTML-related options. Unless you need to make some changes to meet the requirements of your Web development program, I suggest you use the defaults.

The Output Settings defaults are fine with this one exception — one feature in Output Settings that you should consider using when applicable. Normally when you create a file with Save for Web, the image displays as, well, an image in a Web browser. You can, however, also generate backgrounds in Save for Web, comprising small files that are *tiled* (repeated as many times as necessary) to fill the background of a Web page. And you don't even need to open the Output Settings dialog box to access the feature. Here's how:

1. **Select your various Save for Web optimization options.**
2. **Click the Save button in Save for Web.**
3. **In the Save As dialog box that appears, choose**
    - Format: HTML and Images
    - Settings: Background Image

    The HTML file contains Web-specific information that tells the Web browser how to display the image. HTML is the language of the Web.

    When you open the HTML file in a Web browser, the image repeats to fill the background of the page.

Compare using an image as a background (left) and as a simple image (right) in Figure 17-8.

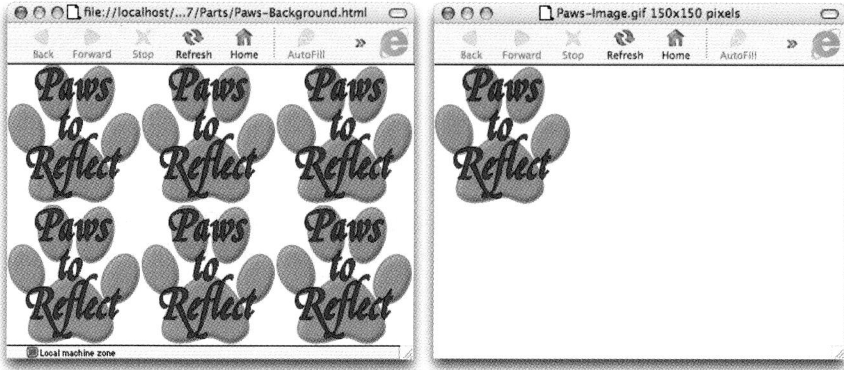


Figure 17-8: Save both HTML and images when creating a tiled background image.

## Image size, resolution, and color for the Web

*Web browsers,* the programs used to view Web sites, are not particularly sophisticated when it comes to graphics. They can't zoom or scale an image the way you can in, for example, Photoshop. Many of the Web browsers available don't use ICC profiles to ensure correct color. (ICC profiles — *color profiles* — are embedded in images to make colors uniform from device to device.) Here are a few things to keep in mind when preparing images for the Web.

Use an image size that's appropriate for display in a Web browser. Generally speaking, you don't want your viewer to have to scroll the browser window to see parts of your image. When deciding how tall to make each image, consider your target audience. If you think the folks you're targeting might have older computers or laptops, plan your Web pages and images around a monitor set to 800 x 600 pixels. If you expect a more current audience, you might want to assume a monitor resolution of 1024 x 768 pixels. And don't forget to allow for the Web browser interface! Subtract about 100 pixels from the height of your planned window.

Always measure Web images in pixels, ignoring print dimensions and "resolution." An image that's 450 pixels tall and 350 pixels wide displays exactly the same in a Web browser at 300 ppi as it does at 72 ppi.

When it comes to color management and the Web, I'm from the school of *None is Better.* Because not all Web browsers can convert colors using ICC color profiles, using profiles can result in a significant difference in image appearance between Photoshop and the Web. In Photoshop's Color Settings dialog box, you can select Color Management Off and work in a completely unmanaged environment. Alternatively, when preparing an individual image for the Web, use the Edit⇨Assign Profile command and select Don't Color Manage This Document. In Save for Web, click the triangle to the upper right of the preview area and select Uncompensated Color. When saving a JPEG file, do not mark the ICC Profile check box.

Also on the subject of Web color, you might hear talk of using *the Web-safe palette,* which is a collection of 216 specific colors that belong to the system-level color table for both Macintosh and Windows. The Web-safe palette is a holdover from the days when computer monitors typically displayed 8-bit color, restricting the number of different colors to 256. These days, there's little need for the Web-safe palette. Even Web-surfing PDAs and cellular phones do a good job with color.

To actually use this background, you copy/paste the HTML code from the HTML file into your Web page's HTML file (`.html` extension) in the appropriate location and then save the image file in the Web site's Images folder.

### Optimizing in ImageReady

When working in ImageReady, you select a file format and your options in the Optimize palette, and then use the File➪Save Optimized As command to generate your Web image file. The format-specific options in the Optimize palette mirror those in Save for Web with one major difference: ImageReady has the capability of maintaining an image's metadata. *Metadata* can include file descriptions, source information (camera make, model, settings, and so on), keywords and categories, and even the image's edit history.

Generally speaking, you might want to add a file description and copyright information to a Web image (the Add Custom ImageReady Metadata option). However, adding full metadata can create a much larger file than necessary. (If the people with whom you're sharing files need metadata, send them the real file rather than posting it as an image on a Web site.)

## Slicing and Adding Image Maps

*Slices,* which can be created in either Photoshop or ImageReady, divide a single image into two or more functional areas. Slicing an image permits you to optimize each section according to that section's needs. When saving, you must generate both HTML and images so that you have the Web code (HTML) to create a table as well as its images. (The table tells the Web browser, using an HTML file, how to arrange and align the individual image files generated from the slices.) *Image maps,* which you create in ImageReady, identify *hot spots* in the image: that is, links to other Web pages or Web sites. When the visitor clicks a hot spot in an image map, that Web browser is redirected to the linked page.

### Creating slices: How and why

If your image has areas with different optimization requirements, you might want to slice it up, subdividing it into smaller images to be reassembled in a Web page. You might, for example, have artwork that contains both a photo (best optimized as JPEG) and areas of solid color (best optimized as GIF). Or your design might include static areas and an area that contains an animation or rollovers.

Both Photoshop and ImageReady allow you to create slices either by using the Slice tool or by creating *layer-based slices* (slices based on the content of a layer). When you drag the Slice tool to create a slice, the program automatically generates the other necessary slices to ensure that the entire image is properly divided into rectangles. (Like all graphic files, slices are rectangular.) When you use the Layer⇨New Layer Based Slice command (Photoshop or ImageReady), a new user-defined slice is created (through all layers) based on a rectangle that includes all the content of the current layer. And, as with the Slice tool, other slices are automatically generated for the rest of the image.

Figure 17-9 shows a sliced image. Note that slice numbers and borders of the slice at the top and in the bottom left are gray, indicating slices generated automatically by the program rather than user-defined or layer-based slices.

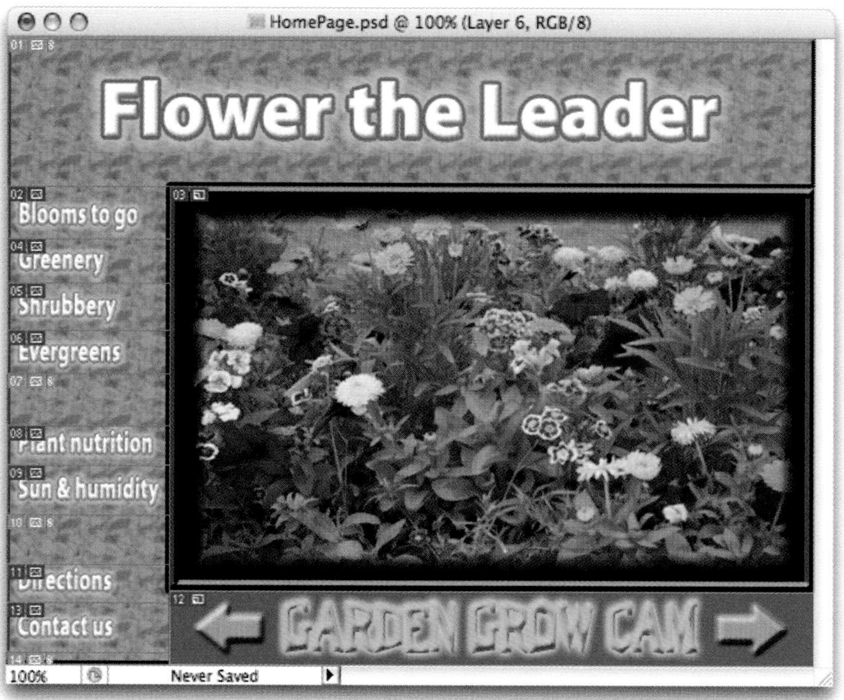


Figure 17-9: Slice a complex image to optimize parts individually or create rollovers.

Creating individual slices for each of the links in the left column lets you easily create rollover effects (discussed later in this chapter). Creating separate slices for the Garden Grow Cam window and its panning controls lets you replace those images in the table with the actual functional elements in your Web development program. (A live camera link and its panning controls are beyond the scope of Photoshop/ImageReady.)

### Designating links with image maps

Unlike a slice, an image map can be any shape and doesn't generate a separate image in a table. Instead, *image maps* create locations in your image that serve as links to other Web pages or sites. When the visitor clicks a point in the image map, the Web browser goes to the designated Web page.

Figure 17-10: Image maps are clickable links to other Web pages.

Create image maps in ImageReady with any of the three Image Map tools. If you need a simple rectangle or circle for your clickable area, not a problem — just grab the appropriate Image Map tool. If you need an irregularly shaped image map, such as that shown in Figure 17-10, use the Polygon Image Map tool. Click to create a series of path-like segments that define the clickable area for the image map. When the visitor clicks within the shape, the Web browser goes to the URL (Uniform Resource Locator — the Web address) that you specify in the Image Map palette. (The Image Map palette, by default, nests with the Slice and Table palettes. Like all palettes, you can show and hide it through the Window menu.)

## Creating Rollover Buttons

A *rollover* is a button (or other part of your Web page) that changes appearance when the visitor's mouse rolls over that spot. The appearance can change when the mouse is over the spot, the mouse button is pressed down, the mouse button is released, the cursor moves off the spot, or all the above. (Consider, if you will, links on a Web page that change color after you click them.)

### Adding a rollover state

In ImageReady (not Photoshop), you use the Web Content and Layers palettes to create rollovers. Click the Create Rollover State button at the bottom of the Web Content palette (second from right), and then show/hide layers in the Layers palette to change the appearance of the image. In Figure 17-11, the Normal rollover state (how the button appears when the page opens) has three layers visible. The Down state (when the visitor clicks the button) has another layer visible, which dramatically changes the appearance of the button. Double-click the rollover state's name in the Web Content palette if you want to change the mouse action that triggers the change in appearance. When added to your Web page, the button will show the Down appearance as long as the cursor is over the button and the mouse button is pressed. When the mouse button is released, the button returns to the Normal appearance.

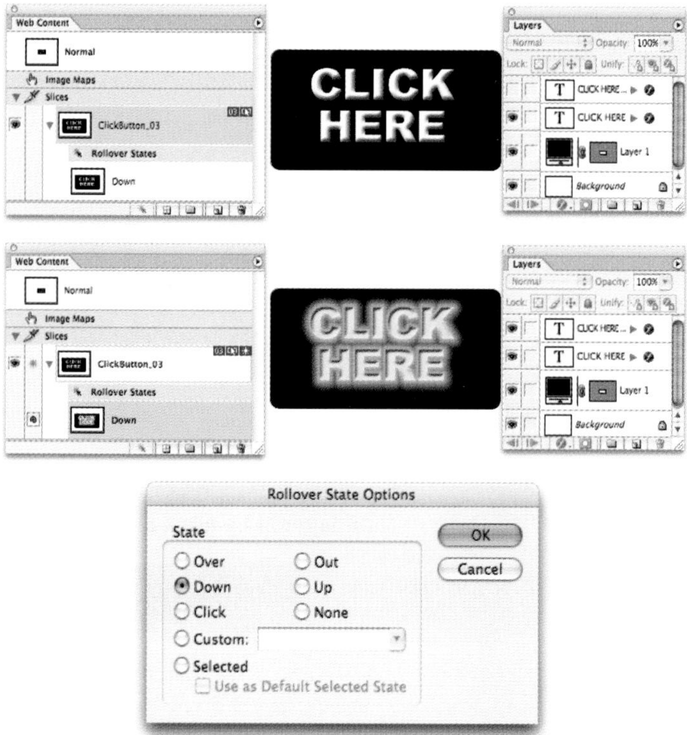


Figure 17-11: Rollover buttons use the Web Content and Layers palettes.

### Saving a rollover button

Like slices, rollovers require that you choose Format: HTML and Images in the Save Optimized As dialog box. To use the button in a Web page, you copy the content of the Images folder to the Web site's Images folder and copy/paste the HTML from the HTML document into the appropriate place in the Web page's HTML document. If you choose the Web site's main folder as the save location, the images are added to the existing Images folder. Although this saves a step, you won't have a backup copy elsewhere on your hard drive. You can use GIF or JPEG for the file format in the Optimize palette when creating rollovers.

Rollovers are perhaps a bit easier to comprehend and plan when you know how the process works. The HTML code that you generate with the Save Optimized As command contains a series of instructions to the Web browser. In effect, those instructions tell the browser to pay attention to the visitor's cursor. When it's over the button, load one image. When the mouse button is down, load a different image. When the mouse moves away, load a third image. A rollover is simply a number of different images, with different appearances, that load at different times according to the mouse behavior.

## A Moving Experience: Animation

Animated GIF files (yes, they must be GIFs, never JPEGs or PNGs) are similar to rollovers in that both are layer-based — you change the appearance of the image in the Layers palette. You use the Animation palette in ImageReady or in Photoshop along with the Layers palette to create individual frames. You also control *playback rate* (how fast the frames change) in the Animations palette.

### Creating a basic animation

Animations can record a number of changes to the image from frame to frame. Layer position, opacity, and layer style are a few of your basic tools for changing the appearance of the image between frames. In Figure 17-12, the four frames of the animation have only one difference: namely, the color of the Outer Glow layer effect. When the animated GIF file loads into a Web page, the Best Prices logo appears to flash in four neon colors, which are sure to catch the viewer's eye. (Best of all, because of the progression of colors, the words *Best Prices* appear to pulse and change size.)

Figure 17-12: Changing a layer style from frame to frame creates a basic animation.

The process is simple:

1. **Open the artwork in Photoshop or ImageReady.**

   You can create an animation from just about any image.

2. **Open and arrange the Animation and Layers palettes.**

   Because you'll be moving back and forth between these palettes, having then conveniently located is a boon.

3. **Click the Duplicate Selected Frame button.**

   This button is located to the left of the Trash icon at the bottom of the Animation palette.

   Always add the new frame before changing the image appearance.

4. **Change the appearance of the artwork.**

   Move a layer, show/hide a layer, change the layer style, or otherwise alter the content of the image.

5. **Repeat for each frame.**

   Add a new frame, change the appearance. Add a new frame, change the appearance. Repeat as necessary until you have all the frames.

6. **Adjust the timing of each frame.**

   Below each frame in the Animation palette, click the downward-pointing triangle to assign *timing* — how long the frame is visible before the next frame appears. You can click and Shift-click to select a series of frames and assign the same timing to all of them at once.

7. **Select a looping option.**

   In the lower-left corner of the Animation palette, decide whether you want the animation to endlessly cycle, play only once, or play for a specific number of repetitions before stopping.

8. **Save as GIF.**

   Use Photoshop's Save for Web or ImageReady's Optimize palette and Save Optimized As command to create a GIF file. You don't need to generate an HTML file; rather, just save the image itself.

## Adding frames easily with tweening

Adding frame after frame to an animation can be tedious work. When your animation includes a progression of movement or visibility, let the Animation palette do most of the work for you. You create the first frame and the last, and then use the Tween feature to create the intermediate frames.

In the example in Figure 17-13, I created a two-layer image, with a cave as the background and a skull as the foreground. The first frame of the animation shows the skull at the top of the cave. After clicking the Duplicate Selected Frame button (think of it as the New Frame button), I dragged the upper layer until the skull touched the top of the background. Next, I clicked the Tween button (third from right at the bottom of the Animation palette), as shown at the bottom of Figure 17-13.

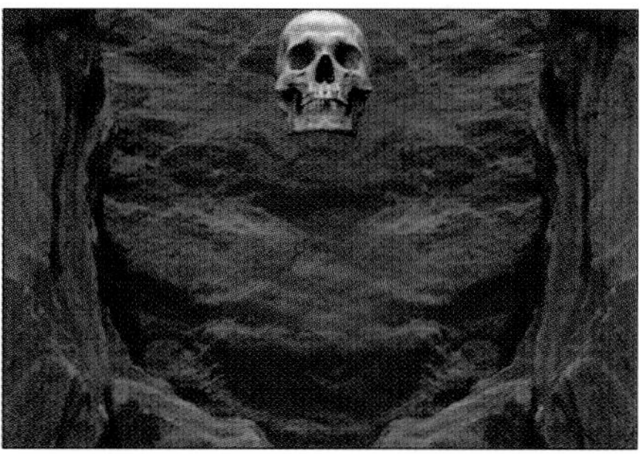

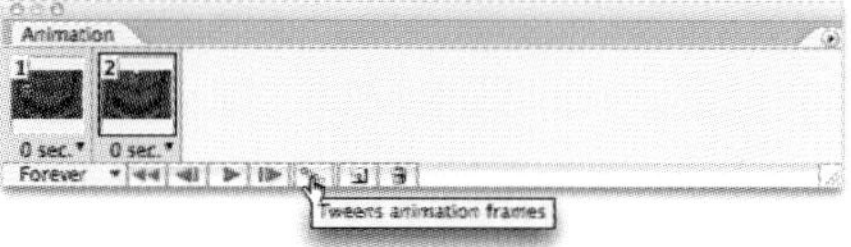


©1998 PhotoSpin, PhotoSpin image #0010032
©2001 PhotoSpin, PhotoSpin image #0490059

**Figure 17-13:** Select two frames and then click Tween to create intermediary frames.

Clicking the Tween button presents me with the Tween dialog box, as shown in Figure 17-14. Because this simple animation involves only a change in position (not opacity or layer styles) and because the moving element is rather large (for the total image size), I elected to enter **4** in the dialog box's Frames to Add text box. The four additional frames are added to the existing frames, giving the animation at this point a total of six frames (see Figure 17-14).

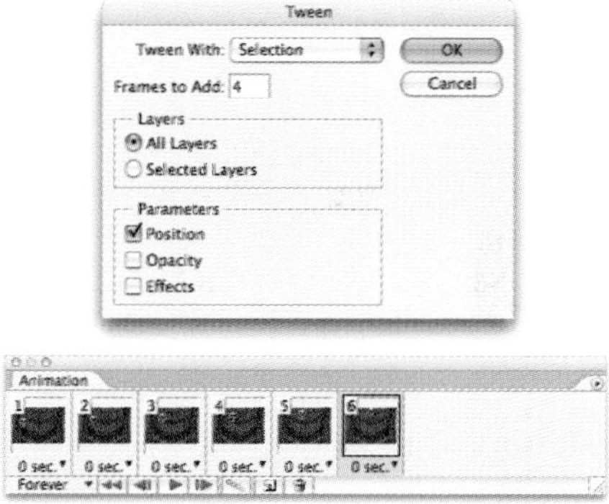


**Figure 17-14:** Tween lets you select several elements to blend position, opacity, and style.

I added a new frame, moved the skull to the far right, and then tweened four more frames by Option/Alt-clicking the Tween button (which automatically applies the last settings). After moving the skull to the bottom, I added another four frames with Tween. Finally, I selected the frame showing the skull at the bottom and the very first frame and added the last four frames. (Click the last frame, and then ⌘/Ctrl-click the first frame to use Tween to finish a looping sequence.) The final animation shows the skull bouncing in a diamond shape, as you can see in the composited image in Figure 17-15.

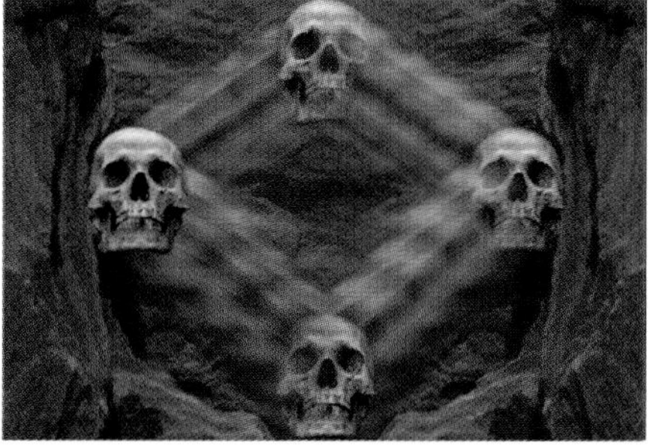

**Figure 17-15:** Final animation, created using two layers, four frames, and lots of tweening.

# Part V
# The Part of Tens

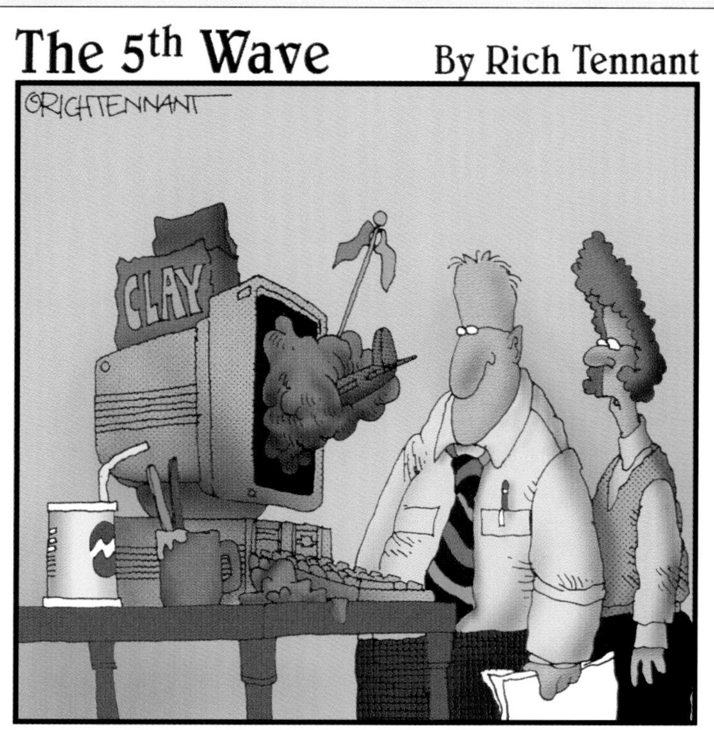


"I couldn't say anything. They were in here with that program we bought them that encourages artistic expression."

## In this part . . .

Don't get nervous — this is The Part of *Tens* and not The Part of *Tense!*

In Chapter 18, I present you with ten of my favorite Photoshop tricks and techniques. Chapter 19 contains a list of some of the presents that I'd give you (if I could) to make working in Photoshop easier and more efficient. (Because I can't give you the hardware and software listed in the chapter, I give you the list instead. Feel free to hand it to a friend shortly before your birthday.)

Chapter 20 provides you with ten reasons to shoot digitally. If you already own and use a digital camera, loan it to an analog colleague.

# Chapter 18

# Pete's Top Ten Favorite Photoshop Tips and Tricks

### In This Chapter

- Playing with artistic and creative tricks
- Exploring a few useful tips

I have literally thousands of Photoshop tips and tricks to share with you, but space here allows for only ten. (Okay, I manage to sneak in a few more tips and tricks here and there in other chapters, but don't tell!) Actually, just about anything you do that doesn't use Photoshop's default values or presets could be considered a tip or a trick. However, you're likely interested in creative and productive shortcuts rather than something like this: *Save copies of your custom brushes, styles, and other such bits and pieces somewhere other than the Photoshop folder so you don't lose them should you ever need to reinstall the program.* (Oops! I snuck in an extra tip, didn't I?)

In this chapter, I present ten of my favorite creative and useful techniques. Some of these tricks I developed while helping solve problems in my role as Help Desk Director for the National Association of Photoshop Professionals (NAPP), and others are tried-and-true helpers that have been around for years.

## Adding Artistic and Creative Effects

Surely you'd prefer to read *Fill a layer with brown, use the Add Noise filter (Gaussian Distribution, Monochrome), and then apply a Motion Blur filter to create a wood grain effect* rather than *If you need to apply a grayed-out filter to a CMYK image, apply it to one channel, and then the other three individually using ⌘+F/Ctrl+F.* (Okay, if I don't cut it out, somebody is going to notice I'm exceeding my Tips and Tricks quota!) Here are some of my favorite (and most useful) creative tips.

## Smoothing skin perfectly

When you see glamour shots — you know, photos of The Beautiful People who look so absolutely perfect — one of the things you're *not* seeing is the texture of the skin. No wrinkles. No creases. No *pores?* Indeed, the skin appears to be perfectly smooth (see Figure 18-1).

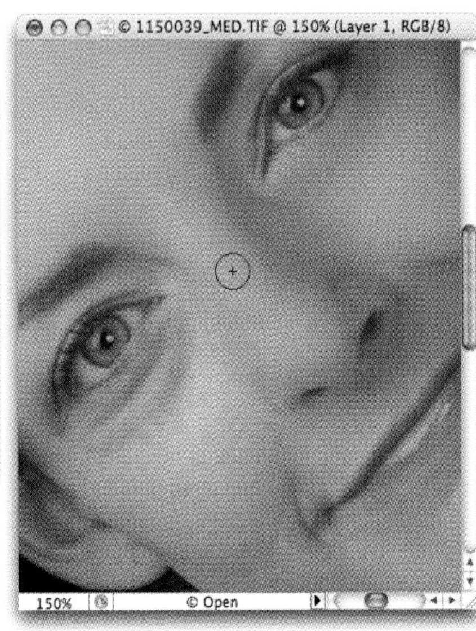


*© 2003PhotoSpin, PhotoSpin image #1150039*

**Figure 18-1:** Use the Healing Brush and a plain-color source area to smooth skin.

Here's how you can achieve that effect without blurring:

1. **Open a copy of your image.**

   Whenever you use a technique that makes permanent changes to the pixels in your image, *you should work on a copy.* That preserves the original image, which not only protects you from any errors that you (or Photoshop) might make but also keeps that original for different techniques and tricks in the future. (Does that count as a tip?)

2. **Add a new layer by clicking the New Layer button in the Layers palette.**

3. **Make a selection.**

   The selection should be away from the face area, and sized at least one-half the width and height of the face.

4. **Fill the selection with color.**

   Press Option+Delete (Mac)/Alt+Backspace (Windows) to fill it with the foreground color (it doesn't matter what color); then deselect.

5. **Select the Healing Brush and set the source point.**

   Make sure that the Use All Layers option is selected in the Options bar and that Aligned is deselected. Option/Alt-click in the center of the filled selection.

6. **Paint over the skin.**

   Click and drag with the Healing Brush to smooth areas of skin. The Healing Brush replaces the texture of the skin (pores and all) with the texture of the source area (smooth). Use short strokes that follow the contour of the face. Make sure that you *don't* paint over eyebrows, nostrils, lips, and other areas of critical detail.

## From a photo to a painting

You have dozens of ways to create a "painterly" effect in Photoshop. Here is one of my favorites, as illustrated by Figure 18-2.

**Figure 18-2:** Blur shadows, sharpen highlights, and add texture for a "painterly" effect.

1. **Open a copy of your image.**

   As always, because this technique makes changes to your pixels, work on a copy of your image.

2. **Select the shadows and blur.**

   Open the Channels palette and ⌘/Ctrl-click the channel at the top (RGB or CMYK or Lab) to make a selection according to the brightness of each pixel. Use the shortcut ⌘+Shift+I/Ctrl+Shift+I to *invert* the selection (select shadows rather than highlights). Apply a slight Gaussian Blur, perhaps 1 or 2 pixels, to blur detail in the darker areas. (Remember that you can use the shortcut ⌘+H/Ctrl+H to hide the "marching ants" and make the selection border disappear — and that's *not* a tip!)

3. **Select the highlights and sharpen.**

   Use the shortcut ⌘+Shift+I/Ctrl+Shift+I to again invert the selection (again selecting the highlights). Apply the Sharpen⇨Smart Sharpen filter with initial settings of Amount: 200% and Radius: 2 pixels. (Adjust the values to match the content of your image and your artistic vision.)

4. **Add a canvas texture to the image.**

   Deselect with the shortcut ⌘+D/Ctrl+D (so that the texture is applied to the whole image), then use the Texture⇨Texturizer filter to add a slight canvas texture, enhancing the "painterly" effect.

## Creating a sketch from a photo

Simulating a painting in Photoshop is great, but sometimes you might need line art or a sketch. Photoshop has a couple of filters that do a nice job of creating pencil sketches, but none of them really do a great job with outlines. Here's an easy way to create line art from a photo (see Figure 18-3).

1. **Open a copy of your image.**

   Again, this is a destructive technique — it makes permanent changes to the pixels in the file — so work from a copy to play it safe.

2. **Apply the Smart Blur filter.**

   Set the filter to Quality: High and Mode: Normal, and use settings that remove all the tiny detail in your image (such as pores and individual hairs or blades of grass) but maintain edges and major detail (such as eyes, noses, golf balls, and trees).

3. **Define edges with Smart Blur.**

   Reopen the Smart Blur dialog box and set the Mode pop-up menu to Edge Only. Adjust the sliders until the white-on-black preview shows approximately the amount of detail you want in the final image; then click OK.

4. **Invert the colors.**

   Use the shortcut ⌘+I/Ctrl+I to swap black and white in the image.

5. **Blur the lines.**

   Apply a 1- or 2-pixel Gaussian Blur to soften the edges of the lines.

6. **Adjust the thickness of the lines with Levels.**

   In the Levels dialog box, drag the middle slider control left and right until you're satisfied with the image's appearance. If desired, you can further refine the sketch with the Sharpen➪Unsharp Mask filter.

*©2003PhotoSpin, PhotoSpin image #1150039*

**Figure 18-3:** You can use the versatile Smart Blur filter to produce line art from a photo.

## *Creating snow or rain*

Here's a multi-use technique that you can use to create falling snow or rain (as shown in Figure 18-4):

1. **Add a new layer to your image by clicking the New Layer button in the Layers palette.**

2. **Still in the Layers palette, change the layer's blending mode from Normal to Screen.**

   The Screen blending mode makes the layer appear to be empty.

   Because this technique uses a separate layer, consider it to be non-destructive (you can always delete the layer later), so you don't have to work on a copy of your image.

3. **Use the Edit➪Fill command to fill the layer with black.**

4. **Add Noise to the layer.**

   Use the Noise➪Add Noise filter to add some variation to the layer. Use Amount: 20%, Distribution: Gaussian, and mark the Monochromatic check box.

5. **Crystallize the noise.**

   Use the Pixelate➪Crystallize filter to turn the little noise into larger chunks. Use Cell Size: 3 for small snow or rain; try 7 or 10 for larger flakes. You can also apply a slight Gaussian Blur to increase the size.

6. **Sharpen the edges.**

   Using the Unsharp Mask filter, sharpen until the snowflakes have distinct edges. Use Amount: 100%, Radius: 2, Threshold: 0. When you create rain, use Amount: 40%.

7. **Apply a Levels adjustment.**

   In the Levels dialog box, drag the middle slider about halfway to the left; then drag the left slider slowly to the right until you see the amount of snow or rain that you want. Afterward, if desired, you can apply the Motion Blur filter to the falling snow/rain. And, of course, you can add a layer mask to control visibility.

Figure 18-4: Use the Noise and Crystallize filters to produce snow or rain.

### The Glass Text effect

Perfect for adding a large copyright notice right across the center of your image (while allowing the image's beauty to still show through), this technique is so easy it doesn't even need a step-by-step explanation. Simply type your copyright info (or any other text), and add a Bevel and Emboss layer style (perhaps with a slight Inner Shadow and maybe a 1-pixel black Stroke effect). Then, at the top of the Layers palette, reduce the Fill slider (not the Opacity slider) to 0 (zero). The pixels on the layer become transparent, but the layer style remains visible.

## Useful Tricks to Make Life Easier

Here are five techniques that make life easier and your work look snappier and more professional.

### Changing product colors in a snap

Use Photoshop's Replace Color feature (in the Image➪Adjustments menu) to quickly and easily make variations of a single image by changing color. Replace Color is especially handy in production environments, letting you shoot one shot and produce numerous color variations. (See Figure 18-5.)

Open Replace Color and Shift-drag the Eyedropper tool through the color you want to change. Adjust the Fuzziness slider to fine-tune the selection; then adjust the Hue/Saturation and Lightness sliders to change the color.

©1998 PhotoSpin, PhotoSpin image #0070004

**Figure 18-5:** Photoshop's Replace Color adjustment makes quick work of color changes.

If the target color appears in more than one part of the image, perhaps a red blouse and red lipstick, make a loose selection around the area you want to change (excluding the other areas) before opening Replace Color.

## Deleting a plain white background

Lots of stock photography comes as a subject shot against a plain white background. Clip art also generally comes on a plain white background. Most of these images have clipping paths or alpha channels that you can use to extract the subject from the background to add it to another image. And when there is no path or channel? Open both images in Photoshop and drag the stock photo's *Background* layer from the Layers palette to the window of the destination image. Make sure that the upper layer is active in the Layers palette and then open the Blending Options panel of the Layer Style dialog box. In the Blend If area at the bottom, drag the upper-right slider handle to the left until the upper layer's white background is completely gone. (See Figure 18-6.)

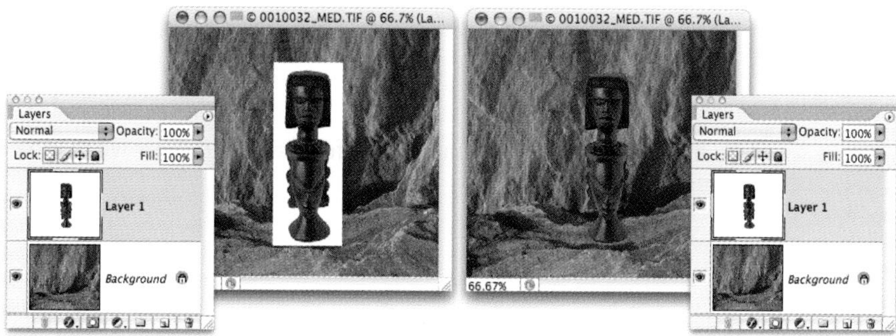


Both images ©1998 PhotoSpin, PhotoSpin image #0010032 (background) and image #0120013 (foreground)

**Figure 18-6:** Use the Blend If sliders to hide a white background.

## Making dashed and dotted lines

Changing a couple of settings in Photoshop's Brushes palette enables you to create dashed and dotted lines with ease. In the Brush Tip Shape pane, increase Spacing to a value higher than 100% to separate the individual imprints of the brush tip (the *brush tip instances*). Switch to the Shape Dynamics pane and select Direction from the Angle Jitter pop-up menu. For best results, make a selection and use the Edit➪Stroke command to apply your dotted or dashed brush along the selection border.

## Quick and easy edge effects

Need some way to make your images stand out? Try this:

1. **Add a new layer to your image by clicking the New Layer button in the Layers palette.**

   To avoid making any permanent change to your image (primarily so you can change your mind about the border later), work on a new layer.

2. **Select a border area around the image.**

   Use the Select➪All command, followed by the Select➪Modify➪Border command. Enter a value twice the width that you want for your edge effect.

3. **Fill the selection with black, gray, or white.**

   - *Black:* Makes your image look brighter and more saturated
   - *Gray:* Minimizes any perceived color shift
   - *White:* Mutes the image somewhat but allows it to stand on its own

   Alternatively, use any color from the image (or its inverse).

4. **Apply filters to the layer.**

   Open the Filter Gallery and apply one or more filters to the border to create an interesting edge effect (such as the samples in Figure 18-7).

## Professional-looking contact sheets

You can use this trick to produce a more traditional-looking contact sheet with a black background and white type:

1. **Set up Contact Sheet II.**

   Use the File➪Automate➪Contact Sheet II command to open the dialog box. Select your source folder, make decisions on page size and layout, pick a font for the filenames, and so on.

Figure 18-7: Filtering a border area creates interesting edge effects for your images.

2. **Clear the Flatten All Layers check box.**

   Before running Contact Sheet II, make sure you clear this check box to ensure that your contact sheet retains its layers.

3. **Generate the contact sheets.**

   Select your page size, source folder, and other settings as I describe in Chapter 16. Click OK.

4. **Fill the *Background* layer with black.**

   In the Layers palette, select the layer named *Background,* press D to set your foreground color to black, and then press Option+Delete/Alt+Backspace to fill the layer with black.

5. **Change the type to white.**

   In the Layers palette, ⌘/Ctrl-click each of the type layers to select them all, click the Link Layers button at the bottom of the Layers palette, and then Shift-click the color swatch in the Character palette to open the Color Picker. Set the color to white (or bright yellow or whatever color suits your fancy) and then click OK. You can now flatten the image (if desired).

# Chapter 19

# Ten Extras You Should Consider

### In This Chapter

- Discovering equipment to add to your wish list
- Checking out software to complement Photoshop

Although Photoshop CS2 is indeed a dandy product all by itself, it doesn't have to live in a vacuum. Hundreds of pieces of hardware and software are available to make working with Photoshop faster, easier, and even perhaps more profitable. (As your birthday approaches, please feel free to leave this book open to this chapter in some conspicuous place around the house or office, perhaps with some great big red circles and arrows.)

After all, there are goodies, and then there are *goodies!* Of the many, many accessories available for Photoshop, these are the ones that I put at the top of my list.

## New Toys: Hardware

Unpack it. Hook it up. Plug it in. Screw it down. Drag it around. Hardware accessories come in a lot of shapes, sizes, and price ranges. Assuming that you have a limited budget or cash flow, here's how I suggest you prioritize your wish list:

- **RAM:** Photoshop CS2 can recognize some 4GB of *RAM* (computer memory). If you work with large images or multiple images — especially if you apply complex filters — add more RAM to work faster and more efficiently. Online retailers like Crucial Technology (`www.crucial.com`) can help you choose the correct memory chips for your computer. And make *sure* you get the right chips!
- **Wacom tablet:** A pressure-sensitive drawing tablet is great for more than painting. Tracing an outline with the Magnetic Lasso using a mouse can be tough, as can creating a complex layer mask with the Brush tool. A Wacom tablet lets you use a pen-like

## • B •

stylus instead of a mouse. The Wacom site (www.wacom.com) has a Tablet Wizard to help you choose the correct tablet for your needs. My tip: If you're a traditionally trained artist, you likely use longer strokes and will be happier with a larger tablet. Likewise, if you have a huge monitor, get a big tablet. Otherwise, a 6 x 8" Intuos$_3$ is great.

- **Tripod:** Photographers (digital or film) need a good, strong, steady tripod. You might be surprised by the amount of time you save retouching photos shot with a camera that's perfectly steady. And to help prevent exposure tremors even more, get a cable release or wireless control for your camera, too!
- **Second monitor:** With a second video card (or a dual-head video card), you can hook up a second monitor that extends the work area (not just for Photoshop) across both screens. Mac users use the two monitors as a single workspace, and Windows users can move palettes to the second monitor but not image windows.
- **Large(r) format printer:** An 8 x 10" photo is great, but sometime a 13 x 19" print is much more powerful (and sells at a better price, too). If your inkjet doesn't print on paper larger than letter size, consider investing in a printer that does. Take a look at Epson online (www.epson.com) for the latest models.

## Extra Capabilities: Software

There are some things that Photoshop does well that additional software does, well, *better.* Here are five great ways to make Photoshop work better:

- **Masking software:** Fly-away hair, glass, shadows . . . lots of very tough selection and masking challenges face you. Mask Pro from Extensis (www.extensis.com) and KnockOut from Corel (www.corel.com) are both excellent.
- **Fonts:** Sure, you have the various fonts installed with your operating system and on various programs, but more can be better! Check out Chank! (www.chank.com), Fonthead Design (www.fonthead.com), Fonts.com (www.fonts.com), and Adobe (www.adobe.com).
- **nik Color Efex Pro:** An amazing product, Color Efex from nik multimedia (www.nikmultimedia.com) maintains relationships among colors while enhancing your image.
- **nik Sharpener Pro:** Another great product from nik multimedia, Sharpener Pro takes the guesswork out of sharpening your image. Your image is analyzed and evaluated for its content, color, resolution, and destination.
- **Scaling software:** If you want to make large prints, perhaps poster size or larger, consider either pxl SmartScale (www.extensis.com) or Genuine Fractals (www.genuinefractals.com).

# Chapter 20

# Ten Reasons to Own a Digital Camera

### In This Chapter

- Five professional-life reasons to go digital
- Four personal-life reasons to go digital
- One good-for-the-future-of-the-planet reason to go digital

It's hard to pick just ten reasons to own and use a digital camera. In an effort to play heartstrings everywhere, I've included ideas about job-related shooting, uses in the home, travel considerations . . . the list goes on and on, but only up to ten. After that, you have to use your imagination.

## Ten Reasons You Should Shoot Pixels

The gap in capability between 35mm film and high-end digital cameras disappeared some time ago. The technology that allows digital cameras to match 35mm quality is now found in quite reasonably priced equipment. (Admittedly, only the most expensive digital camera backs can even think about competing with medium or large format film.) If you haven't yet gone over to the digital side, here are some convincing arguments to make the jump. If you already are digital in mind, body, and lens, read the list anyway — it might give you a few points for future discussions with traditionalists.

### Shooting digital for your work

In the field, in the studio, and even in the home and on the road, digital offers a number of advantages over film.

- **No processing time (or cost):** You don't wait to start editing your images because you download to your computer and open the images in Photoshop. No longer do you have those pesky delays for processing/printing/scanning. (And no bills for film processing.)
- **Instant feedback:** You can evaluate the shot immediately on the camera's LCD screen, which allows you to quickly delete any boo-boos before anyone else sees them. Oh, and that frees up storage space, too, of course! (And don't forget about LCD previews available on many cameras, and operating your camera from the computer, which let you makes decisions even before you shoot.)
- **Create libraries of textures and patterns:** Shoot digital images of clouds and bark and grass and fabric and concrete and bricks and whatever to create libraries of textures to use in Photoshop.
- **Remote control:** Use your computer's monitor (if your camera/software allows) to adjust and perfect the shot before shooting. The screen is a lot larger and more accurate than the camera's LCD.
- **Multiple exposures for one image:** Bracket the exposure, and then combine the images automatically in Photoshop with Merge to HDR.

### Shooting digital for yourself

Owning a digital camera comes in handy for your personal life, too.

- **Travel convenience:** With a digital, you eliminate worries about x-ray machines, baggage scanning, and film storage. And don't forget how much easier it is to carry a half-dozen Flash cards than dozens of rolls of film!
- **Home inventory:** Do it. Really. Do it. Go around the house and take photos of the important stuff. (Don't forget the jewelry!) If your camera has a date/time stamp, use it. You don't even need to print these shots. Just drop that Flash card (or whatever storage device your camera uses) in the safe deposit box at the bank. Or mail it to your family attorney. Or put it in an envelope at the office. But have it safe, just in case Mother Nature (or Human Nature) requires you to file an insurance claim.
- **Family gatherings:** Hey, aren't you the Photoshop expert? Doesn't that make you the perfect person to take this group photo? (Read about instant feedback in the preceding section.)
- **Explore your artistic boundaries:** It really doesn't cost anything (dollar-wise) to shoot digitally. Take the off-angle shot. Play with aperture and exposure. Have fun, play, experiment, and learn. And see what you *really* have inside you.

## Shooting digital for the rest of us

Digital photography is so much more environmentally friendly than film that it boggles the mind! No toxic waste related to film production. No processing chemicals to dispose of (or illegally dump down the sink). Really, truly, a more Earth-friendly way to shoot. And isn't that a nice thought with which to end this book?

We wish you peace, love, health, and happiness!

# Index

## A

## • B •

## • C •

## • D •

• E •

## • J •

## • L •

## • N •

## O



## P

• Q •



• R •

## • S •

• Z •

# Notes

# Notes

## BUSINESS, CAREERS & PERSONAL FINANCE

0-7645-5307-0

0-7645-5331-3 *†

Also available:

- Accounting For Dummies †
  0-7645-5314-3
- Business Plans Kit For Dummies †
  0-7645-5365-8
- Cover Letters For Dummies
  0-7645-5224-4
- Frugal Living For Dummies
  0-7645-5403-4
- Leadership For Dummies
  0-7645-5176-0
- Managing For Dummies
  0-7645-1771-6
- Marketing For Dummies
  0-7645-5600-2
- Personal Finance For Dummies *
  0-7645-2590-5
- Project Management For Dummies
  0-7645-5283-X
- Resumes For Dummies †
  0-7645-5471-9
- Selling For Dummies
  0-7645-5363-1
- Small Business Kit For Dummies *†
  0-7645-5093-4

## HOME & BUSINESS COMPUTER BASICS

0-7645-4074-2

0-7645-3758-X

Also available:

- ACT! 6 For Dummies
  0-7645-2645-6
- iLife '04 All-in-One Desk Reference For Dummies
  0-7645-7347-0
- iPAQ For Dummies
  0-7645-6769-1
- Mac OS X Panther Timesaving Techniques For Dummies
  0-7645-5812-9
- Macs For Dummies
  0-7645-5656-8
- Microsoft Money 2004 For Dummies
  0-7645-4195-1
- Office 2003 All-in-One Desk Reference For Dummies
  0-7645-3883-7
- Outlook 2003 For Dummies
  0-7645-3759-8
- PCs For Dummies
  0-7645-4074-2
- TiVo For Dummies
  0-7645-6923-6
- Upgrading and Fixing PCs For Dummies
  0-7645-1665-5
- Windows XP Timesaving Techniques For Dummies
  0-7645-3748-2

## FOOD, HOME, GARDEN, HOBBIES, MUSIC & PETS

0-7645-5295-3

0-7645-5232-5

Also available:

- Bass Guitar For Dummies
  0-7645-2487-9
- Diabetes Cookbook For Dummies
  0-7645-5230-9
- Gardening For Dummies *
  0-7645-5130-2
- Guitar For Dummies
  0-7645-5106-X
- Holiday Decorating For Dummies
  0-7645-2570-0
- Home Improvement All-in-One For Dummies
  0-7645-5680-0
- Knitting For Dummies
  0-7645-5395-X
- Piano For Dummies
  0-7645-5105-1
- Puppies For Dummies
  0-7645-5255-4
- Scrapbooking For Dummies
  0-7645-7208-3
- Senior Dogs For Dummies
  0-7645-5818-8
- Singing For Dummies
  0-7645-2475-5
- 30-Minute Meals For Dummies
  0-7645-2589-1

## INTERNET & DIGITAL MEDIA

0-7645-1664-7

0-7645-6924-4

Also available:

- 2005 Online Shopping Directory For Dummies
  0-7645-7495-7
- CD & DVD Recording For Dummies
  0-7645-5956-7
- eBay For Dummies
  0-7645-5654-1
- Fighting Spam For Dummies
  0-7645-5965-6
- Genealogy Online For Dummies
  0-7645-5964-8
- Google For Dummies
  0-7645-4420-9
- Home Recording For Musicians For Dummies
  0-7645-1634-5
- The Internet For Dummies
  0-7645-4173-0
- iPod & iTunes For Dummies
  0-7645-7772-7
- Preventing Identity Theft For Dummies
  0-7645-7336-5
- Pro Tools All-in-One Desk Reference For Dummies
  0-7645-5714-9
- Roxio Easy Media Creator For Dummies
  0-7645-7131-1

**Separate Canadian edition also available**
**Separate U.K. edition also available**

ailable wherever books are sold. For more information or to order direct: U.S. customers visit www.dummies.com or call 1-877-762-2974.
K. customers visit www.wileyeurope.com or call 0800 243407. Canadian customers visit www.wiley.ca or call 1-800-567-4797.

## SPORTS, FITNESS, PARENTING, RELIGION & SPIRITUALITY

0-7645-5146-9

0-7645-5418-2

**Also available:**

- Adoption For Dummies 0-7645-5488-3
- Basketball For Dummies 0-7645-5248-1
- The Bible For Dummies 0-7645-5296-1
- Buddhism For Dummies 0-7645-5359-3
- Catholicism For Dummies 0-7645-5391-7
- Hockey For Dummies 0-7645-5228-7
- Judaism For Dummies 0-7645-5299-6
- Martial Arts For Dummies 0-7645-5358-5
- Pilates For Dummies 0-7645-5397-6
- Religion For Dummies 0-7645-5264-3
- Teaching Kids to Read For Dummies 0-7645-4043-2
- Weight Training For Dummies 0-7645-5168-X
- Yoga For Dummies 0-7645-5117-5

## TRAVEL

0-7645-5438-7

0-7645-5453-0

**Also available:**

- Alaska For Dummies 0-7645-1761-9
- Arizona For Dummies 0-7645-6938-4
- Cancún and the Yucatán For Dummies 0-7645-2437-2
- Cruise Vacations For Dummies 0-7645-6941-4
- Europe For Dummies 0-7645-5456-5
- Ireland For Dummies 0-7645-5455-7
- Las Vegas For Dummies 0-7645-5448-4
- London For Dummies 0-7645-4277-X
- New York City For Dummies 0-7645-6945-7
- Paris For Dummies 0-7645-5494-8
- RV Vacations For Dummies 0-7645-5443-3
- Walt Disney World & Orlando For Dummies 0-7645-6943-0

## GRAPHICS, DESIGN & WEB DEVELOPMENT

0-7645-4345-8

0-7645-5589-8

**Also available:**

- Adobe Acrobat 6 PDF For Dummies 0-7645-3760-1
- Building a Web Site For Dummies 0-7645-7144-3
- Dreamweaver MX 2004 For Dummies 0-7645-4342-3
- FrontPage 2003 For Dummies 0-7645-3882-9
- HTML 4 For Dummies 0-7645-1995-6
- Illustrator CS For Dummies 0-7645-4084-X
- Macromedia Flash MX 2004 For Dummie 0-7645-4358-X
- Photoshop 7 All-in-One Desk Reference For Dummies 0-7645-1667-1
- Photoshop CS Timesaving Technique For Dummies 0-7645-6782-9
- PHP 5 For Dummies 0-7645-4166-8
- PowerPoint 2003 For Dummies 0-7645-3908-6
- QuarkXPress 6 For Dummies 0-7645-2593-X

## NETWORKING, SECURITY, PROGRAMMING & DATABASES

0-7645-6852-3

0-7645-5784-X

**Also available:**

- A+ Certification For Dummies 0-7645-4187-0
- Access 2003 All-in-One Desk Reference For Dummies 0-7645-3988-4
- Beginning Programming For Dummies 0-7645-4997-9
- C For Dummies 0-7645-7068-4
- Firewalls For Dummies 0-7645-4048-3
- Home Networking For Dummies 0-7645-42796
- Network Security For Dummies 0-7645-1679-5
- Networking For Dummies 0-7645-1677-9
- TCP/IP For Dummies 0-7645-1760-0
- VBA For Dummies 0-7645-3989-2
- Wireless All In-One Desk Reference For Dummies 0-7645-7496-5
- Wireless Home Networking For Dummi 0-7645-3910-8

## HEALTH & SELF-HELP

0-7645-6820-5 *†

0-7645-2566-2

**Also available:**

- Alzheimer's For Dummies 0-7645-3899-3
- Asthma For Dummies 0-7645-4233-8
- Controlling Cholesterol For Dummies 0-7645-5440-9
- Depression For Dummies 0-7645-3900-0
- Dieting For Dummies 0-7645-4149-8
- Fertility For Dummies 0-7645-2549-2
- Fibromyalgia For Dummies 0-7645-5441-7
- Improving Your Memory For Dummies 0-7645-5435-2
- Pregnancy For Dummies † 0-7645-4483-7
- Quitting Smoking For Dummies 0-7645-2629-4
- Relationships For Dummies 0-7645-5384-4
- Thyroid For Dummies 0-7645-5385-2

## EDUCATION, HISTORY, REFERENCE & TEST PREPARATION

0-7645-5194-9

0-7645-4186-2

**Also available:**

- Algebra For Dummies 0-7645-5325-9
- British History For Dummies 0-7645-7021-8
- Calculus For Dummies 0-7645-2498-4
- English Grammar For Dummies 0-7645-5322-4
- Forensics For Dummies 0-7645-5580-4
- The GMAT For Dummies 0-7645-5251-1
- Inglés Para Dummies 0-7645-5427-1
- Italian For Dummies 0-7645-5196-5
- Latin For Dummies 0-7645-5431-X
- Lewis & Clark For Dummies 0-7645-2545-X
- Research Papers For Dummies 0-7645-5426-3
- The SAT I For Dummies 0-7645-7193-1
- Science Fair Projects For Dummies 0-7645-5460-3
- U.S. History For Dummies 0-7645-5249-X

## Get smart @ dummies.com®

- **Find a full list of Dummies titles**
- **Look into loads of FREE on-site articles**
- **Sign up for FREE eTips e-mailed to you weekly**
- **See what other products carry the Dummies name**
- **Shop directly from the Dummies bookstore**
- **Enter to win new prizes every month!**

**Separate Canadian edition also available**
**Separate U.K. edition also available**

vailable wherever books are sold. For more information or to order direct: U.S. customers visit www.dummies.com or call 1-877-762-2974. K. customers visit www.wileyeurope.com or call 0800 243407. Canadian customers visit www.wiley.ca or call 1-800-567-4797.